Handwritten annotation: Password 1942
52342

Mastering DOS 6

HERBERT SCHILDT

GLENCOE

McGraw-Hill

New York, New York   Columbus, Ohio   Mission Hills, California   Peoria, Illinois

Library of Congress Cataloging-in-Publication Data

Schildt, Herbert.
   Mastering DOS 6 / Herbert Schildt.
     p.   cm.
  Rev. ed. of: Mastering DOS 5.0.   1993.
   Includes index.
   ISBN 0-02-801905-9
   1. Operating systems (Computers)   2. DOS 5.0.   I. Schildt, Herbert.
Mastering DOS 5.0.   II. Title.
QA76.76.063S3743   1995
005.4'469--dc20
                                                           93-34937
                                                              CIP

Imprint 1997

Send all inquiries to:
Glencoe/McGraw-Hill
936 Eastwind Drive
Westerville, Ohio 43081-3374

ISBN 0-02-801905-9

Printed in the United States of America.

5 6 7 8 9 10 11 12 13 14 15   066   03 02 01 00 99 98 97

Contents

PART 2

ADVANCED SHELL FEATURES

PART 3

INTRODUCING THE COMMAND PROMPT

PART 4

MASTERING ADVANCED DOS COMMANDS

PART 5

MANAGING YOUR SYSTEM

PART 6

APPENDICES

Appendix B, continued

Introduction

This book teaches you how to use DOS version 6. It assumes no prior experience with DOS or computers in general.

DOS is the program that is in charge of your computer, and it is the most widely used program in the world. DOS is involved with everything your computer does. It helps you run programs, manages the components of your system, and organizes your information. Knowing how to run DOS opens a new world of computing because it gives you full control of your system.

DOS is a complex program that contains many commands and features. This book emphasizes the parts of DOS that you will use on a day-to-day basis. The material is presented in a way that lets you begin using DOS as soon as possible. In fact, by the end of Chapter 2 you will already be performing simple DOS operations, and by the end of Chapter 4 you will be able to start using your own application programs. By the time you finish this book, you will be able to run DOS like a pro!

There are two ways to run DOS 6: by using the Shell or by using the command prompt interface. This book examines each. It begins with a thorough discussion of the Shell because it is easiest to understand. The Shell is a graphical interface that provides many visual "clues" and an extensive Help System that make learning to run DOS easy. Once you have mastered the Shell, you will progress to the command prompt interface, where you will learn many advanced DOS commands.

This book includes many hands-on examples. For best results you should work through each example using your own computer.

Finally, DOS 6 contains an integrated Help System that will give you information on any DOS feature and command.

PART 1

Using the DOS Shell

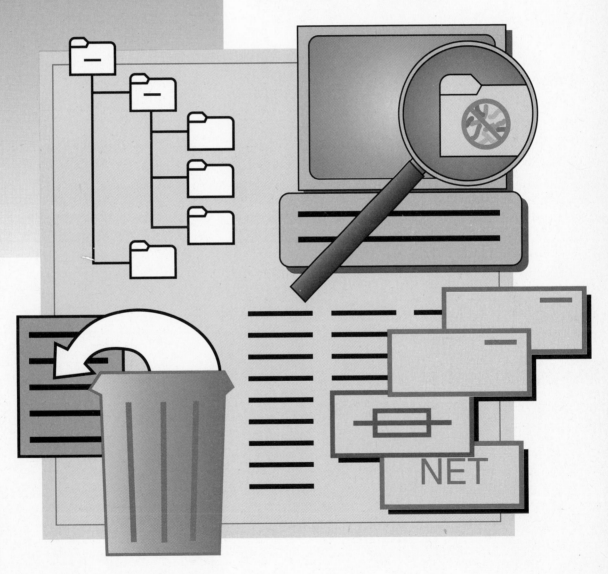

CHAPTER

1

Computer Basics

CHAPTER OBJECTIVES

After completing this chapter, you should be able to:

- Identify the components of a computer system.
- Identify the components of the system unit.
- Understand the differences between disk drives.
- Properly handle and care for diskettes.
- Know what the monitor does.
- Understand the computer keyboard.
- Recognize various peripheral devices.
- Understand the role of software.
- Understand the role of DOS.
- Understand DOS version numbers.

Before beginning your exploration of DOS 6, it is important to understand a few things about your computer, including what the individual pieces of the computer do and how they work together to form the complete system. Although you don't need to understand in detail how a computer works in order to use it, it is helpful to be familiar with its basic operation. In this chapter, IBM-style computers will be used for illustration, but the information will be applicable to virtually all computers capable of running DOS 6.

The Parts of Your System

All microcomputers consist of at least the following three items:

- The system unit

- The keyboard
- The monitor (video display screen)

This is the minimal amount of equipment needed to create a functional computer as illustrated in Figure 1-1. In addition, most computer installations include a printer. Many computer systems also have a modem, which is used to allow two computers to communicate over a telephone line. Your computer could contain other devices, such as a mouse, which is a pointing device. Let's look at these devices now.

The System Unit

The system unit is the heart of the computer and is composed of the following items:

- The central processing unit (CPU)
- Memory
- Disk drives
- Various adapters and options

All other pieces of the computer plug into the system unit through connectors on the back.

The CPU

> **CPU or Central Processing Unit** *The computing part of the computer. Also known as the brain of the computer.*

The *central processing unit*, or *CPU*, is the brain of the computer. It performs all the analytical, computational, and logical functions that occur inside the system. It operates by executing a program, which is a list of instructions (more about these programs shortly).

Memory

> **Byte** *The common unit of storage that holds the equivalent of a single character.*

The memory of the computer stores information that will be processed by the CPU. The memory of your computer is made up of storage units called *bytes*. A byte represents the amount of memory required to store one character. Therefore, if your computer has about 640,000 bytes of memory, it can store approximately 640,000 characters.

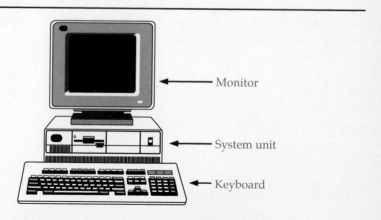

FIGURE 1-1   **The basic elements of a computer**

You will often hear two terms associated with the memory of the computer: RAM and ROM. *RAM* stands for *Random Access Memory*. This is the kind of memory your computer has the most of, and it may be used to store and retrieve any type of information. The one fact you should remember about RAM is that anything stored in it is lost when the computer is turned off. The other type of memory contained in your computer is called ROM, which stands for Read-Only Memory. The contents of this sort of memory cannot be changed; it can only be read. ROM stores information that the computer needs when it is first turned on. (In a way, ROM in the computer is similar to instinct in an animal.) Unlike RAM, the contents of ROM are not lost when the computer is turned off.

Often, you will see the letter *K* after a number when the amount of RAM in a computer is referred to. For example, most computers today come with at least 640K bytes of RAM. Loosely, "K" stands for 1,000 and is the symbol used in the metric system to stand for *kilo*. Therefore, 640K is short for 640,000. (When used with computers, "K" more precisely stands for 1,024, but this distinction is not too significant, except for programmers.)

Disk Drives

A disk drive is used to read and write information to or from a diskette. (The diskette actually holds the information, and the drive is the mechanism that reads or writes data to or from it. You will learn more about diskettes in the next section.) Data that is stored on a diskette is not lost when the computer is turned off. Since anything that is in the RAM of the computer is lost when the power is turned off, information that is important and that you wish to keep must be stored on a diskette.

All disk drives have two elements in common. First, they use a *read/write head* to read and write information to the diskette. This read/write head is similar to the play/record head on a cassette tape recorder. Second, all disk drives have a means of spinning the diskette. Because information is spread over the surface of the diskette, the diskette must turn in order to access all the information on it.

There are two basic types of disk drives: floppy and fixed. Both are housed in the system unit. Most system units are configured in one of these four ways, as illustrated in Figure 1-2:

- One floppy disk drive
- Two floppy disk drives
- One floppy and one fixed-disk drive
- Two floppy disk drives and one fixed-disk drive

Before the advent of the IBM PS/2 Model 60 and Model 80, the system unit of most personal computers sat on the desk beneath the monitor. However, with the Model 60 and Model 80, the system unit is usually placed on the floor away from the monitor and keyboard. These models may also come with an external 5¼ inch drive to allow easy exchange of information with older IBM PC and AT computers.

Random Access Memory (RAM)
The computer's working storage, where programs and data reside before they are processed by the CPU.

K *The abbreviation for* kilobyte, *which stands for 1,000, or more precisely, 1,024 bytes.*

Read/write head
A device that reads and writes information on a disk.

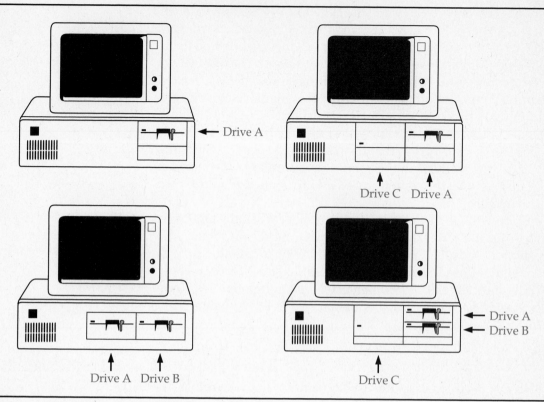

FIGURE 1-2 **Disk-drive configurations**

The drives in a system are referred to by letters, as shown in Figure 1-2. Generally, the fixed-disk drive is drive C.

The *floppy disk* drives use diskettes as their storage media. A diskette is a thin, flat, removable magnetic disk that stores information. There are two types of floppy diskettes. The older one, which is still widely used, is the 5¼ inch minifloppy. This is the type used by the IBM PC, XT, AT, and their compatibles. A newer type of floppy disk is the 3½ inch microfloppy, which is used by IBM's newer PS/2 and PS/1 lines of computers and all modern computers. Diskette elements are shown in Figure 1-3.

> *Floppy disk* *A removable, single, round disk coated with a magnetic material, enclosed in a jacket.*

Minifloppy Diskettes

The 5¼ inch minifloppy diskette, as shown in Figure 1-3, consists of a magnetic medium that actually stores the information, surrounded by a stiff jacket that protects the magnetic medium from harm. The computer accesses the magnetic medium through the read/write opening. The index hole is used by the computer to properly align the diskette. Perhaps the single most important feature of the diskette is the *write-protect notch*. When the write-protect notch is left uncovered (as shown in the drawing), information can be both written to and read from the diskette. However, when this notch is covered using a write-protect tab (supplied along with the diskette), the computer can read the information on the diskette, but cannot write to the diskette. Covering the write-protect notch is a good way to prevent important information from being

> *Write-protect notch* *A small cutout on the side of a 5¼ inch floppy disk or a small sliding button on the back of a 3½ inch floppy disk that determines the disk's read-only status.*

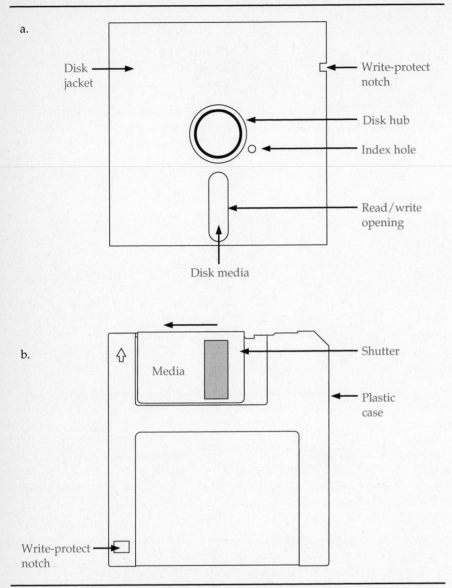

FIGURE 1-3   **Elements of (a) 5¼ inch minifloppy and
(b) 3½ inch microfloppy disks**

accidentally destroyed. Later in this book, you will be instructed to cover the notch for this very reason.

You can insert a minifloppy diskette into a disk drive with the write-protect notch to the left and the read/write hole facing forward. Before the computer can use the diskette, the drive door must be closed or latched. There are three basic types of 5¼ inch drives in general use; the method of closing the drive door for both is shown in Figure 1-4.

Closing the drive door does three things. First, it tells the computer that there is a diskette in the drive. Second, it secures the diskette to the turntable that actually spins the diskette. The diskette must be turning in order for the disk drive to read or write information from or to it. Finally, it enables the read/write head of the drive to access the diskette.

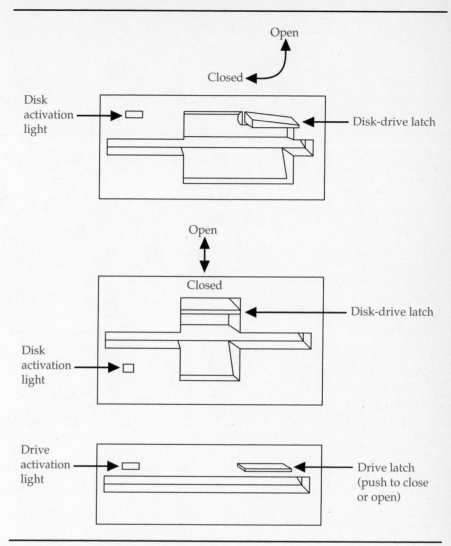

FIGURE 1-4 **Closing the drive door**

Microfloppy Diskettes

The IBM PS/2 and PS/1 lines of computers (and most other modern computers) use microfloppy diskettes. In principle, these work in the same way as minifloppy diskettes, except that they are smaller and provide more protection for the magnetic medium. As Figure 1-3 shows, a microfloppy diskette has a shutter that covers the read/write opening. This shutter is opened by the computer only when access to the diskette is required. This protects the magnetic medium from harm while the diskette is outside the computer and from dust while it is inside the computer.

The write-protect notch in a microfloppy diskette has a built-in slider that is used to cover the notch. The write-protect notch in a microfloppy diskette works in the opposite way to the notch in a minifloppy diskette. When the notch is open, the diskette is write protected; otherwise, it is not.

The microfloppy disk drive does not use a latch. Instead, the diskette drops into place when inserted into the drive. To eject the diskette from the drive, press the diskette eject button on the front of the drive.

Handling Diskettes

All types of diskettes must be protected from harm. The basic rules are no dust, no magnets, and no folding (see Figure 1-5). Dust can cause excessive wear of the magnetic medium, causing premature failure. Magnetic fields can destroy the data on the disk. Be careful; sometimes

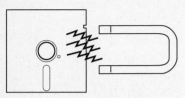

Never place the disk near magnetic devices.

Always place disks back into disk envelopes when you are not using them.

Keep your disk away from telephones.

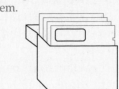

Store floppy disks in a safe location.

Never touch your floppy-disk media.

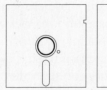

Always make a backup copy of your floppy disk.

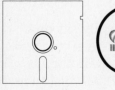

Never smoke near floppy disks.

Keep room temperature in the range 50 degrees F to 110 degrees F.

Never bend floppy disks.

FIGURE 1-5   Protecting your disks

magnetic fields are produced by unsuspected sources. For example, motors in devices such as vacuum cleaners and floor waxers set up strong magnetic fields, which can—given the right circumstances and proximity—erase a diskette. Never store diskettes in the bottom drawer of your desk where they stand the greatest chance of being affected by these appliances. Finally, folding the diskette causes the magnetic medium to be destroyed where the diskette is creased.

Fixed Disks

Hard disk   A non-removable disk that stores much more information than a floppy disk. A hard disk is also called a fixed disk.

Many computers contain a special type of disk drive called a *fixed disk*. You will also see this referred to as a *hard disk*. A fixed disk is a high-speed, large-capacity disk drive. The disk cannot be removed from the disk drive, hence the term *fixed*.

A fixed disk can hold substantially more information than a minifloppy or microfloppy diskette. For example, minifloppy or microfloppy diskettes typically hold between 360,000 and 1,440,000 bytes of information, whereas fixed disks hold from 10 million to more than 300 million bytes. In computer terms, 1 million is referred to by the prefix *mega*; hence, you will often hear the amount of storage available on a fixed disk referred to in terms of megabytes. For example, a disk drive that can hold 20 million bytes of information will be called a 20-megabyte drive.

An important fact to remember about fixed disks is that they do not like jolting vibrations or sharp shocks. A hard blow to the computer while it is accessing a fixed disk can damage the magnetic medium because the read/write head of a fixed disk is positioned extremely close to the surface of the magnetic medium. If you jar it sharply, the head could actually come into contact with the medium and cause a scratch, which could cause a loss of information. You don't have to walk around on tiptoes when using a fixed disk, but you should treat a fixed disk as what it is—a highly sophisticated piece of equipment.

The Monitor

The monitor is the television-like screen that generally sits on top of the system unit (except in the IBM Model 60 and Model 80 and similar computers, where the system unit is usually placed on the floor instead of on the desk with the monitor and keyboard). As you can probably guess, the computer uses the monitor to display information—in other words, it is your window into the computer. The monitor plugs into the back of the system unit. There are two basic types of monitors: black-and-white and color. For the most part, DOS doesn't care what type you have (although appearances will differ between the two).

The Keyboard

The keyboard allows you to communicate with the computer. There are two basic styles of keyboard commonly found with microcomputers:

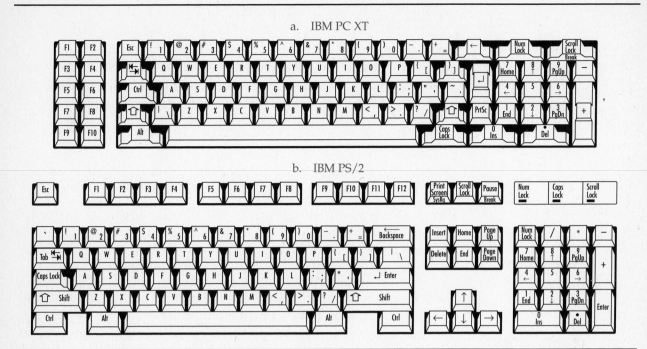

FIGURE 1-6   **The two most common keyboard styles: (a) the PC XT style and (b) the PS/2 style**

PC/XT-style keyboards and AT-style keyboards. The PC/XT-style keyboard was the first one developed by IBM. Later, the IBM AT computer was developed with a slightly different keyboard. The PS/2 and PS/1 keyboards are similar to the AT keyboard. Both types are shown in Figure 1-6. For the most part, these keyboards are like those of typewriters. However, a few special features should be noted.

The 10 keys on the far left of the PC/XT-style keyboard or the 12 keys on the top row of the PS/2-style keyboard, labeled (F1) through (F10) ((F1) through (F12) for the PS/2-style keyboard), are called *function keys*. These, as well as other special keys, are gray instead of white. These keys have special meanings that depend on what the computer is doing. The (ESC) (escape) key can be used to cancel certain operations. The (CTRL) (control) and (ALT) (alternate) keys are used to generate special characters not readily available at the keyboard. The (CAPS LOCK) key operates the same way as it does on a typewriter by forcing all characters to be uppercase.

The numeric keypad has two separate purposes. The first is to allow the rapid entry of numbers; the other is to control the movements of the cursor on the screen. The (NUM LOCK) key determines whether the arrow keys or the digit keys on the number pad are active. By pressing the (NUM LOCK) key, you can toggle between the two uses of the number pad. The (PRTSCR) key causes what is currently on the computer screen to be printed on the printer. The (SCROLL LOCK)-(BREAK) key is used to cancel certain computer operations. You will learn more about these special keys later, as you learn more about DOS.

Function keys *Special keys labeled* (F1) *through* (F12) *whose meanings change depending on the software currently being executed by the computer.*

The Mouse

Mouse A pointing device that allows you to move a locator around the screen and to select options.

A *mouse* is an alternative input device. Unlike the keyboard where you type in information, the mouse is used to select various options. A mouse consists of a small, hand-held unit with one, two, or three buttons and a small ball on the bottom. As you move the mouse across your desk, a small locator symbol, called the mouse pointer, moves across the screen. A typical mouse is shown in Figure 1-7.

Early versions of DOS did not support the mouse. However, DOS 6 is designed to take full advantage of it. Although you do not need a mouse to fully utilize DOS, it does make several tasks much easier.

The Printer

Dot-matrix printer A printer that uses tiny dots to form characters and images.

Letter-quality printer A printer that forms characters that are comparable to those of a typewriter.

Laser printer A desktop printer that uses the electro-photographic method used in copy machines to print typeset-quality output one page at a time.

Most computer installations include a printer, which creates permanent output from the computer. A computer may have more than one printer connected to it because different printers are used for different purposes. The most common printer is called a *dot-matrix printer*. This sort of printer creates printouts quickly, but its print quality is not as good as that of a typewriter. Another type of printer is called either a daisy wheel or *letter-quality printer*. It creates high-quality output and is generally used in word processing applications. Finally, you might have a *laser printer* attached to your computer. A laser printer is capable of producing typeset-quality output and is used when only the very best output quality will do. No matter what type of printer you have, if it is connected to the computer in the standard way, everything you learn in this book will be applicable to it.

The Modem

Modem A device that transmits digital data over a phone line.

For a computer to communicate with another computer over the telephone lines, a piece of hardware called a *modem* is needed. There are two types of modem: internal and external. An internal modem is a special circuit card that plugs into the inside of the computer. All you will see is a telephone cord plugged into the back of the system unit. An external modem sits outside the system. DOS cannot directly communicate with a modem. If a modem is part of your computer, you will need a special communication program to run it.

FIGURE 1-7 **A typical mouse**

Software

So far, only the different pieces of *hardware* that make up a computer system have been discussed. However, there is a saying in the computer business that "a computer without software is, at best, an expensive doorstop." *Software* consists of programs—and programs run your computer. Without programs, the computer hardware can do nothing because it doesn't know what to do. You will probably use several programs, including word processors, accounting packages, and spreadsheets.

Although you do not need to know how to write a program to fully utilize DOS, it is useful to understand what a program is and how a computer executes programs. A program consists of a sequence of instructions that the computer follows. When a program is run, all of its instructions are loaded into the memory of the computer. To begin execution, the CPU fetches the first instruction and performs the specified operation. Next, it gets the second instruction and performs that task; then it gets the third instruction, and so on. The program ends when the last instruction is executed.

Computer programs are represented in machine code, which can be read and executed by the computer. Aside from very experienced, knowledgeable programmers, people cannot read and understand machine code. Other terms for machine code that you might see are "object code" and "executable code."

Hardware   The physical components of a computer system.

Software   Another name for computer programs.

What Is DOS and What Does It Do?

First and foremost, DOS is a program; it is part of the software that your computer needs to function. But it is a very special program because it is in charge of the computer's hardware. With few exceptions, any other program that runs on your computer does so with the help of DOS. Stated a different way, DOS is the program that manages the basic hardware components of the computer and allocates them to your programs as needed. DOS and programs like it are called *operating systems*. In fact, the name DOS is an acronym for Disk Operating System.

Although DOS controls other programs that run in the computer, DOS is under your control and exists primarily to give you a way to communicate your instructions to the computer. You give instructions to DOS via commands that it will recognize. For the most part, these commands consist of regular, English-like words. For example, a few actual DOS commands are ERASE, COPY, and PRINT.

There are two distinctly different ways that you can give a command to DOS. First, you can select a command from DOS's menu-driven interface, which is usually called the DOS Shell, or Shell for short. In essence, the Shell presents you with lists of things that DOS can do, and you simply select the operation desired. For beginners, this is the easiest way to communicate with DOS. However, you can also request a command prompt. From the command prompt, you give DOS commands by typing the name of the command at the prompt.

Operating system (1) The first program loaded into the computer's memory after the system is turned on. (2) The master program that oversees and aids the execution of programs. It is also in charge of the computer hardware.

Early versions of DOS did not have a Shell, and the command prompt was the only way to communicate with DOS. Once you have become familiar with DOS, you may find the command prompt method preferable to using the Shell because it is faster than selecting items from a menu. However, either method can fully utilize DOS.

Because it is easier to learn, the first few chapters of this book focus on the DOS Shell. Later in the book, the command prompt interface is discussed.

DOS Versions

Version number   A number that identifies the specific release of a program.

Like most things, DOS has been improved and enhanced over time. Each time DOS was revised, a new *version number* was assigned. The first version of DOS was 1.00. The latest DOS version, covered in this book, is 6.00. (However, much of what you will learn is applicable to all versions.)

In versions of software, the number preceding the decimal point is called the major revision number. This number is changed only when major alterations take place. The numbers to the right of the decimal point are called the minor revision numbers, and they indicate versions that differ only slightly from the previous one.

> **NOTE**
> Even though this book is specifically about DOS version 6, for the most part it will be referred to simply as DOS, except where a version-related difference may be important.

Summary

You should now be familiar with

- The various pieces of a computer system
- The concept of programs and software
- The function DOS serves in the computer
- The way DOS version numbers are assigned

In the next chapter, you will learn how to start the computer and about the DOS Shell.

Key Terms

Byte   The common unit of storage that holds the equivalent of a single character. Memory is measured in units called bytes.

CPU or Central Processing Unit   The computing part of the computer. Also known as the brain of the computer.

Dot-matrix printer   A printer that uses tiny dots to form characters and images.

Floppy disk   A removable, single, round disk coated with a magnetic material, enclosed in a jacket. The current standard sizes for floppy disks are 5¼ inch diskettes or 3½ inch diskettes.

Function keys   Special keys labeled (F1) through (F12) whose meanings change depending on the software currently being executed by the computer.

Hard disk   A nonremovable disk that stores much more information than a floppy disk. A hard disk is also called a *fixed disk*.

Hardware   The physical components of a computer system.

K   The abbreviation for *kilobyte*, which stands for 1,000, or more precisely, 1,024 bytes.

Laser printer   A desktop printer that uses the electrophotographic method used in copy machines to print typeset-quality output one page at a time.

Letter-quality printer   A printer that forms characters that are comparable to those of a typewriter.

Modem   A device that transmits digital data over a phone line.

Mouse   A pointing device that allows you to move a locator around the screen and to select options.

Operating system   (1) The first program loaded into the computer's memory after the system is turned on. (2) The master program that oversees and aids the execution of programs. It is also in charge of the computer hardware.

Random Access Memory (RAM)   The computer's working storage, where programs and data reside before they are processed by the CPU.

Read/write head   A device that reads and writes information on a disk.

Software   Another name for computer programs. A computer's hardware is not very useful without software.

Version number   A number that identifies the specific release of a program. DOS's version number consists of two parts: the major revision number and the minor revision number. The major revision number is to the left of the decimal point and identifies major revisions. The minor revision number is to the right of the decimal point and identifies minor revisions.

Write-protect notch   A small cutout on the side of a 5¼ inch floppy disk or a small sliding button on the back of a 3½ inch floppy disk that determines the disk's read-only status.

Exercises

Short Answer

1. A computer system is made up of many different components called hardware. What three parts do all computers have in common?

2. The system unit is the core of the computer and is responsible for processing and storing information. What are the four primary parts that make up the system unit?

3. A computer can have two basic types of disk drives. Name the two kinds and briefly explain how they differ.

4. Explain the terms *byte* and *kilobyte*.

5. Explain how to write-protect a 5¼ inch diskette and how to write-protect a 3½ inch diskette.

6. The useful life of a diskette depends on how often you use it, and more importantly, how you treat it. Give three examples of how to properly care for your diskettes.

7. Name some additional devices that may be attached to your computer system.

8. What is DOS an acronym for?

9. Briefly explain the role of DOS.

10. Software version numbers have two parts: the major revision number and the minor revision number. Explain what these numbers mean.

Fill-in-the-Blank

1. The heart of the system unit, also called the "brains," is the _____ _____ _____ or just _____ for short.

2. Memory is often called RAM, an acronym for _____.

3. A byte is just large enough to store one _____.

4. If your computer system has only one floppy disk drive, it is drive _____. If your computer has two floppy drives, one is drive _____ and the other is drive _____. If your computer system contains at least one fixed disk, this disk is drive _____.

5. Monitors can be broken down into two broad classifications: color and _____.

6. The _____ is the main input device for your computer system.

7. _____ is the general term applied to the programs your computer runs. The most common types are word processors, databases, and spreadsheets.

8. _____ is a very special program because it is the program that is in charge of your computer. A program that is in charge of a computer system is called an _____.

Matching

Match the answers in the second column with the terms in the first.

_____ 1. RAM   a. Another name for the fixed disk

_____ 2. Laser printer   b. 256,000 characters

_____ 3. CPU   c. Are numbered (F1) through (F12)

_____ 4. Hard disk   d. Displays visual information

_____ 5. 256K   e. Produces a typeset-quality output

_____ 6. Function keys   f. Random Access Memory

_____ 7. Monitor   g. Central Processing Unit

CHAPTER 2

An Introduction to the DOS Shell

CHAPTER OBJECTIVES

After completing this chapter, you should be able to:

- Know the components of the DOS 6 Shell.
- Make a menu selection using both the mouse and the keyboard.
- Move about the Shell.
- Use the Shell's online help system.
- Understand the Shell's windows.
- Understand dialog boxes.
- Back up your DOS master diskettes.
- Restart DOS.

This chapter introduces the *DOS Shell*, a menu-driven interface that helps you use DOS. It is called a Shell because, conceptually, it encloses DOS. It effectively masks the low-level functioning of DOS and makes it easier to learn to use DOS. Keep in mind that many things introduced in this chapter will be more thoroughly explored later in this book after you know more about DOS.

The DOS Shell is quite powerful and contains many features. The purpose of this chapter is to get you acquainted with several essential concepts and procedures so that you can begin to use DOS. Don't worry if some things are a bit confusing. As you progress, they will start to make sense.

For this and the remaining chapters in this book, it will be best if you are seated at your computer so that you can try the examples.

DOS Shell A menu-driven interface that helps you easily run DOS 6.

19

[/G [:res [N]]] [/B]

Before proceeding with this chapter, you need to get DOS started on your computer. If you don't know how to do this, refer to your DOS user's manual.

What If Things Look Different?

It is possible that the figures in this book will differ slightly from what you see on your computer screen. There are several possible reasons for this. First, there will be minor differences if you are running DOS from a floppy disk rather than a fixed disk. The figures in this book are generated on a computer that uses a fixed disk. If you are running DOS from a floppy disk, the minor differences can, for the most part, simply be ignored. (Any exception to this will be noted in the text.)

A second reason your screen might look slightly different is because the Shell allows you to arrange the layout of the screen in several different ways. The arrangement used in this book reflects the default layout. However, it is possible that your layout has been changed if your computer is used by other people. You will learn how to return your screen to its default configuration shortly.

Third, DOS can be customized to better fit the needs of a specific working environment. (You will learn how to customize DOS later in this book.) If the computer you are using has been in use for a while and is used by other people, it is likely that some customization has occurred. Most customizations will not affect the way you control DOS or use it to help you run programs, but it can cause some things to appear differently on the monitor or not to appear at all. This book assumes that DOS has been installed using standard installation instructions.

As you read this chapter, if you find that your screen looks nothing like what is being shown in the book, you have two choices. First, you can reinstall DOS so that the standard default installation is used. Your screen will then show the examples as they appear in this book. Second, you can just ignore the differences and generalize what is presented here to what you see on your screen. Often, the effect of any customization is so small that the second solution is the better choice. There is, however, one exception, as noted here.

> **NOTE**
>
> **It is possible to configure DOS 6 in such a way that the DOS Shell is not activated. If this has been done, talk to the person who installed DOS on your machine and explain that you are new to DOS and would like to use the Shell to make learning easier. This person should be able to easily reactivate it. If you are on your own and the DOS Shell does not appear when DOS is loaded, refer to the DOS installation instructions and reinstall DOS using the recommended procedure.**

Finally, the way that you use your computer probably is different from the way the one that generated the figures is used. This means that what you see on your screen will be slightly different from what is shown in the figures. (For example, you will have different application programs and directories than those found on the computer used to create the figures.) However, such differences are incidental, and the general appearance of DOS will be the same.

Text Versus Graphics

The DOS Shell can be configured to run in two different modes: text and graphics. If your computer has only a monochrome video adapter, then the Shell will be configured for text mode. Otherwise, it will be configured for graphics mode operation. The differences between these two modes are slight, but the graphics mode version does present a more visually appealing display.

The DOS Shell: An Overview

When the Shell begins execution, you will see a screen that looks like the one shown in Figure 2-1. The Shell consists of these parts:

- The title bar
- The menu bar
- The Disk Drive window
- The Directory Tree window
- The File List window
- The Main group window
- The status bar

In the course of this book, you will learn to use these pieces of the Shell to run DOS, execute your applications programs, and manage your system. If this is your first experience with DOS and computers in general, then the Shell's screen might seem a little intimidating and confusing. Don't worry; very soon you will be navigating the Shell like a professional.

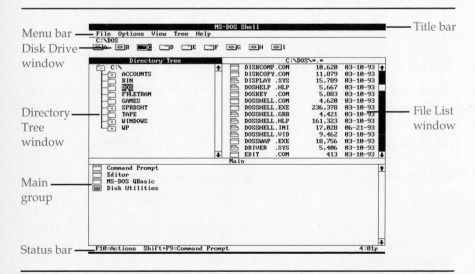

FIGURE 2-1   **The DOS shell screen**

> **NOTE**
>
> **If your screen does not look like the one shown in Figure 2-1, hold down the (ALT) key and press (V) once. Release the (ALT) key. Next, press the (F) key once. Now the layout of your screen should look like that shown in the figure.**

At the top of the screen is the Shell's title bar. The next line down contains the Shell's menu bar. The menu bar provides a means of selecting various operations that pertain to the Shell. As you learn more about the Shell, you will find that menus play a key role in its operation.

In the Disk Drive window, the currently active drive is highlighted. This is the drive that is the focus of DOS.

The Directory Tree window shows a list of all the directories on your disk. You will learn about directories in detail later, after you have learned some fundamentals. But briefly, a directory is a group of related files.

To the right of the Directory Tree window is the File List window. It shows the names and various other bits of information about the files on your disk. In essence, a file is a collection of related information stored on a disk. You will learn more about files in the next chapter.

Main group   *A group that allows you to perform several common DOS activities.*

The *Main group* window contains a list of options associated with the Main group. Groups are used to organize related programs and activities. Note that it is possible to add or delete items to or from the Main group, so your screen may show a different list of options.

Finally, on the bottom of the screen is the status bar. The status bar displays helpful hints related to what you are currently doing as well as displaying the time. As you can see, there are two reminders. First, pressing (F10) activates the menu bar. Second, pressing the (SHIFT) key at the same time you press (F9) activates the DOS command prompt, which provides a different way to run DOS. You will learn about using it after you have learned to run DOS using the Shell.

Now that you have had a short explanation of the Shell, it is time to demonstrate its use.

Making a Menu Selection

Menu   *A list of options from which you may select.*

The operation of the Shell is based on *menus*. Therefore, before you can do much else, you need to know how to make a menu selection. As stated in Chapter 1, the DOS Shell supports both the keyboard and the mouse as input devices. You can run the Shell completely by using the keyboard alone, but the mouse makes a handy addition. This section explores how to make a menu selection using either device.

> **NOTE**
>
> **This section discusses making a menu selection from the Shell's menu bar. However, the selection process is the same for other menus that you will encounter when using the Shell.**

Using the Keyboard

Before you can make a menu selection using the keyboard, you must activate the menu bar. As the status line suggests, to activate the menu bar, press the (F10) key. Try this now. As you can see, the File option is highlighted. You can move the highlight about using the (←) and (→) keys. To select an option, press (ENTER) when the highlight is over the desired object. To deactivate the menu bar, press (F10) a second time. The (F10) key acts as a toggle, alternately activating and deactivating the menu bar each time it is pressed. (The (ALT) key may be used as an alternative to the (F10) key.)

Let's try an example. Activate the menu bar, position the highlight over the Help option, and press (ENTER). You will see this window:

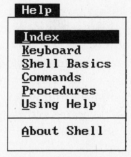

By selecting the Help item, you cause a list of options associated with Help to be displayed. This is called a drop-down menu. Each of the menu bar items has a drop-down menu associated with it. Don't worry about what this drop-down menu contains. We will come back to it shortly.

To make a selection from a drop-down menu, use the up and down arrow keys to position the highlight on the item you want and then press (ENTER). Try moving the highlight at this time, but don't press (ENTER).

Once a drop-down menu has been displayed, you can use the (←) and (→) keys to display the drop-down menus associated with the other menu bar options. Try pressing the (←) key a few times. Notice how the menus change. Return to the Help drop-down menu now.

To deactivate a drop-down menu, press (F10) (or (ALT)). Since you don't actually want to make a selection from the menu, press (F10) at this time. This causes the drop-down menu to go away, but the menu bar is still active. To deactivate the menu bar, press (F10) a second time. Additionally, when a drop-down menu is present, you can cancel the menu bar by pressing (ESC). In fact, pressing the (ESC) key will often cancel whatever you are doing within the Shell.

Deactivate the menu bar at this time, and then reactivate it by pressing (F10). Look closely at the options in the menu bar. Notice that the first letter of each is underscored. Once the menu is activated, you can make a selection from a menu by pressing the key that is underscored in the item of your choice. For example, press (H). This causes Help to be selected and its drop-down menu to be displayed. Notice that each item in the drop-down menu also contains underscored letters for easy selection. In the terminology of DOS, the underscored letters are called hot keys.

Usually hot keys are the first letter in an item's name. However, if a menu contains two options starting with the same letter, then clearly one must use a different hot key. Just look for the underscored letter. The main advantage of using hot keys is that they allow you to make faster menu selections using the keyboard.

At this time, deactivate the menu bar.

Using the Mouse

Using the mouse to select a menu item is somewhat easier than using the keyboard because you don't have to first activate the menu bar. Instead, the menu bar is activated automatically during the selection process. To select a menu bar option, move the mouse pointer to the item you want and click the left button once. The mouse pointer will either be a small arrow or a solid box depending upon what sort of video adapter your system has. The right button of the mouse is not used by the DOS Shell. (However, it is possible that you will have application programs that use it.) To try making a selection using the mouse, move the mouse pointer to the Help entry, and press the left button once. As you can see, the menu bar is activated, the Help entry is selected, and its drop-down menu is displayed—all by a single click of the mouse.

To make a selection from a drop-down menu, simply position the mouse pointer over the desired entry, and press the left mouse button. However, do not try this now.

To deactivate the menu bar using the mouse, move the mouse pointer to a part of the screen that does not contain any menus and press the left mouse button. Do this now. In general, until you have actually made a selection from a menu, you can change what you are doing by moving the mouse to some other part of the screen and single-clicking.

One thing to keep in mind is that you can intermix keyboard and mouse commands. The DOS Shell does not care which you use at any point in time.

Moving About the Shell

In addition to the Shell's menu bar, activity can occur in four other areas. These are the Disk Drive window, the Directory Tree window, the File List window, and the Main group window. However, before one of these windows can become the focus of your commands, it must be activated. When a window is activated, its title is highlighted. (The Disk Drive window highlights the letter of the current drive when it is activated.) The way to activate a window differs depending upon whether you are using the keyboard or the mouse.

When using the keyboard, you change the active window by pressing the (TAB) key. Try pressing the (TAB) key a few times now. Notice that the highlight moves from one window to the next. The window that contains the highlight is active and will be the focus of any input that you give.

cd (change directory)

To activate a window using the mouse, position the mouse pointer in the window you want to activate and press the left button once. Try this now. One small exception to this method is when you are activating the Disk Drive window. This window will become active only when you click on one of the drive symbols. For now, click on only the drive whose letter is currently highlighted.

Making a Selection from the Main Group

Making a selection from the Main group is similar to making a selection from a drop-down menu. To see this in action, activate the Main group window now. To make a selection from a group using the keyboard, use the ⊙ and ⊙ keys to position the highlight on the item you want, and then press (ENTER). For example, move the highlight to the Disk Utilities option and press (ENTER). This causes the options associated with the Disk Utilities entry to be displayed.

To deactivate the Disk Utilities subgroup, either select the Main entry or press the (ESC) key. Either way, the Main group is once again redisplayed. Press the (ESC) key at this time.

If you have a mouse, you can select an option from the Main group by double-clicking on the desired item. A *double click* is two presses in quick succession. You must be careful not to move the mouse between the two clicks. (If the mouse is moved between the first and second click, no command is activated.) To try this, make sure that the mouse is positioned over the Disk Utilities entry and double-click. As you can see, this activates the Disk Utilities group. (If it didn't work the first time, try it again. It can take a couple of tries to learn the art of double-clicking.) Keep in mind that only items in the Main group (or one of its subgroups) require a double click. Other types of menus allow selections with just a single click.

Double click   *Pressing the left mouse button twice in quick succession.*

Although the subject of groups is discussed later in this book, a brief discussion is in order now. The Shell provides the Main group. The Main group may contain two types of items: programs and subgroups. By default, it contains one subgroup, which is the one you just activated: the Disk Utilities group. You make selections from a subgroup in just the same way as you do from the Main group. As you will learn later in this book, it is possible to define your own subgroups and to add items to or remove items from the Main group. Therefore, if your Main group looks different from the one shown in the figures, don't be concerned.

Using the Online Help System

One feature of the Shell that you will want to make extensive use of is its online context-sensitive help system. In general, a help system provides information about a program. In this case, the *online help* system provides information about DOS and the Shell. What makes DOS's help system even more valuable is that it is context sensitive. This means

Online help   *A system that provides instant information about what you are doing at the press of a key. In DOS 6, it provides information about running DOS.*

that it will tell you information about whatever you are doing at the time. Once the help system is activated, you may also request information about other topics. Keep in mind that, in general, the information displayed by the help system is intended to act as a reminder; it cannot be substituted for a good working knowledge of DOS.

Since the help system is especially useful to the beginner, now is a good time to practice using it. To activate the help system, either press F1 or select the Help entry in the menu bar. When you activate the help system using the Help menu bar option, you are presented with a drop-down menu of topics from which you can select your area of interest. However, when you activate the help system by pressing F1, you receive information that relates to what you are currently doing. For example, highlight the File menu bar entry and then press F1. As you can see, a small window appears that tells you about the File option. Your screen will look like the one shown in Figure 2-2. All help windows are organized similarly to the one shown in this example.

At the bottom of the window, a list of the command buttons that relate to the help system is displayed. The first is the Close button. Selecting this command tells DOS that you are done with the help system and you want the window removed. (You can also press ESC to exit the help system.) To the right of Close is the Back button. This button allows you to go back to a previous help screen. Next is Keys; this provides assistance in using the keyboard. After selecting this option, you can return to the original help screen by selecting Back. The Index button presents a list of help topics from which you can select. After selecting a topic, information about it will be shown. Like the Keys option, you can return to the previous window by selecting Back. The final button is Help, and it gives you information about the help system. To move the

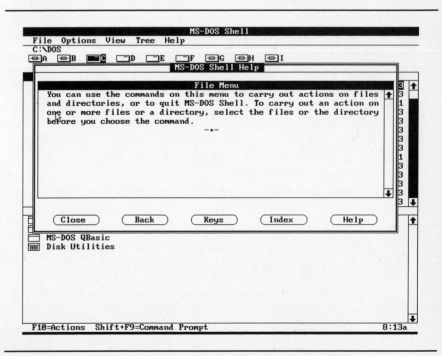

FIGURE 2-2   **The help window for the File Menu bar option**

highlight to the command button you want, use the (TAB) key. To execute the selected command, press the (ENTER) key. You can also execute a command by clicking on a button using the mouse.

Deactivate the help window at this time by pressing (ESC) or by selecting Close.

Understanding the Shell's Windows

In the preceding section, you saw what was called the help window—without further discussion of windows. As you use more of the Shell, you will see that its interface is based upon the window. A *window* is a portion of the screen that is dedicated to one specific task. If you think of the screen as a desk, then you can think of a window as a piece of paper on that desk. For example, if you activate the help window again, you can see that it overlays a portion of the screen. This is like laying one piece of paper over another. When you deactivate the help window, you restore what was previously on the screen. This process of overlaying and restoring is common to all windows used by the Shell. There can be many windows on the screen at the same time, but only one will be active at any one time.

All windows contain the elements shown in Figure 2-3. If the information contained in a window exceeds its height, then the window will include a *scroll bar*. All scroll bars work the same no matter what the window is used for. The components of the scroll bar are shown in Figure 2-4. A scroll bar moves text through the window so that you can see all of it. To use the scroll bar, you must have a mouse.

To move the text in the screen down one line, position the mouse pointer over the down arrow at the bottom of the bar and single-click. To move the text up one line, click on the up arrow at the top of the bar. To move down one full window, click anyplace on the scroll bar that is below the slider box. To move up one full window, click anyplace on the scroll bar that is above the slider box.

Window   A portion of the screen that is dedicated to one specific task.

Scroll bar   A bar on the side and/or bottom of a window that lets you move text through the window.

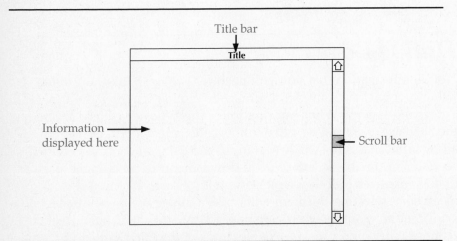

FIGURE 2-3   **The components of a window**

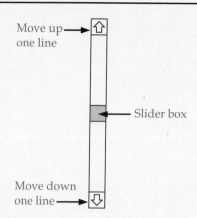

FIGURE 2-4   **The components of the scroll bar**

If you wish to move several lines up or down quickly, position the mouse pointer on the arrow you desire and press and hold the left mouse button. The text inside the window will scroll smoothly until you release the button or reach the end.

If you have a mouse, you can try using a scroll bar by practicing with the one that is (almost certainly) on the right side of the File List window. (In rare situations, you might not have enough files in this window to generate a scroll bar.) Notice that the slider box moves up or down in the direction of the scroll. Its position in the scroll bar is in the same proportion as the position of the text currently in view to the total text. For example, when the slider box is in the middle of its range, the text on the screen is in the middle of the total text.

You can use the mouse to drag the slider box to a new position. To do this, position the mouse on the slider box and press and hold down the left button. Next, move the mouse and the box will follow. The text on the screen will be moved by the same amount. You should try this now.

If you don't have a mouse, you can use the (↑) and (↓) keys to scroll the text one line, or the (PGUP) and (PGDN) keys to scroll the text one full window. To move to the top of the text, press the (HOME) key. To move to the end, press the (END) key.

Dialog Boxes

Not all information that you will need to give to DOS can be entered using menus. For example, it would be clumsy to enter the time or date using a menu. When information of this type needs to be entered, the Shell uses a special type of window called a *dialog box*. Dialog boxes allow input that is not easily accomplished using a menu. As you will see later in this book, many drop-down menu options make use of dialog boxes. If a pull-down menu item is followed by three periods, it means that selecting this item will cause a dialog box to be displayed.

To see an example of a dialog box, activate the menu bar, select the Options entry, and press (ENTER). Next, select the File Display Options item and press (ENTER). You will see this dialog box:

Dialog box   *A special type of window that allows the user to give DOS information that would be awkward to give using a menu.*

```
╔══════════════ File Display Options ══════════════╗
║                                                   ║
║  Name:    ▓*.*▓_____                              ║
║                                                   ║
║                               Sort by:            ║
║                                                   ║
║  [ ] Display hidden/system files   ● Name         ║
║                                    ○ Extension    ║
║                                    ○ Date         ║
║  [ ] Descending order              ○ Size         ║
║                                    ○ DiskOrder    ║
║                                                   ║
║      (   OK   )      ( Cancel )      ( Help )      ║
║                                                   ║
╚═══════════════════════════════════════════════════╝
```

Dialog boxes consist of one or more of the following items:

- Command buttons
- Check boxes
- Input boxes
- List boxes
- Radio buttons

When a dialog box is active, one of these items will be selected and highlighted. The highlighted item is the focus of input. You can move from one item to the next by pressing the (TAB) key or by clicking on the desired item using the mouse. Let's look closely at what each of these items does.

Command buttons display possible courses of action that relate to the dialog box. You saw an example of these in the Help window. Selecting a command button causes that course of action to be performed immediately. Almost all dialog boxes have at least two command buttons. They are OK and Cancel. Most will also have Help. To activate a button using the keyboard, first select the command buttons by pressing (TAB). Next, use the arrow keys to select the button you want and then press (ENTER). If you have a mouse, simply click on the appropriate button.

A check box looks something like this:

[X] *option*

Here, *option* is some option that can be enabled or disabled. When the box has an "X" in it, that option is selected. If the box is empty, then that option is not selected. To change the state of a check box, tab to the box and then press the space bar. The space bar acts as a toggle; each time you press it, the state of the box changes. You can also change the state of a check box by clicking on it with the mouse.

An input box allows you to enter text such as the time or date. To activate the input box, either press (TAB) until the box is active or click on it using the mouse. Once the input box has been selected, enter text using the keyboard and press (ENTER) when you are done. Or, press (TAB) to move to another dialog box option.

When using an input box, it is important to understand that DOS does not have any idea what you are typing until you enter it by pressing the (ENTER) key. In other words, until you press (ENTER), DOS does not know what you have typed. There is a very important advantage to this approach; you can correct mistakes. DOS requires the information and commands you give it to be in a precise format; it does not accept misspellings, for instance. If you see that you have made a typing er-ror—or if you change your mind about the information you want to enter—you can correct it by using the (BACKSPACE) key, which is the gray key with the arrow pointing to the left (labeled BK on some keyboards), as long as you have not yet pressed (ENTER). Each time you press (BACKSPACE), the cursor backs up one space, erasing whatever was in that space. Once you have erased your error, simply begin typing again.

NOTE

As far as DOS is concerned, uppercase and lowercase letters are the same; that is, any time you communicate with DOS, you can enter information without worrying about the case of the letters. However, keep in mind that many programs that run under DOS are case sensitive and require entries to be in either uppercase or lowercase characters.

A list box presents a list of items from which you can choose. (A list box is similar to a drop-down menu.) To activate the list box, either press (TAB) until the box is active or click on it using the mouse. Once the box is activated, select the item you want by moving the highlight to the appropriate item using the arrow keys and then pressing (ENTER), or double-click on the item using the mouse.

Radio buttons are a list of mutually exclusive options that take this general form:

○ option 1
◉ option 2
.
.
.
○ option N

To activate the radio buttons, tab to them. Use the arrow keys to change the selection, or click on the desired selection using the mouse. The circle containing the dot is the item that is selected. One and only one radio button can be selected at any given time.

Before moving on, you might want to try changing some of the information in the Display Options dialog box. However, be sure to end by selecting the Cancel command button. At this stage, you do not want to alter anything controlled by this window. Selecting Cancel means that none of your changes will actually take effect.

Making Backup Copies of Your Master DOS Diskettes

Now that you know something about the Shell, it is time to put that knowledge to use. If your system is new and you are in charge of it, then the most important first step you can take is to back up the master DOS diskettes provided with your copy of DOS. You will want to do this whether you are running DOS from a fixed disk or from a floppy drive. If you are running DOS from a floppy, that diskette could be destroyed or lost. If one of these events occurs, you will need to make a new set of DOS diskettes. If you use a fixed disk, your fixed disk could break. When repaired, it might require that you reinstall DOS on it. For these reasons, it is imperative to have more than one copy of the DOS diskettes. If the backup has already been made by someone else, you should still read this section so you will know how to do it should the need arise.

In general, you should never work with the original DOS master diskettes but always with the backups. It is best to keep the DOS masters in a safe place so that they are not accidentally destroyed.

To begin the backup procedure, activate the Main group and select Disk Utilities. Next, select the Disk Copy option. You will see the dialog box shown here:

> **NOTE**
> **To back up your DOS master diskettes, you will need several blank diskettes.**

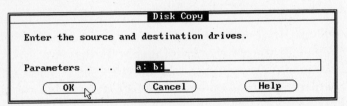

The exact backup procedure varies between systems with two floppy disk drives and those with one floppy drive. Read the section that applies to the configuration of your computer. Be sure to copy all the DOS diskettes by repeating the following procedures. Also, remember to write-protect your master DOS diskettes before backing them up.

Backup With Two Floppy Disk Drives

If your system has two floppy drives, put a DOS master diskette in drive A and a blank diskette in drive B. Since, by default, the Disk Copy option uses these two disk drives, simply press ⟨ENTER⟩ to begin the copying process. The screen will clear and you will see the following messages:

```
Insert SOURCE diskette in drive A:
Insert TARGET diskette in drive B:
Press any key to continue . . .
```

Put a DOS master in drive A and a blank diskette in drive B, then press any key to start the process.

The disk copy process will display some information about what it is doing, but don't worry about it now. Later you will understand what it means. The copy process takes a few minutes on most computers.

After the copy is complete, you will see the message:

```
Copy another diskette (Y/N)?
```

If you wish to make another copy, type **Y** and the copy process will be repeated; otherwise, type **N**. As you will see, many DOS commands require yes or no (Y/N?) responses. (Be sure to copy *all* DOS master diskettes.)

NOTE

To copy a disk using two drives, both drives must be the same size and have the same storage capacity. If this is not the case with your system, follow the instructions for backing up with one floppy drive.

Backup With One Floppy Disk Drive

If your system has only one floppy drive, then you need to change the drive information in the disk copy window to "a: a:". To do this, begin by pressing the Ⓐ key. This will cause the default contents of the Disk Copy dialog box to be cleared. When you have entered **a: a:**, press (ENTER). You will see:

```
Insert SOURCE diskette in drive A:
Press any key to continue . . .
```

You will use drive A for both the source and destination diskettes by swapping them in and out as prompted by the disk copy process. Put a DOS diskette into drive A and close the drive door. Then strike any key. DOS will first read the contents of the DOS diskette into the memory of the computer. Once this has been done, you will see this message:

```
Insert TARGET diskette in drive A:
Press any key to continue . . .
```

At this time, remove the DOS diskette from the computer, put the blank diskette into drive A, and press a key. DOS will then copy the information it read from the DOS diskette onto the blank diskette.

The disk copy will display some information about what it is doing, but don't worry about it now. Later you will understand what it means. The copy process using only one drive can take a few minutes.

After the copy is complete, you will see the message:

```
Copy another diskette (Y/N)?
```

If you wish to make another copy, type **Y** and the copy process will be repeated; otherwise, type **N**. (Be sure to copy *all* DOS master diskettes.) After you type **N**, you will be prompted to press a key to return to the Shell. Do so at this time.

What to Do if Something Goes Wrong

Once in a while, an error will occur when you are copying a diskette, and you will see an error message. Generally, this is caused by a faulty target diskette. The first thing you should do is try the entire process again. Sometimes things will straighten themselves out. If this doesn't work, try a new target diskette. If this still doesn't work, you should seek advice from your instructor or the supplier of your computer.

Labeling the Copies of the DOS Diskettes

Any diskette that contains information should be labeled with the following items:

• A brief description of what is on the diskette

- The copy number
- Your name
- The date

A good title for the DOS operating backup copy is "DOS operating backup disk." Since you might want to have several backup copies, using a copy number is recommended. You can indicate this by calling the first copy "copy: 1," for example. Include the date the diskette was first put in service to help keep diskettes with similar descriptions separate. Finally, putting your name on your diskettes helps to keep them from getting lost. A good layout for the DOS backup label is shown in Figure 2-5. Be sure to prepare the label before you put it on the diskette. Once the label is on, you should use only a felt-tipped pen to make changes or corrections. Using a ballpoint pen or a pencil may result in lost data because of damage to the magnetic surface.

Restarting DOS

It is not necessary to actually turn off your computer and then turn it on again to load DOS. Pressing the keys (CTRL), (ALT), and (DEL) at the same time causes the computer to reload DOS and begin running it. Try doing this now. If you are loading DOS from a diskette, be sure to put the appropriate diskette into drive A. As you can see, DOS restarts.

> **NOTE**
> Restarting DOS in the manner just described is virtually the same as turning the computer off and then back on again. Anything that the computer was doing is completely lost.

You are probably wondering why you would want to restart DOS. There are two possible reasons. First, causing DOS to reload also causes the computer to stop whatever it is doing. Therefore, if the computer begins to do something you think it shouldn't, you can always stop this by reloading DOS. In a sense, pressing the (CTRL), (ALT), and (DEL) keys is an emergency stop signal. For now, since you don't know much about DOS yet, if you think that you have accidentally done something that you shouldn't have, just reload DOS.

You also may need to reload DOS if a program you are running fails. Fortunately, because of the high quality of software available

```
DOS backup diskette
copy: 1
return to: Herbert Schildt
Date: 2/28/94
```

FIGURE 2-5   **A good diskette label layout**

Bug   *Any error found in the software or hardware.*

today, program failures are rare; however, they can still occur. A mistake in a computer program is called a *bug*. Some bugs are simply annoyances, but others are so bad that they can actually cause the computer to stop running. When the computer stops, DOS cannot run, which means you must restart the computer by reloading DOS. It is hoped that you won't have to do this very often.

One last word: In extremely rare situations, a program error can stop the computer so completely that the only way to restart it is to turn it off and then on again.

Turning Off the Computer

When you are ready to turn the computer off, remember to remove all floppy diskettes from the drives. When the power is shut off, there is a fraction of a second when the electricity stored in the power supply of the computer "bleeds" out. During this time of decreasing power, the electronics in the computer are in an unstable state. Although unlikely, the disk drive could possibly write random information onto your diskette. This could destroy valued data. Most computers today have safeguards built in to prevent this, but no safeguard is 100 percent effective.

Summary

At this point you should know how to:

- Start the computer and load DOS and the Shell
- Activate the menu bar and make a selection
- Use the help system
- Use the Shell's windows
- Use dialog boxes
- Move between the Shell's windows
- Make a selection from the Main group
- Make a backup of the DOS diskettes
- Reload DOS
- Safely turn off the computer

In the next chapter you will learn more about DOS files and directories.

Key Terms

Bug   Any error found in the software or hardware.

Dialog box   A special type of window that allows the user to give DOS information that would be awkward to give using a menu.

DOS Shell   A menu-driven interface that helps you easily run DOS 6.

Double click   Pressing the left mouse button twice in quick succession.

Main group   A group that allows you to perform several common DOS activities.

Menu   A list of options from which you may select.

Online help   A system that provides instant information about what you are doing at the press of a key. In DOS 6, it provides information about running DOS.

Scroll bar   A bar on the side and/or bottom of a window that lets you move text through the window.

Window   A portion of the screen that is dedicated to one specific task.

Exercises

Short Answer

1. What keys do you press to restart the computer?

2. Why might you want to restart the computer?

3. What subgroup in the Main group do you select in order to back up a disk?

4. What is a command button?

5. What is a check box?

6. What are radio buttons?

7. What key do you press to activate the help system?

8. Using the mouse, how do you make a menu selection?

9. Using the keyboard, how do you make a menu selection?

10. What does the Directory Tree window show?

True or False

1. DOS 6 does not allow menu selections to be performed using the mouse. _____

2. The purpose of the Shell is to make running DOS easier. _____

3. To move about the Shell you press the (TAB) key. _____

4. The Main group contains commonly used DOS operations and utilities. _____

5. The online help system is not context sensitive. _____

6. A window is a portion of the screen. _____

7. A scroll bar is used to change disk drives. _____

8. A dialog box is a small device attached to the memory of your computer that a modem plugs into. _____

9. A list box contains a list of items from which you may choose. _____

10. All floppy disks that contain information should be labeled. _____

Activities

1. Try restarting your computer by pressing the correct key combination.

2. If you have not yet done so, make a backup of your DOS master diskettes.

3

File Manager Basics

CHAPTER OBJECTIVES

After completing this chapter, you should be able to:

- Explain what a file is.
- Understand file names.
- Understand what the current drive is.
- Understand tree-structured directories.
- Describe what a path is.
- Select the DOS directory.
- Understand the directory listing.
- Identify different file types.
- Differentiate between internal and external commands.
- Understand the concepts of tracks and sectors.
- Interpret DOS error messages.
- Format a diskette.

Although the preceding chapter made little distinction between them, the Shell is comprised of two major components. The first component manages the files on your disks. The second manages your programs. For the sake of discussion, the part of the Shell that works with your files will be called the File Manager, and the part that works with programs will be called the Program Manager. In general terms, the File Manager manages the information on your disks. The Program Manager helps you organize programs.

The File Manager is accessed through a system of three related windows: the Disk Drive window, the Directory Tree window, and the File List window. The Program Manager includes the Main group window and all subgroups. This chapter introduces the File Manager. (The Program Manager is covered later in this book.)

Before you can go much further in your study of DOS, you need to understand how the Shell's File Manager operates. However, in order to understand the File Manager, you will need to know something about the way DOS organizes information on a disk. This chapter introduces several important concepts and terms relating to the File Manager and lays the groundwork for much of the rest of the book, so a careful reading is suggested.

What Is a File?

File   A file is a collection of related information that is stored on a disk.

In the previous chapter, the term *file* was used without any formal definition. Now it is time to provide a more detailed definition.

A file is a collection of related information stored on either a floppy or a fixed disk. (For the rest of this discussion, the word *disk* will refer to both a floppy disk and a fixed disk.) The information stored on the disk is encoded magnetically. The magnetic medium of a disk is essentially the same as recording tape used in an audiotape recorder. The process of putting information onto the disk is very similar to making a tape recording; reading the information from a disk is similar to playing a tape recording.

A disk can hold several files. In a sense, a disk is like a file cabinet, and disk files are like paper files in a file cabinet. For example, the same disk might contain a letter, a mailing list, and a general ledger, each in a separate file. Because they are in separate files, they can't become mixed up. Figure 3-1 illustrates conceptually the way files are stored on a disk. (As you will see later, file storage is a little more complicated than this.)

Information is stored on a disk in much the same way that it is stored in memory: byte by byte. (Remember, a byte is the amount of memory required to store one character.) For example, a file might contain the sentence "This is a test." The individual characters that make up that sentence are stored on the disk one byte at a time.

The single most important fact you should know about disk files is that they are concrete, physical entities. They are as real as paper files. Anything you can do with a paper file can be done with a disk file. This includes copying it, changing it, adding to it, changing its name, and unfortunately, losing it. If you keep this fact in mind, you will have no trouble running DOS.

Filename   The part of a file name to the left of the period.

Extension   The part of the file name to the right of the period.

File Names

Each file on a disk must have a unique name to identify it. A file name can consist of two parts. The first part, traditionally called the *filename*, is what you will think of as the name of the file. It may be from one to eight characters long. The second part of a file name is called the *extension*. Although the extension is optional, it is generally used. The extension

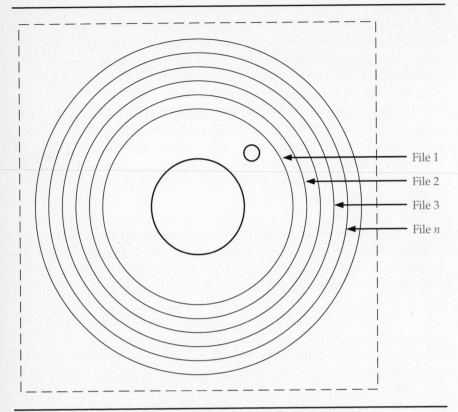

FIGURE 3-1   **A simplified view of files stored on a disk**

exists to help create groups of similar files or to distinguish two files
with the same filename from one another. The extension may be up to
three characters long. In a way, the filename is like a person's first name
and the extension is like a person's last name. You have already seen
some examples of file names in the Shell's File List window.

To fully specify a file, you must use both the filename and the extension. The filename is separated from the extension by a period. An
example of a file name is TEST.TST. In this case, TEST is the filename
and TST is the extension. Although file names are aligned in such a
way in the File List window that some have spaces before the period
and extension, when you specify a file name, you must not use spaces.

In general, most file names are made up of letters and the digits 0
through 9. However, the only characters that cannot be used in a file
name are the following:

." / \ [ ] : | < > + = ; ,

Also, control characters are not allowed. (A control character is generated by holding down the (CTRL) key and pressing another key.)

The Current Drive

Most computers have more than one disk drive. However, only one
disk drive will have the focus of DOS at any one time. You can tell
DOS what drive to use explicitly, as you did when you made backup

copies of the DOS diskettes. For example, if you have two floppy drives, you essentially tell DOS to switch its focus between drive A and B when it copies the disk. If you do not explicitly tell DOS which drive to use, it will use the *currently active drive*, which is usually referred to as the *logged-in* drive. The currently logged-in drive is the one highlighted in the Disk Drive window.

As you should recall from the preceding chapter, when active, the drive identifier window highlights the currently logged-in drive. You may select a different drive by using the ⬅ and ➡ keys and pressing (ENTER) when the highlight is on the drive you want. If you have a mouse, you can simply single-click on the drive you want to log in.

If you are running DOS from a floppy, then by default, drive A is the logged-in drive. If you have a fixed disk, then by default, drive C is logged in. When you switch drives, the information in the Directory Tree and File List windows is automatically updated to reflect this change. That is, you will see the new disk's directory and files. However, do not try switching drives at this time.

DOS's Tree-Structured Directory

All disks have a *directory*. The directory of a disk is a little like the table of contents of a book: it tells what the disk contains. The directory lists the names of the files and each file's length and time and date of creation. The contents of a directory are listed in the File List window.

Although all disks will have at least one directory, a disk can contain several directories, with each directory containing a group of related files.

The one directory that will always be on a disk is called the *root directory*. The root directory is created when the disk is prepared for use.

You can also define subdirectories of the root directory. A *subdirectory* is more or less a directory within a directory. You can think of the root directory as enclosing the subdirectory. A subdirectory usually holds a group of related files. The exact nature of the relationship is purely subjective. For example, a subdirectory could hold all of a certain employee's files—no matter how divergent in purpose and use. Another subdirectory might hold wage information for all the employees of a company. Keep in mind that DOS does not know—or care—how the files are related; it simply treats a subdirectory as a group. Any relationship that files in a subdirectory have to each other is purely for the benefit of you, the user.

It is common for a subdirectory to have its own subdirectories. In fact, assuming there is sufficient disk space, any directory can contain a subdirectory.

You can think of the root directory as being like a filing cabinet with each drawer labeled and used for a specific purpose. The drawers can be thought of as subdirectories. Each drawer (subdirectory) is enclosed by the cabinet (root). Within each drawer, the files can be further organized by topic. This is analogous to a subdirectory within a subdirectory.

Current drive   *The drive that is currently the focus of DOS.*

Directory   *A listing of files on a disk.*

Root directory   *The first and top level directory on a disk.*

Subdirectory   *A directory that is within another directory.*

It is important to understand that a subdirectory is simply a term used to describe a relationship between two directories. The directory that encloses a subdirectory is called the parent directory. The only directory that does not have a parent is the root.

Throughout this chapter and the rest of the book, unless specific clarification is required, the term "directory" will refer to any type of directory—root or subdirectory.

The disk directory structure used by DOS is called *tree structured* because, when drawn in a diagram on paper, the root and subdirectories resemble the root system of a tree. For example, the directory structure of a disk that is used by a small, hypothetical insurance office may look like that shown (conceptually) in Figure 3-2.

In Figure 3-2, the root directory contains three subdirectories: word processing, accounting, and games. Word processing, in turn, contains two subdirectories of its own: form letters and temporary letters. The accounting subdirectory contains three subdirectories: AR (accounts receivable), AP (accounts payable), and GL (general ledger). The games subdirectory has no further subdirectories.

The theory and rationale behind tree-structured directories is that related groups of files can be treated as units of increasing specialization. For example, the directory for word processing branches from the root because word processing is a logically separate task from accounting and games. Word processing itself contains two distinct types of documents: reusable form letters and disposable, single-use correspondence. As you move down the tree from the root, each directory becomes more specialized in what it contains.

Tree-structured directory   *A hierarchical approach to organizing a disk's directory.*

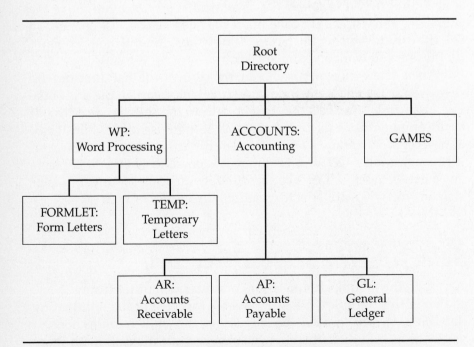

FIGURE 3-2   A diagram of a tree-structured directory

Paths and Path Names

Path   *The route to any given file beginning at the root directory.*

Each directory has a unique *path* from the root to itself. For example, using the directories shown in Figure 3-2, the path to the GL directory, beginning at the root, is first to ACCOUNTS and then to GL. In the language of DOS, you specify a path by using a path name. The path name for the GL directory is \ACCOUNTS\GL. The first backslash is DOS's name for the root. Subsequent backslashes act as separators between each directory in the path and, finally, the file name.

The general form of a path name is shown here:

\dir1\dir2\dir3...\dirN

For example, the full path name for the AP directory is

\ACCOUNTS\AP

Paths and path names will be discussed again later in this book, but you need to know a little about them now so that the title to the File List window makes sense. It displays the path to the current directory. (Don't worry about the "*.*" at this time. It will be explained in a later chapter.)

If your disk contains subdirectories, then they will be displayed in a tree-like fashion in the Directory Tree window. However, in order to save space, the "tree" is displayed sideways.

Selecting a Directory

To select a directory using the keyboard, first activate the Directory Tree window, and then position the highlight on the directory you want by using the ⊕ and ⊕ keys. Each time you move the highlight to a new directory, it becomes the current directory. As you move the highlight, you will see the contents of the File List window change. To select a directory using the mouse, simply position the mouse pointer on the one you want and single-click.

When a new directory is chosen, the contents of that directory are displayed in the File List window. Also, as stated earlier, the title of the File List window reflects the current path to the selected directory. If your computer has a fixed disk and has been in use for a while, it will almost certainly contain a fairly complete directory structure. However, if you are running DOS from a floppy it is possible that it will not have any subdirectories, so don't be surprised if you don't see any. In a later chapter, you will learn how to create subdirectories of your own.

Selecting the DOS Directory

Although the organization of your computer will differ from the one shown in the examples, it is still possible for most of the information displayed on your screen to be the same as that shown in this book. If you have a fixed disk, then to synchronize your displays with those shown in this book, you must simply select the DOS directory. The DOS directory contains those files that are part of DOS. If DOS was

installed on your computer using the normal installation procedure,
then you should see a directory in the Directory Tree window called
DOS. (You may have to scroll the Directory Tree window to find it.)
You should highlight that directory. Your screen will look similar to
that shown in Figure 3-3.

If you don't see a DOS directory, you will need to ask the person in
charge of your computer where the DOS files are stored and select that
directory.

If you are running DOS from a floppy disk, just leave your startup
disk in drive A. What you see will still be similar to (though not the
same as) that shown in subsequent examples.

> NOTE
>
> **If you have a fixed disk,
> then to follow along with
> the examples in this book,
> select the DOS directory
> before proceeding.**

The Directory Listing

Once a directory has been selected, the files that are contained within
that directory are displayed in the File List window. The entry for each
file contains four elements. First is the filename followed by the file's
extension. Next comes the length of the file in bytes. Finally, the creation date of the file is shown.

If the Shell is running in graphics mode, then a fifth element is
included in the directory listing for each file: a small, rectangular icon
at the start of each filename, which tells you if a file contains an executable program. (An icon is a small symbol that represents something.)
If the icon shows a computer screen, then the file contains a program.
If it shows a piece of paper with a corner turned over, the file does not
contain a program. In text mode, no icons are shown.

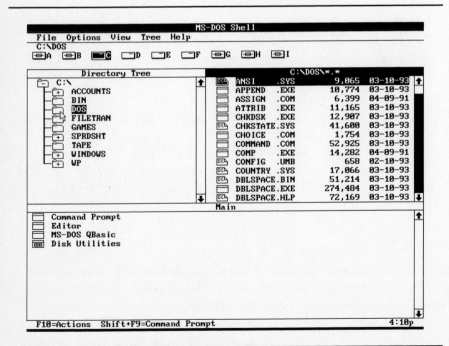

FIGURE 3-3   **The DOS directory**

When a file is selected, its file name is highlighted in graphics mode. In text mode, a small triangle is put in front of the filename.

All files listed in the same directory have unique names. Two files with the same filename and extension will not be allowed. However, two files in different directories can have the same name. (Of course, their full path names will differ.)

REMEMBER

When DOS displays file names, it puts spaces between the filename and extension. However, whenever you need to tell DOS about a file, you must not use any spaces in the name.

Notice the Directory Tree window in Figure 3-3. Each directory has associated with it a small icon that looks like a file folder. Also notice that some folders contain a "+" symbol. If the folder contains a "+", this means that the directory contains one or more subdirectories. In the next chapter you will see how to make the File Manager display all subdirectories. If your computer does not support graphics, then no icons are present. However, in text mode each directory is preceded by two square brackets. If the brackets enclose a "+", then that directory has one or more subdirectories.

File Types

Three types of files can be stored on a disk:

- Text files
- Data files
- Program files

Let's see what they consist of.

Text Files

A text file contains information that you can read. It consists solely of characters that can be displayed on the screen. A common way text files are created is by word processors. In most cases, text files are created and maintained by you. (You will see how later.)

Text files may use any previously unused filename and any extension. However, no text files should use the extension .EXE or .COM because these extensions are reserved for program files. Text files can be displayed on the monitor.

Data Files

A data file contains information that a program, not a person, can read. Most data files cannot be displayed on the monitor because the information they contain is in a form that only the computer can understand. The special internal representation used by the computer for data is sometimes referred to as binary. Binary is a system of representing data as a series of 1s and 0s.

Data files are created and maintained by programs. For example, an inventory management program will create and maintain a data file that holds inventory information.

As with text files, data files may be assigned any previously unused filename and any extension except the extensions .EXE, .COM, or .BAT. Many data files use the extension .DAT.

Program Files

Program files contain programs that the computer can execute. Unlike the two other file types, in DOS all program files use the extension .COM, .EXE, or .BAT. Although some differences exist among program files that use the .COM, .BAT, or .EXE extension, you need to know only that they are program files and are functionally the same. Most program files are created by programmers, although you will learn to create some simple ones yourself.

Many of the programs you will use are application programs. As the name implies, an application program is a program applied to a specific task. For example, a general ledger program is an application program in the area of accounting. In essence, an application program is used to solve a specific problem or to perform a specific task.

Reserved Extensions

DOS reserves a few file name extensions for special purposes. For example, .EXE, .COM., and .BAT are reserved for program files. The .SYS extension indicates files that only DOS uses. The extension .CPI is reserved by DOS for hardware-specific information. The extension .BAS indicates BASIC program files. Other extensions used by DOS include .OVL, .PRO, .VID, .HLP, .GRB, .INF, and .INI. It is best not to use any of the reserved extensions in the file names that you create.

Internal and External Commands

DOS commands are divided into two major groups: internal commands and external commands. An *internal command* is contained in the part of DOS that stays loaded in the memory of your computer. When you execute an internal command, DOS responds almost instantly. The DOS internal commands are those that you are most likely to need frequently as you use the computer.

An *external command* is not loaded into memory with the rest of DOS; rather, it remains on the disk to conserve the computer's memory. DOS includes many seldom-used commands. Instead of having these consume memory that your application programs could use, DOS leaves them on the disk until they are needed. If you are running DOS from floppies, you might need to switch disks to get access to a desired command. Also, because external commands are loaded by DOS as needed, there is a slight delay before DOS responds when you use an external command. After an external command has executed, it is no longer kept in memory; it must be reloaded each time it is used.

Internal command A command that is loaded into memory when DOS is first executed. Internal commands are always ready to be executed.

External command A command that resides on disk until it is needed.

If your computer has a fixed disk, make sure that drive C is logged in and that the DOS directory is selected. If you are using floppies, make sure the DOS Startup diskette is in drive A and that drive A is currently logged in. The directory shown in the directory window is used by DOS. This is where the external commands are stored. Not all files are external commands—just those that end in .COM, .EXE, or .BAT. The other files are essentially data files used by DOS. Keep in mind that an external command is a program supplied by DOS.

The names of the DOS external commands are the same as the filename part of the file names. For example, CHKDSK.EXE corresponds to the DOS command CHKDSK, which is used for checking the status of a disk.

Although the most common DOS functions have been made into menu entries inside the Shell, it is likely that, at some point in time, you will need to specify a command that is not on a menu. Adding commands to the Shell is discussed later, but, in essence, it involves specifying the command's name plus any options the command may require.

The names of the internal and external commands are shown in Table 3-1.

Tracks and Sectors: A Closer Look at How DOS Stores Files

The first part of this chapter provided a simplified explanation of the way DOS stores files on a disk. Here is a closer look. Although understanding the exact method DOS uses to store a file is not technically necessary in order to use DOS, understanding the concepts behind file storage will help you interpret certain DOS messages that refer to them. Also, many books, user manuals, and magazine articles assume that you have a basic understanding of the way DOS files are stored.

Track   A narrow band that forms a complete circle on a disk that is used to hold information.

Sector   A portion of a track.

Information is recorded on a disk in concentric circles called *tracks*. When the disk drive loads a program, you can sometimes hear the read/write head move between tracks. Each track is comprised of a number of *sectors*. (The exact number varies and is not important.) Each sector can hold 512 bytes (characters) and is the smallest accessible unit of storage on the disk. (Actually, DOS can use sector sizes other than 512, but it virtually never does.) When DOS records a file on a disk, it does not necessarily use sectors and tracks that are adjacent to each other. That is, DOS may scatter a file throughout the disk's surface. (This is why even a small amount of physical damage to a disk can destroy several files.) This situation is depicted in Figure 3-4.

The smallest accessible unit of disk storage, the sector, is 512 bytes long. This does not mean, however, that the smallest file is 512 bytes. On the contrary, you can have files of any length, including 0. However, the full 512-byte sector is allocated to each file, and the rest of the space is not used. (For this reason, several small files can sometimes fill up a disk faster than a few large ones.)

As you can guess, when a file longer than one sector is stored on a disk, there must be some way for DOS to know which sector goes with

Internal Commands

BREAK	DATE	MKDIR (MD)	TIME
CHCP	DEL (ERASE)	PATH	TYPE
CHDIR (CD)	DIR	PROMPT	VER
CLS	ERASE (DEL)	RENAME (REN)	VERIFY
COPY	EXIT	RMDIR (RD)	VOL
CTTY	LOADHIGH (LH)	SET	

External Commands

APPEND	DOSSHELL	JOIN	PRINT
ASSIGN	EDIT	KEYB	QBASIC
ATTRIB	EDLIN	LABEL	RECOVER
BACKUP	EMM386	LOADFIX	REPLACE
CHKDSK	EXE2BIN	MEM	RESTORE
COMMAND	EXPAND	MEMMAKER	SETVER
COMP	FASTHELP	MIRROR	SHARE
DBLSPACE	FASTOPEN	MODE	SORT
DEBUG	FC	MORE	SUBST
DEFRAG	FDISK	MOVE	SYS
DELTREE	FIND	MSAV	TREE
DISKCOMP	FORMAT	MSBACKUP	UNDELETE
DISKCOPY	GRAFTABL	MSD	UNFORMAT
DOS	GRAPHICS	NLSFUNC	VSAFE
DOSKEY	HELP	POWER	XCOPY

TABLE 3-1   **DOS's internal and external commands**

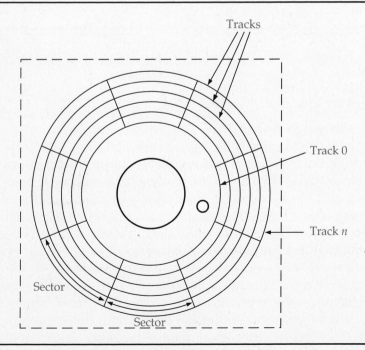

FIGURE 3-4   **Sectors and tracks on a disk**

which file. DOS accomplishes this by storing the location of each sector in a file allocation table, sometimes called the FAT for short. DOS refers to this table when it accesses a file.

The exact physical position of the tracks and sectors on a disk is determined when the disk is formatted. When you made a backup of the DOS master disk, the copy procedure automatically formatted the disk prior to placing information on it. All disks must be formatted before being used. When a disk is not formatted, DOS and the computer have no way of knowing where to put information.

A DOS Error Message

One thing about using a computer that you simply must expect and accept is that from time to time an error will occur. Fortunately, most errors are minor and cause no real damage. However, since you are new to DOS and to the way it reports errors, now is a good time for you to gain a little experience. In this section, we will generate a harmless error so that you can see how DOS responds and what type of response DOS expects from you when an error occurs.

Let's generate an error message. Open the drive door on drive A, and if a diskette is in the drive, remove it. Next, select the A drive using the drive identifier window. Because the drive door is open, DOS will not be able to read the diskette's directory and it will generate the error window shown here:

Notice that there are two options shown in the error dialog window:

1. Try to read this disk again.
2. Do not try to read disk again.

Since there is no disk in drive A, select the second option. Next, log back into drive C if you have a fixed disk and then select the DOS directory again. If you are working from a floppy disk, insert your DOS diskette, close the drive door, and log back into drive A.

In general, errors can occur for a variety of reasons. Some errors, like the one we just generated on purpose, can be fixed by changing something. For example, you could insert a diskette and then select the first option. For these types of errors, you will generally want to change whatever is wrong and then try the operation again. However, there are some types of errors that cannot be rectified at the time. For example, suppose you try to log into a broken disk drive. For this type of error, select the second option and do not retry the operation.

DOS can generate other types of error messages. The most important of these will be discussed as the need arises.

Formatting Diskettes

To follow along with the examples in the next chapter, you will need a blank, *formatted* diskette. Let's make one now.

Before you can use a diskette to store information, the diskette must be formatted. The formatting process prepares the diskette by setting up the tracks and sectors that DOS uses to store information. It also creates the root directory. If you try to use an unformatted diskette, DOS will issue an error message.

To format a disk, first activate the Main group window and select the Disk Utilities option; then select Format. You will see the Format dialog window displayed. It will look like the one shown here:

Format   To prepare a diskette for use.

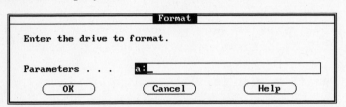

By default, the Format option formats the disk in drive A. (You can change it to drive B if you like.) The formatting option uses an external command called FORMAT, so this command must be on the disk that you are using.

The FORMAT command must be used with care because the formatting process can destroy the data that already exists on a diskette. If you are preparing a new diskette for use, then there is no data to destroy. However, if you accidentally format a diskette that contains data, you run the risk of losing that data forever. Although DOS 6 does contain a command that will, in some cases, unformat a disk and recover your data, you should not rely upon this because it is not possible to undo an accidental format in all cases.

CAUTION

Until you know much more about DOS and your computer, never format your fixed disk. Generally, the fixed disk will already be formatted and will not need to be formatted again. Doing so may irreversibly destroy all files on the disk.

To start formatting, press (ENTER). The screen will clear and you will be told to insert the blank diskette into drive A and press (ENTER). For now, remove any diskette that might be in drive A and put in the blank diskette you are going to format; then press (ENTER). (Note: you must press (ENTER); clicking the mouse has no effect.) This double check is a safety feature that helps prevent you from accidentally formatting the wrong diskette. As the formatting procedure executes, it continually displays the amount of the diskette that has been formatted. Since it takes about a minute to format a disk, this display lets you know that the computer is still working.

When the formatting process is finished, this message will be displayed:

```
Format complete
```

```
Volume label (11 characters, ENTER for none)?
```

The volume label is more or less the disk's name. Although not required, volume labels can be useful in certain situations. Use the name MYDISK for this diskette's volume label and press ⒺⓃⓉⒺⓇ. Next, you will see something similar to this:

```
    1457664 bytes of total disk space
    1457664 bytes available on disk

        512 bytes in each allocation unit.
       2847 allocation units available on disk.
```

```
Volume Serial Number is 341A-15ED
```

```
Format another (Y/N)?
```

The message actually displayed may differ from the one shown here in several ways. First, there are several different types of floppy drives. These drives have different storage capacities, so if the number of bytes of total or available disk space differs, do not worry about it. The message also may differ if part of the floppy diskette was bad and could not be formatted. Although this is not a common occurrence, you are sure to encounter it at some point. If you do, the number of bytes of total disk storage will differ from the amount available, and you will see another line that tells you the exact number of unusable bytes. It is usually best to discard a diskette with bad sectors and use a new one because such a diskette often will deteriorate quickly. Finally, the number of bytes per allocation unit and the number of allocation units per disk depend upon the type of the disk drive. Finally, the volume serial number will almost certainly be different.

Since you need only one diskette, respond to the prompt by pressing **N**. This causes the Disk Utilities group to be displayed once again. To return to the Main group, select the Main option.

Summary

You should now understand:

- What the File Manager is
- What a file is
- How file names are constructed
- The purpose of the directory
- The differences among text, data, and program files
- How to change the current drive
- The difference between internal and external commands
- What tracks and sectors are

- How to interpret a DOS error message
- How to format a diskette

Now that you have seen how DOS stores files, maintains directories, and the differences between files, the next chapter shows you how to use the File Manager to manipulate those files. You will also learn to run external DOS commands and application programs.

Key Terms

Current drive   The drive that is currently the focus of DOS.

Directory   A listing of files on a disk.

Extension   The part of the file name to the right of the period. It can be up to three characters long and is similar in concept to a person's last name.

External command   A command that resides on disk until it is needed.

File   A file is a collection of related information that is stored on a disk.

Filename   The part of a file name to the left of the period. It can be up to eight characters long. It is similar in concept to a person's first name.

Format   To prepare a diskette for use.

Internal command   A command that is loaded into memory when DOS is first executed. Internal commands are always ready to be executed.

Path   The route to any given file beginning at the root directory.

Root directory   The first and lowest level directory on a disk. All disks have a root directory.

Sector   A portion of a track. A sector is the smallest amount of disk space that can be accessed. Sectors are commonly 512 bytes long.

Subdirectory   A directory that is within another directory. Put differently, a subdirectory is a child directory of the directory that encloses it.

Track   A narrow band that forms a complete circle on a disk that is used to hold information. All disks contain several concentric tracks.

Tree-structured directory   A hierarchical approach to organizing a disk's directory.

Exercises

Short Answer

1. Which of these file names are valid?
   a. MYFILE.WP
   b. ACCOUNTS.DAT
   c. MYPROGRAM.EXE
   d. LETTER.FORMLET
   e. ONE+TWO.DAT
   f. [MYFILE].INF
   g. MYFILE

2. What extensions does DOS reserve for program files?

3. What are the three general types of files that you will find on a disk?

4. In a file name, how long can the filename be? How long can the extension be?

5. What directory will all diskettes have?

6. Briefly, what is the current drive?

7. Can two files in the same directory have the same name?

8. In the Shell's directory listing, what information about each file is displayed?

9. Name an extension that is reserved by DOS for a special type of file.

10. What is the difference between an internal and an external command?

11. Explain what a track is. Explain what a sector is.

12. What function does formatting perform?

True or False

1. A file name may be as long as necessary to fully describe the contents of a file. _____

2. Formatting a disk is optional if that disk will be used only in drive B. _____

3. If you see a DOS error message, the best thing to do is to turn off your computer for a few minutes so that it has a chance to cool down. _____

4. A sector is the smallest accessible unit of storage available on a diskette. _____

5. CLS, COPY, DIR, and TIME are internal commands. _____

6. FORMAT is an external command. _____

7. The only difference between internal and external commands is that you must memorize how to use internal commands. _____

8. A text file normally contains information that you can read. _____

9. A program file contains data that a program can read. _____

10. The Shell's directory listing tells you the date of creation of each file. _____

11. Tree-structured directories can only be used with the fixed disk. _____

12. A file is a collection of related information that resides on disk. _____

Activities

1. Format two blank diskettes.

2. Put your Student Data Disk into drive A and then switch to drive A by selecting it using the File Manager. Notice how the File List window changes. (If your computer has only floppy drives, put the Student Data Disk into drive B and switch to drive B.) Before continuing, switch back to the original drive.

CHAPTER

Using the File Manager

CHAPTER OBJECTIVES
After completing this chapter, you should be able to:
- Start running a program.
- Understand the options in the File Manager menu bar.
- View the contents of a text file.
- Copy and move a file using the keyboard and the mouse.
- Erase a file.
- Rename a file.
- Change the directory tree display.
- Use wildcard characters.
- Display detailed information about a file.
- Change the way the Shell arranges the screen.

In Chapter 3 you learned many important concepts about files and directories. In this chapter you will learn to apply those concepts by using the *File Manager*. This chapter introduces several of the most common and fundamental DOS File Manager operations. You will learn how to execute a program and how to view a text file. You will also see how to copy and erase a file and how to change the way that the directory is displayed. By the time you finish this chapter, you will be able to begin running your own application programs.

To follow along with the examples in this and subsequent chapters, you will need a blank, formatted diskette. If you have not yet made one, refer to the end of Chapter 3 for instructions.

File Manager   The part of the Shell that helps you manage your files. It also lets you run programs.

55

Starting a Program

> **NOTE**
> If you are using a fixed disk, log into drive C and select the DOS directory. If you are running DOS from a floppy, make sure that a DOS diskette is in drive A and log into drive A.

It is easy to start a program using the File Manager. The general process is to first highlight the program you want to run in the File List window and then press (ENTER). Or, using a mouse, simply double-click on the program you want to execute. To see an example of this, you will execute a DOS external command. As was mentioned in the last chapter, DOS external commands are actually programs that are supplied by DOS. Thus, the basic method used to execute an external command will also apply to any application program you have.

Let's try running a program now. If DOS has been installed in the normal way, then in the File List window you will see the file CHKDSK.EXE. This is the DOS command that reports on the status of your disk. To execute this command, position the highlight on this command and press (ENTER). If you have a mouse, you can double-click on CHKDSK.EXE to execute it.

Execute CHKDSK.EXE at this time. The screen will clear and the disk drive will be accessed. For some systems, this command may take a few seconds to finish execution. The CHKDSK command will display information about the state of your disk drive as well as the amount of memory in the computer. For the moment, ignore the information. (CHKDSK will be examined closely a little later.) After the information is displayed, you will be told to press any key to return to the Shell. Press a key now. The screen will again clear and the Shell will be reactivated.

For the example just given, and the other examples in this chapter, you are using the DOS directory or disk. However, when you want to run an application program, you will probably need to switch to a different directory or disk, or both, containing the application.

When working with files in the File List window, it is important to understand that there is a difference between selecting a file and executing a file. When you select a file by moving the highlight to it or by single-clicking the mouse on the desired file, you are telling the Shell that you are interested in this file and that you may want to do something with it in the future. However, the file itself is not directly affected. But, when you press (ENTER) or double-click the mouse on a file, you are doing something with the file now—you are executing it. The distinction may seem blurred at this point, but as you learn more about how the File Manager operates, the difference between selecting a file and executing a file will become clearer.

Before continuing, let's execute another DOS command. Using either the scroll bar or the (PGUP) and (PGDN) keys, locate and highlight the file MEM.EXE. This is the DOS command that displays information about the memory in your system. Execute it now. Again, your screen will clear and information will be displayed about the memory in your computer. Press any key to return to the Shell. As with the output of the CHKDSK command, you don't need to worry about what MEM.EXE is telling you. Once you know more about DOS and the system you are using, you will understand it.

A Closer Look at the File Manager Menu Bar

The File Manager menu bar has five options: File, Options, View, Tree, and Help. Each of these options displays a drop-down menu when selected. The following sections present an overview of what each option does.

NOTE

Sometimes an option in a drop-down menu is not always available or applicable to what you are currently doing. When an option is not available for use, it is shown in low-intensity and cannot be selected.

The File Option

Most of the File options relate to a file that you have selected in the File List window. To follow along, activate the File List window and move the highlight to the file called DOSSHELL.HLP.

Select the File option now. You will see this window.

```
┌──────────────────────────────────┐
│ File                             │
├──────────────────────────────────┤
│ Open                             │
│ Run...                           │
│ Print                            │
│ Associate...                     │
│ Search...                        │
│ View File Contents       F9      │
│                                  │
│ Move...                  F7      │
│ Copy...                  F8      │
│ Delete...                Del     │
│ Rename...                        │
│ Change Attributes...             │
│                                  │
│ Create Directory...              │
│                                  │
│ Select All                       │
│ Deselect All                     │
│                                  │
│ Exit                   Alt+F4    │
└──────────────────────────────────┘
```

The File option allows you to perform several operations that relate to files.

The first option is Open, which starts running the program highlighted in the File List window. Selecting this option accomplishes the same thing as starting a program using the files window. This option is only meaningful for program files. You cannot run a non-program file. If the Open command is shown in low-intensity, it means that you forgot to highlight the DOSSHELL.HLP file.

The next option, Run, is similar to Open except that it allows you to specify certain options required by some programs.

If you have a printer, you can use the Print option to print the contents of a text file. If the Print option is shown as not available, you will learn later in this book how to activate it.

The Associate option is used to link one file to another. The Search option lets you search your disk for a specific file (or set of files). If the file is found, then it is displayed.

View File Contents lets you see the contents of a file. This is most useful with text files. Program files with the extension .EXE or .COM contain codes that only the computer can read, so viewing one of these is of little value (except to programmers). Also, some types of data files cannot be read because the information in them is in a special form.

The Move option lets you move a file from one place to another. In general you can move a file between disks or between directories. When you move a file, it is erased from its original position after being copied to its new place.

Copy is like Move except that the original file is not erased. Delete lets you remove (erase) a file from a disk. It also lets you remove a subdirectory. The Rename option allows you to change the name of a file or a subdirectory.

Change Attributes is used to change one or more of a file's attributes. Every file has associated with it a set of parameters that tell DOS certain things about the file. Some of these can be set by you.

The Create Directory option allows you to create a new subdirectory. Select All selects all the files in the current directory. Deselect All deselects all the files in the current directory.

The Exit option removes the Shell and activates the command prompt interface. Do not select this option until you have learned how to run DOS using the command prompt.

Options

Press the ⊙ key to activate the Options menu. This entry allows you to change the way various parts of the Shell operate.

The first option is Confirmation, which lets you control whether various safety check windows are displayed when you Delete or replace a file. The next option is File Display Options. It is used to change the way the files are displayed in the File List window.

The Select Across Directories option allows you to select files in more than one directory. The Show Information option displays information about the current disk and directory. The Enable Task Swapper option allows you to activate DOS 6's Task Manager. (The Task Manager will be discussed in the next chapter.) The Display option lets you change the resolution of your screen so that either more or fewer lines of text can be displayed within the Shell's windows. Colors lets you change the color scheme used by the Shell.

The View Option

Press the ⊙ key to activate the View menu. The options associated with View let you change how the Shell arranges the screen.

The first option is Single File List. Selecting this option causes the Program Manager to be removed from the screen, and the extra room is allocated to the Directory Tree and File List windows. Selecting the Dual File Lists option splits the screen horizontally and lets you display the contents of two separate directories and/or drives at the same time. In this arrangement, the Program Manager is also removed from the screen.

Selecting the All Files option causes the directory structure of the disk to be ignored and all files on the logged-in disk to be displayed. The Program/File Lists option causes the screen to be configured in its default arrangement with both the File Manager and the Program Manager present. Selecting the Program List option causes the Directory Tree and File List windows to be removed with the extra space allocated to the Program Manager.

The Repaint Screen option redisplays the screen. Some types of programs may cause the Shell's screen to be overwritten. If this happens, simply select this option. The Refresh option repaints the screen and updates the Shell's file information.

The Tree Option

Press the ⊝ key to activate the Tree option. The options associated with Tree let you control how a disk's directory is displayed in the Directory Tree window.

The Expand One Level option causes the next level of subdirectories contained within the currently selected directory to be displayed in the Directory Tree window.

The Expand Branch option causes all levels of subdirectories contained within the currently selected directory to be displayed in the Directory Tree window. The Expand All option causes all subdirectories to be shown in the Directory Tree window. The Collapse Branch option causes any subdirectories of the highlighted directory to be removed from the screen. This is the opposite of Expand Branch.

The directory options will be explored in the next chapter when you learn how to create and manage your own directories.

The Help Option

Press the ⊝ key to activate the Help option. This option lets you access the Help system.

The Index option displays an index of help topics. The Keyboard option explains various keys that have a special meaning for DOS. The Shell Basics option displays information about the basic operation of the Shell. The Commands option displays information about the Shell commands. Procedures discusses how to perform various common operations. The Using Help option teaches you how to use the help system, and About Shell causes the DOS version number to be displayed.

Using the Menu Bar's Hot Keys

As you worked through the preceding sections relating to the various menus, you probably noticed that several of the menu options had keys (or key combinations) listed to the right of the menu item. These keys are referred to as *hot keys* which, when pressed, immediately activate the item they are associated with without having to first activate the menu. For example, activate the File menu now. Notice that the

Hot key *A key or key combination that lets you select a menu item without having to first activate the menu.*

Copy option can also be directly activated by pressing the (F8) key. You will want to make mental notes of these hot keys because learning them will make running the Shell easier and faster.

In some cases, instead of a single key, a key combination is shown to the right of the menu option. A key combination is created when two keys are pressed at the same time. For example, the hot key that exits the Shell is (ALT)-(F4). To create this key combination, press the (ALT) and (F4) keys at the same time. Or, if easier for you, press and hold the (ALT) key and then press the (F4) key, finally releasing both keys at the same time. But, don't try this now. As you will see, key combinations are used frequently when running the Shell. In this book, a key combination will be notated using this general form:

special key-key

where *special key* is either (ALT), (SHIFT), or (CTRL). For example, the combination of (ALT) and (H) is shown as (ALT)-(H). This means that you should press both the (ALT) and (H) keys at the same time.

Viewing a File

Now that you have seen the various elements of the File System, let's put them to work. First, if it is not already selected, select the file DOSSHELL.HLP. (Remember, to select a file, activate the File List window and move the highlight to the file—or move the mouse pointer to the desired file name and single-click.) When a file is selected, its icon is highlighted in graphics mode or a small triangle is put in front of its name in text mode.

To view the file, activate the menu bar and select File. From the menu, select View File Contents. This causes the contents of DOSSHELL.HLP to be displayed. The DOSSHELL.HLP file is the one that contains the Shell's help information. You will see the screen shown in Figure 4-1. You can use the (↑) and (↓) keys to scroll the contents of the file up or down one line. You can use the (PGUP) and (PGDN) keys to view the entire contents of the file a screenful at a time. Also, pressing (ENTER) is the same as pressing (PGDN).

If you press (F9) while using the View File Contents utility, the display will show the contents of a file in a format that is used by programmers. Each letter in the file will be shown using its internal machine representation in hexadecimal format. (Hexadecimal is a number system based on 16 instead of 10.) Unless you are a programmer, you will probably not use this version of the View File utility. However, feel free to try it at this time. The (F9) key is a toggle that switches between the two displays each time it is pressed.

The View File Contents window has three items in its menu bar: Display, View, and Help. The Display option's drop-down menu contains two items: ASCII and Hex. Selecting ASCII causes the file to be displayed normally. Selecting Hex causes the file to be shown using the hexadecimal notation discussed in the preceding paragraph. Essentially, the Display menu is simply an alternative to the (F9) key. The View op-

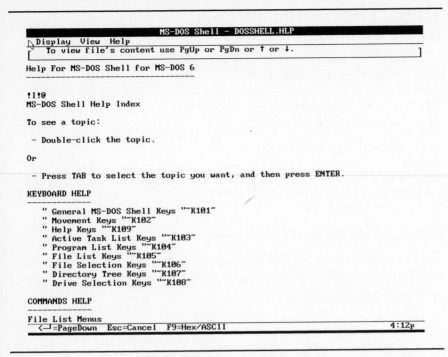

```
                    MS-DOS Shell - DOSSHELL.HLP
 Display  View  Help
[  To view file's content use PgUp or PgDn or ↑ or ↓.            ]

Help For MS-DOS Shell for MS-DOS 6
-------------------------------------

↑I↑@
MS-DOS Shell Help Index

To see a topic:

 - Double-click the topic.

Or

 - Press TAB to select the topic you want, and then press ENTER.

KEYBOARD HELP
-------------
    " General MS-DOS Shell Keys "~K101~
    " Movement Keys "~K102~
    " Help Keys "~K109~
    " Active Task List Keys "~K103~
    " Program List Keys "~K104~
    " File List Keys "~K105~
    " File Selection Keys "~K106~
    " Directory Tree Keys "~K107~
    " Drive Selection Keys "~K108~

COMMANDS HELP
-------------
File List Menus
[ <┘=PageDown  Esc=Cancel  F9=Hex/ASCII                    4:12p ]
```

FIGURE 4-1   **The View File utility**

tion has two entries. You can redisplay the screen by selecting Repaint Screen. The second option, called Restore View, causes the Shell to be redisplayed. The Help option is the same here as it is in the Shell.

Press (ESC) to cancel the View File utility or select Restore View in the View menu.

Drive Specifiers and Path Names

Up to this point you have been selecting files using the File List window and selecting drives using the Drive window. However, many DOS commands require you to enter one or more file names, and it is possible for the file to be on a drive other than the one currently logged in. To tell DOS which drive a file is on, precede the file name with a *drive specifier*. A drive specifier consists of the drive's letter followed by a colon. For example, if the file TEST.TST is on drive B, then you can tell DOS this by using this drive specifier/file name combination:

B:TEST.TST

Here, the "B:" is the drive specifier. Notice that there is no space between the specifier and the file name.

When no drive specifier is present, DOS automatically uses the logged-in drive.

When you select a directory from the Directory Tree window, you are in effect telling DOS to use this directory for all operations unless told otherwise. However, what if you want to access a file in a different directory? You must use the full directory path name of the file.

Drive specifier
A letter followed by a colon that specifies which drive a file is on.

This effectively tells DOS to ignore the logged-in directory and use the one specified with the file name.

Remember that all path names begin with a leading backslash and each directory in the path is separated from the next by a backslash. Also, the file name is separated from the path name by a backslash. For example, if the path to the file TEST.TST is \GAMES\ARCADE, then this is how you would fully specify the file:

\GAMES\ARCADE\TEST.TST

Of course, if TEST.TST is not on the logged-in drive, you must add a drive specifier to the name. For example, if TEST.TST is on drive D, this is its full path name:

D:\GAMES\ARCADE\TEST.TST

Remember that both the drive specifier and the path name are optional. When either or both are absent, DOS uses the current drive and/or directory.

Copying and Moving a File Using the Keyboard

As you continue to use the computer you will find that one of the most common tasks you perform is copying files. You can make multiple copies of a file (but with different names, of course) on the same disk or copy a file to another disk. It is very easy to copy a file using the File Manager. The general procedure using the keyboard is to first select a file in the File List window. Next, activate the File option and select Copy. You will then be prompted for the destination. Before going into too many details, let's try an example.

Select the file called CHKDSK.EXE. Next, activate the menu bar and select File. From the drop-down menu select Copy. You will see a window similar to that shown here:

```
┌──────────────── Copy File ────────────────┐
│                                            │
│   From:  ┌CHKDSK.EXE──────────────────┐    │
│          └────────────────────────────┘    │
│   To:    ┌C:\DOS_───────────────────┐      │
│          └──────────────────────────┘      │
│                                            │
│   ( OK )      ( Cancel )      ( Help )      │
└────────────────────────────────────────────┘
```

Notice that the name of the file you selected (in this case CHKDSK.EXE) is on the From line and the cursor is blinking on the To line. If you are using a fixed disk, the To line will contain "C:\DOS". If you are running DOS from a floppy, the To line will display "A:\". These are the default path names. However, you can specify any path name you like. For this example, if you have a fixed disk, change the To line so that it reads as shown here:

`C:\DOS\CD.EXE`

If you are running DOS from a floppy, change the To line so that it is like the one shown here:

`A:\CD.EXE`

After you have entered the file name correctly, press (ENTER) to begin the copying process. When the process is completed, you will see a directory entry for CD.EXE directly above the one for CHKDSK.EXE. Notice that the only difference between the two entries is the names. Everything else is the same. The Copy command causes an exact copy of the original file to be made. In fact, if you want, execute CD.EXE at this time. As you will see, because it is an exact copy of CHKDSK.EXE, it performs exactly the same function.

Unlike an audiotape in which each copy gets progressively worse, a copy of a disk file is exactly the same as the original. The information in the file does not degrade with each copy.

Probably the most common use of the Copy command is to copy a file to another disk for backup purposes. In general, you will always want at least two copies (three or four are much safer) of important files in case one should be destroyed. Assuming that you have at least two drives in your computer, copying a file to another disk is an easy process. The Copy command allows you to specify the disk drive of the destination file by using its drive specifier. Let's try an example. If you have a fixed disk and a floppy disk drive, insert the blank formatted disk into drive A. To copy CHKDSK.EXE from the fixed disk to the floppy diskette, first select CHKDSK.EXE on the fixed disk, activate the Copy option, and use the following for the To line:

A:\CHKDSK.EXE

If you are running DOS from a floppy, you can copy from drive A (the current drive) to drive B. First select CHKDSK.EXE and then use the following on the To line:

B:\CHKDSK.EXE

If you have two floppy drives, put the blank formatted diskette into B. If you have only one disk drive, you can use the form of the Copy command just given, but you will have to swap diskettes in and out as prompted.

The command just shown to copy CHKDSK.EXE is seldom used in practice because a shorter form exists. When the destination file is going to have the same name as the source file, only the destination drive specifier need be used; there is no need to specify the file name again. For example, this will work fine for the To line:

B:

The only time that you will need to specify a name for the destination file is when it will not be the same as the source file name.

A small variation on copying a file is moving a file. When you move a file, it is deleted from its original location and moved to the new location you specify. If you want to move a file, use the Move option in the File drop-down menu.

Copying and Moving a File Using the Mouse

Dragging   A method of using a mouse in which an object (often a file) is moved from one place or disk to another.

You can use the mouse to copy a file from one disk to another, or from one directory to another on the same disk, by *dragging* the file from one disk or directory to another. In order to follow along, if you are using a fixed disk, make sure you insert a formatted diskette into drive A. If you are running DOS from floppies, then your formatted diskette should be in drive B.

To copy a file using the mouse, first position the mouse pointer on the file you want to copy. Next, press and hold the (CTRL) key. Then, press and hold the left mouse button. A small icon will appear. Now, while continuing to hold the left mouse button and the (CTRL) key, drag the icon to the new directory or drive that you want to copy the file to. When the icon is at the desired location, release the mouse button and then the (CTRL) key, and the file will be copied.

To see how this actually works, let's try an example. Move the mouse pointer to the file you just created called CD.EXE. Press the (CTRL) key and then press and hold the left mouse button. Next, drag the icon to the A drive in the Disk Drive window. (If you are using floppies, drag the icon to drive B, instead.) Once the icon is on the proper drive, release the mouse button and the (CTRL) key. You will see the confirmation dialog box shown here:

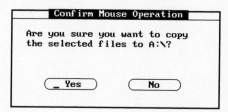

In its default configuration, the Shell double-checks every copy or move operation performed using the mouse because it is easy to accidentally release the mouse button at the wrong spot when dragging the icon to a new location. If you have, indeed, positioned the icon at the correct location, then select Yes to copy the file. Otherwise, select No and try again.

You can use the mouse to copy a file to another directory on the same disk. To do this, drag the file to a directory in the Directory Tree menu.

The procedure for moving a file is almost identical to the one for copying. The only difference is that you do not need to press the (CTRL) key. If you are moving a file to another directory on the same drive, just drag the file to the new directory. (You don't need to press any key.) However, if you are moving the file to a new drive, hold down the (ALT) key and then drag the file to the new drive. On your own, try moving the CD.EXE file to drive A (or B, whichever applies) and then copy it back.

You might want to practice moving and copying files using the mouse before proceeding. It takes a little practice to become proficient.

Erasing Files

Often you will need a file for only a short period of time, or you might want to put a disk to a different use and need to remove those files that no longer relate to the new use. Either way, it is simple to remove a file from a disk by using the File Manager.

To begin, let's erase the file CD.EXE created in the previous section. First highlight the CD.EXE file in the File List window. Next, activate the menu bar and select File. From the drop-down menu select the Delete option. You will then be shown a safety check window that will look like the one shown here:

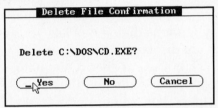

Erasing a file can be a one-way operation; you might not be able to bring it back once it is gone. For this reason, DOS gives you a second chance to change your mind before erasing the file. Since you do, in fact, want to erase the file, select the first option.

Renaming a File

If you have been following along with the examples, then you will have copied CD.EXE to a previously blank disk. Make sure that this disk is in drive A now.

You can change the name of a file by first selecting the file in the File List window and then selecting the Rename option in the File menu. You will then be prompted for the new name of the file. To try this, let's rename the copy of CD.EXE you put on the diskette to TEST.EXE.

First, select drive A using the Disk Drive window. Next, select CD.EXE in the File List window. Activate the menu bar and choose File. Next, select Rename. You will then be prompted for the new name for CD.EXE in the Rename window. Enter **TEST.EXE** and press (ENTER). You will see that the name change takes place.

To change the name back to CD.EXE, repeat the procedure.

If you are running DOS from a fixed disk, then select drive C at this time and activate the DOS directory. If you are using floppies, put your DOS disk back in drive A now.

Remember that when you rename a file, you must give a name that is not already used by another file in the same directory.

Changing the Way Files Are Displayed

You can change what files are displayed in the File List window and the order in which they are displayed using the Options entry. Select

Options at this time. The second entry in the pull-down menu is File Display Options. Select it now. You will see the File Display Options dialog box, which will look like that shown here:

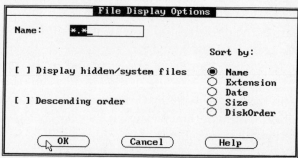

The File Display Options dialog box lets you control four things that affect how files are displayed in the File List window. The first is the Name field, which is used to specify the name of the file or files you want to see displayed. By default, the name is "*.*", which tells DOS to display all files. (You will see why in the next section.) The second option is the Sort by radio buttons. Using these buttons, you can change the way files are ordered in the File List window. The third and fourth items in the File Display Options dialog box are two check boxes. The first allows some files that are not normally shown to be displayed. The second causes the directory to be shown in descending order. Let's take a closer look at these options now.

Looking for Specific Files

Until now, the Shell has displayed the entire contents of the current directory in the File List window. However, you can use the Name option to find a specific file by entering its name. This name is sometimes called the file specifier. You can use this method to quickly determine whether a file is in the directory. For example, enter the file name **SORT.EXE** and press ⟨ENTER⟩. (This is DOS's SORT command.) The File List window will clear, and then only the file SORT.EXE will be displayed. (To have the entire directory displayed again, reactivate the File Display Options option and enter ***.*** at the Name field.)

When you specify a file name, DOS attempts to find a file in the current directory that matches that name. If you specify a file that is not in the directory you will see this message:

```
No files match file specifier
```

If you think that the file you requested is really in the directory, you may have made a typing error. If, after a second try, DOS still reports the file as nonexistent, try listing the entire directory; you may have forgotten the file's name or its exact spelling.

Wildcard File Names

Up to this point, you have learned how to list either the entire directory or a specific file. However, DOS allows you to list groups of related files. Also, you can list a file without knowing its full name. To accomplish these things requires special *wildcard* characters that can

Wildcard   *Either * or ?. These characters are used to match an unknown sequence of characters or a single character, respectively, in a file name.*

be used in place of an actual file name. Let's see how, starting with an example.

Assume that you want to list the names of all the files on a disk that share the .EXE extension. To do this, enter the following at the Name field of the File Display Options window.

*.EXE

This causes DOS to display all files with an .EXE extension. The output will be similar to that shown in Figure 4-2.

When used in a file name that is part of a DOS command, the asterisk (*) is a special character that tells DOS to match any sequence of characters. Specifically, it means that any character can occupy the position of the * and all character positions after it. Note that the filename and extension are separate, so the * applies only to the part of the name in which it is used. This is the reason that the Shell uses *.* by default in the Name field. It causes all files to be matched and, thus, displayed.

You can use the * to find files whose names have one or more initial characters in common by specifying those characters followed by an *. For example, enter this file specifier:

S*.EXE

DOS will display all files that begin with "S" and have the .EXE extension—such as SETVER.EXE, SHARE.EXE, SORT.EXE, and SUBST.EXE. Note that any sequence of characters may follow the "S".

You cannot use the * to find files with filenames that begin with different characters but have common endings. That is, this name

*ST.EXE

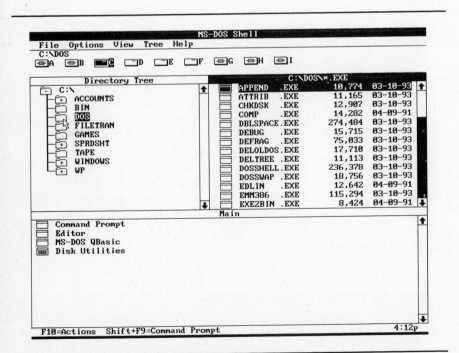

FIGURE 4-2   **The directory displayed using the *.EXE file specifier**

will not find all files with filenames that end in ST. Instead, it will display all files that have the extension .EXE. This is because the * matches any and all characters from its position in the name to the end.

You can use the * in the extension field of a file name. For example, the command

S*.*

reports all files that begin with "S" and that have any extension.

Now try some examples on your own.

The second wildcard character is the question mark (?), which will match any one character in its position. That is, unlike the *, it matches only one character—not a sequence of characters. For example, the following file specifier will find all files whose filenames end with the characters SHELL.

???SHELL.*

To this command, DOS responds with DOSSHELL.COM, DOS-SHELL.EXE, DOSSHELL.GRB, DOSSHELL.HLP, DOSSHELL.INI, and DOSSHELL.VID.

For another example, assume that these files are on your disk (they aren't actually):

TEST1A.DAT
TEST2A.DAT
TEST3A.DAT
TEST1B.DAT
TEST2B.DAT

Giving the file specifier

TEST?A.DAT

causes the files TEST1A.DAT, TEST2A.DAT, and TEST3A.DAT to be found.

Now try some examples of your own using the ? wildcard character. However, before continuing on, reset the Name to *.*.

As you will see later in this book, the wildcard characters are useful in several DOS commands because they allow you to easily handle related groups of files.

Changing the Sorting Order

Reselect the File Display Options entry in the Options menu. Activate the Sort by radio buttons. (Press the (TAB) key three times.) By default, the directory is sorted by the file names. However, you can also have the directory sorted by extension, date, or size. You can also request that the contents of the directory not be sorted, which is accomplished by choosing the DiskOrder entry.

To see the effects of changing the sorting method, choose to sort by extension and press (ENTER). The directory will then look similar to that shown in Figure 4-3.

You might want to try the other sorting methods on your own. However, before moving on, set the Sort by option to Name.

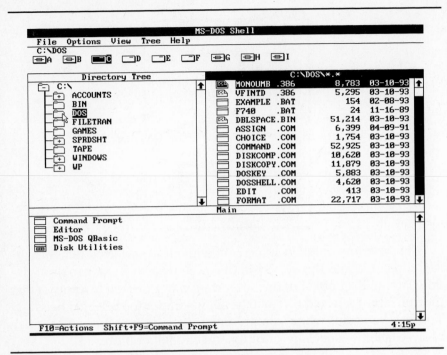

FIGURE 4-3 **The DOS directory sorted by extension**

Displaying Hidden and System Files

It is possible to cause a file not to show up in the File List window. This type of file is called hidden and is commonly referred to as a *hidden file.* DOS contains some hidden files because they are not files that you will ever use. Because these files are part of DOS, they are also referred to as *system files.* In either case, you can cause hidden files to be displayed by activating the Display hidden/system files check box. Unless you are directed to do so by some application program you are using, there is probably no reason to activate this option.

Hidden file   *A file that, by default, does not show in the directory listing.*

System file   *A file that is used by DOS, not by you.*

Display the Directory in Descending Order

By default, the directory is shown in the File List window in ascending sorted order. You can reverse this by selecting the Descending order check box. If you try this, be sure to deactivate it before moving on. If you forget, your screen will not look like the ones shown in this book.

Displaying Information About a File

Select the DOSSHELL.HLP file in the File List window at this time. Now, activate the menu bar and choose Options. From the Options menu, select Show Information. You will see the Show Information window, which will be similar to the one shown here:

```
┌─Options────────────────────────┐
│   Show Information              │
├────────────────────────────────┤
│                                │
│ File                           │
│   Name  : DOSSHELL.HLP         │
│   Attr  : ...a                 │
│ Selected                C      │
│   Number:               1      │
│   Size  :         161,323      │
│ Directory                      │
│   Name  : DOS                  │
│   Size  :       4,570,033      │
│   Files :             134      │
│ Disk                           │
│   Name  : CDISK                │
│   Size  :      33,454,080      │
│   Avail :       9,965,568      │
│   Files :           1,078      │
│   Dirs  :              28      │
│                                │
│  (_Close_)      ( Help )       │
└────────────────────────────────┘
```

This window displays information about the selected file, the current directory, and the logged-in disk. We will come back to this window later in the book, but one important thing for you to know is that the number of selected files will be shown under the Selected heading. This can be useful when you are unsure about how many files have been selected—especially prior to a deletion operation.

Press (ESC) to exit the Show Information window at this time.

Arranging the Screen

As you learned earlier in this chapter, you can have the Shell display the directory in one of five ways by using the View menu bar option. To conclude this chapter, let's experiment with some different screen arrangements. Activate the View drop-down menu at this time.

One useful screen variation is activated by the Dual File Lists option. This option splits the screen and allows you to display the contents of two different directories or disks at the same time. Choose this option now. Your screen will look like the one shown in Figure 4-4. Once the screen is split, you can change which directory or disk (or both) either directory window is displaying. You might want to try this now. (Remember: Use the (TAB) key to activate the various windows.)

Another useful screen arrangement is created by selecting the All Files option. This causes the entire contents of the disk to be displayed, bypassing the directory structure of the disk. Try this option now. Notice that information about the file currently highlighted is shown. As you move the highlight about, the information changes to reflect the new file. Also, notice that the directory that contains the file is displayed.

The All Files option is particularly useful when you forget what directory a file is in. To find the file, activate the All Files option. Next, using the File Display Options selection in the Options menu, change the file name specifier to that of the file you want to find. If the file is on the disk, its name will appear in the File List window. To try this, activate the File Display Options option and enter **CHKDSK.EXE** for the file specifier. As you can see, it will be found.

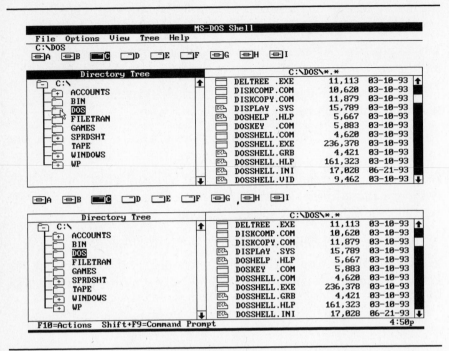

FIGURE 4-4 **The Dual File Lists option**

On your own you should try the other screen arrangement options. However, before moving on be sure to return the screen to its default configuration by selecting the Program/File Lists option.

Summary

You learned about some of the File Manager's most important and common operations in this chapter, including:

- How to start a program
- The various menu bar options
- How to view a text file
- The purpose of drive specifiers
- How to copy files
- How to erase and rename files
- Changing the directory display
- Using wildcard file specifiers
- Arranging the screen

The next chapter will take a look at some of the File System's more advanced features, including creating and managing directories, changing file attributes, and copying files across directories. You will also learn about one of DOS 6's most exciting features: the task switcher.

Key Terms

Dragging   A method of using the mouse in which an object (often a file) is moved from one place or disk to another. To drag, first position the mouse pointer on the object you want, then press and hold the left button while moving the mouse pointer to the desired destination.

Drive specifier   A letter followed by a colon that specifies which drive a file is on. For example, C: specifies drive C.

File Manager   The part of the Shell that helps you manage your files. It also lets you run programs.

Hidden file   A file that, by default, does not show in the directory listing.

Hot key   A key or key combination that lets you select a menu item without having to first activate the menu. For example, pressing (F8) activates the Copy option in the File menu.

System file   A file that is used by DOS, not by you.

Wildcard   Either * or ?. These characters are used to match an unknown sequence of characters or a single character, respectively, in a file name.

Exercises

Fill-in-the-Blank

1. The File Manager menu contains five options. They are called File, _____, _____, _____, and Help.

2. In the File menu, the _____ option displays the contents of a text file.

3. To change the name of a file, use the _____ option in the File menu.

4. To change the way that subdirectories are displayed in the Directory Tree window, use the _____ option in the File Manager menu.

5. A drive specifier consists of a _____ followed by a _____.

6. When dragging a file using the mouse, you hold down the _____ button.

7. To display all files that have the extension .HLP, you must enter the name _____._____ in the File Display Options dialog box.

8. Files that do not display in the directory listing are called _____.

9. To execute a program, you _____-click on it with the mouse or highlight it using the keyboard and then press _____.

Short Answer

1. What File Manager menu bar option do you use to arrange the screen in a dual file list?

2. Can the directory be displayed in reverse alphabetical order?

3. Assume that these files are on your disk: MYFILE.DAT, MYPROG.EXE, JERRY.DAT, and WP.DP. Which files will match this wildcard file name: "*.d*"? Which will match this wildcard file name: "*.da?"?

4. Why does DOS ask if you are sure that you want to erase a file?

5. How does moving a file differ from copying it?

6. How do you tell DOS which drive a file is on?

7. Explain how to run a program using the File Manager.

8. Briefly, what does the CHKDSK command do?

9. Explain the difference between the * and the ? wildcard characters.

10. Can the directory listing be sorted by extension?

11. Does making a copy of a file degrade its quality?

12. In what situation is it unnecessary to specify the name of the destination file when copying a file?

13. How do you execute a program using the File Manager?

14. What is the difference between highlighting a program in the File List window and executing it?

Activities

1. Change the Directory Tree so that it is sorted in reverse alphabetical order.

2. Copy the file MEM.EXE to one called CHKMEM.EXE. Confirm that the copy works just like the original.

3. Arrange the screen into a dual file list.

4. Execute the MEM.EXE command.

5. Put the Student Data Disk into drive A. Using the View File option, view the file called CONST.

6. Put the Student Data Disk into drive A and, if necessary, switch to that drive. Next, using the File Display Options dialog box, display all files that have the .DB extension. (There are three.) Next, display all files that begin with P and have the extension .WK1. (There are two.)

Business Case Study

Your department has just hired a new employee. When he arrives he finds a new computer system on his desk, complete with one fixed disk and one floppy drive. It is suggested that he first make a copy of DOS and store the original in a safe place. He admits he hasn't had much experience working with computers and asks for your help. You yourself have only a little experience but are able to explain enough of the basics to help your fellow employee. Remember that the new employee is a novice, and you don't want your explanation to be too overwhelming.

1. To begin, explain the difference between hardware and software, including the basic role of an operating system. You must also explain the elements of the DOS Shell.

   a. Begin by showing the new employee the parts of the computer system, including the system unit, the keyboard, and the monitor. Next, explain the difference between a floppy disk and the fixed disk and how to properly care for diskettes.
   b. Now it's time to show him how to turn the computer on. Once the DOS Shell has been displayed, explain its various parts, including the Directory Tree window, the File List window, and the Main group. Also, point out the menu bar and the Disk Drive window.
   c. Insert a blank, formatted diskette in drive A and then have the new employee switch to drive A by selecting A in the Disk Drive window. Explain what the current drive is and why it is important.
   d. Now make a duplicate of the master copy of DOS using the Shell's Disk Copy command. Explain how to access this command by first selecting the Main group and then selecting the Disk Utilities option. (Be sure to have a blank disk in drive A before you have the employee try to copy a diskette.)

2. The new employee is catching on fast and since you have explained everything you've been doing in a clear, logical fashion, he asks you to show him a few more things. You gladly oblige.

   a. Show him how to properly label a diskette.
   b. Show him how to change the way files are displayed in the File List window. Also, explain the wildcard characters. Illustrate how they work by displaying all files with the extension .EXE using the * wildcard character.
   c. Explain how to restart the system in case his computer system somehow locks up.

PART 2

Advanced Shell Features

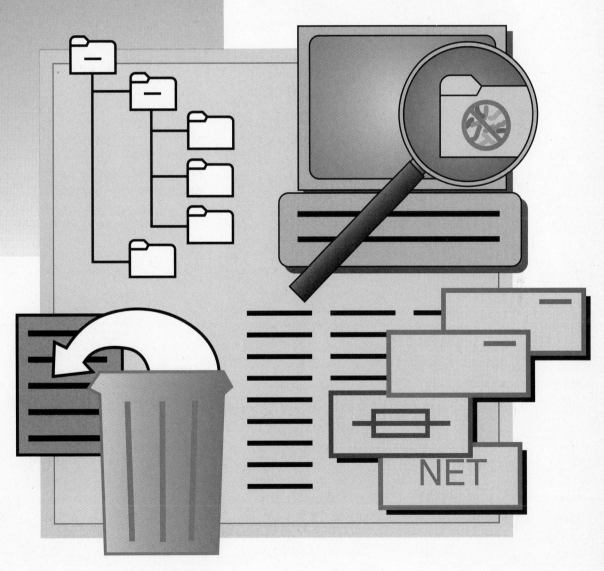

Advanced File Manager Features

CHAPTER OBJECTIVES

After completing this chapter, you should be able to:

- Create directories.
- Remove a directory.
- Use the menu bar Tree option.
- Copy files between directories.
- Replace a file.
- Change a file's attributes.
- Associate a file with a program.
- Work with groups of files.
- Eliminate the confirmation windows.
- Use the Task Manager.

Now that you know your way around the File Manager and can perform many of the most common operations, it is time to unlock some of the system's more advanced features. Even though many of these features are quite powerful, they are not difficult to learn and master.

For the examples in this chapter you will need a blank, formatted diskette. You can use the one you created for Chapter 4 by simply erasing any files you may have copied to it. (To erase a file, just follow the procedure described in Chapter 4.) Put the blank diskette in drive A and log into the A drive at this time.

Creating Directories

You learned the theory behind subdirectories in Chapter 3. Now it is time to learn how to use them. To create a subdirectory using the File Manager, you must use the Create Directory option in the File menu.

In this section, we will create on the disk in drive A the directory structure shown in Figure 5-1. (This is the same directory structure used to introduce directories in Chapter 3.) Before going into much theory, let's begin with an example.

Creating the WP and WP/ FORMLET Subdirectories

> **NOTE**
>
> **Be sure that you are logged into drive A.**

Activate the menu bar and select File. From the File menu, select Create Directory. You will see the Create Directory window shown here:

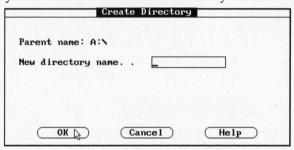

The cursor will be at the line that says "New directory name." At this time enter **WP** and press ⟨ENTER⟩. Here, WP is short for "word processing," which is too long to be a directory name. In the Directory Tree window you will see that the WP directory has been added off the root.

To create the FORMLET directory under the WP directory, first select the WP directory in the Directory Tree window. Next, activate the menu bar and select File. From the File drop-down menu, select Create Directory. When prompted for the directory name, enter **FORMLET** and press ⟨ENTER⟩. (FORMLET is used instead of "form letters,"

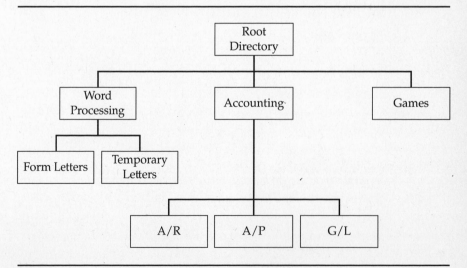

FIGURE 5-1   **The example directory structure**

which is also too long to be a directory name.) After the operation completes, you will see the directory tree displayed here:

```
A:\
  └─WP
      └─FORMLET
```

Creating Subdirectories in General

When you use the Shell to create a subdirectory, you must first select the directory under which you want the subdirectory. That is why when you created the FORMLET directory under WP, you first had to select the WP directory. Put a different way, the directory you specify in the Create Directory window will always be created under the directory currently selected in the Directory Tree window.

Creating the Rest of the Subdirectories

You will now create the rest of the subdirectories that you will need. First, select the WP directory and then activate the Create Directory option. Enter **TEMP** for the name and press (ENTER).

Next, select the root directory and then create the ACCOUNTS directory. With the root still selected, create the GAMES directory. The tree in the Directory Tree window should now look like this:

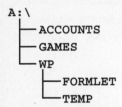

```
A:\
  ├─ACCOUNTS
  ├─GAMES
  └─WP
      ├─FORMLET
      └─TEMP
```

Now, let's fill in the ACCOUNTS subdirectories. Select the ACCOUNTS directory in the Directory Tree window and then create the AR (accounts receivable), AP (accounts payable), and GL (general ledger) subdirectories at this time. When you have finished, your screen should look similar to that shown in Figure 5-2.

Removing a Directory

Now that you have learned to create a subdirectory, it is time to learn how to delete one. To remove a directory, first select the directory you want to remove and then use the Delete option in the File menu. There is one restriction to removing directories: the directory must be empty; it may not contain files or subdirectories.

Switch to the GL directory at this time. Since it is empty, remove it now. You will see a confirmation window, which gives you a second chance to decide whether to delete the directory. Go ahead and delete the directory at this time. You will see that GL no longer appears in the Directory Tree window. Before continuing, recreate the GL directory.

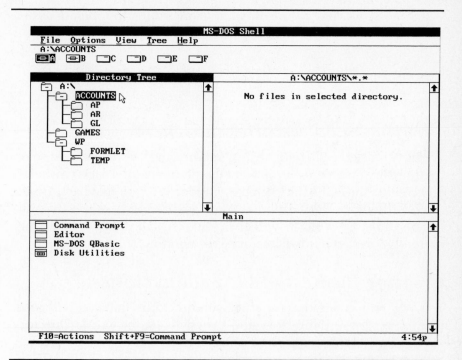

FIGURE 5-2 **The example directory structure as shown on the screen**

If you try to remove a directory that contains files or has its own subdirectories, you will be notified that you cannot delete the directory. If you do, indeed, want to remove that directory, you must erase all the files in it and remove all subdirectories first.

Using the Tree Menu Bar Option

Before moving on to actually using the directories that you just created, you will need to learn how to use the options in the Tree drop-down menu. At this time, activate the Tree option. As mentioned in Chapter 4, this menu affects how the directory of a disk is displayed in the Directory Tree window. In this section, each entry in the menu is examined in detail.

As shown in Figure 5-2, the directory structure of the disk in drive A is fully expanded. This means that all subdirectories are displayed. However, sometimes you will not want to see all subdirectories of a directory. For example, very complex directories can be overwhelming when fully displayed. When this is the case, you can collapse a *branch* using the Collapse Branch option. When you collapse a branch, it means that all subdirectories of a particular directory are no longer displayed. To see how this works, select the WP directory. Next, activate the Tree menu and select Collapse Branch. As you will see, the directories FORMLET and TEMP are no longer displayed.

Branch As applied to directories, a branch is all of the subdirectories that descend from a parent directory.

REMEMBER
When you collapse a branch, only those subdirectories of the directory currently highlighted are affected. All other subdirectories that were displayed are still displayed.

It is important to understand that collapsing a branch does not imply that its directories have been removed from the disk. They are still very much there. It is just that they are no longer displayed in the Directory Tree window. To redisplay these directories, select the WP directory and reactivate the Tree menu. This time select Expand Branch. This causes the subdirectories of WP to be displayed once again.

In general, the Collapse Branch option causes all subdirectories of the selected directory to be removed from the screen. The Expand Branch option causes all subdirectories of the selected directory to be displayed.

At this time, select the root directory and then activate the Tree option and select Collapse Branch. This causes all directories, except the root, to be removed from the screen. Now, reactivate the Tree option and select Expand One Level. Now the Directory Tree window will look like this:

```
A:\
    ├── ACCOUNTS
    ├── GAMES
    └── WP
```

The Expand One Level option causes just the next level of subdirectories to be displayed—not the entire branch.

To see all directories, use the Expand All option. Try this now.

If you have a mouse, you can control how directories are displayed by clicking on the file-folder icons associated with each directory. If the icon has a "+" in it, this means that there is at least one other layer of subdirectories that is not currently displayed associated with the directory. If you click on the folder, another level of directories is shown. If a folder contains nothing, then no more subdirectories are present. If you click on a folder that contains a "–", then the entire branch is collapsed.

You can also use special hot keys to expand and collapse directories. First, move the highlight to the directory you want to affect. Then, to expand one level, press the + (plus) key. To collapse a branch, press – (minus). To expand a branch, press *. Finally, to expand all branches, use (CTRL)-(*).

Copying Files Between Directories

When you copy a file from one directory to another, you must be sure to fully specify the destination path name. For example, let's copy the file CHKDSK.EXE into the FORMLET subdirectory of WP. If you have a fixed disk, switch to drive C and select the DOS directory. If you are running DOS using two floppies, put the DOS disk in drive A and the disk whose directory structure you just created into drive B. If you have only one floppy, put the DOS disk in A and follow the instructions for a dual floppy system. In this case, DOS will prompt you to swap disks.

Fixed disk users: Select the file CHKDSK.EXE and then activate the Copy option in the File directory. When prompted for the destination, enter this at the To line:

A:\WP\FORMLET

To begin the copying process, press (ENTER).

Floppy disk users: Select the file CHKDSK.EXE and then activate the Copy option in the File directory. When prompted for the destination, enter this at the To line:

B:\WP\FORMLET

To start the copying process, press ⟨ENTER⟩. After the copy has been made, remove the DOS disk from drive A and replace it with your directories disk.

After the copy has been made, select drive A and then select the FORMLET directory. You will see that the file CHKDSK.EXE is, indeed, in the directory.

To copy a file from a subdirectory to the root directory, use the backslash as the destination path. For example, to copy the file CHKDSK.EXE from FORMLET to the root, first log into drive A, activate the FORMLET directory, and then select CHKDSK.EXE. Next, activate the Copy option in the File menu and use this as the destination:

A:

Remember that the leading backslash is DOS's name for the root directory. If you check the root at this time, you will see that the file has been copied there.

Earlier in this book, you were told that no two files on the same disk could have the same name. Although this statement is true, it needs to be qualified in light of subdirectories. Put more fully, no two files on the same diskette and *sharing the same path name* can have the same name. That is, *within any directory*, no two file names can be the same. However, files in other directories can have identical names. DOS keeps identical names straight because it always associates a path name with a file name.

Let's do one last exercise. Copy the file CHKDSK.EXE from the FORMLET subdirectory of WP to the WP directory itself, this time giving the destination file a different name. First, select the FORMLET directory and select CHKDSK.EXE. Next, activate the Copy option in the File menu and use this for the To line:

A:\WP\TEST.TST

When you check the WP directory, you will see that the file TEST.TST is there and that its contents are the same as the CHKDSK.EXE file in the FORMLET directory.

Replacing a File

Once again, copy CHKDSK.EXE from FORMLET into WP, calling the destination file TEST.TST again. This time, before the copy commences you will see a confirmation window similar to the one shown here:

Whenever you attempt to copy a file to a destination that already has a file by that name, you will see this window. Since it is easy to accidentally replace a file that you did not mean to replace, confirmation windows act as safety checks, which help prevent mistakes.

At this time, press (ENTER) so that the copy process can proceed.

The Current Directory

If you have a fixed disk, try this: log into the C drive and select the DOS directory. Next, log into the A drive and select the GAMES directory. Now, log back into the C drive. Notice that the DOS directory is selected. Log into A. Notice that the GAMES directory is selected. If you have two floppy drives, put the DOS disk in A and the directories disk in B and try the same process.

The point of this exercise is to illustrate the fact that DOS remembers which directory is active for each disk drive in the system. In the absence of a path name, DOS uses the current directory. Certain DOS commands, like Copy, make use of this fact, as you will see a little later in this chapter.

Directory Capacities

The root directory of a disk can hold a fixed number of entries, depending upon the capacity of the disk. (An entry is either a file or subdirectory name.) Table 5-1 shows the number of entries for the most common disk formats. The root directory of the fixed disk can hold 512 entries.

Unlike the root directory, a subdirectory can hold as many entries as available disk space allows. This is because DOS simply continues to allocate space on the disk to hold the entries. In general, however, you should not have extremely large directories because they are difficult to manage. Once you have more than 100 or so entries, it is time to think about creating a new subdirectory and moving some of the files to it.

Disk Capacity (in bytes)	Maximum Number of Entries in Root Directory
160/180K	64
320/360K	112
720K	112
1200K	224
1440K	224

TABLE 5-1   **Root directory capacity of various disks**

Managing Your Directories

Although the topic of directory management will be examined more closely later in this book, a few pointers will be given now. First and foremost, subdirectories should be used to hold logically related groups of files. Files can be related to each other in several different ways. For example, if a computer is shared by a number of people, then creating a subdirectory for each individual is probably a good idea. Even though all the files in a user's subdirectory may be quite different in purpose from one another, they are all related because they belong to that user. However, if a computer is being used by one person for several separate tasks, as in the example presented earlier in this chapter, then the subdirectories are best organized by functional categories. Generally, the way the computer is used should dictate the directory design.

It is important to remember that each subdirectory uses disk space. Creating an unnecessarily large number of subdirectories wastes disk space. Also, subdirectories that are deeply nested and require long path names slow DOS's access time to any files they contain. You must balance these factors against the advantages that subdirectories have to offer.

Changing a File's Attributes

File attribute   A quality associated with a file.

All files have a number of attributes associated with them. Some of these *file attributes* are meaningful only to DOS and may not be changed by you. However, four of them can be viewed and set by you. Before seeing how to change a file's attributes, you need to know what they are.

The four file attributes that you can set are these:

- Hidden
- System
- Read-only
- Archive

Each attribute is either on or off. If the hidden attribute is on, then the file will not be displayed in the Shell's File List window. However, as you saw in Chapter 4, you can cause hidden files to be displayed by selecting Display hidden/system files in the Display Options option of the Options menu. The hidden attribute is off by default.

If a file is part of DOS, it will have its system attribute on. System files, by default, are not displayed in the File List window.

Archive   The file attribute that, when set, indicates that the file will be automatically copied when some types of backup procedures are used.

When the *archive* attribute is set, the file will automatically be copied by some types of backup operations. The types of backup procedures that use the archive attribute will be discussed later in this book.

Read-only   The file attribute that, when set, allows a file to be read but prevents a file from being changed.

When the *read-only* attribute is set, the file can be read but it cannot be modified or erased. This attribute is off by default. If you wish to safeguard a file from accidental erasure or intentional tampering, setting the read-only attribute is a very good idea.

To change a file's attribute, use the Change Attributes option in the File menu. To see an example, switch to the root directory of drive A and select CHKDSK.EXE at this time. Activate the menu bar, select File, and then select Change Attributes. Your window will look like the one shown here:

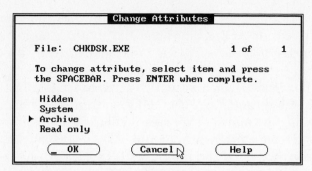

To change an attribute, first press the (TAB) key until the list of attributes is highlighted. Next, using the arrow keys, position the highlight on the attribute you want to change and press the space bar. The space bar works as a toggle. Each time you press it, it changes the state of the highlighted attribute. When an attribute is on, it has a small diamond just to the left of it. You can also toggle the state of an attribute by clicking on it using the mouse.

For now, since there is no reason to change any attribute, exit the dialog box by selecting Cancel or by pressing (ESC).

Associating Files

You can associate a program file with a group of other files that share a common extension. For example, a word processing program can be associated with all files that have the extension .WP. After this association has been made, each time you select a .WP file, the word processor is automatically executed and you can then begin editing the file.

As you know from preceding chapters, you cannot execute non-program files. If you try to do so by highlighting the file in the File List window and pressing (ENTER) or by double-clicking, the Shell will beep at you and do nothing else. However, when a non-program file is associated with a program, then you can "execute" the file. When you do this, the program associated with that file is actually executed and the file you selected is used by that program.

To see an example of associated files, return to the DOS directory on drive C if you have a fixed disk, or put the DOS disk in drive A if you are running DOS from a floppy. Next, find the file EDIT.COM in the File List window and highlight it. EDIT is the DOS 6 text editor. You will learn how to use it later in this book, but for now the text editor will help demonstrate associated files. Next, activate the File menu and select Associate. You will see an Associate File window that will look similar to the one shown here:

You will be prompted for the extensions of the files you want to associate with the editor. At this time enter **HLP** (with no period before the "H") and press (ENTER). Now EDIT is associated with any file that ends in HLP.

To see how the association works, activate the File List window, move the highlight to DOSSHELL.HLP, and press (ENTER) or double-click on it using the mouse. The screen will clear and you will see the DOS editor screen, as shown in Figure 5-3. As you can see, the DOS editor has been activated and the DOSSHELL.HLP file has been automatically loaded into the editor. (DOSSHELL.HLP is the file that contains the help information that is used by the Shell's help system.)

Although you will learn about the DOS editor later in this book, a few features will be mentioned here. You can use the arrow keys to move through the DOSSHELL.HLP file a line at a time. Using (PGUP) and (PGDN), you can move the file a screen at a time.

To leave EDIT, press the (ALT) key to activate the editor's menu bar. Select the File entry and the Exit option. This causes the Shell to return.

To disassociate a set of files from a program, select the program file and then activate the Associate option. When prompted for the extensions, you will see the current associations. Simply remove the one you no longer want. Try this now by removing HLP from EDIT's association list.

How you will use the Associate option or whether you will use it at all depends upon what you are going to be using the computer for. For example, in addition to word processing, another area that lends itself to associated files is a spreadsheet program. You could associate the spreadsheet with its files; however, associated files may not make much sense if you are using the computer primarily for an accounts payable program.

> **CAUTION**
> **Do not do any other operations on the DOSSHELL.HLP file.**

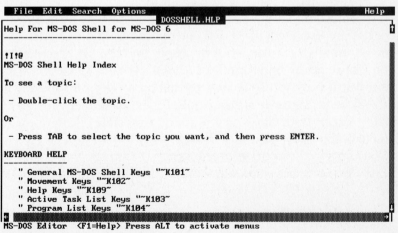

FIGURE 5-3   **The DOS editor screen**

Working With Groups of Files

So far, you have used the File List window to select and work with only one file at a time. However, it is possible to work with two or more at the same time. In this section, you will learn how to work with groups of files.

Selecting Multiple Files

Before you can work with a group of files, you need to know how to select them. By default, only one file in the File List window can be highlighted at any one time. However, in this section you will learn how to highlight multiple files. The method by which this feat is accomplished varies between the keyboard and the mouse. Both variations are examined here.

To select multiple files using the keyboard, first activate the File List window. Next, press (SHIFT)-(F8). After doing this, you will see the word "ADD" just to the left of the time at the bottom of the screen. To select a file, press the space bar. To add another file, move the highlight and press the space bar again. The space bar acts as a toggle. Therefore, if you accidentally select a file you don't want, simply move the highlight to it and press the space bar a second time. When you have selected all the files you want, press (SHIFT)-(F8) a second time.

If you want to select a range of adjacent files, follow this procedure. First, press (SHIFT)-(F8) and then move the highlight to the first file. Next, press and hold down the (SHIFT) key while you use the ⬇ key to move the highlight to the last file in the list. All files between the two ends will be selected. Press the (SHIFT)-(F8) key combination to stop selecting files. You can use (SHIFT)-(PGUP) and (SHIFT)-(PGDN) to select an entire window full of files.

To select multiple files using the mouse, press the (CTRL) key and then single-click on the files you want. To select a range, click on the first file. Then hold down the (SHIFT) key and click on the last file.

Selecting and Deselecting All Files

Sometimes you will want to perform a file operation on all of the files in a directory. The easiest way to select them all is to use the Select All option in the File menu or to press (CTRL)-(/). Try this now. As you can see, all the files are selected.

To deselect all files, use the Deselect All option in the File menu or press (CTRL)-(\). Deselect all files at this time.

One good use for the Deselect All option is when you are working with a directory containing many files and you are not sure which have been selected. By using Deselect All, you can be assured that no files are selected.

Now that you know how to select multiple files, it is time to see why they are useful.

Copying Groups of Files

As you continue to use DOS, you will frequently want to copy groups of files. Using the Shell, this is easy to accomplish.

To copy more than one file at a time, first select all the files you want to copy. Next, activate the Copy option in the File menu and specify the destination. All the specified files will be copied. For example, assuming that you have a fixed disk, put the directories disk created in the first part of this chapter into drive A and log into the DOS directory of drive C. Next, select a few small files and then activate the Copy command. For the destination, simply specify **A:** and press (ENTER). This causes the selected files to be copied into the root directory of the disk in drive A.

You can also move multiple files in the same way. Simply select those you want to move, and activate the Move command.

Deleting Groups of Files

Another common DOS operation is the erasure of two or more files. Using the Shell, you accomplish this operation easily by first selecting the files that you want to erase and then using the Delete option in the File menu. When you do this, all selected files will be erased. However, you will be prompted by the Delete confirmation window for each file individually.

As you continue to use DOS, you will find more ways that manipulating groups of files can make things easier.

Eliminating the Confirmation Windows

As you have seen in the examples, whenever you delete a file or replace a file in a copy operation, a confirmation window is displayed, which gives you a chance to change your mind. A confirmation window is also displayed each time you copy or move a file using the mouse. However, once you become experienced with DOS and its Shell, these extra steps can become tedious. For this reason, the Shell lets you disable the confirmation windows using the Confirmation selection in the Options menu. Select this option now. As you can see, three options appear in this window:

Confirm on Delete
Confirm on Replace
Confirm on Mouse Operation

By default all confirmation windows are on. If you deselect the Confirm on Delete option, then no confirmation window will be displayed when you delete a file or a directory. Deselecting Confirm on Replace means that there will be no safety check when you copy a file to a destination that already has a file by the same name. Deselecting Confirm on Mouse Operation prevents the confirmation window from appearing when using the mouse.

As long as you know what you are doing, there is no harm in deactivating these saftey check windows. However, you might want to leave them active for the first few weeks that you run DOS just to avoid making a disastrous error.

Selecting Files Across Directories

By default, when you change directories, any files selected in the previous directory are automatically deselected. However, you can change this by selecting the Select Across Directories option in the Options menu. When this option is activated, files that you have selected stay selected until you explicitly turn them off. The principal advantage to this is that it allows you to perform operations on files in different directories at the same time.

A Closer Look at the Show Information Window

If you have a fixed disk, select the DOS directory. If you are using floppies, put your DOS disk in drive A. Next, select CHKDSK.EXE in the File List window. Then activate the Show information option in the Options menu. The Show Information window was discussed briefly in the previous chapter. Let's explore it more thoroughly now.

The Show Information window is divided into four main sections: File, Selected, Directory, and Disk. The File section displays the name of the currently selected file (if any) and shows that file's attributes. When the hidden attribute is on, an "h" is displayed. When the read-only attribute is set, an "r" is shown. When the archive attribute is on, an "a" is displayed. When the system attribute is on, an "s" is displayed.

The Selected section tells you which disk drives are active and how many files (if any) are currently selected. It also tells you the size of those files.

The Directory section shows you the name of the current directory, the amount of space the files in that directory take up, and the number of files contained in the directory.

The Disk section reports the name of the disk, the capacity of the disk, and the number of bytes not currently in use. It also displays the number of files and directories on the disk.

Using the Task Manager

DOS 6 includes an important feature not found in earlier versions of DOS prior to version 5: the Task Manager. (A *task* is essentially another name for a program.) After activating the Task Manager, you can rapidly switch between different programs without having to first terminate one program to execute the next. The Task Manager simply

Task   *In simple terms, a task is another name for a program.*

pauses one program while you run another. For example, without the Task Manager, if you are using your word processor and you want to do a quick calculation using your spreadsheet program, you need to terminate the word processor and execute the spreadsheet. However, with the Task Manager, you can simply switch between the two programs without having to end either. As you can imagine, this is quite a useful feature.

NOTE

You may have heard about multi-tasking operating systems like Windows or OS/2. In these operating systems, it is possible to actually run more than one program simultaneously. However, this is not the case with DOS—even when using the Task Manager. DOS suspends execution of one program while you run another. Although DOS does not actually execute programs concurrently, the Task Manager still makes it much easier for you to switch between your application programs.

Task swapper   The part of the Task Manager that actually switches between programs.

To activate the Task Manager, first activate the menu bar and choose Options. Next, select Enable Task Swapper. The *task swapper* is the part of the Task Manager that allows you to switch between programs. After doing so, your screen will look like the one shown in Figure 5-4. Notice that a new window has been added. The new window, although blank now, is used to hold a list of active tasks in the system. We will come back to it in a moment.

Starting a Task

After the switcher is activated, simply execute a program in the normal way to start a task. For example, highlight the file LABEL.EXE in

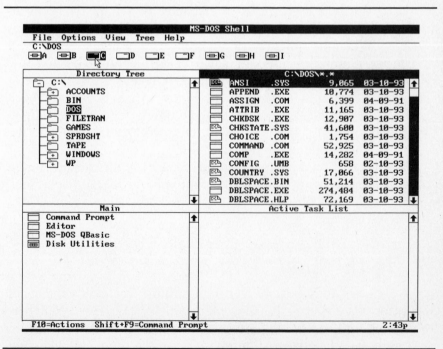

FIGURE 5-4   **The shell after activating the Task Manager**

the File List window and execute it. This is the DOS command that gives a disk a label. (You will learn about LABEL later in this book.) Your screen will clear and you will see the following prompt:

```
Volume label (11 characters, ENTER for none)?
```

Don't enter anything at this prompt. The only reason that you are using LABEL.EXE is that it will continue to execute in the computer until it receives a file name. This provides time to illustrate the Task Manager. (CHKDSK, for example, would have terminated before you had time to explore the Task Manager.)

As you can see, starting a task is just the same as starting a program. The only difference is how DOS treats it.

Switching Between Tasks

There are now two active tasks in your computer: LABEL.EXE and the Shell. To switch between tasks, press and hold the (ALT) key and then press (TAB). (Continue to press the (ALT) key.) The screen will clear and you will see the following line:

```
MS-DOS Shell
```

While still holding down the (ALT) key, press the (TAB) key a second time. This time the line changes to "LABEL.EXE". Press the (TAB) key again, and "MS-DOS Shell" is displayed. Each time you press the (ALT)-(TAB) combination, the task switcher displays the next task in the list of active tasks. At this point the MS-DOS Shell task should be displayed. (If it is not, then press (TAB) again.) Now, to select a task, simply stop pressing the (ALT) key. This will cause the Shell to return to the screen.

When the Shell returns, you will see that LABEL.EXE is in the Active Task List window. When you are in the Shell, you can activate a task listed in the Active Task List window in just the same way that you execute a program from the File List window. First highlight it and press (ENTER) or double-click on it using the mouse. Try this now by activating LABEL.EXE again. The screen clears and LABEL's prompt is once again displayed on the screen.

Let's add another task. To do this, press (ALT)-(TAB) once to return to the Shell. This time, execute CHKDSK.EXE. However, before it has a chance to terminate, press (ALT)-(TAB) again. This time you will find three tasks that you can switch between by pressing (ALT)-(TAB). Try pressing (TAB) a few times now. When you are ready again, select the Shell. Now you will find two items listed in the Active Task List window: LABEL.EXE and CHKDSK.EXE. This time, select CHKDSK.EXE. The CHKDSK command resumes execution at the point at which you left it.

When CHKDSK finishes, the Shell is resumed and CHKDSK.EXE is no longer shown in the Active Task List window because it has terminated.

You can switch between tasks in several other ways that make task switching easier. You can return directly to the Shell without having to select it from the list of tasks by pressing (CTRL)-(ESC). Pressing (ALT)-(ESC) activates the next application task. (The Shell cannot be selected using (ALT)-(ESC).) Pressing (SHIFT)-(ALT)-(ESC) activates the previous application task.

When you are in the Shell, pressing (ALT)-(TAB) activates the previous task. Finally, you can activate several applications at the same time without leaving the Shell by holding down the (SHIFT) key when you start each program. You will simply see their names added to the Active Task List window.

> **REMEMBER**
> Once the Task Manager is active, to start a task, simply run a program in the normal manner. To switch between tasks, press (ALT)-(TAB). To return directly to the Shell, press (CTRL)-(ESC).

Terminating a Task

By far the best way to terminate a task is to let it end normally. This is what happened to CHKDSK in the preceding example. Since LABEL.EXE is still active in the system, let's terminate it, too. First, activate it by pressing (ALT)-(TAB) or selecting it in the Active Task List window. Now press (ENTER) and then **N**. You will then see the keypress prompt. Press another key and the Shell will be reactivated and LABEL.EXE will no longer be in the Active Task List window. If you press (ALT)-(TAB) now, DOS will simply beep at you since there are no other tasks to switch to.

Once in a while, for various reasons, a program might not be able to terminate normally. If this happens, you can still remove that program from the computer by first highlighting it in the Active Task List window and then using the Delete option in the File menu.

Running Out of Disk Space

All disks have a finite amount of storage capacity so it is possible to fill one. If a disk is full or nearly full and you try to copy a file to it that is bigger than the amount of free space on the disk, you will see this error message inside the Copy window:

```
The disk is full.
```

If this occurs, your only immediate option is to cancel the Copy operation. Next, you must decide whether to use a new disk or to remove unneeded files from the disk. Then you must repeat the Copy operation.

You can determine the amount of free space on a disk by selecting the Show information option in the Options menu.

Summary

In this chapter you learned about several advanced File System features, including these:

- Creating subdirectories
- Removing a directory
- Copying files between directories

- Working with groups of files
- File attributes
- Associating files
- Eliminating the confirmation windows
- Using the Task Manager

The next chapter continues the discussion of the Shell. It includes information on how to configure the Shell and how to print the screen, and a discussion of some special editing keys.

Key Terms

Archive   The file attribute that, when set, indicates that the file will be automatically copied when some types of backup procedures are used.

Branch   As applied to directories, a branch is all of the subdirectories that descend from a parent directory.

File attribute   A quality associated with a file. The file attributes include hidden, system, read-only, and archive.

Read-only   The file attribute that, when set, allows a file to be read but prevents a file from being changed.

Task   In simple terms, a task is another name for a program.

Task swapper   The part of the Task Manager that actually switches between programs.

Exercises

Short Answer

1. When creating a directory, what File menu option do you use?
2. When deleting a directory, what restriction applies?
3. What Tree menu option do you use to show the entire directory structure of a disk?
4. Can two files, each residing in a different directory of the same disk, have the same name? If so, why? If not, why not?
5. How many files can the root directory of a fixed disk hold?
6. If a file has its read-only attribute set, can the file be erased or modified?
7. What does the Associate option do?
8. How are multiple files selected (in the File List window) when using the keyboard? When using the mouse?
9. How do you copy groups of files?
10. How do you activate the Task Manager?

11. How do you switch between tasks?

12. How do you terminate a task?

13. What are your options if you run out of disk space?

14. What directory does DOS assume if no directory is specified?

True or False

1. Subdirectories can only be created on a blank diskette. _____

2. A subdirectory must be empty before it can be removed. _____

3. The root directory cannot be removed. _____

4. The Collapse Branch option causes all files and subdirectories that are collapsed to be erased from the disk. _____

5. When copying a file from one directory to another, the copy must be given a different name. _____

6. The file attributes are hidden, system, read-only, and archive. _____

7. When a non-program file is associated with a program, that program is automatically executed if you double-click on that non-program file with the mouse. _____

8. Using the Shell, you may copy only one file at a time. Specifically, it is not possible to copy a group of files. _____

9. The Task Manager multi-tasks two or more programs. _____

10. Using the Task Manager, you can switch between programs by pressing (ALT)-(TAB). _____

Activities

1. Experiment with the various Tree options.

2. Activate the Task Manager and experiment with it by executing multiple copies of the LABEL command.

Using the Program Manager and Miscellaneous Topics

CHAPTER OBJECTIVES

After completing this chapter, you should be able to:

- Execute programs using the Run option.
- Understand the Program Manager.
- Add a program to the Main group.
- Understand program properties.
- Use program parameters.
- Create and use program subgroups.
- Add a password.
- Use some DOS editing keys.

This is the last chapter of the book that deals exclusively with the Shell. Here you will learn how to run programs that require additional information. You will also learn to add programs and groups to the Program Manager. Read these discussions carefully because some important concepts are introduced, which will be expanded upon later in this book.

Executing Programs Using the Run Option

Up to now, when you have run a program you have simply selected it from the File List window. While this works for many programs, some programs take certain options and others may require that additional information be specified in order to run properly. Each piece of extra information used by a program is called a *parameter*. One way to execute a program that uses parameters is to use the Run option in the File menu. In this section you will see how to accomplish this.

Let's begin with an example. First, make sure that either the Directory Tree or File List window is active. Now activate the menu bar and select the File menu. (There is no need to highlight a file in the File List window.) Next, select the Run option. You will see the dialog box shown here:

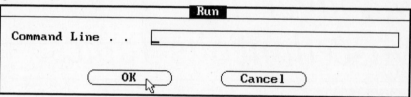

When using the Run option, you must enter the name of the command you want to execute in the Command Line input box. For example, to execute the CHKDSK command, enter **CHKDSK** in the box and press (ENTER). You do not need to use the .EXE extension. It won't hurt to use the extension, but it is completely unnecessary. Try this now. As you can see, the CHKDSK command is executed. Notice also that when CHKDSK terminates, you will see this prompt:

```
Press any key to return to MS-DOS Shell
```

When you run a command using Run, the Shell will not return after the command terminates until you press a key. This gives you time to read any information displayed by the program on the screen.

Although the preceding example is a valid use of Run, there is no advantage over simply selecting CHKDSK in the File List window. What makes the Run option important is that it also allows parameters to be applied to a program. To see how, if you have a fixed disk, put a formatted diskette in drive A. If you are running DOS from a floppy, put a formatted diskette in drive B. Now reactivate the Run option, and enter this command if you have a fixed disk:

CHKDSK A:

Enter this command if you use floppies:

CHKDSK B:

Both these commands use one parameter—a drive specifier. This parameter causes the CHKDSK command to check the disk specified by the drive specifier. That is, CHKDSK A: causes the A drive to be tested, and CHKDSK B: causes the B drive to be checked. By default, CHKDSK operates on the currently logged-in disk, but by using a parameter, it can be made to operate on any drive in the system. As you will see, by using a drive specifier in the same general way as shown with CHKDSK, you can make many DOS commands operate on drives other than the one that you are currently logged into.

Here is another example. Remember that in Chapter 2 when you made copies of your master DOS diskettes, you used the Disk Copy option in the Disk Utilities group. However, there is another way to accomplish this using DOS's DISKCOPY command. The command takes the general form:

DISKCOPY *from to*

where *from* and *to* are drive specifiers that tell DISKCOPY which drive to use as the source and which drive to use as the target. For example, in the Command Line input box of the Run option, this command tells DISKCOPY to copy the disk in drive A to the disk in drive B (don't actually try this):

DISKCOPY A: B:

This is an example of a command that takes two parameters. It is also another example of how a DOS command uses drive specifiers as parameters to determine which drives are the focus of the command.

Later in this book, when you learn about using the command prompt interface, you will learn more about specifying parameters and options. For now, however, just remember that if you need to run an application program that requires parameters, use the Run command in the File menu.

Running a Series of Commands

Using the Run option, it is possible to string together several programs and/or DOS commands on one single command line. To do this, simply separate each command from the next by using a semicolon. For example, activate the File menu and select Run. At the Command Line, enter the following:

CHKDSK ; MEM ; VER

Make sure that each semicolon has at least one space on each side of it. Now press (ENTER). As you will see, first the CHKDSK command is executed, and then the MEM command. As you should recall, the MEM command reports information about your system's memory, including such things as the total amount of memory and the size of the largest program that can be run. Finally, the VER command executes. The VER command displays DOS's version number.

As you have seen, executing multiple commands on one command line is very easy. There are only two things to remember. First, no command line may exceed 255 characters. Second, each semicolon must have at least one space on each side of it.

Using the Program Manager

Program Manager
The part of the Shell that helps you manage your programs.

The final major part of the Shell that we will explore is the *Program Manager*. As you know, the Program Manager is the window on the bottom of your screen that is titled Main. In this and the next few sections, you will learn how to add programs and groups to the Program Manager, how to execute programs using the Program Manager, and how to prompt for parameters. You will also learn about several options that control the way programs are executed.

> **NOTE**
>
> **Highlight the Main window of the Program Manager at this time.**

Groups Versus Subgroups

The Program Manager uses a main group/subgroup approach to its organization. A group may contain both programs and subgroups. For example, by default, the Main group contains one subgroup called Disk Utilities and three programs: the Command Prompt, the Editor, and MS-DOS QBasic. In a way, groups and subgroups are similar in concept to directories and subdirectories.

In the Program Manager, any group can have a subgroup. Except where the distinction is important, the term "group" will apply to both groups and subgroups.

The theory behind the group method is that you can put related programs into their own group. For example, you might create a word processing group and put the word processor, spelling checker, and thesaurus programs in that group. The Program Manager lets you manage and structure your programs by allowing you to keep related programs in separate groups.

> **NOTE**
>
> **Although they are conceptually similar, don't confuse subgroups with subdirectories. The subgroup in which a program appears in the Program Manager window has nothing whatsoever to do with what directory the program is in on the disk.**

Adding a Program to the Main Group

If you haven't yet done so, activate the Program Manager and make sure that the Main group window is displayed.

You can add a program to a group so that you may execute it from the Program Manager window instead of having to use the File Manager. Not only can this be more convenient, saving you time and keystrokes, but it can also help ensure that the program is started correctly. Furthermore, you can add any DOS command, whether internal or external, to a group.

Since all of DOS's external commands are programs, let's add CHKDSK to the Main group. Activate the menu bar and select the File option. You will see a menu that has the following entries:

New
Open
Copy
Delete
Properties
Reorder
Run
Exit

NOTE

When the Program Manager is active, the contents of both the menu bar and the File option, specifically, are different from when the File Manager is in use. Also, there is no Tree option. The View and Help options are the same as in the File Manager.

Select the New option. You will see the dialog box shown here:

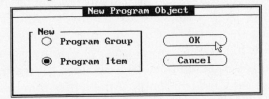

Since you can add either a program or a subgroup to a group, this dialog box lets you select which type of item you are adding. Because you are adding a program, select Program Item and press (ENTER). You will see the dialog box shown here:

```
╔══════════════════ Add Program ══════════════════╗
║                                                  ║
║  Program Title . . . . [_____]║
║                                                  ║
║  Commands  . . . . . . [_____]║
║                                                  ║
║  Startup Directory . . [_____]║
║                                                  ║
║  Application Shortcut Key  [_____]   ║
║                                                  ║
║  [X] Pause after exit      Password . . [_____] ║
║   ( OK )    ( Cancel )    ( Help )  ( Advanced...)║
╚══════════════════════════════════════════════════╝
```

Each program has five fields of information associated with it, along with one check box. The first two input boxes must be filled in. The others are optional.

The first piece of information you must enter is the title of the program, which will be displayed in the group window. For CHKDSK, use this title: **Check the Disk**. Titles can be up to 23 characters long. The second thing you must enter is the command you want to execute. The Commands line is similar to the Command Line input box of the Run option. The command line may be up to 255 characters long. Therefore, to execute CHKDSK, enter **CHKDSK** now. Notice that the check box labeled "Pause after exit" is checked by default. You will see the effect of this shortly. Now, either press (ENTER) or select the OK command button.

If you inspect the Main group, you will see that the "Check the Disk" title is present.

To verify that you did everything correctly, execute Check the Disk by highlighting it and pressing (ENTER) or by double-clicking on it. The screen will clear and the disk is checked. After the CHKDSK command terminates, you will again see the prompt to press a key to return to the Shell. This message is displayed because the Pause after exit option was turned on in the Add Program dialog box.

NOTE

You can quickly tell whether an entry in a group is a program or a group by looking at the icon associated with it. Program icons look like blank folders, and group icons look like folders that contain other folders.

Program Properties

Program properties *Information associated with your program that the Program Manager uses to better manage and utilize your programs.*

As you saw in the preceding example, when you add a program to a group you must specify certain bits of information. In the language of DOS, these pieces of information are called *properties*. In the preceding example, only two properties were used. However, the Program Manager has several others and they are the subject of this section.

Instead of adding another program to the Main group just to illustrate the other properties that can be associated with a program, you can simply reuse the CHKDSK entry. After a program has been added to a group, it is possible to modify or enhance its properties. This is accomplished by using the Properties option in the File menu. You can make use of this option to explore the other properties supported by the Program Manager.

To view or change the properties associated with a program, first highlight the desired program in the Program Manager. Next, select the Properties option in the File menu. You will see a dialog box that is virtually identical to the Add Program box. For the example at hand, first highlight Check the Disk and then select the Properties option in the File menu. You will see that the first two input boxes contain the information you entered when you added CHKDSK to the Main group. Let's explore the other properties in this box now.

The Startup Directory input box lets you specify a disk and/or directory that you want to switch to before the command you entered in the Commands box begins execution. This is useful when a program exists in one place and its data files are in another. For example, your word processing program might be on the C drive, but you keep your files on the disk in drive A. By specifying "A:\" in the Startup Directory input box, you will cause your word processor to use that disk and directory for your files. You may enter up to 63 characters in this field. Since there is no need to switch directories at this time, simply leave this field blank.

The Application Shortcut Key lets you specify one special key combination that, when pressed, causes the task switcher to automatically switch directly to that program. The key combination must be constructed by using the (ALT), (CTRL), or (SHIFT) key in conjunction with a letter of the alphabet. For example, (ALT)-(F) or (CTRL)-(G) are valid Application Shortcut keys. If you like, enter a shortcut key in this box.

If you deactivate the Pause after exit, once a program terminates (in this case CHKDSK), the Shell is immediately redisplayed. For now, leave this box as it is.

You can give a program password protection if you like, by using the Password input box. The password can be up to 20 characters long. If you add a password each time you try to run the program, you will first be prompted for the password. Any time you try to change that program's properties, you also will be prompted for the password. If you want to try adding a password, go ahead; just make sure that you don't forget it! (Passwords will be discussed again later in this chapter.)

Advanced Properties

Notice that one of the command buttons in the Program Item Properties window is labeled Advanced. While the properties shown in the Program Item Properties window are the ones that you will use the most often, programs can have other properties, as well. To see them, select the Advanced command button now. You will see a window like the one shown here:

```
┌──────────────────── Advanced ─────────────────────┐
│                                                    │
│  Help Text      [_                              ]  │
│                                                    │
│  Conventional Memory   KB Required   [        ]   │
│                                                    │
│  XMS Memory  KB Required  [        ]   KB Limit [        ] │
│                                                    │
│  Video Mode    ● Text      Reserve Shortcut Keys [ ] ALT+TAB │
│                ○ Graphics                       [ ] ALT+ESC │
│  [ ] Prevent Program Switch                     [ ] CTRL+ESC │
│        (    OK    )      ( Cancel )        ( Help )  │
└────────────────────────────────────────────────────┘
```

The first item is the Help Text input box. This box lets you enter some helpful information about the program. This information can be up to 255 characters long. As you enter text past the end of the window, the text will automatically be scrolled to the left. If you want, you can use this for the help information:

The CHKDSK program checks the disk drive for errors. It also reports the size of the disk, the size of memory, and amount of each that are free.

When this text is displayed, the help system will automatically format it for you.

The next three input boxes have to do with the memory of your computer and require technical knowledge that is beyond the scope of this book. Unless your situation is very unusual, the defaults provided for DOS for these properties are adequate.

If you will be using the Task Manager, you may need to change the setting of the Video Mode option. By default, the Program Manager assumes text mode, and this is the mode that you will want to use with CHKDSK. However, if the program uses graphics, then change this option to Graphics. Keep in mind that once the Shell returns, the video mode is reset. Therefore, you define the video mode for *each program* you add to a group. (That is, this option does not permanently affect your computer's display mode. It is in effect only for the time that a program is executing.)

As you know, the task switcher uses (ALT)-(TAB) to switch between tasks and (CTRL)-(ESC) to return directly to the Shell. You can go to the next task by using (ALT)-(ESC). However, some application programs may need to use these key combinations. Therefore, if you want to reserve one or more of these keys for use by your application program, you need to check the appropriate box or boxes in the Reserve Shortcut Keys list. When you reserve a key combination, the task switcher will no longer respond to it.

Finally, if you check Prevent Program Switch, the task switcher will not be able to switch out of this program. The only way to return to the Shell will be to terminate the program. Normally, you will not want to use this option unless one of your application programs instructs you to do so.

Specifying Program Parameters Using the Program Manager

Earlier in this chapter you learned how to use the Run command in the File Manager's File menu to specify one or more parameters when executing a program. In this section, you will see how to specify various parameters and options when running a program using the Program Manager.

Let's begin with an example. Highlight the Check the Disk entry and activate the File menu. Next, select the Properties option. Now change the Commands input box so that it contains the following (use B: if you are running DOS from a floppy):

CHKDSK A:

Once you have made the change, press (ENTER) or select the OK command button. Now try selecting Check the Disk. As you will see, it checks the disk in drive A.

In this case, the Program Manager used the A: drive specifier to tell CHKDSK which disk to test, thus allowing it to check a drive other than the default. You could, in theory, create several slightly different CHKDSK commands, each testing one of the drives in your system (that is, one for drive A, one for drive B, and so on). However, as you will soon see, such an approach is quite inefficient and unnecessary.

Although being able to add a built-in parameter to CHKDSK using the Program Manager might be convenient in some situations, a more flexible approach would be even better. For example, wouldn't it be nice if you could simply activate the CHKDSK command and the Shell would automatically prompt you for the drive you wanted to test? For most situations, the answer is yes. And it is possible for the Program Manager to do this using the Shell.

Before discussing any theory, let's begin with an example. First, highlight the Check the Disk entry. Next, activate the Properties option in the File menu. Finally, change the Commands line so that the

"A:" is replaced by "%1". (For now, don't worry what the "%1" means.) Your Commands input box should contain this:

CHKDSK %1

Once you have made the change, press (ENTER). Now you will see a new dialog box called Program Item Properties, as shown here:

```
┌──────────────────Program Item Properties───────────────────┐
│                                                             │
│  Fill in information for % 1   prompt dialog.               │
│                                                             │
│  Window Title  . . . .  [_                              ]    │
│                                                             │
│  Program Information .   [                             ]    │
│                                                             │
│  Prompt Message  . . .   [                             ]    │
│                                                             │
│      Default Parameters . .  [                         ]    │
│                                                             │
│        (   OK  ⌖ )      ( Cancel )        ( Help )          │
│                                                             │
└─────────────────────────────────────────────────────────────┘
```

This box is displayed because the "%1" tells the Program Manager that you want to be prompted for additional information needed by the program when it is executed. This dialog box lets you specify how you want the dialog box associated with CHKDSK to appear.

The title of the dialog box that will prompt for the additional option may be entered in the Window Title input box. The title may not be more than 23 characters long. If you want instructions to appear above the prompt, enter those instructions in the Program Information input box. This field may not exceed 180 characters. You can define a prompting message in the Prompt Message input box. This message may not exceed 18 characters and will be displayed to the left of the input box. Finally, if you want a parameter that will be displayed as the default selection (which the user may, of course, override), specify it in the Default Parameters input box.

To see an example, enter:

Which Drive?

in the Window Title box. Enter:

Choose the drive you want to test.

for Program Information and

Enter Drive:

in the Prompt Message input box. Finally, enter:

B:

for Default Parameters. The dialog box should now look like this:

```
┌──────────────────Program Item Properties───────────────────┐
│                                                             │
│  Fill in information for % 1   prompt dialog.               │
│                                                             │
│  Window Title  . . . .   [Which Drive?                 ]    │
│                                                             │
│  Program Information .    [oose the drive you want to test.]│
│                                                             │
│  Prompt Message  . . .    [Enter Drive:               ]    │
│                                                             │
│      Default Parameters . .  [B:_                      ]    │
│                                                             │
│        (   OK  ⌖ )      ( Cancel )        ( Help )          │
│                                                             │
└─────────────────────────────────────────────────────────────┘
```

Once you have entered the information correctly, press (ENTER) (or select OK).

Now try the Check the Disk program again. This time you will see the dialog box as shown here:

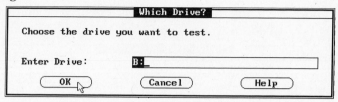

Try entering **A:** to respond to the prompt. As you will see, this causes the disk in drive A to be tested. Let's see why.

When you entered A: in response to the prompt, you caused A: to be automatically substituted for the %1. If you had simply pressed (ENTER), then B:, the default, would have been substituted for the %1. In the language of DOS, the %1 is called a *replaceable* or *dummy parameter*. Its sole purpose is to act as a placeholder in the Commands line until you fill in the actual parameter when the program is run. You might want to try this command again at this time, seeing how it responds to different input.

The key point to remember is that the %1 is a placeholder that will be substituted with the information that you enter when you run the program.

> **Replaceable parameters** *Parameter placeholders that take on the values you specify when you execute a program using the Run option.*

Specifying Multiple Parameters

You can specify more than one replaceable parameter. DOS supports ten replaceable parameters called %0 through %9, of which %1 through %9 can be used. (%0 cannot be used in the Shell.) Using these parameters, you can specify up to nine parameters to any program you execute using the Program Manager. In this section, you will see how to use multiple replaceable parameters.

Again, let's begin with an example by adding another command to the Main group. First, activate the menu bar, select File, and then select New. Since you will be adding a program, select the Program Item. Now, in the Add Program dialog box, enter:

Copy Disk

into the Title box, and

DISKCOPY %1 %2

into the Commands box. This is the DOS command that copies two diskettes. Although this feature is already part of the Disk Utilities group, it is used here for illustration. (It also will give you insight into how the default options in the Main group were created.) Next, press (ENTER) or select the OK command button.

Now, you will be prompted to fill in information relating to the %1 replaceable parameter. For Window Title enter:

Copy Disk

In the Program Information window, enter:

This program copies a disk.

In the Prompt message, enter:

Source drive

Don't enter anything in the Default Parameters box. Now, press (ENTER).

You will see the dialog box that lets you define information about the second replaceable parameter, %2. For the first two input boxes, use the same text as you did for the %1 dialog box. However, for Prompt Message enter the following:

Target drive

Again, leave the Default Parameters box blank, and press (ENTER).

Before trying the Copy Disk program, have both your work disk and a blank diskette ready. Now execute the Copy Disk command. You will be prompted first for the source drive. Enter **A:**. Put your work disk in drive A and (if you have two floppy drives) the blank disk in drive B. (If you have only one floppy, you will need to swap diskettes.) Next, you will be prompted for the target drive. Enter **B:**. As you can guess, the A: you enter for the source drive replaces %1 and the B: you enter for the target drive replaces %2. After you have completed the prompts, the diskette in drive A is copied to the one in drive B.

In general, the replaceable parameters are replaced in the order in which you are prompted for information. Therefore, if you have some application program called MYAPP that takes four parameters, you will specify a Commands line that looks like this:

MYAPP %1 %2 %3 %4

You will be prompted for four pieces of information when the program is run.

As a final example, one common use for a replaceable parameter is as a placeholder for a file name. For example, your word processor might require that the name of the file that you will be editing be specified when the program is executed. Therefore, if your word processor is called WDPRC, then this is the Commands line that you should specify when adding this program to a group:

WDPRC %1

Then, when you run the word processor, you will be prompted for the name of the file you want to edit.

Later in the book, you will learn more about the replaceable parameters and how they relate to a powerful DOS feature called batch files. Until then, you can use replaceable parameters to run your application programs and other DOS commands.

Creating a Subgroup

You will probably want to add only a few programs to the Main group. For example, if your most common task is using a spreadsheet, then you will want to be able to start that spreadsheet from the Main group

Subgroup   *A group of related programs or other subgroups that descend from a parent group.*

in order to save yourself the extra step of first selecting a subgroup before selecting the program. However, in general, you will not want to add programs to the Main group, but rather to *subgroups* so that you can keep your programs organized.

To create a subgroup, activate the Main group window, activate the File menu, and select New. When the New Program Object dialog box is displayed, select Program Group. You will see the Add Group window, as shown here:

```
┌──────────────────────────────────────────────┐
│                   Add Group                    │
│                                                │
│  Required                                      │
│                                                │
│    Title  . . . .        [_            ]       │
│                                                │
│  Optional                                      │
│                                                │
│    Help Text  . .        [             ]       │
│                                                │
│    Password   . .        [         ]           │
│                                                │
│    (   OK   )        ( Cancel )     ( Help )    │
└──────────────────────────────────────────────┘
```

As the dialog box suggests, the only thing that you must do is give the group a title. The title can be up to 23 characters long. For now, use **My Group**. If you want, you can also enter help information about the group and a password. The help text can be up to 255 characters long, and the password can be up to 20 characters long.

Once you are done, press (ENTER) or select the OK button. Now you will see that "My Group" has been added to the Main window. Select My Group at this time. Notice that the first, and only, entry is Main. The Shell automatically makes Main an entry in any subgroup's list of items. In general, whenever you create a subgroup, the parent group's name will always be the first entry in the subgroup's menu.

Adding a Program to a Subgroup

Adding a program to a subgroup is exactly like adding a program to the Main group. First, select the subgroup that you want to add the program to and then activate the File menu. From this menu select New to add the program.

For illustration, let's add the MEM command to the My Group group. This is an external command; it must be on the currently logged-in disk.

If you haven't done so, select My Group at this time. Next, activate the menu bar, select the File menu, and activate the New entry. Since you are adding a program, select Program Item from the New Program Object. The Add Program dialog box will be shown. In the Title input box, enter **Report System Memory**. For the Commands line, use:

MEM

Leave the rest of the input boxes blank and either press (ENTER) or select the OK command button. You will see that a new program entry is in your My Group subgroup. You might want to try executing it now, just to prove that it works.

Copying Programs Between Groups

You can copy a program's entry from one group to another by using the Copy command in the File menu. The general method to accomplish this is as follows. First, highlight the program that you want to copy inside its own group and then select the Copy option. Next, select the group that you want to copy the program into. Finally, press F2 to actually copy the program entry.

Let's try this by copying CHKDSK from the Main group into My Group. First, activate the Main group and highlight the Check the Disk entry. Activate the File option and select Copy. Next, activate My Group and press F2. As you can see, the information for the CHKDSK command has been copied into the My Group group.

The Copy operation does not erase the original entry for the program. To perform a move operation, you must first perform a copy followed by a delete, as described in the next section.

Deleting a Program From a Group

To delete a program from a group, first highlight the program you want to remove and then activate the File option. Next, select the Delete option. You will then see a confirmation window that gives you one last chance to change your mind before the program is deleted.

Keep one fact firmly in mind: Removing a program's entry from a group does not remove it from the disk.

To try removing a program, let's remove the copy of the CHKDSK program from the Main group. First, activate the Main group and highlight the Check the Disk entry. Next, activate the File option and choose Delete. When the safety check window appears, choose to delete the program.

Deleting a Group

You can remove a group by using the Delete option in the File menu. First, highlight the name of the group and then activate the Delete option. The subgroup must be empty before it can be deleted.

Reordering Programs Within a Group

You can change the order of items in a group by using the Reorder command in the File window. The basic procedure is as follows. First, activate the group you want to reorder and then highlight the item whose position you want to change. Next, activate the File option and select the Reorder option. Move the highlight to the position where you want the item to be put and press ENTER, or double-click using the mouse. The item will be moved and the list will reflect the new order. You might want to try this feature on your own.

Password   *A word that you use to restrict access to certain programs or groups when using the Shell.*

Using a Password

You can restrict access to a program by giving it a *password* when you enter the program into a group. If you use a password, then only those people who know the password can activate the program from the Shell. (The program can still be executed using the Run option, however.)

You can use any characters you like for a password. Be sure to remember the password because you will also need it to activate the Properties option in the File menu. That is, to alter any properties associated with a program protected by a password—such as removing the password—also requires the use of the password.

You can also control access to an entire group by giving the group a password when you define it. The password will then be needed to modify any properties associated with the group.

CAUTION

The password controls access to a program only if that program is executed from the Shell. Anyone who knows how to use the DOS command prompt interface will still be able to run the program. Therefore, a password is at best a mild deterrent—not real protection. At worst, a password may tip someone off that a sensitive program is on your computer. A better security approach is to lock up the computer when it is not in use.

The Program Manager's Run Option

In the Program Manager's File menu, the Run option performs in the same way as it does in the File menu of the File Manager.

Some More Shell Editing Keys

Before concluding this chapter, a few additional editing keys that relate to the Shell's input boxes will be discussed. To follow along, activate the File Manager, activate the menu bar, select File, and then select the Run option. Although you won't actually be running a program, this input box makes a good place to experiment.

When you enter information into an input box, some special keys can be used to make changing or fixing what you have entered easier. These keys are (HOME), (END), the ← and → keys, (BACKSPACE), and (DEL). Let's see how they work.

First, enter this into the Command Line input box:

this is a test

Now, press the (HOME) key. The cursor will move to the beginning of the line. Next, press the (END) key. This time the cursor moves to the end of the line. In general, whenever you press the (HOME) key, the cursor moves to the start of an input box. Pressing the (END) key causes the cursor to move to the end of the text.

If you want to change something in the middle of what you have entered, you may use the ← or → keys to move the cursor to the point you want to change without erasing what is already there. For example, press (END) and then press the (←) key five times. The cursor will be under the space before the "t" of "test." When you are in the middle of text, you can add characters simply by typing them. Whatever is to the right of what you enter will be moved over, making room for the new characters. To see an example, enter:

a small

at this time. Now the input box contains:

```
this is a small test
```

To delete a character to the left of the cursor, press the (BACKSPACE) key. If you want to delete the character that is under the cursor, use the (DEL) key.

You might want to experiment with the input box editing keys for a while. However, when you are through, be sure to exit the Run dialog box by selecting Cancel or by pressing (ESC).

Summary

In this chapter you learned the following:

- How to execute programs using the File Manager's Run option
- How to add programs to a group
- How to execute programs using the Program Manager
- How to execute a program that requires parameters
- How to use replaceable parameters
- How to create a subgroup
- How to copy programs between groups
- How to reorder a group
- About using passwords with programs and groups
- About some additional editing keys

The next chapter contains a discussion of DOS's text editor.

Key Terms

Password   A word that you use to restrict access to certain programs or groups when using the Shell.

Program Manager   The part of the Shell that helps you manage your programs.

Program parameters   Extra information used by a program.

Program properties   Information associated with your program that the Program Manager uses to better manage and utilize your programs.

Replaceable parameters   Parameter placeholders that take on the values you specify when you execute a program using the Run option.

Subgroup   A group of related programs or other subgroups that descend from a parent group.

Exercises

Matching

Match the answers in the second column with the terms in the first.

_____ 1. Parameter

_____ 2. Percent sign

_____ 3. Group

_____ 4. Shortcut key

_____ 5. The (HOME) key

_____ 6. The (END) key

_____ 7. Subgroup

a. Analogous to a subdirectory except that it applies to groups.

b. Extra information used by a program when it begins executing.

c. A key combination that is used to switch directly to a specific program when using the task switcher.

d. The character that replaceable parameters begin with.

e. The editing key that moves the cursor to the beginning of the line.

f. A collection of related programs and/or subgroups.

g. The editing key that moves the cursor to the end of the line.

Short Answer

1. When using an input box, what key do you press to delete the character to the left of the cursor? What key do you press to delete the character that is at the cursor?

2. To execute a program that requires additional information, you use what File menu option?

3. How do you run a series of commands using the Run option?

4. How do you create a new group in the Program Manager?

5. How do you add a program to a group in the Program Manager?

6. Name three properties that a program may have.

7. Assume that you have a spreadsheet program called SP. You want to add it to the Program Manager so that when you execute it, you are automatically prompted for the file that you want to work with. What is the text that you must put in the Commands field of the Add Program dialog box?

8. Why do passwords provide only limited security?

Activities

1. If you haven't already done so, add the CHKDSK program to the Main group of the Program Manager as described in the text. Next, add a password to this program.

2. Add a shortcut key to the CHKDSK program and experiment with it.

Using the DOS Editor

CHAPTER OBJECTIVES

After completing this chapter, you should be able to:

- Invoke the DOS editor and enter text.
- Delete characters, words, and lines.
- Move, copy, and delete blocks of text.
- Use the clipboard.
- Find and replace text.
- Save and load your file.
- Print the file.
- Set various editor options.

Until now, you have not created any new files. However, as you advance in your study of DOS, it will be necessary to create and modify short text files. Also, there will almost certainly be times when you will want to create a text file, such as a memo, and print it on the printer. To handle both these needs, DOS 6 includes a text editor. The DOS editor is activated from the Main group.

A *text editor* is a special program that lets you manage text files. If you have used a word processor, you can think of a text editor as a very limited word processor. Typically, word processors are designed to handle special formats, type fonts, and the like. But a text editor simply allows you to maintain a text file; it provides no special features.

The DOS 6 editor contains about 35 commands and is quite powerful. However, you will not have to learn all the commands at once. The most important commands deal with inserting, deleting, and moving text; others include searching and replacing text. Once you have mastered these basic areas, you will easily be able to learn the rest of the editor commands and put them to use as you need them. Learning

Text editor   A program that lets you create, manage, and maintain text files.

113

to use the editor will be surprisingly simple because you will have DOS's online context-sensitive help system at your disposal.

Editor Commands

Before beginning it is important to explain how you give commands to the DOS 6 editor. Like the Shell itself, the DOS editor allows many operations to be selected from menus within the editor. In addition, hot keys are supported, which are shortcuts to menu selection. However, unlike the Shell, not all editor options may be selected using the menus; some can be activated only by using special keystrokes. Many of the shortcut and keystroke commands are formed by using *control characters*. In this book, control characters are written like this: (CTRL)-(X). This is pronounced "control X." A control character is formed by holding down the (CTRL) key and pressing another key. For example, to type (CTRL)-(F), hold down the (CTRL) key, press (F), and then release both keys. Many editor commands are control characters or begin with a control character. For example, pressing (CTRL)-(Y) causes a line of text to be erased.

Many editor commands may also be entered using the mouse.

Control character
A character formed by holding down the (CTRL) *key and then pressing another key.*

Invoking the Editor and Entering Text

To execute the DOS 6 editor, activate the Program Manager and select the Editor option. You will see this dialog box.

```
┌────────────────────████ File to Edit ████────────────────┐
│                                                          │
│   Enter the name of the file to edit. To start MS-DOS    │
│   Editor without opening a file, press ENTER.            │
│                                                          │
│   File to edit?        ┌──────────────────────────────┐  │
│                        │_                             │  │
│                        └──────────────────────────────┘  │
│    ┌────────────┐      ┌────────────┐    ┌────────────┐  │
│    │   OK       │      │  Cancel    │    │   Help     │  │
│    └────────────┘      └────────────┘    └────────────┘  │
└──────────────────────────────────────────────────────────┘
```

Inside the editor dialog box, you must enter the name of the file that you want to edit. You can enter the name of an existing file or create a new file. For now, since you have no preexisting files, you will enter a new file name. Enter **MYTEXT.TXT** and press (ENTER). In a few seconds, your screen will look like the one shown in Figure 7-1.

The top line of the editor window contains the editor's menu bar. The title of the editor window is the name of the file currently being edited. At the bottom right of the editor window, the current line and column position of the cursor are displayed. Along the right side of the window is the vertical scroll bar, and along the bottom is the horizontal scroll bar. The vertical scroll bar scrolls text up and down. The horizontal scroll bar scrolls text left and right.

When you are not in the middle of giving the editor a command, it is ready to accept input. This means that when you strike keys on the keyboard, they will appear in the editor window at the current cursor location.

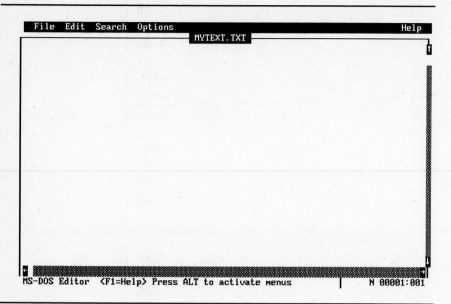

FIGURE 7-1   **The DOS editor screen**

By default, the editor is in *insert mode*. This means that as you enter text, it will be inserted in the middle of what (if anything) is already there. The opposite is called *overwrite mode*. In this mode of operation, new text can overwrite existing text. You can toggle between these two modes by pressing the (INS) key. You can tell which mode is currently active by the shape of the cursor. In insert mode, the cursor is represented as a blinking underscore. In overwrite mode, it is a blinking rectangle.

Make sure that the editor window is active and type the following lines:

This is a
test of the
DOS editor.

Be sure to press (ENTER) after the last line. If you make a mistake, you can use the (BACKSPACE) key to correct it. Your screen will now look like that in Figure 7-2. Notice the position of the cursor and the values associated with the line and column display at the lower right of the editor window.

Because the DOS editor is a screen editor, you can use the arrow keys to move the cursor about the text at random. Also, when you click the mouse, the cursor moves to the position of the mouse pointer. At this time, use either the arrow keys or the mouse to position the cursor at the far left side of the line "test of the". Now type **very small** and then press (ENTER). As you do so, watch the way the existing line is moved to the right instead of being overwritten. This is what happens when the editor is in insert mode. Had you toggled the editor into overwrite mode, the original line would have been overwritten. Your screen will now look like Figure 7-3.

Insert mode   An editor mode in which characters you type do not overwrite existing characters. Existing text is moved to the right to make room for the new characters.

Overwrite mode An editor mode in which characters you type replace (i.e., overwrite) existing characters.

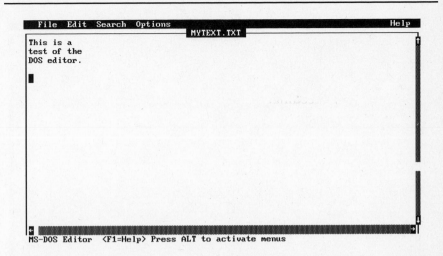

FIGURE 7-2   **Editor screen with text entered**

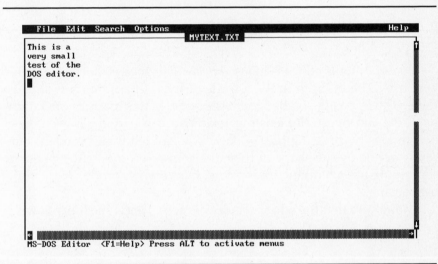

FIGURE 7-3   **Editor screen after inserting a line**

Deleting Characters, Words, and Lines

You can delete a single character to the left of the cursor by pressing the (BACKSPACE) key or (CTRL)-(H). To delete the character that the cursor is on, press either the (DEL) key or (CTRL)-(G). To try each method, first position the cursor on the "i" of "is" in the first line and press (BACKSPACE). Notice that the preceding space is removed. Reenter the space now. Next, position the cursor on the "i" again and try pressing (DEL). This time the "i" is removed. Reenter the "i" at this time.

You can delete an entire word that is to the right of the cursor by typing (CTRL)-(T).

You can remove an entire line by typing (CTRL)-(Y). It does not matter where the cursor is positioned in the line—the entire line is deleted. You should try deleting a few lines and words at this time. Before continuing, however, reenter the lines that you deleted.

If you wish to delete from the current cursor position to the end of the line, type the sequence (CTRL)-(Q) (Y). To see how this works, position the cursor on the "s" of "small" in the second line and enter the sequence (CTRL)-(Q) (Y). Notice that the word "very" is still there, but the rest of the line beginning with the "s" in "small" is deleted. Reenter "small" before proceeding.

Moving, Copying, and Deleting Blocks of Text

The DOS editor allows you to manipulate blocks of text. You can move or copy a block to another location or delete it altogether. In order to do any of these things, you must first define a block. A *block* can be as short as a single character or as large as your entire file. Typically, a block is somewhere between these two extremes.

You can define a block of text in two different ways: using the keyboard or using the mouse. To define a block using the keyboard, move the cursor to the start of the block, hold down the (SHIFT) key, and use the arrow keys to move the cursor to the end of the block; release the arrow and (SHIFT) keys. The block you defined will be highlighted. To define a block using the mouse, first position the mouse pointer at the start of the block. Next, press and hold the left mouse button and move the mouse to the end of the block. Finally, release the button.

For example, move the cursor to the "t" at the start of the third line, press the (SHIFT) key, and press (↓) twice. Your screen should look like Figure 7-4.

Once you have defined a block of text, you can move it using this sequence. First press (SHIFT)-(DEL). This causes the text to be removed from the screen and put into the *clipboard*, which is a temporary storage area used by the editor. Next, move the cursor to the point in your file where you want to move the text and press (SHIFT)-(INS). You may also move text

> **Block**   *As it applies to text editing, a block is a group of characters that can be as short as a single character or as long as the entire file.*

> **Clipboard**   *A temporary repository for text that will be used later.*

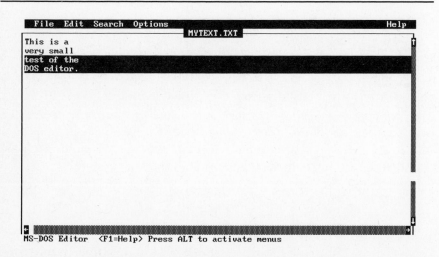

FIGURE 7-4   Editor screen after defining a block

using menu commands. To do this, first define a block, then activate the Edit menu and select Cut. This removes the selected text and puts it in the clipboard. Move the cursor to the new location, activate the Edit menu again, and this time select Paste. This moves the text to the new location.

To copy a block, first define the block. Next, press (CTRL)-(INS). This copies the block into the clipboard but does not remove the block from the screen. Next, move the cursor to where you want the text to be copied and press (SHIFT)-(INS). You can also use the Edit menu to copy a block. After you have created a block, first select the Copy option to copy the text into the clipboard. Next, move the cursor to where you want the text copied and select the Paste option.

To delete the currently marked block, either press (DEL) or select the Clear option on the Edit menu. The deleted text is *not* put into the clipboard.

Before moving on, let's copy a block of text. First, define a block of text that consists of the first two lines of the sample text you have in the editor. (To do this, position the cursor at the start of the first line, hold down (SHIFT), and press (↓) twice.) Next, press (CTRL)-(INS). Now, move the cursor to the bottom of the file and press (SHIFT)-(INS). Your screen will look like Figure 7-5.

More on the Clipboard

As stated in the previous section, the clipboard is a temporary depository for fragments of text that have been moved or copied. To move text into the clipboard, you need to mark the region and then either move or copy that block.

To retrieve a block of text from the clipboard, use the Edit menu's Paste command or press (SHIFT)-(INS). This causes the most recently moved or copied block of text in the clipboard to be copied into the editor

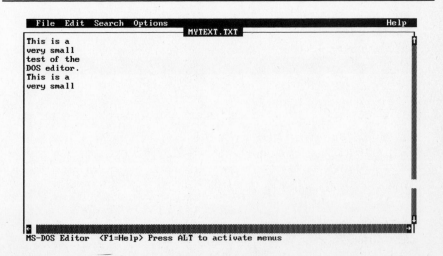

FIGURE 7-5 **Editor screen after copying a block**

window at the current cursor location. However, this does not remove the text from the clipboard. You can press (SHIFT)-(INS) as often as you like, producing multiple copies of the text.

Each time you move or copy a new block of text, that text replaces any text previously held in the clipboard.

More on Cursor Movement

The DOS editor has a number of special cursor commands. These commands are summarized in Table 7-1. You should experiment with these commands now. Of course, you may also move the cursor by positioning the mouse pointer at the desired location and clicking.

> **NOTE**
>
> By holding down the (SHIFT) key, you can use any of the cursor commands (except for the scrolling commands) to help define a block. For example, (SHIFT)-(CTRL)-(→) highlights the word to the right of the cursor.

Finding and Replacing

Often, you will want to find a specific sequence of characters in your file. This will be especially true when working with larger files. To find a sequence of characters, use the (CTRL)-(Q) (F) command or select the

Action	Command
Move left one character	(←) or (CTRL)-(S)
Move right one character	(→) or (CTRL)-(D)
Move left one word	(CTRL)-(←) or (CTRL)-(A)
Move right one word	(CTRL)-(→) or (CTRL)-(F)
Move up one line	(↑) or (CTRL)-(E)
Move down one line	(↓) or (CTRL)-(X)
Scroll up	(CTRL)-(↑) or (CTRL)-(W)
Scroll down	(CTRL)-(↓) or (CTRL)-(Z)
Move up one page	(PGUP) or (CTRL)-(R)
Move down one page	(PGDN) or (CTRL)-(C)
Move to start of line	(HOME) or (CTRL)-(Q) (S)
Move to end of line	(END) or (CTRL)-(Q) (D)
Move to top of screen	(CTRL)-(Q) (E)
Move to bottom of screen	(CTRL)-(Q) (X)
Move to top of file	(CTRL)-(Q) (R) or (CTRL)-(HOME)
Move to bottom of file	(CTRL)-(Q) (C) or (CTRL)-(END)
Move to start of next line	(CTRL)-(ENTER)
Scroll screen left	(CTRL)-(PGUP)
Scroll screen right	(CTRL)-(PGDN)

TABLE 7-1   **The cursor commands**

Find option on the Search menu. You will then be prompted by the dialog window shown here:

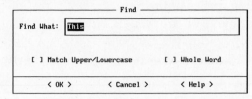

The editor will automatically copy the word that the cursor is on or near in your file into the Find What box. If this is the text you want to search for, then you do not need to enter anything. Otherwise, just enter the text you want to find. The sequence of characters you are looking for is generally referred to as a string, and it may be up to 127 characters long.

If the string you are looking for is found, then the cursor is moved to the start of that string. If no matching string is found, the message "Match not found" is displayed, and the cursor will remain in its previous location.

You can specify two options that affect how the search for the string you entered is conducted. By default, the search is not case sensitive. This means that for the purposes of the search, "test" and "TEST" will be treated as the same. You can cause the search to be case sensitive by selecting the Match Upper/Lowercase checkbox. (Remember, to select a checkbox, tab to the box and press the space bar.) Also, by default, substrings are found. For example, if you search for the word "other," a match will be found with the word "Another" because it contains the word you are looking for. You can prevent these types of matches by selecting the Whole Word option.

The search proceeds from the current cursor location forward (toward the end) in the file.

You can repeat the search by pressing (CTRL)-(L) or (F3), or by selecting the Repeat Last Find option on the Search menu. Repeating the search allows you to find multiple occurrences of a string within a file.

You can replace one string with another. To activate the Replace command, type (CTRL)-(Q) (A) or select the Change option on the Search menu. Its operation is identical to the Find command except that it allows you to replace the string you are looking for with another. You will see the dialog box shown here:

```
┌─ Change ─┐
Find What: [                    ]

Change To: [                    ]

[ ] Match Upper/Lowercase    [ ] Whole Word
< Find and Verify >  < Change All >  < Cancel >  < Help >
```

As you can see, the options available in the Change dialog box are similar to those available with Find. However, the replace operation can be executed in two ways. By selecting Find and Verify, the editor will ask you before making each change. You can turn off this feature by selecting Change All.

Setting and Finding Place Markers

You can set up to four place markers in your file by pressing CTRL-K *n*, where *n* is the number of the place marker (0–3). After a marker has been set, the command CTRL-Q *n*, where *n* is the marker number, causes the cursor to go to that marker. Place markers are especially convenient in large files.

Saving and Loading Your File

To save your text to disk using the same name you specified when you started the editor (in this case, MYTEXT.TXT), activate the File menu and select Save. Your file will then be saved to disk.

You can save your file under a different name by selecting the Save As option. You will see the following Save As dialog box.

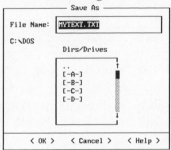

Simply enter the new name in the File Name box. The directory that the file will be saved to is shown immediately below the File Name box. You can change the directory or the drive your file is saved to by first activating the Dirs/Drives box and then selecting the directory or the drive from the list.

Once you have finished editing one file, you can move on and edit other files without having to leave and reenter the editor. Furthermore, you can edit a preexisting file or create a new one.

To edit a preexisting file, select the Open option on the File menu. This causes a dialog box to be displayed, and you are prompted for the name of the file you wish to load. You can specify the file name in several ways. First, you can type it in. Second, you can tab to the list of files shown in the dialog box and make a selection. If you have a mouse, you can also double-click on the desired file and it will be loaded. By default, all files with the .TXT extension are displayed. However, if you change the file name in the File Name box, the file list will reflect those that match the new name. You can use the wildcard characters in the file name. For example, to list all files in the current directory, specify *.* as the file name.

You can change the directory or drive that the file is to be loaded from by using the Dirs/Drives box.

If you try to load a file that is nonexistent, you will receive an error message, and the file currently being edited will be left unchanged in the editor window.

If the file you are currently editing has had changes made to it but has not yet been saved, you will be prompted to save the file before loading another.

If you want to create a new file, select the New option on the File menu. The file will not have a name until you give it one when you save it.

Printing the File

To print the file that is currently being edited, select the Print option on the File menu. You will see the dialog box shown here:

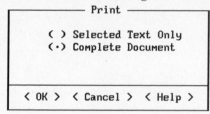

```
┌─────────── Print ───────────┐
│                             │
│    ( ) Selected Text Only   │
│    (•) Complete Document     │
│                             │
├─────────────────────────────┤
│  < OK >   < Cancel >   < Help >  │
└─────────────────────────────┘
```

If no block of text is selected, then the entire file will be printed. If you have defined a block and you select the Selected Text Only option, then only that block will be printed. However, even if you have selected a block, you can still print the entire file by selecting the Complete Document option.

Auto-Indentation

Auto-indentation An editing feature that causes the cursor to return to the same indentation level as the previous line each time you press (ENTER).

The DOS editor includes a feature called *auto-indentation*. To understand what it does, enter this text exactly as it is shown:

This
  is
    an
      example of auto-indentation.

As you enter the text, you will notice that the cursor returns to the position of the previous indentation level. This feature makes the creation of tables and lists much easier because you don't need to manually enter several spaces.

When you press (BACKSPACE) at the start of an indented line, the cursor moves to the left one full indentation level.

Entering Control Characters

You can enter a control character into a file by first typing (CTRL)-(P) followed by the control character you want. For example, (CTRL)-(P) (CTRL)-(T) inserts a (CTRL)-(T) into your file. It will appear as the paragraph symbol. In general, you should not enter control characters into your file unless an application program requires you to do so.

Command Summary

Table 7-2 lists all the DOS 6 editor commands.

Setting Some Editor Options

You can change some aspects of the way the editor operates by selecting the Options menu. This menu contains two selections, Display and Help Path. The Help Path option is used to specify the path to the editor help files. If DOS has been installed correctly on your computer, you will not need to use this option.

The Display option lets you change the way some things in the editor work and look. Activate the Display option at this time. You will see the dialog box shown in Figure 7-6. You can change the foreground (text) and background colors used by the editor. If you don't use a mouse, you can remove the scroll bars from the editor window by deselecting the Scroll Bars option. You can also change the size of a tab.

Summary

In this chapter you learned how to

- Start the DOS editor and enter text
- Delete characters, words, and lines of text
- Move, copy, and delete blocks of text

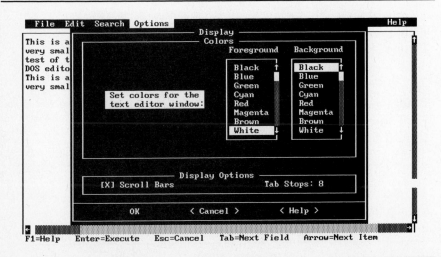

FIGURE 7-6   **The Display option dialog box**

Cursor Commands

Action	Command
Move left one character	← or CTRL-S
Move right one character	→ or CTRL-D
Move left one word	CTRL-← or CTRL-A
Move right one word	CTRL-→ or CTRL-F
Move up one line	↑ or CTRL-E
Move down one line	↓ or CTRL-X
Scroll up	CTRL-↑ or CTRL-W
Scroll down	CTRL-↓ or CTRL-Z
Move up one page	PGUP or CTRL-R
Move down one page	PGDN or CTRL-C
Move to start of line	HOME or CTRL-Q S
Move to end of line	END or CTRL-Q D
Move to top of screen	CTRL-Q E
Move to bottom of screen	CTRL-Q X
Move to top of file	CTRL-Q R or CTRL-HOME
Move to bottom of file	CTRL-Q C or CTRL-END
Move to start of next line	CTRL-ENTER
Scroll screen left	CTRL-PGUP
Scroll screen right	CTRL-PGDN

Insert Commands

Toggle insert mode	INS or CTRL-V
Insert a blank line	ENTER or CTRL-N
Enter control character	CTRL-P or CTRL-*character*

Delete Commands

Delete entire line	CTRL-Y
Delete to end of line	CTRL-Q Y
Delete character on left	BACKSPACE or CTRL-H
Delete character at cursor	DEL or CTRL-G
Delete word to right	CTRL-T
Delete block	DEL
Delete block and put in clipboard	SHIFT-DEL
Delete leading spaces	SHIFT-TAB

Find Commands

Find	CTRL-Q F
Find and replace	CTRL-Q A
Repeat find	CTRL-L or F3

Miscellaneous Commands

Toggle overwrite/insert mode	INS or CTRL-V
Set a place marker	CTRL-K n
Find a place marker	CTRL-Q n

TABLE 7-2 **DOS 6 editor command summary by category**

- Use the clipboard
- Find and replace text
- Set and find place markers
- Save and load files
- Print your files
- Set various options

In the next chapter, you will learn to use DOS's command prompt interface.

Key Terms

Auto-indentation   An editing feature that causes the cursor to return to the same indentation level as the previous line each time you press (ENTER).

Block   As it applies to text editing, a block is a group of characters that can be as short as a single character or as long as the entire file.

Clipboard   A temporary repository for text that will be used later.

Control character A character formed by holding down the (CTRL) key and then pressing another key.

Insert mode   An editor mode in which characters you type do not overwrite existing characters. Existing text is moved to the right to make room for the new characters.

Overwrite mode   An editor mode in which characters you type re-place (i.e., overwrite) existing characters.

Text editor   A program that lets you create, manage, and maintain text files.

Exercises

Matching

Match the answers in the second column with the terms in the first.

_____ 1. (←)   a. Toggles insert mode

_____ 2. (CTRL)-(→)   b. Deletes a line

_____ 3. (CTRL)-(HOME) c. Activates the Find dialog box

_____ 4. (CTRL)-(END)   d. Moves to the end of the file

_____ 5. (INS)   e. Deletes the word to the right of the cursor

_____ 6. (CTRL)-(Y)   f. Moves to the beginning of the file

_____ 7. (CTRL)-(T)   g. Moves left one character

_____ 8. (CTRL)-(Q) (F) h. Moves right one word

Fill-in-the-Blank

1. The DOS editor is invoked by first activating the _____ _____ and then choosing the Editor option.

2. When using a mouse, you can move text vertically through the editor window by using the _____ _____ _____.

3. To copy text into the clipboard (without deleting it from the original text), first define a block and then press _____.

4. You can repeat a search by pressing _____.

5. To replace one string with another, either press _____ or select the _____ option in the Search menu.

Short Answer

1. How do you define a block of text using the mouse?

2. What is the clipboard?

3. By default, string searches are not case sensitive. How do you make such searches case sensitive?

4. What is a place marker?

5. In your own words, explain what auto-indentation is.

6. How do you enter a control character into a file?

Activities

Experiment with the DOS editor. Try several commands. Also, experiment with setting some editor options.

Business Case Study

You have been given the job of installing a new inventory manager on drive C of your company's computer. The inventory manager requires a directory structure like this:

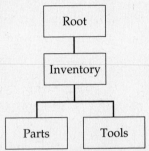

1. First, you must create the necessary directories on your fixed disk. You perform the following steps using the DOS Shell.

   a. First, make sure that drive C is the current drive. If not, select its icon in the Disk Drive window. Also, make sure that the root directory is current.
   b. Next, activate the File menu bar option and select Create Directory.
   c. Now, create the INVTRY directory.
   d. To create the subdirectories of INVTRY, first select the INVTRY directory in the Directory Tree window. Next, activate the File menu bar option and use Create Directory to create the PARTS directory. Select Create Directory a second time to create the TOOLS directory.

2. Now that the directory structure has been created, you will need to copy the inventory manager program from its master floppy disk to your fixed disk. In this case, all files on the master disk must be copied into the INVTRY directory on drive C.

   a. To begin you put the master diskette into drive A, switch to drive A, and then select all files on drive A using the Select All option in the File menu.
   b. Next, activate the File menu and select Copy. When the Copy dialog box is displayed, you specify as its target C:\INVTRY. This causes all the files to be copied from drive A to the INVTRY directory of drive C.

PART 3

Introducing the Command Prompt

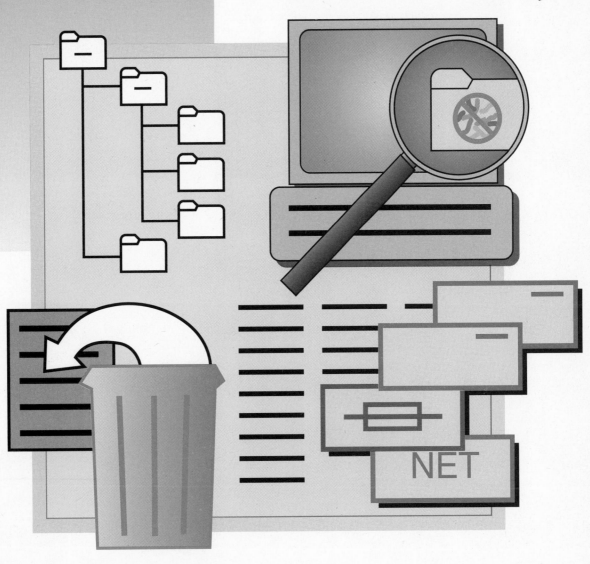

CHAPTER

8

Using the Command Prompt

CHAPTER OBJECTIVES

After completing this chapter, you should be able to:

- Activate the command prompt.
- Understand the DOS prompt.
- Issue the DIR command.
- Return to the Shell.
- Change the current drive.
- Stop the display from scrolling when using DIR.
- Understand command prompt error messages.
- Use the VER, CLS, COPY, and TYPE commands.
- Understand several DIR options.
- Use the DOS command prompt editing keys.

As you may know, earlier versions of DOS did not include the Shell. Instead of supplying menu options and dialog boxes to accomplish most common operations, these earlier versions displayed a *command prompt* and waited for the user to enter a command. Although DOS versions 5.00 and later have supplied the Shell, it is still possible to activate the command prompt and operate DOS directly from this prompt. (DOS version 4 supplied a Shell that was somewhat different than that supplied by later versions of DOS, but DOS 4 was never widely accepted or used.)

This chapter will begin exploring the command prompt and its command-based interface. To follow along with the examples, you will need a blank, formatted diskette.

Command prompt
The traditional interface to DOS.

Why Use the Command Prompt?

You might be wondering why you would want to use the command prompt interface when the Shell is available. There are four main reasons to learn and use the command prompt. Perhaps the most important is that the Run option in the File menu of the File Manager accepts the same command line as the command prompt interface. Therefore, to make full use of the Run option, you need to understand how to enter a command at the command prompt. Second, many computers will not be immediately upgraded to a version of DOS that supports the Shell. Therefore, if you will be working with a wide variety of computers, it is a good idea to know how to run DOS using only the command prompt. Third, once you know how to use the command prompt, it is actually faster (and sometimes easier) than using the Shell. In general, the Shell trades away some power and performance for ease of use. Finally, a few commands cannot be easily activated using a Shell menu selection.

Activating the Command Prompt

The command prompt can be activated in two general ways from within the Shell. First, you can choose the Command Prompt option in the Main group or press (SHIFT)-(F9). The screen is cleared and the command prompt interface is activated. What actually happens when you use this method of activating the command prompt is that the Shell stays in memory waiting for you to come back to it. To go back to the Shell, you must use the EXIT command, which in essence tells DOS to leave the command prompt and resume the Shell.

You can also activate the command prompt by pressing (F3) or (ALT)-(F4) while the Program Manager window is active, or by selecting the Exit option in the File menu of the Program Manager. Activating the command prompt in this way causes the Shell to be removed from memory. Thus, there is nothing to return to, so the EXIT command has no effect. To restart the Shell after activating the command prompt in this way, you must use the DOSSHELL command.

Generally speaking, it is best to activate the command prompt by pressing (SHIFT)-(F9). This is the method used in this chapter.

No Mousing at the Command Prompt

Put bluntly, the mouse does not work with the command prompt. The mouse may work with programs that you run from the command prompt, but there is no way to use it to communicate with DOS.

The Sign-On Message and the DOS Prompt

Activate the command prompt by pressing (SHIFT)-(F9) at this time. When the command prompt is activated, you will see a sign-on message. The message contains a statement of copyright and also tells you the version number of DOS that you are using. Some commands work only with later versions of DOS, so you need to know what version you are running. You should make a mental note of it at this time.

Beneath the sign-on message and on the far left, you will see either "A>" or "C>". If you loaded DOS from a diskette, then you will see "A>". If you loaded it from a fixed disk, you will see "C>". This letter and symbol combination is called the DOS prompt. Whenever the cursor is positioned immediately after the prompt, DOS is ready to accept a command.

If your system has a fixed disk and has been in use for a while by other people, your DOS prompt may look somewhat different. As you will see later in this book, you can tell DOS exactly what style of prompt you want. Thus, if your prompt differs, don't worry about it.

A Note to Fixed Disk Users

If you are running DOS from a fixed disk, then you will need to log into the DOS directory after activating the command prompt in order to follow along with the examples. To do this, type the command

CD \DOS

and then press (ENTER). This causes the DOS directory to become current. The CD command stands for Change Directory. You will learn more about it later in this book.

A First Look at the DIR Command

When you are running DOS from the command prompt, you tell DOS what you want it to do by giving it a command. Many of the commands have direct parallels in the Shell. A few do not. Before learning the theory of operation, let's try some commands.

One of the most useful commands is *DIR*, which displays the directory of the disk. At the prompt, type **DIR** followed by (ENTER). (If you make a typing mistake, use the (BACKSPACE) key to correct your error before pressing (ENTER).) This causes the file directory to be displayed on the screen.

Because there are more files on the disk than there are lines on the monitor, the first part of the list scrolls off the top of the screen. Don't worry about this; it is supposed to happen. Later you will learn ways to control how information is displayed. The output displayed on your screen will be similar to that shown in Figure 8-1.

DIR   The command that lists the directory.

```
MEMMAKER EXE    118660 03-10-93    6:00a
SIZER    EXE      7169 03-10-93    6:00a
MONOUMB  386      8783 03-10-93    6:00a
TEST     TXT        15 01-16-93    4:09p
MSTOOLS  DLL     13424 03-10-93    6:00a
MOUSE    SYS     34581 10-04-90    3:22p
MSAV     EXE    172198 03-10-93    6:00a
MSAV     HLP     23891 03-10-93    6:00a
MSAVHELP OVL     29828 03-10-93    6:00a
MSAVIRUS LST     35520 03-10-93    6:00a
VSAFE    COM     62576 03-10-93    6:00a
COMMAND  COM     52925 03-10-93    6:00a
CONFIG   UMB       658 02-10-93    3:51p
MSBACKUP INI        43 11-25-92    3:31p
SYSTEM   UMB      1589 11-20-92    2:23p
MSAV     INI       248 01-20-93   10:17a
DEFAULT  SET      4250 01-21-93    1:33p
DEFAULT  SLT       784 01-21-93   10:51a
QBASIC   INI       132 01-13-93    4:52p
MSBACKUP LOG     39883 02-21-93    4:11p
MOUSE    INI        28 12-19-92    2:10p
      136 file(s)    4713872 bytes
                     8617984 bytes free
```

FIGURE 8-1   **Sample output of the DIR command**

NOTE

Keep in mind that in this and other examples throughout this chapter, the actual output you see will be somewhat different from what is shown in this book.

Notice that once the directory has been listed, DOS returns the prompt to the screen. Whenever DOS finishes a command, it redisplays the prompt. This lets you know that it has completed the task. When DOS is accessing a diskette, the small, red drive-active light comes on. Never remove a diskette from the drive when this light is on; if you do, you might destroy some of the information on the diskette.

The directory listing includes the following items from left to right: the name of the file, the size of the file (in bytes), and the date and time the file was created. The directory listing is similar to the one displayed in the File List window except that the Shell does not display a file's time of creation.

Besides listing the directory, the DIR command tells you three other things. First, it displays the number of files in the directory. Second, it tells you how many bytes of disk storage are allocated to the files. Finally, it tells you the amount of free space on the disk. The amount of storage capacity of a diskette or of a fixed disk varies greatly; you should consult your owner's manual for specific information.

> **NOTE**
>
> Two important points: First, as stated earlier, DOS does not care whether you enter commands using uppercase or lowercase letters. This book uses uppercase letters so that you can easily distinguish commands from surrounding text, but in actual practice you will probably use lowercase letters most of the time. Second, as you enter information using the Shell or enter a command at the command prompt, DOS knows nothing about what you type until you press (ENTER). Therefore, you can fix typing errors or change your command any time before pressing (ENTER).

Returning to the Shell

Before moving on, try returning to the Shell by typing the command **EXIT** at the DOS prompt and then pressing (ENTER). In a few moments, the DOS Shell will again be displayed. Now press (SHIFT)-(F9) to reactivate the command prompt. You might want to try this a few times until you are comfortable moving between the Shell and the command prompt.

> **EXIT** *The command that leaves the command prompt and returns to the Shell.*

    Remember that if you activate the command prompt by pressing (F3), (ALT)-(F4), or by selecting the Exit option in the File menu in the Program Manager window, you cannot use EXIT to return to the Shell. Instead, you must use the DOSSHELL command.

    Reactivate the command prompt at this time.

Another Command

One of the simplest commands in DOS is the VER command, which displays the version number of DOS you are using. To see how it works, type **VER** and press (ENTER). You will see a message similar to this:

```
MS-DOS Version 6.00
```

Changing the Current Drive

When you type the DIR command, you get a directory listing of the drive that corresponds to the letter in the prompt. If you have two floppy disk drives or a fixed disk and a floppy disk drive, you can switch to the other drive by typing its drive letter followed by a colon and pressing (ENTER). For example, if you have a fixed disk, then try switching to the A drive. If you are using floppies, then try switching to drive B. Be sure that you have a formatted diskette in the target drive. For example, to switch to the A drive, you enter **A:** followed by (ENTER). As you can see, the DOS prompt has been changed to reflect the switch to a new drive.

    To switch back to either the A or the C drive, you follow the same format as before, substituting the proper drive designation. Switch back to either the A or C drive now. (If you have two diskette drives, be sure that the DOS diskette is in drive A.)

A Closer Look at DIR

Earlier, you learned the simplest form of the DIR command. However, as you will soon see, DIR is much more flexible and contains several options. Let's take a look at two of those options now. The DIR options discussed here are applicable to all versions of DOS. Later in this chapter, several DIR options specific to DOS 6 will be explored.

Two DIR Options

As you know from using the Shell, many DOS commands allow one or more options that alter slightly the meaning or effect of the command. When you are running DOS from the command prompt, a command option begins with a slash (/) followed by the specific option. The / signals DOS that an option follows.

The first DIR option is /P, which tells DOS to temporarily stop listing the directory when the screen is full. Remember that when you listed the directory, some file names scrolled off the top of the screen. The /P option prevents this. At each pause, you will see the message

```
Press any key to continue . . .
```

This means that when you are ready to see more of the directory, press any key.

To execute the DIR command with the Pause option, enter the command line like this:

DIR /P

Try this now.

Since the output of the DIR command did not scroll off the screen, the first few lines are still present. These lines tell you the disk's volume name (which is loosely the disk's name), the serial number (which is determined when the disk is formatted), and the path to the directory being listed.

Often, all you will want is a list of the files on a disk, and you will not be interested in all the other information that DIR displays. When this is your goal, you can use the /W option, which causes DOS to display only the file names in the directory. The file names are displayed in five columns across the screen so that many more file names than usual are visible at one time. To use this option, enter the command line like this:

DIR /W

Try this now. You can remember the /W option as the Wide-listing option.

Looking for Specific Files Using DIR

Until now, you have been using the DIR command to list the entire contents of the directory. However, you can use the DIR command to find a specific file by specifying its name after the command. This

ADRIL 24th

method quickly determines whether a file is in the directory. For example, try this command:

DIR DISKCOPY.COM

DOS will display

```
Volume in drive C is CDISK
Volume Serial Number is 1624-8258
Directory of C:
```

```
DISKCOPY COM    11879    03-10-93    6:00a
       1 file(s)     11879 bytes
                     7118848 bytes free
```

As you can see, DOS displays information only about the file you request, and not the entire directory.

If you specify a file that is not in the directory, you will see this message:

```
File not found
```

For example, see what happens when you enter

DIR GARBAGE

Wildcard File Names

You can use the wildcard characters to allow DIR to list groups of related files. The wildcard characters work the same for the DIR command as they do in the File Manager.

Assume that you want to list the names of all the files on a disk that share the .COM extension. To do this, enter the following, exactly as shown:

DIR *.COM

This causes DOS to display all files with a .COM extension.

REMEMBER

When used in a file name that is part of a DOS command, the asterisk (*) is a special character that tells DOS to match any sequence of characters. Note that the filename and extension are separate, so the * applies only to the part of the name in which it is used. The second wildcard character is the question mark (?), which will match any one character in its position. That is, unlike the *, it matches only one character—not a sequence of characters.

As you will see later, the wildcard characters are very useful in commands other than the DIR command because they allow you to easily handle groups of related files.

Listing Other Directories Using DIR

You can have DIR list the contents of disks or directories other than the current one by using a drive specifier, pathname, or both. The drive specifier and/or pathname follows DIR on the command line. For example, to list the contents of the current directory on drive B, use this command line:

DIR B:

To see the contents of a directory called ACCTING on drive C, use this command:

DIR C:\ACCTING

For a final example, this command searches the current directory of the disk in drive A for the file SORT.EXE.

DIR A:SORT.EXE

Another Way to Stop the Directory Display

The /P option to the DIR command provides a convenient way to stop the display when listing a directory, but there is another way that you probably will use more frequently. If you press CTRL-S, the display will stop until you press another key (or CTRL-S again). The CTRL-S key sequence acts as a toggle that you can remember as stop/start. To try the CTRL-S command, list the directory and then stop the listing at various points.

DOS also lets you stop the display by pressing CTRL-NUM LOCK on PC-type keyboards or PAUSE on AT, PS/2, or PS/1 keyboards. If you stop the display by using CTRL-NUM LOCK or PAUSE, you must restart it by pressing a different key—these commands are not toggles like CTRL-S. (Note: Some PC-compatible computers may behave slightly differently when these keys are pressed.)

Not all application programs that run under DOS recognize the CTRL-S or CTRL-NUM LOCK keys. Therefore, it may not always be possible to stop the display of some programs.

A Command Line Error Message

Many error messages appear differently at the command prompt than they do in the Shell. To see an example, let's generate the same type of error as in Chapter 3.

Open the door on drive A and enter this command:

DIR A:

Since the drive door is not latched, DOS cannot access the disk directory. In a few seconds you will see the following message:

```
Not ready reading drive A
Abort, Retry, Fail?
```

Let's examine what this message means.

First, DOS is telling you that it cannot access (read) the diskette in drive A. This is, of course, because the drive door is open. However, DOS does not know the exact cause of the problem; it knows only that the drive is not ready to be used. Several conditions could cause this error in addition to the drive door being open. For example, a faulty or unformatted diskette could cause this error message to be displayed.

DOS gives you three ways to respond to this error. You may abort the command, retry the command, or ignore the error. Let's look at these now.

To abort the DIR command, type **A**. This causes DOS to stop trying to read the diskette. You should use the Abort command when there is no way to remedy the condition causing the error.

The Retry command lets you correct the condition causing the error. To retry the command, insert a formatted diskette, close the drive door, and then press **R**. The disk directory will be displayed. Use Retry when you can eliminate the error.

The Fail command loosely tells DOS to ignore the error. It has limited applications. It tells DOS to ignore the immediate error and continue on with the command. Generally, once one error has occurred, more will follow. The Fail command is most often used only by programmers because considerable knowledge about how the computer and DOS function are needed to use it successfully.

If you have not done so, insert a formatted diskette, close the drive door, and press **R** for Retry.

Command Prompt Error Messages: An Overview

In the previous section, you saw an example of a DOS error and its associated message. In reality several occurrences other than a drive door being open can cause DOS to issue an error message. As you continue to use DOS, you will likely see one or more of these error messages. It is important to respond correctly when presented with an error, so let's take a look at some of the most common errors at this time. (Your DOS user manual contains a complete description of all DOS error messages.) Many errors are followed by one of these prompts:

```
Abort, Retry, Fail?
Abort, Ignore, Retry, Fail?
```

The options in the first prompt have been discussed in the preceding section. Some errors, like the one that we just generated, do not offer the Ignore option because it is not applicable. However, for those errors that do, choosing the Ignore option causes DOS to ignore the error and continue. However, this is not generally a wise choice because it could lead to loss of data. (Like Fail, Ignore is most applicable for programmers.) How you respond is in many ways determined by exactly what error has occurred.

Bad Command or File Name

The "Bad command or file name" error message is easily the most common error message you will see. It tells you that DOS does not understand the command that you just entered at the prompt. This message requests no response—you simply reenter the command properly. Generally, this message results from misspelling a command. For example, if you type the command "DUR" instead of "DIR", you will see this message.

General Failure

The "General failure" error message appears when you attempt to access a diskette that has not been formatted, is damaged, or is not intended for use by DOS or in a DOS-compatible computer. To remedy the problem, either abort the operation or insert a correct diskette and try again.

Insufficient Disk Space

As you know, a disk has only a finite amount of space on it. When you run out of space, you will see the "Insufficient disk space" message. To correct this error, either use a new disk or remove files from the existing disk.

Invalid Drive Specification

The "Invalid drive specification" message appears when you try to specify a drive that does not exist. For example, if you type "Z:" in an attempt to reach the (nonexistent) drive Z, you will see this message. Simply retry your command with the proper drive letter.

Non-DOS Disk

The "Non-DOS disk" message appears when you try to use a damaged diskette. Usually, it means that the diskette directory is completely or partially destroyed or is intended for use by another operating system, such as UNIX. Either abort your command or retry it with a different diskette.

Nonsystem Disk or Disk Error

The message "Nonsystem disk or disk error" appears when you try to load DOS from a diskette that does not contain DOS. To correct this error, insert the DOS diskette and strike any key.

Sector Not Found

The "Sector not found" error message is displayed when a sector that is part of a file cannot be found. Because the locations of the sectors are stored in the file allocation table, DOS won't know where to find one or more sectors if this table becomes damaged. Generally, all you can do is try a different diskette. If this error occurs on a fixed disk, then you will have to use a new copy of the file.

Seek Error

The "Seek error" message indicates that the disk drive was unable to find a track. This problem can be caused by three errors. First, the disk drive may be out of alignment—this problem requires repairs by a professional technician. Second, the diskette may be improperly inserted in the drive. If so, try inserting it again. Finally, the disk may be physically damaged. In this case, replace the disk.

Clearing the Screen

It's time to take a little break and look at one of DOS's simplest commands: *CLS*. CLS clears the monitor's screen. Try this now. As you can see, the screen is cleared and the DOS prompt is redisplayed in the upper-left corner of the screen. The CLS command is not meaningful when the Shell is in use.

CLS   The command that clears the screen.

The CLS command is useful for three reasons. First, you may have sensitive information on the screen that you do not want everyone to see. When you are done with the information, executing the CLS command is an easy way to wipe it off the screen. Second, occasionally an application program will leave the screen looking "messy." Clearing the screen is a good way to remedy this situation. Finally, if you are not going to be using the computer for a while, it is advisable to clear the screen in order to save the phosphors in the picture tube from undue wear. (The phosphors in a picture tube slowly burn out as they are used.)

An Introduction to the COPY Command

The command prompt version of *COPY* operates in essentially the same way as it does in the Shell. The only difference is that the command prompt version is more powerful.

COPY   The command that copies a file.

The basic form of the COPY command is

COPY *source-filename destination-filename*

You can remember this format as

COPY *from to*

The COPY command copies the contents of the first (source) file to the second (destination) file. For example, this command copies the file CHKDSK.EXE into one called TEMP.EXE:

COPY CHKDSK.EXE TEMP.EXE

Try this now. As the COPY command begins execution, the disk drive will start, and the drive-active light will be on. After the DOS prompt returns, list the directory and you will see the file TEMP.EXE. (Using the Shell, erase the file TEMP.EXE before continuing.)

Using Wildcards With COPY

For this section you will need a blank, formatted diskette. If you have a fixed disk, then put this disk in drive A. If you have only floppy drives, put the disk into drive B.

It is common to want to copy several files from one disk to another. Although you can copy each file separately, often you can use the wildcard characters to simplify the process and copy several files at once. To see how this works, let's first begin with an example. Try the following command, adjusting the drive specifiers to suit your system. (As the command is shown, it will work for fixed-disk systems.) Make sure that you have a formatted work disk in drive A.

COPY *.EXE A:

This command tells DOS to copy to the A drive all files with the .EXE extension. During the copy process, DOS prints on the screen the name of each file copied. A directory listing of the target diskette will show that all the .EXE files have been copied.

One of the first things you should notice about the command just given is that the destination file name is missing—only the drive specifier is present. When you do not specify a destination file name, DOS assumes that you want the destination file to have the same name as the source file. This same principle applies to wildcard copies. Each file copied to the destination disk has the same name as it did on the source disk. It would be perfectly valid to use the command "COPY *.EXE A:*.EXE", but it is redundant.

In general, you can use the ? and * wildcard characters with the COPY command in the same way you use them with the DIR command. If you are unsure exactly which files will be copied using a wildcard file name, first execute the DIR command using the same wildcard characters to see what DOS reports.

NOTE

The File Manager Copy option does not allow you to use the wildcard characters. This is an example of a situation in which the command prompt version is more powerful than the Shell equivalent.

If you wish to copy all the files listed in the directory of one disk to another, use the wildcard characters *.*. For example, to copy the contents of the diskette in drive A to the diskette in drive B, type the following command:

COPY A:*.* B:

Although this may seem obvious, it must be stated: You cannot copy a file onto itself. That is, a command such as this is invalid:

COPY SORT.EXE SORT.EXE

Also, if you try to copy a file that does not exist, DOS will display this message:

```
File not found
```

At this point, you should be able to copy files between disks without any trouble. If you do not feel confident, try some examples before continuing. The COPY command, as you will learn later, has several more features and options that make it one of the most powerful DOS commands.

The TYPE Command

In the Shell, you used the View option in the File menu of the File Manager to see the contents of a file. The command prompt's similar command is *TYPE*, which displays the contents of a text file on the screen.

> **TYPE**   *The command that displays a file on the screen.*

In order to follow along with the examples in this section, return to the Shell. Next, use the DOS editor to create a short text file called MYTEXT.TXT, containing these lines (or any other of your own choosing):

When, by chance, perfection is attained,
we try in vain to recreate the same.

Once you have saved the file, return to the command prompt interface.

Next, try this command:

TYPE MYTEXT.TXT

This command displays the contents of the MYTEXT.TXT file.

In general, you can use the TYPE command to list on the screen the contents of any text file. (Actually, TYPE can list any sort of file, but only text files will display meaningful information.) The sample file that you used is very short; longer text files will quickly scroll off the screen unless you stop them. You can freeze the display by using the same control keys that you used to stop the DIR command: (CTRL)-(S), or (CTRL)-(NUM LOCK), or (PAUSE).

An important point to remember is that DOS has no way of knowing which files are text files. That is, as far as DOS is concerned, a file is a file, and text, data, and program files all look pretty much alike to it. It is your responsibility to remember which files are which.

Although you won't be using TYPE again soon, you will find that in actual practice it is one of the most useful DOS commands because it lets you easily peek into a file to see what's in it.

Some More DIR Options

Before concluding this chapter, let's take a final look at the DIR command. As you know, the Shell makes it possible to display the directory sorted in a number of different ways. It is also possible to display selected groups of files based upon their specific attributes. As you will see, you also can perform these and other types of operations using the command prompt.

Sorting the Directory Using DIR

By default, when you issue the DIR command, the directory is displayed in the order in which the files occur on the disk. However, using the /O option, you can have DIR sort the directory in a number of different ways. The /O option takes this general form:

/O:*order*

where the value of *order* determines how the /O command sorts the directory. The values of *order* are shown here.

Order	Sort By
C	compression ratio
–C	reverse order by compression ratio
D	date and time
–D	reverse order by date and time
E	extension
–E	reverse order by extension
G	display directories before files
–G	display directories after files
N	name
–N	reverse order by name
S	size
–S	reverse order by size

For example, this command displays the directory sorted by name in reverse order:

DIR /O:–N

This example first displays all files and then any subdirectories.

DIR /O:–G

You should try various combinations of the /O option at this time. Keep in mind that all /O options are mutually exclusive (that is, you can use only one /O option at a time). Also, sorting by compression ratio applies only to compressed drives, which are discussed later in this book.

If you want to see only files that have certain attributes, use the /A option. It takes this general form:

/A:*attr*

Here, *attr* must be any combination of the following:

attr	Files Listed
A	files with archive attribute on
–A	files with archive attribute off
D	directories only
–D	files only
H	hidden
–H	non-hidden
R	read-only files only
–R	non-read-only files
S	system
–S	nonsystem

This command displays all system files:

(handwritten: To view from dir.)   *(handwritten: ; more)*

DIR /A:S

This command displays all read-only files that are also hidden:

DIR /A:RH

Listing All Files on a Disk

As you know, the Shell allows you to view a system file list. This is a listing of all files without regard to the directory structure of the disk. You can perform a similar function using DIR by specifying the /S option. This causes the current directory and all subdirectories to be searched for the specified file or files. (Wildcards may be used.) When matches are found, the file(s) and the directory (or directories) containing the file(s) are displayed. Using the /S option is an excellent way to find a lost file when you can't remember what directory you put it in. The /S option also displays the total number of matching files.

This DIR command searches the current directory and all of its subdirectories and displays all the files (and the directories that contain them) that start with X:

DIR X*.* /S

This command performs the same function but also sorts all matching files by name (per directory):

DIR X*.* /S /O:N

Miscellaneous DIR Options

DIR allows three further options. First, you can cause only the filenames and extensions to be displayed without any further information by specifying the /B option. When you use this option, file names are displayed with a period separating the filename and the extension. You might find this option useful as you become more experienced with using DOS.

The /C option displays a file's compression ratio. This option applies only to compressed drives.

Finally, you can display DIR's output in lowercase using /L.

The DOS Editing Keys

Up to this point, when you made a mistake while typing a command you used the (BACKSPACE) key to back up to the error and then retyped the rest of the line. Also, if you wished to re-execute a command, you retyped it. In this section you will learn how to use some special keys that will make the entry of DOS commands a little easier. These special keys are called editing keys because they allow you to edit (make changes to) what you type on the command line. This is especially important because your command lines will start to become longer.

Fundamental to using the editing keys is the concept of the *input buffer*. The input buffer is a small region of memory that is used by DOS to hold the commands that you enter from the keyboard. The

Input buffer   A small region of memory that holds what you enter on the command line using the keyboard.

important thing to understand is that the input buffer will contain the last command that you typed until you enter a new one. This lets you reuse, alter, or fix the immediately preceding command through the use of the DOS editing keys.

The DOS editing keys and a synopsis of their functions are shown in Table 8-1. Let's look at each in turn.

> **NOTE**
> For the remainder of this section, disregard the "Bad command or file name" error message. Some of the examples will send DOS unknown commands. This will hurt nothing, but it will cause an error message to be displayed.

The (F1) Key

At the DOS prompt, enter the following sequence of characters: **123456789**. Be sure to press (ENTER). Doing this loads the DOS input buffer with "123456789". Once the DOS prompt returns, press the (F1) key three times. Your command line will look like this:

```
C>123
```

As is obvious from the example, the (F1) key redisplays one character at a time from the input buffer. Continue to press the (F1) key until the "9" appears. At this point, pressing (F1) again has no effect because you have reached the end of the buffer. (DOS does not store the (ENTER) key in the buffer.) Press (ENTER) now.

The (F2) Key

The (F2) key redisplays all characters in the input buffer up to the character that you specify. To use the (F2) command, you first press (F2) and then the character. For example, if you press (F2) followed by a **6**, the command line will look like this:

```
C>12345
```

Key	Function
(F1)	Redisplays one character from the input buffer each time it is pressed.
(F2)	Redisplays all characters up to, but not including, a specified character in the input buffer.
(F3)	Redisplays all characters in the input buffer.
(F4)	Deletes all characters up to, but not including, a specified character from the input buffer.
(F5)	Re-edits the line you just typed.
(DEL)	Deletes a character from the input buffer.
(ESC)	Cancels the current line just typed prior to pressing (ENTER).
(INS)	Inserts the next character typed at the current location in the input buffer.

TABLE 8-1 **The DOS editing keys**

Try this now. DOS has redisplayed all characters up to the "6". At this time press ⒡⒈ until the "9" is redisplayed and then press ⒠⒩⒯⒠⒭.

The ⒡⒊ Key

Probably the most useful editing key is ⒡⒊ because it redisplays the entire input buffer. This is especially helpful because it lets you re-execute the previous command without retyping it. Press ⒡⒊ at this time. The command line will look like this:

```
C>123456789
```

Do not press ⒠⒩⒯⒠⒭.

The ⒠⒮⒞ Key

At this point, the cursor should be immediately following the "9" on the command line. Press ⒠⒮⒞ now. As you can see, DOS prints a "\" (backslash) and positions the cursor directly under the "1". The command line will look like this:

```
C>123456789\
```

The ⒠⒮⒞ key cancels whatever is on the command line. DOS uses the "\" to indicate this cancellation. The DOS prompt is not redisplayed, but the cursor is placed directly under the location it occupied when the prompt was present.

After canceling a command with ⒠⒮⒞, you may still use all the editing keys to redisplay or change the previous command. For example, press ⒡⒊ followed by ⒠⒩⒯⒠⒭ at this time.

The ⒟⒠⒧ Key

If you wish to delete a character from the input buffer, use the ⒟⒠⒧ key. Each time you press it, a character will be deleted. You will not see the characters you delete, so use this key with caution. By way of example, press ⒟⒠⒧ three times and then press the ⒡⒊ key. The command line will look like this:

```
C>456789
```

If you press ⒠⒮⒞ prior to pressing ⒠⒩⒯⒠⒭, you can cancel the effects of the ⒟⒠⒧ key. Press ⒠⒮⒞ followed by ⒡⒊ and ⒠⒩⒯⒠⒭ now.

Using ⒡⒋ to Delete Several Characters

If you wish to delete several characters, the ⒡⒋ key can be used. It is somewhat similar to the ⒡⒉ key in that you first press ⒡⒋ and then a character. DOS will then delete all characters from the current position up to but not including the character you typed. For example, press ⒡⒋, then **4**, and then ⒡⒊. The command line will look like this:

```
C>456789
```

Keep in mind that nothing is displayed when you use the ⒡⒋ command, so it is a little easy to forget what you have deleted; use ⒡⒋ with caution.

The (INS) *Key*

At the DOS prompt enter this line: **This a test**. Assume, for the sake of example, that you wished to enter "This is a test". You can correct the command by first using (F1) to position the cursor after the space that follows "This", pressing (INS), typing **is** followed by a space, and then pressing (F3). When you press the (INS) key, DOS lets you insert any number of characters at that point without overwriting what is already in the buffer. You should try some examples of this process.

The (F5) *Key*

All the other editing keys let you manipulate the command that is already in the input buffer. Let's suppose, however, that you begin typing a new command and make a mistake. By pressing the (F5) key, you will cause DOS to load the input buffer with what you just typed—giving you a chance to correct it—without executing it.

Summary

In this chapter you learned the following:

- How to activate the command prompt
- How to use the DIR command
- About the VER command
- How to change the current drive
- How to freeze the display
- About some error messages
- How to clear the screen
- How to use the COPY command
- How to view a file using the TYPE command
- How to use the command prompt editing keys

The next chapter will continue exploration of DOS's command prompt.

Key Terms

Command prompt   The traditional interface to DOS. To use the command prompt to communicate with DOS, you issue commands. Unlike the Shell, the command prompt does not use menus.

CLS   The command that clears the screen.

COPY   The command that copies a file.

DIR   The command that lists the directory.

EXIT   The command that leaves the command prompt and returns to the Shell.

Input buffer   A small region of memory that holds what you enter on the command line using the keyboard.

TYPE   The command that displays a file on the screen.

Exercises

True or False

1. When using the command prompt, you may use the mouse. _____

2. From the command prompt, you may return to the Shell by entering the EXIT command. _____

3. When using the DIR command, you may pause the display by using the /P option. _____

4. To see a listing of all files in the current directory that begin with P and have the extension .EXE, you would use this command: DIR P*.EXE. _____

5. When you see an error message that prints the prompt "Abort, Retry, Fail?" it doesn't really matter which option you choose. _____

6. The message "Bad command or file name" means that you gave DOS a command that it does not understand (possibly because you simply misspelled it). _____

7. The general form of the COPY command is "COPY *source target*". _____

8. In general, the TYPE command performs the same function as the Shell's View File option. _____

9. Using DIR, it is possible to display only those files that have been recently erased. _____

10. Pressing the ⒡⒋ key causes all characters on the command line to be converted to uppercase. _____

Short Answer

1. What effect does pressing the ⒡⒊ key have when at the command prompt?

2. What command copies the file MYFILE from the current directory of drive C to the current directory of drive A?

3. What command displays the directory sorted by date and time?

4. What command displays the directory sorted in reverse order?

5. What command displays the DOS version number?

6. What command clears the screen? Why might you want to clear the screen?

7. What command displays only system files?

8. Assuming that the root is the current directory, what command lists all files on a disk?

9. What does the TYPE command do?

10. What does the (F1) key do when using the command prompt?

11. What extra piece of information is displayed using the DIR command that is not displayed in the Shell's File List window?

For the following exercises, put your Student Data Disk in drive A and log into A.

12. Try this command: **DIR *.DOC**. How many files are displayed?

13. There are four files that have the extension .DOC. Which of these are text files? (Hint: Use the TYPE command to find out.)

14. Copy MYFILE to TEMP. Next, list the directory. Is TEMP the same size as MYFILE? Does it contain the same information?

Activities

1. Generate a DOS error message by opening the door to drive A and then attempting to list its directory. Experiment with different responses to the "Abort, Retry, Fail?" message.

2. Try listing the directory using various DIR options.

The DOS Command Prompt: A Closer Look

CHAPTER OBJECTIVES

After completing this chapter, you should be able to:

- Print a text file on the printer using PRINT.
- Use various PRINT options.
- Use the ERASE command.
- Change the name of a file using RENAME.
- Cancel a command.
- Verify COPY operations.
- Manage directories using the command prompt interface.
- View the directory structure using TREE.
- Use the DOS help system

In the preceding chapter, the DOS command prompt was introduced. In this chapter, you will continue to explore it as well as some commands that are specific to the command prompt.

Unless noted otherwise, this chapter assumes that if you are running DOS from a fixed disk, you are logged into the C drive and you have selected the DOS directory. If you are running DOS from floppies, make sure that the DOS disk is in drive A.

Printing a Text File on a Printer

> **NOTE**
> This section assumes that you have a printer attached to your system and that it is attached in the standard fashion. If this is not the case, you should still read this section but do not try the examples. If you have a specialized printer, contact your instructor or other knowledgeable person to find out how to print files.

When you wish to make a printed copy of a text file, you can do so by using the *PRINT* command. PRINT is an external command. The simplest form of PRINT is:

PRINT *file name*

PRINT   The command that prints a text file on the printer.

where *file name* is the name of the text file to be printed.

Let's begin with an example. First, create a short text file called TEST.TXT. It can contain anything you like. (If you want, you can reuse the file you created in Chapter 8.) Once you have created TEST.TXT, enter this command:

PRINT TEST.TXT

When the PRINT command begins, you will probably see this message:

```
Name of list device [PRN]:
```

The PRINT command is an installed command. This means that the first time it is executed, it loads itself into memory and then stays resident. However, when it is first executed, you must specify what device the printer is connected to. (This is what "list device" refers to.) If your printer is attached in the standard way, then just press ENTER at this prompt. (If your printer is nonstandard, ask your instructor how to respond to this prompt.) If you do not see this prompt, it simply means that the PRINT command has already been installed.

Once PRINT is installed, you will see a message similar to this and the printer will begin printing.

```
C:\TEST.TXT is currently being printed
```

(If you are using a floppy disk, the drive and path part of the message will be A:\.)

The command prompt will be redisplayed immediately, even though the printing is not yet complete. The PRINT command is one of the few DOS commands that operates in the background, allowing you to continue using the computer to do other things. A background task is a simple form of multi-tasking in which the computer performs two (or more) operations at essentially the same time.

You can use a drive specifier in the file name to print a file that is not on the current disk. For example, with a file called TEST.TST on drive B, you would use a command like this to print:

PRINT B:TEST.TST

Canceling a Printout

Suppose that you are in the middle of printing a long file and you decide that you don't need the printout. To cancel the PRINT command, enter the following:

PRINT /T

The /T is a PRINT command option; it stands for terminate.

Printing Multiple Files

You can give PRINT a list of files to print. You can do this in two ways. You can execute the PRINT command repeatedly, specifying one file at a time, or you can specify a list of files all at once. To see how this works, copy the file TEST.TXT into the files TEST1, TEST2, and TEST3. (For these files, don't use any extensions.) Now execute this PRINT command:

PRINT TEST1 TEST2 TEST3

PRINT will respond as follows:

```
C:\TEST1 is currently being printed
C:\TEST2 is in queue
C:\TEST3 is in queue
```

PRINT creates a *print queue* of the files you want printed and then prints them one at a time in the order they are specified. Using the DOS default setting, you can queue up to ten files. Later, you will learn how to set the queue size to fit your needs.

Print queue   A list of files to be printed.

If you decide that you need to print a file called TEST4 while the other files are still being printed, you can add it to the print queue by entering:

PRINT TEST4

This will add TEST4 to the list of files to be printed.

Removing Files From the Print Queue

Suppose that you have just specified a list of files to be printed and you decide that one of the files doesn't need to be printed after all. You can remove a specific file from the queue by using the /C PRINT option. To remove a file from the queue, use the general form

PRINT *file-name* /C

For example, to remove TEST2 from the print queue, enter

PRINT TEST2 /C

NOTE

If you wish to cancel the printing of all files, the easiest way is to use the /T option. This terminates the PRINT command and removes all files from the queue. Only use the /C option when you want to terminate one or more specific files.

Setting the Queue Size

By default, the PRINT command can queue up to ten files. However, using the /Q option, you can set the size of the queue anywhere in the range of 4 to 32. The /Q option must be specified the first time PRINT is executed. If you try to use it after that, an error message will be displayed and the option will be ignored. The general form of the /Q option is shown here:

PRINT /Q:*size*

where *size* is between 4 and 32. For example, this sets the queue size to 20:

PRINT /Q:20

You should experiment with the PRINT command at this time.

Using the Shell's Print Option

This section digresses from the command prompt interface in order to discuss how to print a file from the Shell. While printing a file from the Shell is similar to printing a file from the command prompt, you need to know a few things.

For this section, reboot your computer by pressing (CTRL)-(ALT)-(DEL). (The reason for rebooting is to return your system to its start-up state.)

When the Shell returns to the screen, first select the file TEST.TXT and then activate the File menu. It is likely that the Print option is not available because the PRINT command has not yet been installed. (Be sure that you have, indeed, highlighted the TEST.TXT file.) Therefore, before you can print a file using the Shell, you must execute the PRINT command. The easiest way to do this from within the Shell is to use the Run option in the File menu, using the same form you would use if running PRINT from the command prompt interface. After you have installed PRINT, the Print option will then be available within the Shell.

Once the Print option is available to print a file using the Shell, simply select the file or files that you want to print and activate the Print option. However, if you want to terminate the printing of a file or files, you must execute PRINT using the Run option, specifying the appropriate option.

> **NOTE**
> If the Shell's Print option is not available, then you must install the PRINT command in order to activate it.

Removing Files From a Disk

The command to remove a file from a disk is called *ERASE*. DOS allows a second name for ERASE called DEL, but this book will continue to use ERASE. (You can use whichever form you like.) The general form of the ERASE command is

ERASE *file name*

where *file name* is the name of the file to be erased. The ERASE command is similar to the Delete option found in the File menu.

> **ERASE** *The command that removes a file from the disk.*

For a simple first example, execute this command:

ERASE TEST1

(TEST1 is the name of the file created in the previous section.) You can verify that TEST1 is no longer present by listing the directory.

You can erase groups of files by using the wildcard characters. For example, this command erases all files that share the .BAK extension:

ERASE *.BAK

You can erase all files in the current directory with this command. (Don't try this!)

ERASE *.*

DOS will prompt you with the message:

```
All files in directory will be deleted!
Are you sure (Y/N)?
```

If you do want to erase all the files in the current directory, enter **Y**; otherwise, enter **N**.

When using wildcard characters with the ERASE command, it is wise to first execute a DIR command with the same wildcards just to make sure you know exactly what you are erasing—*before* you erase it!

If you want, you can have ERASE ask you before erasing a file. To cause this, specify the /P option. This option might be valuable when using wildcards to erase files.

Changing File Names

You can change the name of a file by using the *RENAME* command. DOS allows a short form of this command called REN; however, this book will use RENAME to avoid confusion. The general form of the command is:

RENAME *old-name new-name*

You can use RENAME to alter any part of a file's name, including the extension. The RENAME command is equivalent to the Rename option in the File menu of the Shell.

For example try this command, which assumes that you have the file TEST2 (created earlier) on the current disk:

RENAME TEST2 RALPH

Once the DOS prompt returns, execute the DIR command. You will see that the file TEST2 is no longer in the directory, but the one called RALPH is. By typing **RALPH**, you can be assured that the contents of the file are the same; only the name has changed.

Since RALPH is a pretty silly name for a file, use RENAME to change it to SAMPLE.TXT by entering this command:

RENAME RALPH SAMPLE.TXT

RENAME The command that changes the name of a file.

You can use drive specifiers with the RENAME command. For example, if you have a file called TEST on drive B, then the following command changes its name to OLDTEST:

RENAME B:TEST B:OLDTEST

If you try to rename a file to a file name that already exists, or if you try to rename a file that does not exist, DOS will respond with an error message.

Canceling a Command

Sometimes you will enter a command, change your mind, and want to cancel the command. Many, but not all, DOS commands can be canceled by pressing CTRL-C or CTRL-BREAK. For many purposes, CTRL-C and CTRL-BREAK are equivalent, but in some situations CTRL-BREAK is more effective. For this reason, you should generally use CTRL-BREAK. To try canceling a command, execute DIR and then press CTRL-BREAK before the directory listing has finished. As soon as you press CTRL-BREAK, the screen displays "^C" (short for cancel), and the DOS prompt returns. Try this now.

As stated, not all DOS commands can be canceled in this way. For example, because the PRINT command runs as a background task, you must use the /T option to stop it. Also, most commands cannot be canceled in the middle of their execution. That is, most DOS commands have a point of no return. After this point, you cannot stop the command from proceeding. For example, once the RENAME command has begun to actually change a file's name, you cannot cancel it until it is done. In more technical language, most DOS commands have a critical section that, once entered, cannot be aborted because doing so would corrupt the structure of the disk. You don't need to worry about destroying anything by trying to cancel a command because DOS will not let you cancel at an inappropriate time.

A COPY Option

You can have the COPY command automatically verify that the file it has just copied is exactly the same as the original. Although it is quite rare, occasionally a file copy will not be successful. This can happen for several reasons. By far the two most common reasons are a transient power loss or fluctuation that causes the disk drive to temporarily write incorrect data or bad magnetic media on the target disk. To guard against this sort of trouble, you can tell COPY to check the destination file against the target file as the copy process proceeds. This will make the COPY operation take longer, but this extra time can be worthwhile for very important files.

To tell COPY to verify the destination file, specify the /V option. You enter this option after the rest of the command. For example, to copy with verification the file SORT.EXE from drive C to drive A, enter this command:

COPY SORT.EXE A: /V

NOTE
The verify option is not available for the Shell Copy option in the File menu. It only works at the command prompt or by using the Shell Run option.

Working With Directories

Although the structure of the disk is unchanged, the way you work with directories in the Shell and the way you work with them at the command prompt will seem rather different. In this section you will see how to create, use, and delete directories from the command prompt.

For this section, you will need a blank, formatted diskette. Put this diskette into drive A and log into drive A at this time.

Creating a Directory

To create a subdirectory from the command prompt, use the *MKDIR* (or MD, for short) command. The general form of this command is:

MKDIR *directory-name*

MKDIR (or MD)   The command that creates a directory.

In this section, you will create a directory structure equivalent to that shown in Figure 9-1.

A directory name must conform to the same conventions and restrictions as a file name. The name may not exceed eight characters, and the extension cannot be longer than three characters. Most directories are not given extensions, and this convention is used in this book.

To begin building the example directory structure, enter the following command:

MKDIR SPRDSHT

Here, SPRDSHT is short for "spreadsheet," which is too long to be a directory name. Once the prompt returns, enter **DIR**. The only entry will look similar to this:

```
SPRDSHT    <DIR>      01-29-94      9:25a
```

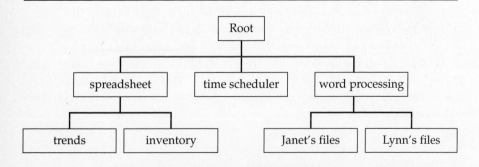

FIGURE 9-1   **The example directory structure**

(Of course, your date and time will be different.) The "<DIR>" signifies that SPRDSHT is a directory rather than a file. Keep in mind that you are still in the root directory.

Before moving on, create the other two directories that branch from the root. Enter these two commands:

MKDIR SCHEDULE
MKDIR WP

Here, SCHEDULE is short for "time scheduler" and WP is short for "word processing." You can list the directory again to see the effect of these commands.

Changing Directories

Now that you have created three subdirectories, it is time to see how to activate one. The *CHDIR* (or CD) command is used to change the current directory. The general form of CHDIR is:

CHDIR *new-directory*

where *new-directory* is a valid path name to the new directory.

For example, to make the WP directory current, enter

CD WP

Try this now. (When a short form of a command exists, this book generally uses the long form to avoid confusion. However, since CD is almost universally used instead of CHDIR, it will be used in this book.)

Once the prompt returns, list the directory. You will see something similar to the following:

```
Volume in drive A is MYDISK
Volume Serial Number is 4124-14CD
Directory of  A:\WP


.          <DIR>       01-29-94      1:10p
..         <DIR>       01-29-94      1:10p
      2 File(s)    1456128 bytes free
```

Take a close look at this display. One of the first features you should notice is that the directory name is shown in the line that reads "Directory of A:\WP." When you list the root directory, only the backslash is displayed. In DOS the backslash is used to represent the root directory, which has no name. The combination \WP specifies the path to the WP directory. That is, begin at the root and then go to WP.

The two entries in the directory are in DOS shorthand. The single period is shorthand for the current directory, and the two periods represent the parent directory—which, in this case, is the root directory. For example, if you enter:

DIR ..

the root directory will be displayed. Typing:

DIR .

CHDIR (or CD) The command that changes the current directory.

lists the current subdirectory. Remember that to list the current directory (subdirectory or root), you need only enter **DIR**. The period is redundant.

Creating Subdirectories Within a Subdirectory

You create a subdirectory inside of a subdirectory in exactly the same way that you created a subdirectory from the root. Let's create the two subdirectories to WP at this time. Make sure that you are in the WP directory and then enter the following commands.

MKDIR JANET
MKDIR LYNN

A directory listing will now look like this:

```
Volume in drive A is MYDISK
Volume Serial Number is 4124-14CD
Directory of  A:\WP

.            <DIR>      01-29-94      1:10p
..           <DIR>      01-29-94      1:10p
JANET        <DIR>      01-29-94      1:12p
LYNN         <DIR>      01-29-94      1:12p
      4 File(s)    1455104 bytes free
```

(Again, your date and time will differ.)
    Switch to the JANET directory by entering:

CD JANET

and then list the directory. The path line will now look like this:

```
Directory of A:\WP\JANET
```

As you might guess, \WP\JANET specifies the path to the JANET directory. It is interpreted like this: Start at the root and go to the WP directory; from the WP directory, go to the JANET directory.

Returning to the Parent Directory

You can move from a subdirectory to its parent in two ways. The first, and by far the most common, is to issue this command:

CD ..

Since the two periods are shorthand for the parent's directory name, this works no matter what the parent directory is called.
    The second way to return to the parent directory is to explicitly specify its full path name. For example, to go from the JANET directory to the WP directory, you can enter:

CD \WP

The backslash is necessary for reasons that will soon become clear.

Returning to the Root Directory

No matter how deep you are in subdirectories, you can always return to the root directory by entering this command:

**CD **

Because the backslash is DOS's name for the root directory, this causes DOS to make the root directory active.

Of course, you can always return to the root directory by entering repeated CD.. commands until you reach the root.

Creating More Directories

If you haven't yet done so, return to the root directory and then switch to the SPRDSHT directory at this time. To continue setting up the directories on the disk, enter these commands:

MKDIR TRENDS
MKDIR INVNTRY

Moving Between Directories

You can move between directories in several ways. One way that will always work, no matter what directory is currently active, is to enter the CD command followed by the complete path name of the directory to which you wish to go. For example, return to the root directory by entering **CD **, then move to the WP directory by entering **CD WP**. Now, to move from the WP directory to the TRENDS subdirectory of SPRDSHT, you can use this command:

CD \\SPRDSHT\\TRENDS

Return to the WP directory now, using this command:

CD \\WP

If you type an invalid path or misspell a directory name, DOS will respond with the message "Invalid directory". In this case, enter the command again, correcting the error.

To move from the WP directory to its LYNN subdirectory, you *cannot* use this command:

CD \\LYNN (this is incorrect)

(If you try this command, DOS will respond with the message "Invalid directory.") This command will not work because the backslash preceding LYNN tells DOS to start at the root and then move to the LYNN directory. However, LYNN is not a subdirectory of the root—it is a subdirectory of WP. Hence, to move from WP to LYNN, you must use one of these commands:

CD LYNN
CD \\WP\\LYNN

The first command is essentially a shorthand version of the second. Because the WP directory is active and LYNN is a subdirectory of WP, you can simply use CD LYNN because DOS already knows the rest of the path. The second form works, of course, because the entire path is explicitly stated. In general, any time you move from a parent directory to a subdirectory, you need to specify only the subdirectory name. However, the reverse is not true. To move from a subdirectory back to the parent, you must use either the CD.. command or a complete path name.

Displaying the Current Directory Name

In addition to allowing you to change directories, the CD command also displays the current directory and path if it is executed with no arguments. To try this, enter **CD** at this time. If you ever have any doubts about being in the proper directory, using this command is the way to find out.

For example, switch to the LYNN subdirectory of WP and enter **CD**. Your display will look like this:

A:\WP\LYNN

Removing a Directory

To remove a directory, you must use the *RMDIR* (or RD, for short) command. The general form of the RMDIR command is

RMDIR *directory-name*

where *directory-name* specifies a valid path to the directory you wish to remove.

Directories cannot be removed using ERASE. Although you use the Delete option in the File menu to erase both files and directories when using the Shell, these are two distinct operations. (The Shell simply masks this from you.) Therefore, when using the command prompt interface, you must use ERASE when deleting a file, but you must use RMDIR (or RD) when removing a directory.

There are two restrictions to removing directories. First, the directory must be empty; it cannot contain files or other subdirectories. When you list the directory, you should see only this:

```
.          <DIR>
..         <DIR>
```

Second, the directory cannot be the current directory. That is, you cannot remove a directory that you are currently using.

For example, you can remove the SCHEDULE directory by using this command:

RMDIR SCHEDULE

If you try this, be sure to re-create SCHEDULE before continuing.

If you try to remove the current directory or a nonexistent directory, you will see an error message.

RMDIR (or RD)
The command that removes a directory.

The TREE Command

You can display a directory tree, which looks much like that displayed in the Directory Tree window of the File Manager, by using the *TREE* command. The simplest form of the TREE command is

TREE *path*

The *path* is unnecessary if you want the structure of the disk in the current drive beginning at the current directory. TREE is an external command, which means that you must have it on your disk.

To see how TREE works, copy the file TREE.COM into the root directory of your work disk in the A drive and enter **TREE**. (Make sure that drive A is active.) You will see output similar to that shown in Figure 9-2.

TREE Options

The TREE command allows two options. If you want a list of the files in each directory, use the /F option. For example, the following command lists both the directory structure and files in each directory:

TREE /F

On a full disk, the output from this command will be quite lengthy, but it can still be useful when you are trying to find a file on a disk.

By default, the TREE command uses text mode graphics characters. For English-speaking countries, in standard text mode a PC does provide a limited set of simple graphics figures, including vertical and horizontal lines. If you live in an English-speaking country, these characters will be used by TREE. However, some foreign languages use an extended character set, which preempts these block graphics characters. For this reason, TREE allows the /A option, which uses an alternate set of characters that are valid in any language.

You can display a subtree by specifying a starting point and passing TREE a path. For example, to have TREE display the WP subtree, use this command:

TREE \WP

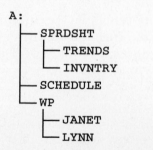

FIGURE 9-2 **The output of the TREE command**

Getting Help

As you have probably guessed, because the Shell is not active when you use the command prompt interface, the Shell's help system is also not available. However, you can still receive help about DOS commands when using the command prompt interface. One way to obtain information about a DOS command is to follow the command with the /? option. This causes Help information to be displayed, but the command itself is not executed. For example, to receive information about the DIR command, enter this at the command prompt:

DIR /?

The /? option works with all DOS commands, but this option will not work with most application programs.

    Another way to obtain information about a command is by using the HELP command. You can execute HELP in one of the following two ways:

HELP
HELP *command*

    Here, *command* is the command that you want help about. If you execute HELP without a command, then a list of commands is displayed from which you may select the one that you want information about.

    The HELP program is a window/menu-based system that is operated in the same way as the Shell. It will work with either the keyboard or the mouse and its use is self-explanatory and largely intuitive.

> **NOTE**
> **Although the information supplied by HELP is useful, it should not and cannot substitute for a good working knowledge of DOS.**

    For a short description of each DOS command, you can use the FASTHELP command. You can use one of these forms:

FASTHELP
FASTHELP *command*

When you use the first, you receive a short synopsis of each command. When you specify a command, you receive information specifically about that command.

/? *An option of all command prompt commands that causes information about that command to be displayed.*

Summary

In this chapter, using the command prompt you learned how to do the following:

- Print a file
- Erase a file
- Rename a file
- Cancel a command
- Verify a COPY

- Create, manage, and delete directories
- Use the TREE command
- Get help about commands

In the next chapter you will learn about more DOS commands that may be used from either the Shell or the command line.

Key Terms

/?   An option of all command prompt commands that causes information about that command to be displayed. (When this option is used, the command itself does not execute.)

CHDIR (or CD)   The command that changes the current directory.

ERASE   The command that removes a file from the disk.

MKDIR (or MD)   The command that creates a directory.

PRINT   The command that prints a text file on the printer.

Print Queue   A list of files to be printed. Files are printed in the order in which they are specified.

RENAME   The command that changes the name of a file.

RMDIR (or RD)   The command that removes a directory.

TREE   The command that displays the directory structure of a disk.

Exercises

Short Answer

1. Assume that you have three text files called LET1, LET2, and LET3. What command would print all three?

2. What PRINT option cancels the printing of all files still in the print queue?

3. What makes PRINT an unusual command relative to DOS?

4. When using the Shell, if the Print option is not available, what must you do?

5. To erase all files that begin with TH and have the extension .DAT, what command must you use?

6. Before erasing files using wildcards, what preliminary step is a good idea and why?

7. What command changes the name of a file and what is its general form?

8. If you wish to verify that a COPY operation was successful, what option must you specify?

9. What command creates a directory called MYDIR?

10. What command deletes a directory called MYDIR?

11. Assume that the current directory is \WP\LARRY. What command switches to the directory \DB\TOD?

12. What does the TREE command do?

13. How can you receive help information about a DOS command when using the command line interface?

14. What command always returns to the root directory?

True or False

1. To view the current directory name, simply enter CD by itself. _____

2. When using TREE, you can have it also display all files in each directory by specifying the /F option. _____

3. It is not possible to use ERASE to erase groups of files using wildcard characters. _____

4. If you try to cancel a command when it is in its critical section, you will destroy your disk. _____

5. You can have ERASE prompt you before erasing a command by specifying the /P option. _____

6. Assuming that the file TEST is in the print queue, this command will remove it: **PRINT TEST /C**. _____

7. The command CD .. always returns to the root directory. _____

8. Using RMDIR, you can remove a directory even if it contains files. _____

9. The TREE command rearranges the directory structure of your disk so that it is in alphabetical order. _____

10. The PRINT command must be installed before you can print files using the Shell. _____

Activities

1. Using the directories disk that you created in Chapter 5, experiment with changing directories, copying files between directories, and removing directories using the command prompt directory commands.

2. When you use the verify option with the COPY command, all COPY operations take longer. To see this for yourself, try copying a long file. First, specify the /V option. Then, copy it again without the

option. You will notice that the second copy took far less time. (Be sure to erase the copy of the file before continuing.)

3. Put your Student Data Disk in drive A. Print the files CONST, MYFILE, and YOURFILE. Experiment with the PRINT command options by canceling the printing of MYFILE before it prints. Also, try adding files to the print queue.

CHAPTER 10

More DOS Commands

CHAPTER OBJECTIVES

After completing this chapter, you should be able to:

- Understand labels and use the LABEL command.
- Use VOL.
- Format diskettes using FORMAT.
- Transfer system files using SYS.
- Use VERIFY to confirm disk operations.
- Understand XCOPY.
- Replace files using REPLACE.
- Print the screen.
- Check the disk using CHKDSK.
- Copy disks using DISKCOPY.
- Compare files using COMP.
- Compare files using FC.
- Compare diskettes using DISKCOMP.
- Set the date and time using DATE and TIME.
- Set file attributes using ATTRIB.

Now that you know your way around the command prompt interface, it is time for you to learn about some more DOS commands that give you greater control over the computer. Some of these commands are fairly complicated, but they yield great returns for the time you invest in learning them.

LABEL and VOL

When you list the directory from the command prompt, the first line looks something like this:

```
Volume in drive C is CDISK
```

Also, if you select the Show Information option from the Options menu in the File Manager, you will see that a name is specified in the disk portion of the window. Until now you have been ignoring the name of the disk. Here you will learn what a disk's name means and how to give a disk a label.

What Is a Volume Label?

A volume label is essentially a name for a disk—either floppy or fixed. It can be up to 11 characters long and may consist of any characters allowed in a file name. In addition, you can use a space in a volume label. However, a period is not allowed.

A disk may have a volume label for two reasons. The first is that it helps you to positively identify the disk. This can be useful when you are trying to remember which disk is which. However, the volume label should never take the place of the external stick-on label. The second reason is that, in the future, new versions of DOS may allow you to access a disk by its volume name instead of by drive letter.

Using LABEL

*LABEL   The command
that sets a disk's volume
label.*

To change the name of a disk, use the external DOS *LABEL* command that has this basic form:

LABEL *name*

where *name* is the name that will be given to the disk.

> **NOTE**
>
> **Before trying an example, note the current name of the disk you are using. In the next example, you will change the name, so you will want to restore the original name when you are through with this section.**

Let's begin with an example. This command changes the volume label of the default disk to MYDISK. Try this now.

LABEL MYDISK

To confirm that the change has been made, once again execute the LABEL command, but this time do not specify any additional parameters. You will see something similar to this (the disk drive letter may differ, as well as the serial number):

```
Volume in drive C is MYDISK
Volume Serial Number is 1250-2236
Volume label (11 characters, ENTER for none)?
```

When you execute LABEL without a volume name as a parameter, it first reports the existing volume name and serial number and then prompts you for a new name. If you just press (ENTER), the existing name is kept. Press (ENTER) now. Next, you will see this line:

```
Delete current volume label (Y/N)?
```

Technically, a disk does not have to have a volume name, so LABEL gives you a chance to delete the current name. Pressing Y deletes the label. Press **N** now.

You can place a drive specifier in front of the label in the command line version to change the volume label of a disk other than the current one. For example, the following command sets the volume label of the diskette in drive B to SAMPLE:

LABEL B:SAMPLE

VOL

If you are using the command prompt and just want to see the volume label, enter the *VOL* command. VOL is an internal command.

For example, enter **VOL** now and you will see the following:

```
Volume in drive C is MYDISK
Volume Serial Number is 1250-2236
```

You can use a drive specifier with VOL to see the volume label of a disk in a drive other than the current one. For example, the following command displays the volume label for drive B:

VOL B:

VOL   The command that displays a disk's volume label.

Remember that if you are using the Shell, then you can view a disk's volume name by first selecting the File Manager, then selecting the desired drive, and finally selecting the Show Information option in the Options menu.

Formatting Diskettes

Earlier in this book, you saw how to format a disk using the Shell. This section will look more closely at this important command.

To format a diskette from the command prompt, you must use the *FORMAT* command. FORMAT is an external command. The simplest form of the FORMAT command is:

FORMAT *drive-specifier*

FORMAT   The command that formats a diskette.

where *drive-specifier* determines which drive will be used to format the diskette. For example, to format the disk in drive A, you would use a command like this:

FORMAT A:

To try this command, insert a blank diskette in drive A and enter the command. When FORMAT begins, it displays the size of the diskette that it is formatting. As the formatting proceeds, FORMAT displays the percentage of the diskette that is formatted. When the process is complete, FORMAT asks you for a volume label. If you don't want to give the diskette a name, then you just press (ENTER). Next, you will see information about the diskette you just formatted. FORMAT reports the total number of bytes of storage, the number of bytes in bad sectors (if any), and the amount of usable storage. It also tells the size of each *allocation unit*, and the number of allocation units on the disk. Finally, it displays the disk's serial number. FORMAT assigns a unique serial number to each disk. At this time, the serial number has no purpose, but in later versions of DOS it may be of value.

Allocation unit
A group of sectors. Also called a cluster.

The FORMAT command accepts a number of different options that greatly expand its capabilities. All FORMAT options follow the drive specifier, and more than one option can be present. Although some of FORMAT's options are applicable only to programmers and system integrators, several may be valuable to you. In the next few sections, the most important and commonly used FORMAT options are discussed.

Specifying a Volume Label

As you know, FORMAT requests a volume label when you format a diskette. However, you can specify a volume label for a disk on the command line by using the /V option. It takes this general form:

FORMAT *drive* /V:*vname*

Here, *vname* is the volume label. Using this option, you won't be prompted to enter a volume label.

Putting the System Files on a Diskette

For a diskette to be able to load DOS, at least these three files must be present on the disk:

COMMAND.COM
IO.SYS
MSDOS.SYS

On some systems, these files may have slightly different names.

Collectively, they are called the DOS system files, or system files for short. Loosely, they form different parts of the DOS program. Only COMMAND.COM will show up when the directory is listed; the other two will be hidden. You can have FORMAT automatically copy COMMAND.COM, IO.SYS, and MSDOS.SYS onto the newly formatted diskette. The option to specify this is /S. Once the formatting has been completed, in addition to the other messages, the message "System transferred" will be displayed and the amount of disk space used by the system will be shown.

FORMAT must have access to the system files in order to transfer them to the new diskette. If they are not on the current disk, you will be prompted to insert a system diskette so that the system files can be copied.

Although a diskette formatted with the /S option can start the computer and load DOS, you will have access only to DOS's internal commands because the external ones are not transferred to the new diskette. However, you can copy the external commands onto the diskette. Also, other files are needed if the Shell is to be used.

Leaving Room for the System Files

DOS is a copyrighted program that you may use but may not give or sell to anyone else except as described in the DOS license agreement. Therefore, you may need to create a diskette that reserves room for the DOS system files but does not actually copy them to the diskette. For example, you might wish to prepare a diskette for a friend that contains several of your files, but you want to make sure that he or she can put a system on it if necessary. (This is done with the SYS command, which we will discuss next.) If you don't reserve room, the system cannot be put on the diskette.

Use the /B option during formatting to cause storage for the system to be reserved. No additional messages are displayed, but room is set aside for the system files.

Two Ways to Format

The FORMAT command has two options that allow you to format a disk in radically different fashions. The first is the /Q option, which causes a disk to be formatted very quickly. When a quick format is performed, the only thing done to the disk is that the file allocation table is cleared. Because a quick format simply clears the file allocation table, it must be used on a previously formatted diskette. That is, you cannot quick format a previously unformatted diskette.

The opposite of the quick format is the unconditional format. An unconditional format performs an actual, low-level format of the diskette. An unconditional format irretrievably destroys all information on the diskette. To unconditionally format a disk, specify the /U option.

Transferring the System With SYS

If a diskette has been formatted with the /B option or if there is sufficient room on the diskette, you can copy the system files to it by using the *SYS* command. SYS is an external command. The simplest form of the SYS command is

SYS *drive-specifier*

SYS   The command that transfers the DOS system files.

where *drive-specifier* determines the drive that will receive the system files. This form of the command reads the system files from the default drive. This implies that the system files must be present on the default disk.

To see how SYS works, format a fresh diskette using no options whatsoever.

Now, if you do not have a fixed disk, make sure that A is the current drive and that your DOS work diskette is in it. Put the blank formatted diskette into B. (If you have only one disk drive, you will need to swap diskettes.) If you have a fixed disk, put the freshly formatted diskette into A and make sure that C is the current drive. Now, execute SYS using A: as a drive specifier if you have a fixed disk or B: if you do not. Once the system files have been transferred, you will see the message:

```
System transferred
```

If you want SYS to read the system files from a disk other than the default, use this form of the command:

SYS *source target*

Here, the system files will be read from the drive and/or path specified by *source* and written to the drive specified by *target*.

The VERIFY Command

Disk write operations are usually successful. However, on certain rare occasions, such as a power surge, an error can occur, and the contents of the disk file will not be exactly what they are supposed to be. Because of the possibility of error, you can make DOS verify that the data has been written correctly. To do this, DOS actually reads the section of the file just written and compares it to what is in memory. If a discrepancy is found, a write error is reported. The command that turns on or off the verification process is called *VERIFY* and it takes this general form:

VERIFY *on/off*

VERIFY is an internal command.

By default, VERIFY is off. To turn it on, enter:

VERIFY ON

VERIFY   The command that turns on or off the DOS disk verify option.

You might think it a good idea to always have VERIFY turned on, but it isn't. The reason is that each write operation would take about twice as long because of the extra work that DOS must do. Turn on VERIFY only when you are working with very important files. Remember that disk errors are rare. If you are experiencing frequent errors, your computer should probably be checked by a qualified service technician.

You can see if VERIFY is on or off by entering "VERIFY" with no argument. For example, entering

VERIFY

now will result in the message

```
VERIFY is on
```

(assuming that VERIFY is ON).

XCOPY: An Expanded COPY Command

Assume that you have a diskette with directories organized like those shown in Figure 10-1. How can you copy the entire contents of the WP directory, including the contents of the JOHN and MARY subdirectories plus JOHN's subdirectory FORMS, and still maintain the directory structure? With the standard COPY command, you must copy each directory individually, making sure that all files are copied into the correct destination directory. This approach is clearly error prone and tedious. For this reason, DOS includes the *XCOPY* command, which, in addition to having many other useful features, lets you automatically copy complete sets of directories and subdirectories.

> *XCOPY   An expanded version of the COPY command.*

XCOPY is an external command. In its simplest form XCOPY works much like COPY. For example, to copy a file called SAMPLE from drive A to drive B, you could use the following command:

XCOPY A:SAMPLE B:

However, XCOPY goes far beyond this. XCOPY takes the general form

XCOPY *source destination options*

where *source* and *destination* may be a drive specifier, a file name, or a directory name—or any combination of the three. The *options* let you control exactly what and how XCOPY copies.

Let's look at how XCOPY functions with its various options.

Copying Files

Although it is faster to copy files with the internal COPY command, you can copy files using XCOPY. The wildcard characters * and ? are allowed. Also, the /V (verify) option is supported.

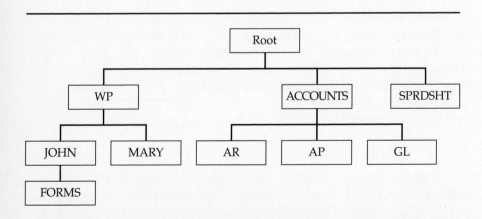

FIGURE 10-1   **A sample disk directory structure**

Copying Groups of Directories

You can use XCOPY to copy the contents of the current directory plus the contents of any subdirectories. To see how this works, format two diskettes and label them ONE and TWO. On diskette ONE, create these two subdirectories using the following commands (fixed-disk users: do *not* use your fixed disk for this example):

**MKDIR WP
MKDIR ACCOUNTS**

Switch to the WP directory and issue the following command:

MKDIR LETTERS

The directory structure of diskette ONE should now look like this:

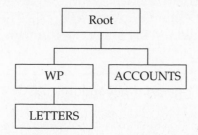

Copy the file TEST.TXT into the root directory of this disk, but call the destination file SAMPLE.TXT. You created the TEST.TXT file in Chapter 9. (Use a command similar to **COPY TEST.TXT A:SAMPLE.TXT**.) Then copy SAMPLE.TXT to the WP directory and call it SAMPLE2.TXT. (Use the command **COPY SAMPLE.TXT \WP\SAMPLE2.TXT**.) Next, copy SAMPLE.TXT to the WP\LETTERS directory, calling it SAM-PLE3.TXT. Finally, copy XCOPY.EXE into the root directory of dis-kette ONE. If not already there, put diskette ONE in drive A. If you have a dual-floppy system, put diskette TWO into drive B. Otherwise, you will need to swap it in and out of drive A as prompted by DOS.

As a first example, try the following command:

XCOPY A: B:

After the command is finished, only the files SAMPLE.TXT and XCOPY.EXE from the root directory will have been copied to diskette TWO. (You can confirm this by listing the directory of the target disk.) The reason for this is that, in its simplest form, XCOPY operates just like COPY and copies only those files that are in the current directory.

In order for XCOPY to copy the contents of a group of directories, you must use the /S option. Try the following command now:

XCOPY A: B: /S

After the command has finished, list the directory of diskette TWO. As you can see, the directory WP has been created. If you change to WP, you will see that SAMPLE2.TXT has been copied to that directory and that the subdirectory LETTERS has been created. SAMPLE3.TXT will be found in WP\LETTERS.

The /S option tells XCOPY to copy the contents of the current directory plus all subdirectories. If necessary, it will create the subdirectories on the destination diskette.

You might wonder why the directory ACCOUNTS was not found on diskette TWO. The reason is that ACCOUNTS had no files in it. If a directory contains no entries, by default XCOPY will not create it on the destination diskette. If you want all directories created, whether empty or not, you must specify the /E option. For example, the following command will cause the empty ACCOUNTS directory to be created on diskette TWO:

XCOPY A: B: /S /E

You can copy less than the entire disk by specifying the directory to begin with. For example,

XCOPY A:\WP B: /S

will copy only the contents of the WP directory plus its subdirectory.

Using the Archive Attribute

The archive file attribute is turned on whenever a file is created or changed. You can use this fact to selectively back up only those files that have been created or changed since the last time you performed a backup. To accomplish this, use XCOPY with either the /A or the /M option. The difference between the two options is what happens to the archive attribute on the source files.

If you use /A, the archive attribute is not changed on the source files, which means that you could make repeated copies of those files with the archive attribute turned on. However, /M causes the archive attribute of the source files to be turned off after they are copied. The reason for this is to allow you an easy way to copy only those files that have changed since the last time a copy was made.

DOS provides a better command, called MSBACKUP, which also uses the archive attribute to perform backup operations. (You will learn about it later in this book.) It is best to leave this sort of backing up to MSBACKUP, which is designed expressly for this purpose.

Using the Date Option

You can use XCOPY to copy files based upon their creation dates by using the /D option. This option takes the general form

/D:mm-dd-yy

Only those files with creation dates the same as or later than the specified date will be copied. For example,

XCOPY A: B: /S /D:12-12-91

will copy all files with creation dates of 12-12-91 or later.

The /D option applies only to files. Directories will be established on the destination disk without regard to their creation dates.

Query Before Copy

The /P option causes XCOPY to prompt you before each file is copied. The message will take the general form

file-name (Y/N)?

If you press Y, the file is copied. Press N to cause that file to be skipped.

The /W Option

As you have noticed, XCOPY begins to copy files immediately. If you need to switch diskettes before the copying takes place, specify /W, which causes XCOPY to issue the following prompt prior to starting the copying process:

```
Press any key to begin copying file(s)
```

After switching diskettes, press a key.

Verifying the Copy

You can have XCOPY verify that the copy of each file on the target has been copied without error by specifying the /V option. Keep in mind, however, that copy errors are rare and that the /V option will slow down XCOPY considerably.

Replacing Files

As you continue to use DOS, you will find that there are two common situations involving copying files that neither COPY nor XCOPY can handle. The first occurs when you want to replace only those files on the destination disk with files of the same name from the source disk. For example, a work disk may contain several files for which a new version exists. The second situation is the opposite of the first. Sometimes you will want to add files to a disk without overwriting any file already on the disk. You can accomplish both of these activities with *REPLACE*.

The general form of REPLACE is

REPLACE is the command that replaces existing files on a disk with new versions.

REPLACE *source destination options*

where *source* and *destination* specify the source and destination file names, directories, or drives, which may include the wildcard characters * and ?. REPLACE is an external command.

In its simplest form, REPLACE behaves much like COPY. For example,

REPLACE A:SAMPLE.TXT B:

copies the file SAMPLE.TXT from A to B. However, REPLACE really shines when wildcards are used.

Using the two diskettes that you created for the XCOPY examples, copy the file REPLACE.EXE to diskette ONE. Now insert diskette ONE in drive A and, if you have two floppies, diskette TWO in drive B. If you only have one floppy, DOS will alternate that drive between A and B and you will be prompted to swap the two diskettes. Now enter:

REPLACE A:*.* B:

You will see this message:

```
Replacing B:\SAMPLE.TXT
Replacing B:\XCOPY.EXE
2 File(s) replaced
```

As you can see, REPLACE copied SAMPLE.TXT and XCOPY.EXE but not REPLACE.EXE. By default, REPLACE will replace only those files that it finds on the destination diskette. Because REPLACE.EXE did not exist on the destination disk, it was not copied. In this example only the files in the root directory were replaced. However, if you specify the /S option, then all files in all subdirectories on the target diskette will also be examined and replaced if possible. For example, enter:

REPLACE A:*.* B: /S

As you can see, this replaces all files on the destination diskette in all directories.

You can use REPLACE to add to a disk only those files that are not currently on the destination disk. This prevents existing files from being overwritten. To do this, you use the /A option. Try this command now.

REPLACE A:*.* B: /A

You will see the following:

```
Adding B:REPLACE.EXE

1 File(s) added
```

This time the only files copied were those that *did not* already exist on diskette TWO.

If you need to insert a different diskette before REPLACE begins, use /W, which causes REPLACE to wait until you press a key before beginning.

The /P option causes REPLACE to prompt you before a file is replaced. For example, if you enter

REPLACE A:*.* B: /P

you will see the following prompt:

```
Replace B:\SAMPLE.TXT (Y/N)
```

If you press Y, the file will be replaced; otherwise, it will not.

You can replace only those files on the target diskette that are older than the ones on the source diskette by using the /U option.

By default, REPLACE will not replace files that are marked as read-only on the target. However, if you specify the /R option, then read-only files will also be replaced.

Here are some points to remember:

- You cannot use the /A and /S options together.
- You cannot use the /A and /U options together.
- The source and destination need not be on different disks—they may simply be different directories on the same disk.

Printing the Screen

It is sometimes useful to print what is displayed on the screen. DOS lets you do this with the Print Screen command. Unlike most other DOS commands, you do not need to enter a command at the command prompt—you simply press the (PRINT SCREEN) key. (For some computers, to reach (PRINT SCREEN) you must use the (SHIFT) key.) To try this, display a directory listing. Once the DOS prompt is displayed, press (PRINT SCREEN). The information that is on the screen is printed at the printer.

Printing Graphics Images

When you press the (PRINT SCREEN) key, whatever is on the screen is printed on the printer. However, this will work correctly only for screens that contain text and no graphics. Here, the term "graphics" is used to mean such things as lines, circles, boxes, charts, and the like. To print a screen that contains graphics, you must first execute the *GRAPHICS* command. GRAPHICS is an external command.

GRAPHICS The command that allows the (PRINT SCREEN) key to print some types of graphics images.

The GRAPHICS command has the general form

GRAPHICS *printer option*

where the name of the *printer* is one of the names listed in Table 10-1.

If no printer name is specified, the IBM Personal Graphics Printer is assumed. The Epson MX-70, MX-80, MX-100, and like printers are commonly used with microcomputers and also work with the default setting.

For example, to allow graphics to be printed on a color printer with a red, green, blue, and black ribbon, enter:

GRAPHICS COLOR4

By default, white on the screen is printed as black on the printer and black on the screen is printed as white. The /R option causes black to print as black and white to print as white. This option is seldom used.

The background color of the screen is usually not printed. However, if you have a color printer, you can print the background by specifying the /B option.

If you have an IBM PC Convertible Liquid Crystal Display, use the /LCD option.

Finally, the GRAPHICS command includes the /PRINTBOX option. This option requires significant technical knowledge to use. However, if you have an application program that requires this option, just follow that application program's instructions.

Printer Type	Name
IBM Personal Graphics Printer	**GRAPHICS**
Wide-carriage IBM Personal Graphics Printer	**GRAPHICSWIDE**
IBM Proprinter	**GRAPHICS**
IBM PC Convertible Printer	**THERMAL**
IBM Color Printer with black ribbon	**COLOR1**
IBM Color Printer with red, green, blue, and black ribbon	**COLOR4**
IBM Color Printer with black, cyan, magenta, and yellow ribbon	**COLOR8**
Any Hewlett-Packard DeskJet printer	**DESKJET**
Hewlett-Packard LaserJet	**LASERJET**
Hewlett-Packard LaserJet II	**LASERJETII**
Hewlett-Packard PaintJet	**PAINTJET**
Hewlett-Packard QuietJet	**QUIETJET**
Hewlett-Packard QuieJet Plus	**QUIETJETPLUS**
Hewlett-Packard PCL printer	**HPDEFAULT**
Hewlett-Packard Rugged Writer	**RUGGEDWRITER**
Hewlett-Packard Rugged Wide Writer	**RUGGEDWRITERWIDE**
Hewlett-Packard ThinkJet	**THINKJET**

TABLE 10-1   **Printer names for use with the GRAPHICS command**

Checking a Diskette Using CHKDSK

Whether you are using a floppy diskette or a fixed-disk drive, the state of the magnetic medium that holds your information is of crucial importance. Unless physical damage is obvious, it is impossible to determine whether the information on a diskette is valid simply by looking at it. To verify that the magnetic information on a disk is correct requires the use of a computer and the command *CHKDSK*. You have used CHKDSK in several examples earlier in this book; now it is time to take a formal look at it. CHKDSK is an external command, so you will need to have a copy of it on the disk that is in the current drive.

> **CHKDSK**   *The command that checks the status of a disk. It can also fix certain types of disk errors.*

The general form of CHKDSK is

CHKDSK *drive-specifier options*

where *drive-specifier* is the drive to be checked and *options* is one or more options. Both the drive specifier and options are optional. If no drive specifier is used, the current drive is checked.

To execute the simplest form of CHKDSK, simply run it with no options. The output of the CHKDSK command will be similar to that shown in Figure 10-2.

As you can see, the CHKDSK command reports the number of bytes of total disk space, the number of bytes used by DOS's hidden files, the amount of space used by directories, the number of bytes used by user (accessible) files, and the amount of storage space still available

```
Volume CDISK       created 10-21-1993 4:54
Volume Serial Number is 72AD-AD7E

33419264 bytes total disk space
   71680 bytes in 3 hidden files
   63488 bytes in 22 directories
18634752 bytes in 888 user files
  122880 bytes in bad sectors
14526464 bytes available on disk

    2048 bytes in each allocation unit
   16318 total allocation units on disk
    7093 available allocation units on disk

  655360 total bytes memory
  594496 bytes free
```

FIGURE 10-2   **Sample output from the CHKDSK command**

on the diskette. The term "user file" refers to a file that the user can display and manipulate. CHKDSK also reports the number of bytes in each allocation unit, the total number of units on the disk, and the number of units available. CHKDSK reports both the total system memory and the amount of free memory. The difference between the total free memory and the total system memory is the amount of memory used by DOS itself. CHKDSK also reports the disk volume label, if one is defined, and the serial number. It also shows the amount of disk space lost, if any, to bad sectors.

Disk Errors

Aside from actual physical damage, a disk may become partially unusable for either of two reasons. First, an application program could have an error in it that causes that part of the disk to become detached from the directory. Second, a system fault or unplanned power loss may cause the links between the sectors that comprise the disk to contain incorrect values. In most cases, these types of errors can be detected and corrected by CHKDSK, although information may be lost. In CHKDSK's default mode, presented earlier, errors are detected but not corrected. To make CHKDSK correct errors, you need to specify the /F (Fix) option after the CHKDSK command. For example,

CHKDSK /F

will cause any error detected to be fixed (if possible).

One of the most common errors you will encounter is reported with this message:

```
X lost allocation units found in Y chains.
Convert lost chains to files (Y/N)?
```

where *X* is the number of lost allocation units and *Y* is the number of chains. You may recall from Chapter 2 that DOS organizes files into sectors. An allocation unit (also referred to as a *cluster*) is a group of sectors that are all in one track, and a *chain* is a group of allocation units. If one becomes disassociated from the directory, then it is said to be lost because DOS no longer knows what file it belongs to. What CHKDSK does with this space is up to you. If you answer Yes to the question in the error message, then new files composed of the lost chains will be created. They will be called by file names of the form FILE*num*.CHK, where *num* is the number of the file. The files will be numbered 0 through 9,999. In theory, you can examine these files to determine whether they contain useful information; if they do not, you can erase them. In practice, however, these files seldom contain information that is usable and, even if they do, in most cases you won't be able to tell simply by looking at the file. For these reasons, you should generally answer No to the prompt. CHKDSK will then free the space for future use.

Cluster   *A group of sectors.*

Chain   *As it applies to DOS, a chain is a collection of clusters.*

You should run CHKDSK frequently to make sure that your disk is in good working condition. Once a day is normally sufficient unless you have reason to suspect that an error has occurred.

Remember that although CHKDSK can clean up certain types of disk errors, it can do nothing to help a disk that has been physically damaged.

Another CHKDSK Option

By using the /V option, CHKDSK will display the full path and the name of each file on the disk in this format:

drive:path\file name

You might want to try this now.

Backing Up a Diskette

Just as you made a backup copy of the DOS master diskette in Chapter 2, you can make backup copies of any diskette using *DISKCOPY*. The general form of the DISKCOPY command is

DISKCOPY *source destination*

DISKCOPY   *The command that copies an entire diskette.*

For example, to copy the contents of the diskette in drive A to the one in drive B, you enter

DISKCOPY A: B:

If the destination diskette is not formatted, DISKCOPY will format it prior to copying the source diskette. However, the formatting process does increase the time it takes to copy a diskette, so it is often helpful to have a number of formatted diskettes on hand.

If you have only one floppy disk drive, use this form of the DISKCOPY command:

DISKCOPY A: A:

Technically, you can omit either the destination drive specifier or both drive specifiers because DISKCOPY will use the current drive by default. However, it is safer to fully specify the drive specifiers to avoid any misunderstanding.

You cannot use DISKCOPY to copy to or from a fixed disk. However, you can still use floppy diskettes created using DISKCOPY on a system that has a fixed disk.

As stated earlier in this book, several different types of diskettes and disk drives are in use, and these all have different storage capacities. The general rule for applying DISKCOPY is this: The capacity of the source diskette must be equal to the capacity of the destination diskette. If this is not the case, DOS will issue a warning message. Generally, you need not worry when you are simply backing up a diskette that was created on the system that is performing the backup.

It is important to understand that DISKCOPY creates an exact copy of the source diskette. That is, sector by sector, the source diskette and the destination diskette are exactly the same. On the other hand, executing a COPY *.* command will copy all the user files, but the resulting destination diskette, although containing the same files, will not be an exact duplicate of the original. Most of the time this difference does not matter, but in some special situations one method of copying the contents of a diskette is more desirable than the other. (For example, an application program may specify which method of copying is best for it.) For now, however, when you want to copy an entire diskette, you should use DISKCOPY.

Although several things can go wrong during the disk copy process, fortunately, they seldom do. If an error does occur, your course of action is determined by the nature of the error. If DISKCOPY reports an error *reading* the source diskette, you should abort the DISKCOPY command and try a different diskette, if a duplicate is available. If a duplicate diskette is not available, try removing the source diskette from the drive and reinserting it. Sometimes a diskette is simply misaligned in the drive. As a last resort, tell DOS to ignore the error and continue. This may lead to the loss of data, however. If DISKCOPY reports an error *formatting* or *writing* the destination diskette, start over again with a new target diskette.

DISKCOPY offers the /1 option, which causes it to copy only one side of a diskette, even if the diskette is double sided. Using both sides of a diskette effectively doubles the storage capacity. Virtually all disk drives in service today are double sided, but the original drives issued when the first IBM PCs came out were single sided. You will use the /1 option only when you need to copy a single-sided diskette to a double-sided diskette. Most likely you will never need this option.

If you wish to have DISKCOPY verify that the disk has been copied correctly, you can specify the /V option. Keep in mind that the verification process will slow down DISKCOPY considerably.

If you purchase a program, the diskette it comes on may be copy protected. Copy protection prevents the unauthorized duplication of programs. In general, you cannot use DISKCOPY to copy a copy-protected diskette.

When to Back Up Diskettes

Although you are new to DOS, it is never too early to learn about the importance of backing up diskettes. When you made the backup copy of the DOS masters in Chapter 2, it was to protect the originals from harm. This concept can be generalized. Whenever you have valuable data on a diskette, you should make one or more copies in case the original diskette is lost, destroyed, or accidentally erased.

Most computer professionals, such as programmers, systems analysts, and maintenance personnel, recommend a system of rotating backups. In this method, you create one master diskette and two backup diskettes: a primary and a secondary. At the end of each work period in which the master diskette is altered, the master diskette is copied to the primary backup diskette. Periodically—weekly, for example—the master diskette is copied to the secondary backup diskette. Finally, occasionally—monthly, for example—the secondary diskette is "retired" and put in a safe place. A new secondary backup diskette is then created. This reduces the chances of losing important information. Later, this book will look at the backup and protection of diskettes in greater detail.

Comparing Two Files Using COMP

From time to time you may be unsure whether two files on different diskettes but with the same name are, indeed, the same file. For example, imagine that you have an inventory program that creates and maintains a file called INV.DAT. If you have two copies of this file, how do you know that they both contain the same information? Another related situation arises when you suspect that two files with different names may actually be the same file. How can this be determined? Finally, sometimes you will want to be sure that a file has, indeed, been accurately copied. How can you be sure that the destination file is 100 percent the same as the source file? These are not trivial questions. Although you can type or print text files and visually compare them, some types of files do not lend themselves to visual inspection. One way to be sure that two files are the same is to use the COMP (Comparison) command. COMP is an external command.

So that you can work along with the examples in this chapter, you need to create a small text file called COMPTEST.TXT that contains the following text:

**This is a sample
text file.**

Execute the following command with your work disk in the current drive (or use drive C if you have a fixed disk):

COPY COMPTEST.TXT TEST1.TXT

There are two ways to execute COMP. One is simply to execute it with no options. You will then be prompted for the two files to compare.

NOTE
Your copy of DOS 6 may or may *not* include the COMP command. If it does not, skip this section and proceed to "Comparing Two Files Using FC."

COMP   *A command that compares two files.*

As a first example, compare the file COMPTEST.TXT with TEST1.TXT by typing **COMP** and then pressing (ENTER). The first prompt is

```
Name of first file to compare:
```

Respond by entering **COMPTEST.TXT**. Next you will see the prompt

```
Name of second file to compare:
```

Respond with **TEST1.TXT**. Next, you will be prompted for an option. At this time no option is needed, so simply press (ENTER). COMP will then compare the files. Since the files are the same, they will compare and you will see this message and prompt:

```
Files compare ok
Compare more files (Y/N)?
```

If you answer Y to this prompt, you can compare another set of files. However, at this time, answer **N**.

You should give no special significance to which file is first and which is second. Either file can be first or second.

A much easier way to invoke the COMP command is by specifying the two files when you execute COMP. For example, in order to compare COMPTEST.TXT and TEST1.TXT, use this command:

COMP COMPTEST.TXT TEST1.TXT

This form of the command does not prompt you for the file names or options—it simply performs the comparison.

Keep in mind that when you use the command line form of the command, the files you are comparing must be on disks that are already mounted in the drives because the comparison operation begins immediately. If you must switch diskettes, then use the form of COMP that prompts you for the file names. This will allow you to insert the proper diskettes.

A Comparison Showing Differences

If you enter the command

COMP COMPTEST.TXT SORT.EXE

you will see the message "Files are different sizes," and no comparison will be performed. The COMP command will not compare files that have different sizes because it assumes (rightfully) that different-sized files cannot be the same.

To see what happens when two files of the same length differ, you will need to modify the TEST1.TXT file so that the content differs, but the length is the same. At this time, edit TEST1.TXT so that the word "sample" is changed to "simple" and "text" is changed to "test", as shown here:

This is a simple
test file.

TEST1.TXT now differs from COMPTEST.TXT by the "i" in "simple" and by the "s" in "test". However, the length of the files is identical. If you compare the two files, you will see this output:

```
Compare error at OFFSET B
File 1 = 61
File 2 = 69
Compare error at OFFSET 14
File 1 = 78
File 2 = 73
```

This rather odd-looking output is telling you that the two files differ in byte numbers 11 and 20. Although hard to believe, it further reports that COMPTEST has an "a" where TEST1 has an "i" and that COMPTEST has an "x" where TEST1 has an "s". For rather murky reasons, by default the COMP command reports the position and contents of bytes that differ using *hexadecimal* numbers. Hexadecimal is a number system based on 16. The commonly used decimal number system is based on 10. The hexadecimal digits are the standard digits 0 through 9 plus the letters A through F, which correspond to the numbers 10 through 15. The number 10 in hexadecimal format is 16 in decimal format; the number 1A in hexadecimal format is 26 in decimal format. Therefore, the message "Compare error at OFFSET B" means that there was a difference between the two files at character number 11. COMP reports the characters at the point of difference using the internal code used by the computer to represent the character set. For example, hexadecimal 61 (97 in decimal format) is the code for the letter "a", and hexadecimal 69 (105 in decimal format) is the code for the letter "i". Unless you intend to become a programmer, you need not worry about hexadecimal format or character codes. What you do need to understand is that the two files differ; it usually doesn't matter how they differ. As you will soon see, it is possible to make COMP display a more civilized output.

> **Hexadecimal**
> *A number system based on 16 that is used primarily by programmers.*

Although the COMP command uses the term "error" when two files differ, this is really not a proper usage of the word. Just because two files are not the same does not mean that one is in error—it just means that they are different. It is certainly possible that the files differ because of an error, but it is neither the only nor the most likely reason.

Comparing Files on Separate Diskettes

It is very easy to compare a file on one disk to one of the same name on another disk. For example, to compare the file TEST on the fixed disk to the file TEST on the floppy disk in drive A, you can enter

COMP C:TEST A:TEST

Because both the file names are the same except for the drive specifier, you can shorten this command to

COMP C:TEST A:

Of course, when files are called by different names, you must fully specify both names.

Some COMP Options

As you just saw, by default COMP displays any differences between two files in hexadecimal. However, if you use the /D option, the differences will be displayed in decimal. Although decimal is an improvement over hexadecimal, COMP can still behave more rationally. If you specify the /A option, then any differences are shown using the actual letters (rather than numbers). However, you should only use the /A option on text files.

You can have COMP tell you the line number of each line that contains a discrepancy by using the /L option.

By default, COMP considers uppercase and lowercase letters to be different. However, by using the /C option, COMP will ignore case differences (that is, a capital C and a lowercase c will match).

Finally, you can have COMP compare only the first part of two files by using the /N option, which has this general form:

COMP *file1 file2* /N:*num*

Here, *num* is the number of lines to compare.

Comparing Files Using the FC Command

As stated earlier, you may or may not have the COMP command included in your copy of DOS 6. Either way, you will have a stronger, more flexible file comparison command called *FC*. It takes this general form:

FC *file1 file2*

where *file1* and *file2* are the files being compared. FC is an external command.

> *FC A command that compares two files.*

Even if your copy of DOS 6 included COMP, there are two principle advantages to using FC instead. First, it can compare files that are of different sizes. Although different size files are implicitly different, sometimes one file is actually just a minor variation of another or it can be a completely different version. Therefore, you can use FC to see how much different size files actually vary in content. For example, you may have two files (on different disks), both called INVOICE but differing in size by 12 bytes. Using FC you can determine if these files are simply slightly different versions of each other or if they are completely different files.

The second advantage is that FC can *resynchronize* itself when an error occurs. Resynchronization is the process by which FC attempts to find comparisons between the two files after a mismatch has occurred. For example, look at these two files:

File 1		File 2
A		A
B		B
C	← mismatch →	D
D		E
E		F
F		

Using a command like COMP, once the mismatch between the third characters (C and D) has been flagged, all other comparisons in the file will be flagged as mismatched. However, FC will resynchronize. In essence, resynchronization lets FC continue to compare files that differ only slightly.

The value of resynchronization is that it allows FC to provide a more accurate report of the differences between two files. This can be valuable in a number of situations. For example, you might have two versions of the same inventory file that differ only in the fact that one has an extra entry somewhere in the middle. Using COMP, after the mismatch (caused by the extra entry) occurs, everything else in the two files will be reported as mismatching. However, FC will resynchronize, and more accurately report only the first mismatch.

In general, only text files can be resynchronized. By default, FC compares all files that have an extension of .COM, .OBJ, .EXE, .SYS, .LIB, or .BIN as binary files and no resynchronization will occur. However, by specifying the /L option, these files can be compared as if they were text files, in which case these program and program-related files will be compared using resynchronization.

FC displays mismatches in text files like this. First, it displays the first file name. Next it displays the last matching lines followed by those lines that mismatch. Then it displays the first matching line. This process continues until the end of the shorter file is reached. For example, the output of an FC on the two files shown above looks like this:

```
Comparing files TEST and TEST1
***** TEST
B
C
D
***** TEST1
B
D
*****
```

Mismatches in comparisons of binary files use this sort of display:

offset x y

Here, *offset* is the relative position of the mismatched bytes in the files, *x* is the value of the byte in the first file, and *y* is the value in the same position in the second file. The output is in hexadecimal.

When comparing text files, you can tell FC to ignore case difference by using the /C option. To display the line numbers of mismatches, use the /N option.

You can cause text files to be compared as binary by specifying the /B option.

FC has some other options that are most useful to programmers and system integrators and are not discussed here. (You may want to explore these options on your own.)

Comparing Diskettes

In some situations, it may be easier to compare an entire diskette than to compare individual files. For example, if you back up your data diskettes using DISKCOPY, you must compare all files on the diskette to determine whether the backup disk is current. This can be tedious if there are several files. To solve this problem, DOS provides the *DISKCOMP* command, which compares two diskettes. DISKCOMP is an external command.

DISKCOMP The command that compares diskettes.

The general form of the DISKCOMP command is

DISKCOMP *source destination*

where *source* and *destination* are the drive specifiers for the disks to be compared.

If you have two diskette drives, you can easily compare two diskettes by using this form of the DISKCOMP command:

DISKCOMP A: B:

You will then be prompted to insert the two diskettes that you wish to compare into the drives.

If you have only one floppy disk drive, use this form of the command:

DISKCOMP A: A:

You will then be prompted to insert the first diskette into drive A. As DISKCOMP runs, it will prompt you to swap diskettes.

If the two diskettes are identical, then DISKCOMP will display the message "Compare OK." If there are differences, DISKCOMP reports the sides and tracks in which the differences occur. Knowing the side and track is not too meaningful (except occasionally to programmers). Generally, though, all you need to know is whether the diskettes are the same.

Two diskettes of different capacities cannot be compared using DISKCOMP. As has been mentioned, several different types of disk drives are in general use. The smallest-capacity diskette holds about 160,000 bytes, and the largest holds about 1,440,000 bytes. Generally, diskettes formatted and used on the same computer will be of the same size, so size is not often a problem when comparing diskettes. However, be prepared for this trouble when comparing diskettes created on different computers.

It is not possible to compare the fixed disk. Even if you have two fixed disks in your system, they cannot be compared.

One particularly good use for DISKCOMP is for verifying that DISKCOPY successfully copied the contents of an important diskette. Although DISKCOPY performs its own error-checking operation, if the data on a backup diskette is extremely important, executing the DISKCOMP command to compare the original diskette and the copy is a good idea—even if only for peace of mind.

The DATE and TIME Commands

As you are probably aware, your computer contains a clock that keeps track of the time and date. To set or change the time and date, you must use DOS's *TIME* and *DATE* commands. Depending upon your computer, you might need to reset the time and date each time you turn on the computer.

To execute either command, simply enter its name. The DATE command first displays the current system date and then prompts you for a new date. You can just press (ENTER) if you do not wish to change the date after all. Otherwise, enter the correct date using digits in the format shown when the date is displayed. If you live in an English-speaking country, then enter the date using the format month-day-year. If you live in a non-English-speaking country, enter the date using the form common to your country. Separate the parts of the date using the dash.

You can also specify the new date on the command line after the DATE command. If you do this, you will not be prompted for the date. For example, this command sets the date to January 1, 1994.

DATE 01-01-94

To set the time, enter **TIME**. The TIME command displays the current system time and then prompts you for a new time. If you wish to leave the time unchanged, simply press (ENTER). DOS displays the time on the normal 12-hour clock, using "a" for A.M. and "p" for P.M. DOS 6 allows you to enter the time using either a 24-hour (military-style) approach or the 12-hour method. When using the 12-hour method, for times after 12 noon, put a "p" or "pm" on the end of the time you enter. For example, 2:45 in the afternoon would be entered as "2:45p". Without the p or pm, DOS assumes that the time you enter is A.M. If you use the 24-hour approach, then hours after 12 noon range from 13 to 23. This means, for example, that 9 A.M. will be entered as "9", but 1 P.M. must be entered as "13", 2 P.M. as "14", and so on. Some older versions of DOS require that you enter the time using a 24-hour clock.

To enter the correct time, separate the hours, minutes, and seconds using a colon. (Both the seconds and minutes are optional.) When you have entered the correct time, press (ENTER).

Aside from allowing you to change the current system date and time, the DATE and TIME commands are useful when you simply want to know the time of day.

TIME   The command that sets the system time.

DATE   The command that sets the system date.

ATTRIB

ATTRIB   The command that sets file attributes.

You learned about file attributes when you studied the File Manager. Recall that DOS associates a set of file attributes with each file on the disk. As you saw when learning about the Shell, you can examine and change certain of these attributes. DOS also provides a command prompt version of this operation called *ATTRIB*. With it, you can examine and set the archive, read-only, system, and/or hidden attributes. ATTRIB is an external command.

The general form of the ATTRIB command is

ATTRIB *attribute file-name*

where *attribute* is either not present or is one of the following:

+R	**Turn on read-only attribute**
–R	**Turn off read-only attribute**
+A	**Turn on archive attribute**
–A	**Turn off archive attribute**
+H	**Turn on hidden attribute**
–H	**Turn off hidden attribute**
+S	**Turn on system attribute**
–S	**Turn off system attribute**

The *file-name* is the name of the file (including drive and path specifiers) that will have its attributes changed or examined.

You can examine the attribute setting of a file with the ATTRIB command by not specifying an attribute. For example, enter the following:

ATTRIB ATTRIB.EXE

DOS will respond with

```
A       C:\DOS\ATTRIB.EXE
```

assuming that you are running DOS from a fixed disk; otherwise, the path will be different.

The "A" signifies that the archive attribute is turned on.

To set a file to read-only mode, use the +R argument. For example, enter the following command:

ATTRIB +R ATTRIB.EXE

Now examine the attribute settings of ATTRIB.EXE again by using ATTRIB without any attribute arguments. You will now see the display

```
A   R   C:\DOS\ATTRIB.EXE
```

which tells you that ATTRIB.EXE is now in read-only mode.

To summarize: When an attribute is turned on, its first letter is displayed; when it is turned off, nothing is displayed.

To see the effect of the read-only attribute, try to erase ATTRIB.EXE. DOS will respond with "Access denied." DOS will not let you erase a read-only file.

To turn off the read-only attribute, use the following command:

ATTRIB –R ATTRIB.EXE

You can use the wildcard characters * and ? in the file name, but you should do so with caution because you will be setting the attributes of all the files specified.

You can change the attributes of all files in a directory, plus those in any subdirectories, by placing /S after the end of the file name. (Be sure to leave a space between the file name and the /S.) For example, the following command will set the archive attribute of all files with the .TXT extension on a disk in drive A. **Don't try this example.**

ATTRIB +A A:*.TXT /S

Summary

This chapter introduced a number of powerful DOS commands that expand the control you have over the system. These are the commands:

- ATTRIB
- CHKDSK
- COMP
- DISKCOMP
- FC
- FORMAT
- GRAPHICS
- LABEL
- REPLACE
- SYS
- VERIFY
- VOL
- XCOPY

In the next chapter, you will learn about a powerful feature of DOS that lets you create your own commands.

Key Terms

Allocation unit　A group of sectors. Also called a *cluster*.

ATTRIB　The command that sets file attributes.

Chain　As it applies to DOS, a chain is a collection of clusters.

CHKDSK　The command that checks the status of a disk. It can also fix certain types of disk errors.

Cluster　A group of sectors.

COMP　A command that compares two files.

DATE　The command that sets the system date.

DISKCOMP　The command that compares diskettes.

DISKCOPY　The command that copies an entire diskette.

FC　A command that compares two files.

FORMAT   The command that formats a diskette.

GRAPHICS   The command that allows the (PRINT SCREEN) key to print some types of graphics images.

Hexadecimal   A number system based on 16 that is used primarily by programmers.

LABEL   The command that sets a disk's volume label.

REPLACE   The command that replaces existing files on a disk with new versions.

SYS   The command that transfers the DOS system files.

TIME   The command that sets the system time.

VERIFY   The command that turns on or off the DOS disk verify option.

VOL   The command that displays a disk's volume label.

XCOPY   An expanded version of the COPY command.

Exercises

Matching

Match the answers in the second column with the terms in the first.

_____ 1. ATTRIB	a.	An expanded version of COPY.
_____ 2. DATE and TIME	b.	Copies an entire disk.
_____ 3. DISKCOMP	c.	Prepares a diskette for use.
_____ 4. FC	d.	Sets the system time and date.
_____ 5. DISKCOPY	e.	Compares two files.
_____ 6. REPLACE	f.	Sets a disk's volume label.
_____ 7. XCOPY	g.	Displays and sets a file's attributes.
_____ 8. FORMAT	h.	Compares two diskettes.
_____ 9. LABEL	i.	Replaces existing files on the target disk.

Short Answer

1. What command sets the volume label of a disk to MYDISK?

2. How long can a volume label be and what purpose does it serve?

3. What command formats the diskette in drive A and gives it the volume label WORDPROC?

4. What option causes FORMAT to copy the DOS system files to the diskette being formatted?

5. Briefly explain the /Q and the /U FORMAT options.

6. Why isn't it necessarily a good idea to keep the DOS VERIFY option turned on at all times?

7. What XCOPY command copies all files on the diskette in drive A that have creation dates on or after 7/9/92 to the diskette in drive B?

8. Name all of the XCOPY options and briefly describe what they do.

9. What does REPLACE do that neither COPY nor XCOPY can?

10. How do you print the screen? What command must you execute if you want to print graphics screens?

11. What does the CHKDSK command do and why should you use it from time to time?

12. What does the CHKDSK option /F do?

13. If you want to copy an entire diskette, why is DISKCOPY a better command than COPY or XCOPY?

14. What command compares these two files: LARRY.DAT and LARRY.BAK?

15. What COMP option causes case differences to be ignored? What option causes any differences to be shown using the actual letters instead of hexadecimal numbers?

16. Can DISKCOMP compare diskettes that have different storage capacities?

17. What command sets a file called PRIVATE.DAT to read-only?

Activities

1. Using DATE and TIME, check that your computer has the correct date and time. If not, correct them.

2. Put your Student Data Disk into drive A. Set the file called MYFILE to read-only. Next, try to erase the file. (You can't.) Finally, turn off read-only before continuing.

3. Using DISKCOPY, make a copy of the Student Data Disk. Next, verify that the copy is accurate by comparing the diskettes using DISKCOMP.

4. Experiment with printing the screen.

Business Case Study

You are the manager of a word processing department. It has been decided that all the secretaries' systems will be upgraded from systems with a fixed disk and a 5¼ inch disk drive to systems with a fixed disk with a higher memory capacity and one 3½ inch disk drive. Your own computer system has both 5¼ inch and 3½ inch disk drives, which will make the transition easy.

Your job is to organize the steps each secretary will follow to copy his or her documents from the hard drive to the floppy drive. When done, he or she will give the copied diskette to you, and you will copy it to a 3½ inch diskette on your system. You will then give the secretary the new 3½ inch diskette, and he or she will copy the information from the new 3½ inch drive to the new hard drive.

1. Assume that all secretaries have a fixed disk on their old systems called drive C, that DOS is installed in a DOS directory, and that their word processing program is in a directory called WP. Further assume that each secretary has turned on his or her computer system, and the system prompt reads "C:\>".

   You instruct the secretaries to do the following:

   a. Change to the DOS subdirectory.
   b. Format one floppy diskette in drive A. When DOS prompts you for the volume label, use the first eight characters of your last name to identify the disk.
   c. When you are finished formatting the disk with a label in drive A, change to the WP directory.
   d. Display the directory in a way that both pauses and displays the files across the width of the screen. After looking at the directory listing, copy only data files (assume the extensions .DOC and .TXT) to the floppy disk in drive A.
   e. Display the directory of drive A to make sure the copy was successful.

   If the copy was successful, go on to Part 2.

2. You are now going to take the secretaries' 5¼ inch diskettes and copy the files for them onto 3½ inch diskettes. You will concurrently make a permanent copy of these data files on your drive C.

   Assume that your system is on, and you are currently at the C:\> prompt.

   a. Format a new 3½ inch diskette in drive A.
   b. Put the first secretary's diskette into drive B, which is the 5¼ inch disk drive, and copy the files from this drive to drive A.
   c. Display the directory of drive A to see that the copy was successful.
   d. Make a new directory in drive C called NEWFILES.
   e. Change to the NEWFILES directory.
   f. Copy the files from drive A to the NEWFILES directory on drive C.

You have successfully copied the files to the NEWFILES directory in drive C, and you have copied a 3½ inch diskette for each secretary. Label the diskettes and give them back to the secretaries.

Now it's time to instruct them how to copy their 3½ inch diskette files onto their new hard drives. Be sure they change to the word processing directory (assume the program has already been installed) and locate the appropriate subdirectory to copy their data from drive A.

PART 4

Mastering Advanced DOS Commands

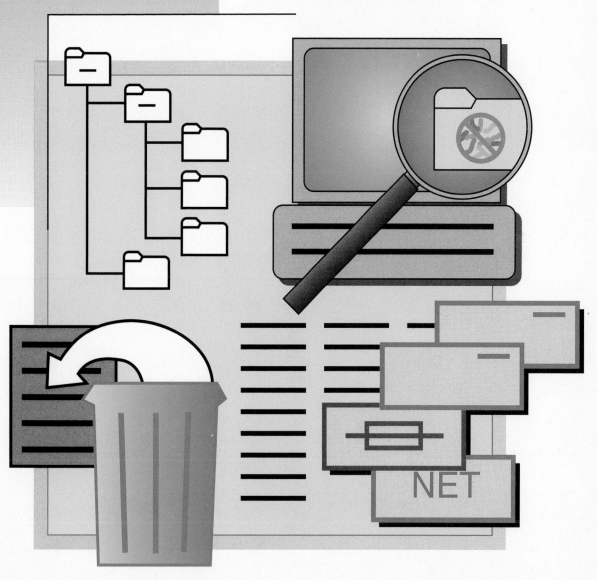

NET

Batch Files

CHAPTER OBJECTIVES

After completing this chapter, you should be able to:

- Understand batch files.
- Use parameters in batch files.
- Use the ECHO command.
- Use the PAUSE command.
- Add remarks.
- Use the IF command.
- Control execution flow using GOTO.
- Execute one batch file from within another using CALL.
- Use the FOR command.
- Use the SHIFT command.
- Process user input with CHOICE.
- Understand AUTOEXEC.BAT.

You will sometimes want to give the computer a list of commands all at once and then have it whir away on its own without further interaction from you until the list of commands has been executed. For example, you might want to tell the computer to prepare payroll information, print checks, and create weekly backup files without having to wait for each task to be completed before giving the next command. The creation of lists of commands is the subject of this chapter.

If you have a fixed disk, make sure that it is logged in and that the DOS directory is selected. If you are working with floppies, make sure that your DOS work disk is in drive A.

Batch file *A file that contains one or more DOS commands that will be executed automatically by DOS.*

What Are Batch Files?

DOS allows you to create lists of commands through the use of *batch files*. A batch file is simply a text file that contains one or more DOS commands. All batch file names must have the extension .BAT. Once you have created a batch file, you cause DOS to execute the commands in the file by executing the file like any other external command. You can think of batch files as custom commands that you create.

As you will see, batch files are useful whether you are running DOS from the Shell or from the command prompt interface.

To execute a batch command from the command prompt, simply enter its name. For example, if the batch file is called MYBATCH.BAT, you would enter **MYBATCH** at the prompt. From the Shell, you may either select the batch file using the File Manager or put it in a group menu in the Program Manager window. However, when using the Shell, it is easiest to execute the batch files from the File Manager using the Run option in the File menu.

Two Simple Batch Files

As an easy first example, use the DOS editor (or another text editor) to create a file called TEST.BAT that contains the following lines:

DIR
CHKDSK

Now execute this file by entering **TEST**. As you can see, DOS first lists the directory and then executes CHKDSK. (Note that you do not use the extension when you enter a batch file name at the prompt.)

How It Works

When you execute a command, a sequence of events begins. First, DOS checks to see if the string of characters that you entered matches one of DOS's internal commands. If it does, then that command is executed. Otherwise, DOS checks the current disk to see if what you executed matches one of DOS's external commands or an application program. (Remember that all DOS external commands and programs end with the .EXE or .COM extension.) If the command or program is found, it is executed. Otherwise, DOS checks to see if there is a batch file that matches. If one exists, DOS sequentially executes the commands in the batch file, starting with the first and finishing with the last.

Batch file commands must not have the same name as any other DOS command or application program that you are using. If you accidentally create a batch file with the same name as a DOS command, DOS will always execute the command—never the batch file.

A Second Example

You will find that you often execute the same sequence of commands over and over again. For example, if you are using an accounting program, then you may make copies of all the data files at the end of each day. Assume that the data files are called REC.DAT, EMP.DAT, INV.UPD, WITHHOLD.TAX, and PAYABLE.DAT. To copy these files from drive C to A, you would enter the following commands:

COPY *.DAT A:
COPY INV.UPD A:
COPY WITHHOLD.TAX A:

However, if you created a batch file containing these commands and called it BKUP.BAT, then you could just execute BKUP to copy the files.

To see how such a command will work, create three files called SAMPLE1.TXT, SAMPLE2.TXT, and SAMPLE3.TXT. Enter a few characters of your own choosing into each. Now create the BKUP.BAT file that contains the following commands:

COPY SAMPLE1.TXT A:
COPY SAMPLE2.TXT A:
COPY SAMPLE3.TXT A:

(If you have two floppies, use B as the destination drive.) Place a diskette into drive A (or B for two-floppy systems) and execute BKUP. You will see DOS copy the files.

Although creating a batch file command certainly saves some typing, the command's main advantage is reliability. Once you have created a batch command, it will always do exactly what you want it to do. You needn't worry about it accidentally forgetting to copy a file, for example.

Canceling a Batch Command

The easiest way to cancel a batch command once it begins is to press (CTRL)-(BREAK). ((CTRL)-(C) also works.) Depending on what commands make up the batch command, DOS may wait until the current command finishes before stopping the batch command. DOS will prompt you with the following message:

```
Terminate batch job (Y/N)?
```

If you really want to stop execution of the batch command, press Y; otherwise, press N and the command will continue to run. If any of the commands that make up the batch file have already been executed by DOS, their effects will not be nullified by canceling the batch command. For example, if the first command erases some file, subsequently stopping the batch command will not prevent the file from being erased.

Adding Parameters

You will often want to create a batch command that will operate slightly differently depending on how it is used. For example, consider these two batch files.

Batch File 1	Batch File 2

Batch File 1
COPY SAMPLE1.TXT A:
FC SAMPLE1.TXT A:

Batch File 2
COPY SAMPLE2.TXT A:
FC SAMPLE2.TXT A:

As you can see, the only difference between file 1 and file 2 is the file name used in the COPY and FC commands. In this section, you will learn how to create one batch file that can replace these two batch files by using placeholders instead of actual file names.

Replaceable Parameters

DOS allows you to use up to ten replaceable parameters (sometimes called dummy parameters) as placeholders in a batch file. These replaceable parameters are %0 through %9. Each piece of information that you pass to the batch file is called an argument and is placed on the command line immediately after the batch file name or as an option when you start the batch file using the Shell. For this reason, these are called command arguments. Each replaceable parameter in a batch file is replaced by its corresponding argument. Parameter %0 will be replaced by the name of the batch file. Parameter %1 will contain the first argument, %2 will contain the second argument, and so on. For example, create a batch file called CPYFILE.BAT that contains the following lines:

COPY %1 %2
FC %1 %2

When you execute this command,

CPYFILE SAMPLE1.TXT A:

parameter %1 will contain SAMPLE1.TXT and %2 will have the value A:. (In this and the rest of the examples in this book, the %0 parameter is not needed and is not used.) Try this now. As you can see, CPYFILE.BAT provides a general version of the two batch files it replaces.

When you specify the arguments to a batch file, you must separate them from each other. The most common way to do this is by using spaces, as the examples in this section have shown. However, tabs and commas will also work.

Special Batch File Commands

DOS allows you to use some special batch file commands that give you greater control over how a batch file is interpreted or operates. These special commands let you create batch files that are actually much like programs. These commands are discussed now.

The ECHO Command

ECHO The batch command that outputs a message to the screen. It also controls what is displayed when a batch file executes.

The *ECHO* command has two uses. First, it is used to control whether DOS displays the commands in a batch file. By default, ECHO is on, which means that DOS displays each command in the batch file as it is executed. If ECHO is turned off, the batch commands will not be displayed, but any output produced by the commands will still be shown. The second use of the ECHO command is to print messages to the screen while the batch file is executing.

The ECHO batch command takes the general form

ECHO *on/off/message*

To turn ECHO off, enter:

ECHO OFF

To turn it on, enter:

ECHO ON

For example, create a file called E.BAT and enter these lines into it:

ECHO OFF
VER

When you execute this batch file, you will see the output of the VER command, but you will not see DOS actually execute the command. The output displayed by this batch file looks like this:

```
C>ECHO OFF
MS-DOS Version 6.00
C>
```

For comparison, remove the ECHO command and try the batch command again. This time the VER command is displayed as it is executed. The output now looks like this:

```
C>VER
MS-DOS Version 6.00
```

To summarize, when ECHO is off, only the output of the commands is displayed on the screen. When ECHO is on, DOS also displays each command as it executes.

When a batch file command sequence concludes, the ECHO function is automatically turned on.

You can also use ECHO to display a message on the screen. To do this, simply place the message after the ECHO command. For example, the following batch file tells the user what to do if errors are found in a file comparison operation.

ECHO OFF
FC %1 %2
ECHO If errors have been reported, call the office manager.

Keep in mind that the message will be displayed whether ECHO is on or off.

Suppressing Echo One Line at a Time

If you wish to suppress the display of only certain commands, it may be easier to accomplish this on a line-by-line basis. To prevent a single batch command from displaying, simply place "@" in front of the command. For example, DOS will echo all commands except the second one in this batch file:

```
DIR
@COPY %1 %2
CHKDSK
FC %1 %2
```

The PAUSE Command

PAUSE The batch command that temporarily stops execution of a batch file.

You can temporarily stop a batch command by using the *PAUSE* command, which takes the general form

PAUSE *remark*

The *remark* is optional. When a PAUSE is encountered, DOS displays

```
Press any key to continue . . .
```

DOS will now wait until any key is pressed on the keyboard. After a key is pressed, the batch command will continue. You can also cancel the batch command by pressing (CTRL)-(BREAK).

The PAUSE command is useful when a precondition must be met before processing can continue. For example, the following batch file can be used to copy the files on the disk in drive A to the one in drive B. It first prompts you to place the proper diskettes in the drives.

```
ECHO OFF
ECHO Put source diskette in A and destination diskette in B
PAUSE
COPY A:*.* B:
```

Your screen will look like this:

```
Put source diskette in A and destination diskette in B
Press any key to continue . . .
```

Adding Remarks

REM Embeds a remark into a batch file.

Sometimes you may want to embed messages and/or notes to yourself (or others) in the batch file to help you remember precisely what the file does. You can do this with the *REM* command, which has the general form

REM *remark*

The *remark* can be any string from 0 to 123 characters in length. No matter what the remark contains, it will be completely ignored by DOS.

The following batch file command uses remarks to show who created the file and what it is used for.

```
REM Purpose: weekly accounting backup batch file
REM Author: Herbert Schildt
REM Date of creation: 7/25/94
COPY *.DAT B:
COPY *.INV B:
COPY *.BAK B:
```

It is a good idea to identify your more important batch file commands, as shown in this example, especially when several people will be sharing the same system.

As you begin to write larger batch file command sequences, you will find that remarks help you remember the what and why behind them. Sometimes it is useful to use remarks to give a "play-by-play" description of what a batch file is doing.

The IF Command

It is often useful to create a batch command that does different things depending on certain conditions. To accomplish this, DOS supports the *IF* batch file command, which takes the general form

IF *condition command*

Here, *condition* is one of three possible types of conditions and *command* is any other DOS command. If the condition evaluates to TRUE, the command following the condition is executed. Otherwise, DOS skips the rest of the line and moves on to the next line (if there is one) in the batch file.

DOS allows the IF command to test for three different types of conditions. First, you can test two strings for equality. Second, you can check to see if a file exists. Finally, you can see if the previously executed program (or command) terminated because of an error. Let's look at some examples of these now.

Checking Strings for Equality

In DOS, a *string* is simply a sequence of characters. You can use the IF command to check two strings for equality by using the general form

IF *string1* == *string2 command*

If *string1* equals *string2*, the condition is true; otherwise, it is false. To see a simple example, create a file called CHKSTR.BAT that contains the following lines:

IF RED == YELLOW ECHO This will not be printed.
IF RED == RED ECHO This you will see.

Try this batch command now. As you can see, only the second ECHO statement is executed.

The IF command is case sensitive. This means that "IF RED == red" will be false.

Of course, comparing two strings as shown in the previous example is of little practical value. However, you can use this feature to compare command arguments. For example, change the CHKSTR.BAT file like this:

IF %1 == YELLOW ECHO The color is yellow.
IF %1 == RED ECHO The color is red.

Now try executing CHKSTR with an argument of RED. As you can probably guess, it reports that the color is red.

> **IF**   *The batch command that executes another command based upon the outcome of a certain conditional test.*

For a more useful example, imagine that a computer in a small office is used by George, Fred, and Mary, with each having his or her own directory. Assume further that Mary does word processing, George is in charge of accounting, and Fred uses a spreadsheet. You could write one backup batch file command that will back up the files in the proper directory given the name of the person. Such a batch command might look like this:

IF %1 == MARY COPY \WP*.* A:
IF %1 == FRED COPY \SPSHEET*.* A:
IF %1 == GEORGE COPY \ACC*.* A:

assuming that this file is called BK.BAT; then to back up her files, Mary need only place a diskette into drive A and enter:

BK MARY

Checking for a File

You can check to see if a file or set of files exists by using the EXIST condition of the IF command, which takes the general form

IF EXIST *file-name command*

where *file-name* is the name of the file that you are checking for. The *file-name* may include both a drive specifier and a pathname. You may also use the question mark (?) and asterisk (*) wildcards if you wish.

For example, enter the following lines into a file called EXTEST.BAT.

IF EXIST GARBAGE.FIL ECHO This should not be found.
IF EXIST SORT.EXE ECHO SORT.EXE is on the disk.

Run this now. As you can see, only the message "SORT.EXE is on the disk" is displayed.

You can also use the EXIST condition to provide a double check when you are copying files. In the following batch file, if the file already exists on the destination diskette, the batch file will allow the user to cancel the command if the file should not be overwritten.

IF EXIST B:%1 PAUSE B:%1 exists - press Control-Break to cancel
COPY %1 B:

Checking for Errors

An application program can set an internal DOS variable that indicates whether the program terminated normally or because of an error. For the sake of discussion, call this variable the *error variable*. If a program terminates normally, it sets the error variable to zero, indicating that everything went all right. If it terminates because of an error, it sets the error variable to a number greater than zero. If a program does not actually set the value of the error variable, it is zero by default. DOS lets you check this variable through the use of the ERRORLEVEL condition in the IF command, which takes the general form

IF ERRORLEVEL *n command*

where *n* is a number greater than or equal to zero and represents the error number set by the application program. If the value of the error variable is equal to or greater than *n*, the condition is true.

The use of ERRORLEVEL is somewhat complicated, and the command is used most frequently by programmers. However, all programs will set ERRORLEVEL to zero if they terminate normally. Therefore, you can use the following form of the IF command in any batch file you create to check for normal program termination before proceeding. (Keep in mind that not all application programs will set this variable when they terminate because of an error, so some errors could be missed.)

REM Check to see that the previous program terminated
REM normally.
IF ERRORLEVEL 1 PAUSE Abnormal program termination.

Using the NOT

You can precede the IF condition with the word *NOT*, which will then reverse the outcome of the condition. For example, if

EXIST TEST.DAT

is true, then

NOT EXIST TEST.DAT

is false.

NOT   Reverses the effect of an IF conditional test.

To understand how the NOT works, assume that you have an application program that requires that the file INFO.DAT be present on the current disk. You could use the following batch command to check for the file before the program is run.

IF NOT EXIST INFO.DAT PAUSE Insert the program disk.

Using the GOTO

As you have seen in the preceding examples, batch files execute their commands in the order in which they occur in the file. However, by using the *GOTO* batch command, the commands in a batch file can be executed in a nonsequential order. The general form of the GOTO is

GOTO *label*

GOTO   The batch command that lets batch files execute commands in nonsequential order.

where *label* is a label defined elsewhere in the batch file. When the GOTO is executed, DOS goes to the specified label and begins executing commands from that point. Using the GOTO, you can cause execution to jump forward or backward in the file.

For example, create a file called GOTOTEST.BAT and enter the following lines:

IF %1 == RED GOTO RED
IF %1 == BLUE GOTO BLUE
:RED
ECHO You chose the color red.

```
DIR
GOTO DONE
:BLUE
ECHO You like blue.
CHKDSK
:DONE
REM The batch file is now finished.
```

Try this batch command with the arguments of BLUE and RED.

As you can see from the previous example, all labels must begin with a colon. Although a label may be up to 125 characters long, DOS will use only the first eight because, in the language of computers, only those characters are significant. This means that the following labels will appear the same to DOS:

```
:longlabel1
:longlabel2
```

You may not use a period in a label name.

As the example illustrated, you can use the GOTO in conjunction with IF to create blocks of commands that will be executed only if the condition controlling the IF command is true. Notice that you must provide a GOTO around other blocks of commands—as was done with the GOTO DONE in the RED block—if you don't want execution to "fall through" into the next block.

You can use the GOTO and label to create a loop. For example, the following batch file continues to list the directory until you press CTRL-BREAK, which cancels the command.

```
:ONE
DIR
GOTO ONE
```

The CALL Command

> **CALL** *The batch command that executes another batch command.*

Sometimes you will want to execute another batch file command from within a batch file. The best way to do this is with the *CALL* command. The general form of this command is

CALL *batch-file*

where *batch-file* is the name of the batch file command that you wish to execute.

As a first simple example, create a file called ONE.BAT containing the following lines:

```
ECHO OFF
ECHO This is in batch file ONE
CALL TWO
ECHO This is back in batch file ONE
```

Now create the file TWO.BAT, which contains the following line:

```
ECHO This is in batch file TWO
```

Now execute batch file ONE. After it has run, your display will look like this:

```
This is in batch file ONE
This is in batch file TWO
This is back in batch file ONE
```

A batch file can call itself, but you must make certain that some terminating condition eventually stops the process.

A good use for CALL is to allow the creation of master batch files that simply consist of calls to other batch files. Such a master file looks somewhat like an outline and provides a quick way for you to see what is actually happening. (As you create your own batch files, you will be surprised at how long and complicated they can become.) For example, a master batch file for word processing might look like this:

**REM First create the document
CALL WORDPROC
REM Next, check it for spelling
CALL SPELL
REM Now, print it
CALL PRNT**

You can pass command arguments to the called batch file by specifying them after the name of the batch file. For example, this CALL statement passes the arguments "one" and "two":

CALL MYBATCH one two

One final point about calling other batch file commands—canceling a called command cancels all batch files, including both the one currently executing and the one that called it.

Repeating Commands With FOR

You can repeat a series of commands using different arguments through the use of the *FOR* command, which takes the general form

FOR %%*var* IN (*argument list*) DO *command*

where *var* is a single-letter variable that will take on the values of the arguments. The arguments must be separated by spaces, tabs, or commas. (Spaces are the most commonly used.) The FOR will repeat the *command* once for each argument. Each time the FOR repeats, *var* will be replaced by an argument—moving from left to right.

One important point: There must be a space on either side of the IN and the DO. Neither can be touching a parenthesis.

For a first simple example, create a file called SIMPFOR.BAT that contains the following commands:

**ECHO OFF
FOR %%I IN (%1 %2 %3) DO ECHO %%I**

This batch file will print the first three command arguments it is called with. For example, execute it with the arguments "ONE TWO THREE". The output produced by the FOR command will look like this:

FOR   The batch file command that executes a series of commands.

```
ONE
TWO
THREE
```

As a second example, create a file called FORTEST.BAT that contains the following commands:

ECHO OFF
FOR %%H IN (FORTEST.BAT ONE.BAT TWO.BAT) DO DIR %%H

Run FORTEST now. As you can see, the DIR command is executed three times, each time with a different file name. Each time the FOR repeats, %%H is replaced by the next argument in the list. That is, the first %%H equals FORTEST.BAT, the second %%H equals ONE.BAT, and so on. The FOR continues to repeat until the last argument is used.

You can use FOR to execute a list of commands by placing the commands in the argument list. For example, the following command will first clear the screen, then list the directory, and finally check the disk:

FOR %%C IN (CLS DIR CHKDSK) DO %%C

You may not use a FOR command as the object of the DO. That is, FOR cannot be used to execute another FOR command.

Using SHIFT

SHIFT *The batch command that lets you use more than ten replaceable parameters.*

As you know, there are only ten replaceable parameters: %0 through %9. You can use the *SHIFT* command to gain access to command arguments greater than ten. Each time SHIFT is executed, the contents of the replaceable parameters are shifted down one position with whatever was in %0 being lost and %9 containing a new argument if one exists. For example, given these beginning values,

Replaceable Parameter	Value
%0	TEST
%1	A
%2	B
%3	C
%4	<empty>

after one SHIFT, they will have the following values:

Replaceable Parameter	Value
%0	A
%1	B
%2	C
%3	<empty>
%4	<empty>

As a simple first example, create a file called SHFT.BAT that contains the following commands:

ECHO OFF
ECHO %0 %1 %2 %3
SHIFT
ECHO %0 %1 %2 %3

Execute the following command as shown here:

SHFT ONE TWO THREE

You will see this output:

```
SHFT ONE TWO THREE
ONE TWO THREE
```

You can use a loop to make accessing a large number of arguments easier. For example, change the SHFT.BAT file so that it contains the following commands:

ECHO OFF
:LOOP
ECHO %1
SHIFT
IF NOT %1 == END GOTO LOOP
REM This will loop until an argument containing
REM the word END is reached.

Now execute this batch file as shown here:

SHFT THIS IS A TEST THAT ACCESSES EACH ARGUMENT END

This will display the following:

```
THIS
IS
A
TEST
THAT
ACCESSES
EACH
ARGUMENT
```

Processing User Choices Using CHOICE

New to DOS 6 is a batch command that lets you present the user with a choice and obtain a response to which your batch file can respond. This is accomplished using the *CHOICE* command. CHOICE is a powerful, flexible command that has several forms and options. The most basic form is:

CHOICE *prompt*

Here, *prompt* is a message that is displayed on the screen. The prompt may be either quoted or not. (Generally, quoted prompts are used.) The prompting message is then followed by "[Y,N]?". When executed, the CHOICE command displays the prompt and then waits until the user presses either Y or N. For example, this CHOICE command:

CHOICE "Do you want to continue "

causes this prompt to be displayed on the screen:

```
Do you want to continue [Y,N]?
```

CHOICE The batch command that processes a user's response.

NOTE
CHOICE is only available if you are using DOS 6 or a later version.

The command will then wait for you to press either Y or N. Any other key will cause the console to beep, and the keypress will be ignored.

The choice that the user selects is returned to your batch file as an ERRORLEVEL value. This means that the value can be tested using an IF statement. If the user presses Y, then the error value 1 is returned. If the user presses N, then the error value 2 is returned. To see how these values can be used, try this batch file:

```
REM A simple example of CHOICE
ECHO OFF
CHOICE "Which Key "
IF ERRORLEVEL 2 GOTO TWO
IF ERRORLEVEL 1 GOTO ONE

:ONE
ECHO You pressed Y
GOTO DONE

:TWO
ECHO You pressed N
GOTO DONE

:DONE
```

When run, this file displays this prompt:

```
Which key: [Y,N]?
```

Depending upon which key you press, the appropriate response is displayed. By default, CHOICE lets you enter the response in either uppercase or lowercase.

Notice how the IF statements are arranged in the preceding example. Remember, an IF ERRORLEVEL will be true if the error value is equal to or greater than the value specified in the statement. This means that your batch files must always test for the larger values first.

Technically, the prompting string is optional. When not used, only the "[Y,N]?" is displayed. From a practical point of view, however, the prompting string is almost always needed.

Using Case-Sensitive Responses

As mentioned, by default, you may enter your response in either uppercase or lowercase. However, if you want the response to be case-sensitive, then specify the /S option. To see its effect, change the CHOICE line in the foregoing example so that it looks like this:

CHOICE "Which Key " /S

Now, try the batch file. As you will see, you must enter the response in uppercase.

Using Other Responses

By default, CHOICE requests either a Y or an N (corresponding to a Yes or No) response. However, you can specify the letters that you want CHOICE to respond to. Also, you can prompt the user for more than two possibilities. This allows CHOICE to respond to something other than Yes or No. To specify the letters CHOICE will accept, use the /C option. It has this general form:

/C*chars*

where *chars* are the letters that you want to use. You may use as many characters as you like. For example, here is a batch file that lets the user choose between three options that are represented by the letters A, B, and C.

```
REM Respond to three choices.
ECHO OFF
CHOICE "Press a key now: " /CABC
IF ERRORLEVEL 3 GOTO THREE
IF ERRORLEVEL 2 GOTO TWO
IF ERRORLEVEL 1 GOTO ONE

:ONE
ECHO You pressed A
GOTO DONE

:TWO
ECHO You pressed B
GOTO DONE

:THREE
ECHO You pressed C

:DONE
```

In this example, A has the value 1, B has the value 2, and C has the value 3. More generally, the first character specified in the /C option returns the error value 1, the second character returns 2, and so on.

You are not limited to only letters of the alphabet when using the /C option. You can also use numbers and certain punctuation characters. However, don't use the following characters because DOS reserves them for special purposes: <, >, and |.

Suppressing the Character Prompt

In some cases, you might not want CHOICE to display the response letters (the characters inside the square brackets). You can suppress this prompt by specifying the /N option. For example, change the CHOICE line in the preceding example so that it looks like this:

CHOICE "Press a key now: " /CABC /N

When you run the file, only the message "Press a key now:" will be displayed; no prompting letters will be shown.

Using a Timeout

Sometimes you will want to give the user a chance to make a selection, but if the user does not make a choice in a reasonable length of time, you want the batch file to continue on, using a default selection. To accomplish this, use the /T option. Its general form is shown here.

/T*char,seconds*

Here, *char* is the character that will be used by default if the user does not make a selection within the specified number of seconds. The number of seconds to wait is given in *seconds*. Here is an example that uses a timeout.

```
REM A timeout example.
ECHO OFF
CHOICE "Select now (timeout in 3 secs.): " /CABC /TC,3
IF ERRORLEVEL 3 GOTO THREE
IF ERRORLEVEL 2 GOTO TWO
IF ERRORLEVEL 1 GOTO ONE

:ONE
ECHO You pressed A
GOTO DONE

:TWO
ECHO You pressed B
GOTO DONE

:THREE
ECHO You pressed C

:DONE
```

In this example, if the user does not make a selection within 3 seconds, the default value linked to C (in this case, the value 3) is returned automatically and the batch file continues execution.

Once the user presses any key (even if invalid) in response, the /T is disabled and the timeout feature is no longer active.

Using CHOICE to Build Menu Batch Files

One excellent use of the CHOICE command is to create menu batch files that allow the user to choose between two or more selections. Although your own situation and work environment will dictate what type of menu-based batch files are appropriate, the following short example helps illustrate their use. This file allows the user to either display the DOS version number, check the disk, or display the directory tree.

```
REM A simple menu file.
ECHO OFF
CHOICE "Version, Check-disk, or Tree: " /CVCT
IF ERRORLEVEL 3 GOTO TREE
IF ERRORLEVEL 2 GOTO CHKDSK
IF ERRORLEVEL 1 GOTO VER
GOTO DONE
```

```
:VER
VER
GOTO DONE

:CHKDSK
CHKDSK
GOTO DONE

:TREE
TREE

:DONE
```

Your use of menu files is limited only by your imagination.

Executing a Batch File from Within a Batch File

You can start another batch file command from within a batch file without using the CALL command. However, executing a batch file command without using CALL produces different results than when CALL is used. To cause one batch file to execute another, simply use the name of the batch file like any other command. When the batch file name is encountered, DOS will automatically stop executing the first batch file and begin executing the second. However, when that file terminates, control returns to DOS and the prompt is displayed—in other words, DOS does not return to the original batch file.

For example, assume that BKUP is the name of a batch file. Then, given the following batch file:

```
CLS
CHKDSK
BKUP
DISKCOMP A: B:
```

the final line will never be executed. If you want control to return to the original batch file, use the CALL command.

Adding a Batch Command to the Program Manager

You add a batch command to a group in the Program Manager window just like any other program by using the New option in the File menu.

AUTOEXEC.BAT

There is one special batch file, *AUTOEXEC.BAT*, that you will probably want to use. This is the batch file that DOS automatically executes when DOS first begins running. You will often want DOS to perform one or more tasks when the computer is first started. Place these tasks in the AUTOEXEC.BAT file.

AUTOEXEC.BAT
The batch file that is automatically executed when DOS begins running. This file must be in the root directory of the disk that loads DOS.

If DOS was installed following the normal procedure, then an AUTOEXEC.BAT file already exists. You are free to add to this file, but you should not delete anything in it. Also, anything you add must go before the line that contains DOSSHELL. DOSSHELL is the program that is the DOS Shell.

You can use the AUTOEXEC.BAT file to create a "custom look" for your system. For example, a computer dedicated to word processing might add these lines to the AUTOEXEC.BAT file:

ECHO OFF
CLS
ECHO WELCOME TO WORD PROCESSING
ECHO   AT WIDGET CORP.
PAUSE

You can also use the AUTOEXEC.BAT file to confirm that the proper programs are available for use. For example, assume that the program ACCOUNT.EXE is required for the operation of the computer and that it must be located on drive A. The following will wait until you put a diskette containing ACCOUNT.EXE into drive A.

:LOOP
IF EXIST A:ACCOUNT.EXE GOTO OK
ECHO Insert program diskette into drive A
PAUSE
GOTO LOOP
:OK

Later in this book, you will learn several ways to customize DOS, and some of these customization commands are perfect candidates for inclusion in the AUTOEXEC.BAT file.

Summary

In this chapter you learned how to create custom DOS commands through the use of batch files. You learned

- How to parameterize a batch file
- About these special batch commands

    ECHO
    PAUSE
    CALL
    REM
    IF
    FOR
    GOTO
    SHIFT
    CHOICE

- About the AUTOEXEC.BAT file and its special purpose in DOS

In the next chapter you will learn about filters, pipes, and how to redirect input and output. These elements give you control over how information moves about inside the computer.

Key Terms

AUTOEXEC.BAT   The batch file that is automatically executed when DOS begins running. This file must be in the root directory of the disk that loads DOS.

Batch file   A file that contains one or more DOS commands that will be executed automatically by DOS.

CALL   The batch command that executes another batch command.

CHOICE   The batch command that processes a user's response.

ECHO   The batch command that outputs a message to the screen. It also controls what is displayed when a batch file executes.

FOR   The batch file command that executes a series of commands.

GOTO   The batch command that lets batch files execute commands in nonsequential order.

IF   The batch command that executes another command based upon the outcome of a certain conditional test.

NOT   Reverses the effect of an IF conditional test.

PAUSE   The batch command that temporarily stops execution of a batch file.

REM   Embeds a remark into a batch file.

SHIFT   The batch command that lets you use more than ten replaceable parameters.

Exercises

Matching

Match the answers in the second column with the terms in the first.

_____ 1. ECHO

_____ 2. PAUSE

_____ 3. CALL

_____ 4. REM

_____ 5. IF

_____ 6. FOR

_____ 7. GOTO

_____ 8. SHIFT

_____ 9. CHOICE

a. Executes a series of commands.

b. Allows the use of more than ten command line parameters.

c. Stops execution of the batch file until the user presses a key.

d. Embeds a comment.

e. Allows nonsequential execution of your program.

f. Conditionally executes another command.

g. Displays output on the screen.

h. Executes another batch file.

i. Processes user response.

Short Answer

1. What does the @ do?

2. What extension must all batch files have?

3. Write a batch file that performs the following tasks: clears the screen, displays the directory, and then waits for a keypress.

4. What command causes commands not to be displayed as they are executed?

5. In the command COPY A:%1 B:%2, what are %1 and %2 called and to what do they refer?

6. How do you cancel a batch file?

7. What three conditions can the IF command test?

8. Demonstrate that you understand how to use the GOTO command by creating a batch file that contains three lines. Make one line an ECHO statement that is never executed.

9. Briefly describe what the AUTOEXEC.BAT file is.

10. When the IF is used to test for the equality of two strings, does it differentiate between uppercase and lowercase?

11. How can command line arguments be separated from each other on the command line?

12. Assume that you have two batch files called BAT1.BAT and BAT2.BAT. What command in BAT1.BAT will execute BAT2.BAT?

13. When you call another batch file, how do you pass parameters to it?

14. What is wrong with this batch file?

    :LOOP
    PAUSE Put disk in A to continue
    GOTO LOOP
    CHKDSK A:

15. What IF command checks for the existence of SORT.EXE on drive A and then, if it exists, copies it to drive B?

16. What IF command reports whether the previously executed program terminated correctly?

17. Show the general form of CHOICE and explain its operation.

18. Show the CHOICE command that prompts the user with "Press A or B" and times out in five seconds using B as the default.

Activities

1. Create an AUTOEXEC.BAT file that requests the time and date and then waits for you to insert your Student Data Disk into drive A.

2. Create a batch file called RENEXT.BAT that accepts two command line arguments, both of which specify file name extensions. Have RENEXT.BAT change all files with extensions that match the first argument to the extension specified in the second argument. However, it should rename files only after checking to make sure that no file by the new name already exists.

3. Show how these two batch files could be combined by using replaceable parameters.

File 1	File 2
DIR A:	DIR B:
DISKCOPY A: B:	DISKCOPY B: A:
DISKCOMP A: B:	DISKCOMP B: A:
DIR B:	DIR A:

Redirecting I/O

CHAPTER OBJECTIVES

After completing this chapter, you should be able to:

- Understand standard input and standard output.
- Redirect output to a file.
- Redirect input to a file.
- Redirect I/O to other devices.
- Use the DOS filter commands.
- Use pipes.

Data goes into the computer via *input* devices and leaves by way of *output* devices. The transfer of information to or from these *devices* is called an *input/output* operation, or *I/O* operation for short. The computer has several I/O devices including the keyboard, monitor, printer, and disk drives. By using some special DOS commands, you can reroute the flow of data. This is called redirected I/O.

Standard Input and Standard Output

You might be surprised to learn that DOS does not "know" where its commands come from or where its output is sent. That is, DOS does not know that you use a keyboard to enter commands and that you see DOS's response on a monitor. This is because DOS does not deal directly with the I/O devices. Rather, it works through two special, internal pseudodevices called *standard input* and *standard output*. These pseudodevices provide the interface between DOS and the various I/O devices supported by the computer.

When DOS begins execution, standard input is linked to the keyboard and standard output is linked to the monitor. However, you can

Input device *A device, such as a keyboard or a mouse, from which the computer receives information.*

Output device *A device, such as a disk or a printer, that receives output from the computer.*

Device *Any internal or external piece of peripheral equipment.*

I/O *Short for Input/Output.*

Standard input and output *The pseudodevices through which DOS communicates with I/O devices.*

221

change which device is linked with which pseudodevice. For example, you can think of standard input and standard output as depicted in Figure 12-1.

This discussion will look first at the redirection of I/O to and from a disk file. Later you will see how to redirect I/O to the other devices supported by the computer.

For the examples shown in this chapter, if you are using a fixed disk, make sure drive C is logged in and that the DOS directory is selected. If you are running DOS from a floppy, make sure that your DOS work disk is in drive A and that A is the current drive.

Redirecting Output to a File

DOS uses the > and >> operators to redirect the output generated by a DOS command or an application program that would normally be shown on the screen. The general usages of these operators with files are

command >> file-name
command > file-name

where *command* is either a DOS command or an application program and *file-name* is the name of the file that will receive the output generated by *command*. For example, execute the CHKDSK command using this command line:

CHKDSK > OUT

If you are using the Shell, run CHKDSK using the Run option in the File menu. Simply enter the command line as shown when prompted by the Run dialog box.

When the command executes, nothing is displayed on the screen. Now examine the file OUT by using either TYPE at the command prompt or the View option in the File Manager. You will see that the output of the CHKDSK command is contained in the file OUT.

The difference between the > and >> operators lies in how the output file is handled. The > operator always creates a new, empty file to hold the output information. If a file by the specified name already

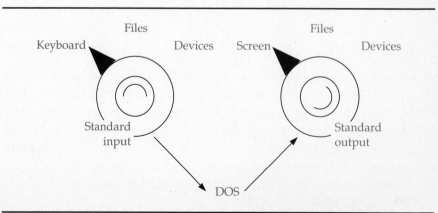

FIGURE 12-1   **A depiction of standard input and standard output**

exists on the disk, it is first erased and then a new, empty one is created. That is, if OUT had already existed on your work disk, the previous example would have erased it, destroying its contents, and then recreated it and put the new information into it. However, the >> operator does not destroy an already existing file. If the specified file already exists, the >> operator causes the output to be put on the end of the file. However, if the file does not exist, it will still be created.

To understand the difference, try the following command:

MEM > OUT

Now, if you examine OUT, you will see the following output (the exact information may vary slightly):

```
Memory Type         Total =  Used  +  Free
---------------     ------   ------    ------

Conventional         640K     45K      595K
Upper                115K     40K       75K
Adapter RAM/ROM      128K    128K       0K
Extended (XMS)      3213K   1241K     1972K
---------------     ------   ------    ------

Total memory        4096K   1454K     2642K

Total under 1 MB     755K     85K      670K

Largest executable program size       595K   (609136 bytes)
Largest free upper memory block        50K   (51040 bytes)
MS-DOS is resident in the high memory area.
```

As you can see, the old contents of OUT are no longer present. Now try the following command:

CHKDSK >> OUT

Entering **TYPE OUT** will result in the following display:

```
Memory Type         Total =  Used  +  Free
---------------     ------   ------    ------

Conventional         640K     45K      595K
Upper                115K     40K       75K
Adapter RAM/ROM      128K    128K       0K
Extended (XMS)      3213K   1241K     1972K
---------------     ------   ------    ------

Total memory        4096K   1454K     2642K

Total under 1 MB     755K     85K      670K

Largest executable program size       595K   (609136 bytes)
Largest free upper memory block        50K   (51040 bytes)
MS-DOS is resident in the high memory area.
Volume Serial Number is 1A88-4B26

  33454080 bytes total disk space
      2048 bytes in 1 hidden files
    118784 bytes in 42 directories
  32876544 bytes in 1804 user files
    456704 bytes available on disk
```

```
 2048 bytes in each allocation unit
16335 total allocation units on disk
  223 available allocation units on disk

655360 total bytes memory
609136 bytes free
```

As you can see, this time the previous contents of the file are preserved and the new output is placed at the end.

You should understand that only the output that would normally go to the screen is being redirected. Other I/O operations performed by the command are not affected. For example, try the following COPY command at the command prompt (you cannot redirect the Shell's Copy command):

COPY OUT TEST > OUT2

This command correctly copies the contents of OUT into TEST. Only the information that COPY sends to standard output will be placed into the file OUT2. In this case, OUT2 will only contain the message "1 File(s) copied".

One of the most common uses of redirected output is to create a log file that records the activity of the computer when you are not physically present. For example, the end-of-month phase of an accounting package might include several lengthy operations that are best run overnight. If you place all the commands in a batch file with output redirected into a log file using the >> operator, you can confirm that all went well when you come in the next morning.

Redirecting Input to a File

You can redirect standard input with the < operator. It has the same basic usage as the > operator. Instead of causing the command to send its output to a file, < causes a command to use the contents of a file as input. When input is redirected, information that is normally entered at the keyboard is read from the specified file.

Although you will seldom need to redirect command input to a file, it is easy enough to do if you are careful. As a simple example, first create a file called INPUT.DAT that contains the word SAMPLE followed by a blank line. Now execute the following command exactly as shown.

LABEL < INPUT.DAT

Recall that LABEL sets the volume label name of the disk. As you can see, DOS no longer pauses and waits for you to enter the label name. Instead, it reads the name from the file INPUT.DAT. To confirm that this actually happened, use VOL to display the volume label. (At this time, you can change the label back to what it was previously.)

You must be careful when redirecting input to a file because if the file fails to contain sufficient input to satisfy the command, the computer will stop running and lock up. If this happens, the only thing that you can do is restart the system.

> **NOTE**
>
> Although DOS commands allow their input and output to be redirected, some application programs do not. Certain programs bypass DOS's standard I/O routines and communicate directly with the hardware—usually to achieve improved performance. In this situation, the redirection operators will not be effective. If you attempt to redirect I/O to an application program and it doesn't work right, this is probably the reason.

Redirecting I/O to Other Devices

You can redirect I/O operations to devices other than disk drives by using their DOS *device names*. These device names and what they refer to are shown in Table 12-1. You cannot create a disk file with the same name as any device name. For traditional reasons, you may place a colon after the device name; however, this book will not do so because it is superfluous.

Device name   A name that DOS uses to refer to a device. For example, PRN refers to the standard printer.

For the most part, you can use the device names anywhere you would use file names. For example, create a short text file called MYNAME that contains your name. Now try the following command from the command prompt (if you have a printer).

COPY MYNAME PRN

As you can see, your name is printed on the printer as long as your printer is configured in the standard manner.

For unknown reasons, the Copy command in the File menu of the File Manager will not accept the DOS device names. This is why you were told to execute the previous example from the command prompt. Later versions of the Shell may correct this shortcoming. For now, execute the next few examples from the command prompt (or execute COPY using the Run option in the File menu).

An alternative to using the TYPE command to display the contents of a text file on the screen is to simply COPY it to CON. For example, the following command prints your name on the screen:

COPY MYNAME CON

CON	**The console, either keyboard or screen**
AUX	**The first asynchronous serial port**
COM1	**Same as AUX**
COM2	**The second asynchronous serial port**
COM3	**The third asynchronous serial port**
COM4	**The fourth asynchronous serial port**
PRN	**The first printer—output only**
LPT1	**Same as PRN**
LPT2	**The second printer—output only**
LPT3	**The third printer—output only**
NUL	**A nonexistent device used by programmers for testing software**

TABLE 12-1   **The DOS device names**

A really slick trick that allows you to use your computer like a very expensive typewriter is the following command:

COPY CON PRN

(To cancel this comand, press (CTRL)-(Z) and then (ENTER).) Using this command, whatever you type will be printed on the printer. However, COPY may wait until you enter a (CTRL)-(Z) and press (ENTER) before printing begins.

You can use the I/O redirection operators on device names as well as file names. For example, this command routes the output of the CHKDSK command to the printer. (This command can be executed from the Shell using the Run option in the File menu of the File Manager.)

CHKDSK > PRN

Using CTTY

DOS allows you to redirect both the input and output to a different device by using the CTTY (short for Change TeleType) command. The command name is traditional and derives from the early days of computing when teletype machines were used instead of terminals. It is possible to hook up a remote terminal to a DOS-based computer and then switch control of the computer to that terminal. For example, if the terminal were connected to the COM1 serial port, you would enter

CTTY COM1

to switch control to it. Don't try this, however, unless you know that the device you are switching to can actually control the computer. For example, a printer cannot.

To switch control back to the console, enter:

CTTY CON

Unless you have a remote terminal attached to your computer, don't used the CTTY command.

Filters

Filter   *A special type of DOS command that performs some type of manipulation on the data it is sent before sending it on to another command or device.*

DOS has three special commands that are called *filters* because they read standard input, perform some manipulations on the information, and write it to standard output. The three filter commands are MORE, FIND, and SORT. Let's look at these now. These are external commands, which you can execute from the Shell or from the command prompt.

MORE

MORE   *The DOS filter command that displays output one screen at a time.*

The *MORE* filter command reads standard input, displays 24 lines at a time on the screen, and waits for you to press a key before displaying the next screenful of information. To see how MORE works, create a text file call BIG.TXT that is 50 lines long, with each line containing its line number. That is, the first ten lines of the file will look like this:

```
1
2
3
4
5
6
7
8
9
10
```

Now try the following command:

MORE < BIG.TXT

As you can see, the first 24 lines of the file are displayed. On the twenty-fifth line is the prompt

```
-- More --
```

To see more of the file, press any key.
    The general form of MORE is

MORE < *file-name/device-name*

Actually, the < and the *file-* or *device-name* are optional. However, if you leave them off, MORE will simply read characters from the keyboard and display them on the screen, which is not very useful.

    If you use the command prompt, MORE provides a better way than TYPE does to browse through large text files because it automatically pages through them 24 lines at a time. If you use the Shell, then the View option in the File System may be more to your liking for simply viewing a file, but as you will see, MORE is more flexible.

FIND

The *FIND* filter command searches a list of files for occurrences of a specified string and displays each line where a match occurs. FIND has the general form

FIND *options "string" file-list*

The *string* is the sequence of characters that you are looking for and must be enclosed between double quotes. The *file-list* is the list of files that FIND will search. You may not use the wildcard characters in the file names.

    Before you can try the examples, you must create a file called SAMPLE.TXT and enter the following lines into it.

**This is a sample text
file that illustrates
the use of the FIND filter command.
Notice that upperCASE
and lowercase
are considered separately by FIND.**

> **FIND**   *The DOS filter command that searches a file for a specific string.*

Now try the following command:

FIND "that" SAMPLE.TXT

FIND will respond with this output:

```
--------- SAMPLE.TXT
file that illustrates
Notice that upperCASE
```

Each time that an occurrence of the search string is found, FIND will respond by printing the line in which the match occurs.

As the contents of the file suggest, FIND treats uppercase and lowercase letters separately. For example, try the following command:

FIND "CASE" sample.txt

FIND will only report a match in the line "Notice that upperCASE"; it will not find the lowercase version.

You can specify more than one file to search. To see how this works, copy SAMPLE.TXT to SAMPLE2.TXT and change the first line so that it reads as follows:

This is a second sample text
Now try the following command:

FIND "second" SAMPLE.TXT SAMPLE2.TXT

FIND will respond like this:

```
--------- SAMPLE.TXT
--------- SAMPLE2.TXT
This is a second sample text
```

Notice that the files are searched in the order in which they appear on the command line. In this case, the word "second" occurs only in SAMPLE2.TXT. However, in response to the following command,

FIND "text" SAMPLE.TXT SAMPLE2.TXT

FIND will display

```
--------- SAMPLE.TXT
This is a sample text
--------- SAMPLE2.TXT
This is a second sample text
```

You may have any number of files in the list, as long as the total length of the command line does not exceed 128 characters.

Sometimes you will want to know only if there are any occurrences of the string and, if so, how many times it appears in the file. To do this, use the /C option. For example, try the following command:

FIND /C "that" SAMPLE.TXT

FIND will respond like this:

```
--------- SAMPLE.TXT: 2
```

As you can see, only the number of occurrences is reported; the line containing the string is not shown.

You can use the /N option to show the relative line number of each occurrence. Try the following:

FIND /N "that" SAMPLE.TXT

The output will now look like this:

```
---------- SAMPLE.TXT
[2]file that illustrates
[4]Notice that upperCASE
```

The line numbers are shown between square brackets. You cannot use the /N and /C options together.

You can have FIND report all lines that do not contain the string by using the /V option. For example, the following command,

FIND /V "that" SAMPLE.TXT

produces this output:

```
This is a sample text
the use of the FIND filter command.
and lowercase
are considered separately by FIND.
```

Finally, you can cause FIND to ignore case using the /I option. When used, the /I option causes FIND to match both uppercase and lowercase.

SORT

The *SORT* filter command sorts information read from standard input and writes the sorted version to standard output. SORT has the general form

SORT *option < input > output*

where *input* and *output* are either file or device names. If they are not specified, the screen is used for output and the keyboard for input. It is not uncommon to have SORT display its output on the screen.

SORT works by sorting information on a line-by-line basis. It treats uppercase and lowercase as the same (that is, SORT is not case-sensitive). Unless you specify otherwise, SORT arranges the information in ascending alphabetical order.

As a simple first example, create a file called SORTTEST.TXT and enter the following lines:

one
two
three
four
five
six
seven
eight
nine
ten

SORT   *The DOS filter command that sorts information.*

Now try the following command:

SORT < SORTTEST.TXT

This will cause SORT to display the sorted file on the screen. The output will look like this:

```
eight
five
four
nine
one
seven
six
ten
three
two
```

You can have the sorted information put in a file by specifying it. For example, the following command will put the information in the file TEMP:

SORT < SORTTEST.TXT > TEMP

You can sort in reverse order by specifying the /R option. The following command displays the SORTTEST.TXT file in reverse alphabetical order:

SORT /R < SORTTEST.TXT

Sorting on a Specific Column

Tables of information are very common. Sometimes it is useful to sort a table using information other than that contained in the first column. Unless directed otherwise, SORT begins sorting with the first character of each line. However, you can tell SORT what character to begin sorting on with the /+n option, where n is the column to begin with.

For example, a hardware store might keep its inventory in a file similar to the one shown here.

item	cost	on hand
pliers	10	10
hammers	8	3
nails	1	100
screws	1	0

The store manager could use SORT to sort the data based on the on-hand column to provide an easy way to see which items are out of stock or running low by using the following command, assuming the file is called INVENT.DAT:

SORT /+23 < INVENT.DAT

The output is as follows:

```
screws        1          0
hammers       8          3
pliers        10         10
nails         1          100
item          cost       on hand
```

The number 23 is used because it is the character position where the on-hand column starts. If you try this example, do not use tabs in the file.

PIPES

You can route the output of one command into the input of another. This process is called *piping* because you can conceptually think of the information flowing from one command to the next through a pipe. To create a pipe between two programs, you use the | operator, which has the general form

command1 | *command2*

where the output of *command1* is automatically redirected to the input of *command2*. For example, try the following command using the command prompt, or use the Run option in the File menu of the File Manager window:

DIR | MORE

This causes the directory listing to be sent as input to MORE instead of to the screen. MORE then displays the directory 24 lines at a time.

It is possible to string together several filter commands. For example, this command causes the directory to be sorted and displayed one screenful at a time.

DIR | SORT | MORE

As you can see, the directory is displayed in sorted order. In this case, two pipes were used. The output of DIR was used as input by SORT, whose output was in turn used as input by MORE. Figure 12-2 should help you visualize how the previous command operates. In general, you can have as many pipes as can fit on the command line.

When a pipe is created, a temporary disk file is established that is automatically erased when the commands are completed. Therefore, there must be room on your disk for this temporary file. The size of the file is governed by the amount of output generated by the command that is putting data into the pipe. A few thousand free bytes are usually sufficient.

A pipe is very helpful in locating a "lost" file when you are using the command prompt interface. From time to time, a file will accidentally be placed into the wrong directory of a disk. If a great many subdirectories exist, it can take a long time to find the file by manually searching each directory. However, the following command will search all directories on a disk and report the path to the file. The file is called TEST here, but in reality you would substitute the name of the file that you are looking for.

> **Pipe** *A means of routing output from one command into the input of another.*

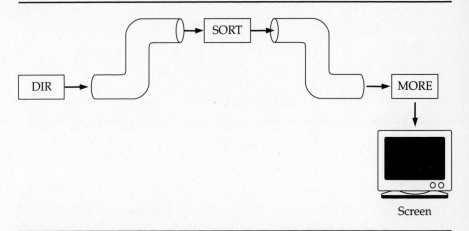

FIGURE 12-2 **A visualization of the DIR | SORT | MORE command**

CHKDSK /V | FIND "TEST"

You can execute this command from the File Manager or from the command prompt.

If you remember, when CHKDSK is used with the /V option, it displays all the files on the disk in the basic form

drive:path\file-name

Hence, when a match is reported, the path to the file is shown.

Putting It All Together—
Creating Simple Databases

You can use I/O redirection and pipes to create simple but effective databases. You can use the FIND command to locate information, the SORT command to sort the database, and the MORE command to browse through it. You will use the DOS editor (or any other editor) to enter information into the database. The only restriction is that each entry in the database must be on one line.

As a simple example, let's develop a quick-reference telephone directory database of frequently called numbers. The database will use the basic format

Last-name, First-name area-code number

For example:

Bell, Alexander 222 555-2222

For the sake of the examples, enter the following information into PHONE.DAT:

Washington, George 111 555-1111
Bell, Alexander 222 555-2222
Newton, Isaac 333 555-3333
Nietzsche, Friedrich 444 555-4444

To find Newton's telephone number, you would use the following command:

TYPE PHONE.DAT | FIND "Newton"

A second or so later, Newton's phone number will appear.

You can sort your phone list by using the following series of commands:

SORT < PHONE.DAT > TEMP
COPY TEMP PHONE.DATA
ERASE TEMP

You can list the numbers for groups of people based on the beginning letters in their names. For example, the following command lists the telephone numbers for both Newton and Nietzsche.

TYPE PHONE.DAT | FIND "N"

You can expand the telephone directory to include addresses, or perhaps remarks, as long as everything fits on one line.

You can use the same basic approach to create databases for other items. The possibilities are limited only by your imagination.

Summary

In this chapter, you learned the following:

- About standard input and output
- How to redirect I/O
- About DOS devices
- About the filter commands SORT, FIND, and MORE
- About pipes
- How to create simple databases using DOS

In the next chapter, you will learn how to configure DOS to best suit your needs.

Key Terms

Device   Any internal or external piece of peripheral equipment.

Device name   A name that DOS uses to refer to a device. For example, PRN refers to the standard printer.

I/O   Short for Input/Output.

Input device   A device, such as a keyboard or a mouse, from which the computer receives information.

Filter   A special type of DOS command that performs some type of manipulation on the data it is sent before sending it on to another command or device. The filter commands are SORT, FIND, and MORE.

FIND   The DOS filter command that searches a file for a specific string.

MORE   The DOS filter command that displays output one screen at a time.

Output device   A device, such as a disk or a printer, that receives output from the computer.

Pipe   A means of routing output from one command into the input of another.

SORT   The DOS filter command that sorts information.

Standard input and output   The pseudodevices through which DOS communicates with I/O devices.

Exercises

Short Answer

1. What is the difference between the > and the >> operators?

2. What command sends the output of the CHKDSK command to a file called CHKDSK.OUT?

3. Assume you have two files called FILE1.DAT and FILE2.DAT and that you want to compare them using this command: **COMP < IN**. What must the contents of IN be? (Hint: Think about the information the COMP command requests.)

4. What command sends the output of the CHKDSK command to the printer?

5. To what device does CON refer?

6. Explain what MORE, FIND, and SORT do.

7. What FIND command searches the file CONST for the word "people"? (To check your answer, use your Student Data Disk.)

8. What command sorts a file called INVTRY.DAT and puts the output in a file called INVTRY.SRT?

9. How do you sort a file in reverse order?

10. What does a pipe do?

11. What command displays the output of the TREE command one screen at a time?

12. How do you sort a file beginning at a certain offset?

True or False

1. By default, when DOS begins execution, standard input is connected to the screen and standard output is connected to the keyboard. _____

2. In general, error messages are displayed on the screen even when output of a command is directed to a file. _____

3. The command DIR TREE.COM > OUT writes output to the file named OUT. _____

4. Use the >> operator to append information to the end of an existing file. _____

5. The FIND command is not case-sensitive. _____

6. The | routes the output of one command into the input of another. _____

7. COM1 refers to the command file that organizes the computer's memory. _____

8. PRN and LPT1 refer to the same thing. _____

9. The command COPY TEST1 TEST2 >> OUT copies the file TEST1 into both the files TEST2 and OUT. _____

Activities

1. Put your Student Data Disk in drive A. Using FIND, locate all the lines in the file CONST that contain the phrase "the right".

2. Put your Student Data Disk in drive A. Sort the file CONST, putting the result in SORT1.OUT. Next, try sorting the file beginning with the tenth character in each line. Call this file SORT2.OUT. Examine the files and notice the differences.

3. Using DIR with the /S option, show the command that will display a sorted directory listing of the entire disk in reverse order.

4. Put your Student Data Disk in drive A. Display the file CONST one screen at a time using MORE.

13

Using DOSKEY to Expand the Command Line Interface

CHAPTER OBJECTIVES

After completing this chapter, you should be able to:

- Access your command history.
- Use DOSKEY's expanded editing keys.
- Use DOSKEY macros.
- Understand some DOSKEY options.

Although DOS's editing keys make using the command line easier, DOS 6 includes a command that lets you take full control. This command is called *DOSKEY*, and it allows you to reuse previous commands and to give a name to a series of commands. As you will see, DOSKEY is a powerful addition to the command line interface.

> **DOSKEY** *The DOS command that expands the capabilities of the command line interface.*

NOTE

The DOSKEY command applies only to the command line interface and has no effect in the DOS Shell. Also, DOSKEY is an external command.

DOSKEY is an installed command. To install it, simply enter **DOSKEY** at the command line. (Do this now so that you can follow along with the examples.)

Accessing Your Command History

As you know, when you press F3 the last command you entered is redisplayed and may be used again. DOSKEY expands this concept by letting you reuse not only the previously entered command, but any of the last several commands you gave DOS. (The exact number of commands that DOSKEY remembers varies depending on several factors, but you can count on at least the last 25 commands.) DOSKEY records your commands as you enter them, creating a *command history.*

Command history
The list of previous commands that you have given DOS.

To see how DOSKEY works, give DOS the following commands, one at a time. (Be sure that DOSKEY is installed.)

DIR
CHKDSK
VER

Once you have entered these commands, press the ↑ key once. You will see VER redisplayed. Now press the ↑ key a second time; this time CHKDSK is shown. Press the ↑ a third time and DIR is displayed. Each time you press the ↑ key, DOSKEY displays the command you entered before the one currently shown.

Each time you press the ↑ key, the next earlier command in your command history is displayed. Therefore, pressing the ↑ essentially moves you backwards through your command history. To move in the forward direction, press the ↓ key. For example, if DIR is currently displayed, then pressing the ↓ causes CHKDSK to be shown. You can execute any command in your command history by displaying it and then pressing ENTER.

To display the first (oldest) command in your command history, press PGUP. To display the last (newest) command you entered, press PGDN.

You can display your command history by pressing the F7 key. Try this now. You will see output similar to this:

```
1: DIR
2: CHKDSK
3:>VER
```

As you can see, all commands are numbered. (You will see how to make use of this fact later.) Also notice that "VER" is preceded by a ">". The command that is preceded by the ">" is the one that is current.

As you can see from these examples, access to your command history can save you considerable time and effort when you need to reissue the various commands repeatedly. However, your command history also provides another valuable service: it lets you verify what commands you actually gave DOS. This can be important when something goes wrong and you think that perhaps you issued a command incorrectly. Using DOSKEY you can find out if that is the case. Also, with DOSKEY installed, you can find out if anyone has tampered with your system. By checking the command history, you can look for commands that you did not give.

As you know, when you press (F7) your command history is displayed with a number associated with each command. You can execute any command in that history by specifying its number. To do this, first press (F9). You will see this prompt:

Line number:

Enter the number of the command. The command associated with the number will then appear on the command line.

Pressing (ALT)-(F7) erases your command history.

Pressing (F8) causes DOSKEY to search your command history for commands that match the first few characters you enter at the prompt.

DOSKEY's Expanded Editing Keys

In addition to the editing keys supported by DOS, several new editing keys are available when DOSKEY is installed. These are listed in Table 13-1. To try these new editing keys, enter this on the command line (but don't press (ENTER)):

This is a test

Now press the (HOME) key. The cursor jumps to the "T" at the start of the line. Press (END). Now the cursor moves to the end of the line.

You can move the cursor forward one word by pressing (CTRL)-(→). To move back one word, press (CTRL)-(←). Try both of these key combinations now.

As you know, pressing (BACKSPACE) erases the character to the left of the cursor. However, you can move the cursor to the left without destroying the character currently there by pressing (←). Try this now. You can also move forward nondestructively by pressing (→). One reason you might want to move the cursor nondestructively is to fix a typing error.

Keys	Action
(HOME)	**Positions the cursor at the start of the current command line**
(END)	**Positions the cursor at the end of the current command line**
(←)	**Nondestructively moves the cursor back one character**
(→)	**Nondestructively moves the cursor forward one character**
(CTRL)-(←)	**Nondestructively moves the cursor back one word**
(CTRL)-(→)	**Nondestructively moves the cursor forward one word**
(INS)	**Toggles between insert and overwrite modes**
(CTRL)-(T)	**Allows multiple commands to be entered on a single command line**

TABLE 13-1   **DOSKEY's expanded editing keys**

By default, DOS uses overwrite editing. This means that when you nondestructively move the cursor into the middle of the command line and then type a character, the character you type overwrites the character that was previously there. However, it is possible to switch DOS to insert mode by pressing the (INS) key. When you do this, the shape of the cursor will change. When using insert mode, each time you type a character, any characters to the right of the current location are shifted right and not overwritten. Thus, insert mode allows you to insert text in the middle of the command line. Insert mode lasts only until you press (ENTER), or until you press (INS) again. Then overwrite mode is resumed.

Without DOSKEY, you may enter only one command at a time on the command line. However, after installing DOSKEY, it is possible to specify several commands on a single command line. To do this, each command must be separated by a (CTRL)-(T), which will be displayed as a paragraph symbol. For example, try this command line; it executes the DIR, CHKDSK, and VER commands:

DIR ¶ CHKDSK ¶ VER

One thing to remember when you string commands together using (CTRL)-(T) is that you will need to press (CTRL)-(C) for each command that you want to cancel. That is, given the previous example, if you want to cancel all three commands, you will need to press (CTRL)-(C) three times.

Using Macros

Macro   As it relates to DOS, a name that represents one or more commands.

The second major feature of DOSKEY is the *macro*. A macro is a name that you define to represent one or more commands. In essence, by defining a macro, you are defining a new command that is comprised of one or more other DOS commands or your own application programs.

To define a macro, use this general form of DOSKEY:

DOSKEY *macro = command sequence*

For a simple first example, execute this command now:

DOSKEY TOM = DIR

Now enter the name **TOM** on the command line. As you might expect, the directory is listed. What has happened is that now TOM is another name for DIR; DIR is still present, but now TOM also causes the directory to be listed. Although this simple first example provides no tangible benefit, the next few examples reveal some of the power of macros.

To create a macro that stands for a series of commands, you need to specify a list of commands. Each command must be separated by this character combination: $T. (The "T" may be in either uppercase or lowercase.) For example, try this command:

DOSKEY MYCOM = DIR $T VER $T CHKDSK

Once you have entered this command, enter **MYCOM** on the command line. As you will see, this causes the directory to be listed, the DOS version number to be displayed, and the CHKDSK command to be executed. In essence, the $T is similar in operation to the (CTRL)-(T) command separator used with the command line.

You can specify as many commands as you like, but no command line can exceed 127 characters.

To see a list of all the macros currently available, use this form of the DOSKEY command:

DOSKEY /MACROS

Try this now. You will see the definitions of the two macros that you just created.

To remove a macro, use this general form of DOSKEY:

DOSKEY *macro* =

When no command sequence is specified, the macro is removed from the system. To remove all macros, press (ALT)-(F10).

It is important to understand that all macros are held in the memory of the computer and are lost when the computer is turned off. However, you can put macro definitions into the AUTOEXEC.BAT file so that they are generated each time you turn on the computer.

Increasing the Power of Macros

You can increase the power of your macros in three ways: by adding pipes, by redirecting I/O, and by using arguments. These functions are accomplished using the $ commands shown in Table 13-2. As you proceed, you will see several similarities between the operation of a DOSKEY macro and a batch file. Let's see how these functions work.

The $B command is DOSKEY's way of specifying the | pipe operator. As you should recall from the previous chapter, the | causes the output of the command on the left to be fed into the input of the command on the right. For example, this macro uses $B to display a sorted directory listing:

DOSKEY SORTDIR = DIR $B SORT

Command	Purpose
$B	**Creates a pipe and stands for the	symbol.**
$G	**Redirects output and stands for the > symbol.**
$L	**Redirects input and stands for the < symbol.**
$1–$9	**These are the replaceable parameters that will receive the values of any arguments specified on the command line. They are similar in function to the batch file parameters %1 through %9.**
$*	**A special replaceable parameter. It will contain all the information you specify after the macro name on the command line.**
$$	**Produces a single $ sign.**

TABLE 13-2   **DOSKEY's $ commands**

When you execute the SORTDIR macro, you will see the following on the command line just before the sorted directory is displayed:

```
C:\>DIR | SORT
```

As you can see, when DOSKEY actually executes the macro, the $B is translated into the |, which DOS can understand.

The $G redirects the output of a command. It is the equivalent of the > DOS operator. Typically, output is redirected into a file or to another device. For example, this macro definition directs the output of the CHKDSK command to a disk file called CHKOUT:

DOSKEY CDSK = CHKDSK $G CHKOUT

The $L redirects input and is the same as the < DOS input operator.

The replaceable parameters $1 through $9 operate just like the batch file parameters %1 through %9. The arguments you enter after a macro name on the command line are copied into the parameters. For example, given the macro definition

DOSKEY CPY = COPY C:$1 D:$2

this command line causes the file called HERE on drive C to be copied to the file THERE on drive D:

CPY HERE THERE

The $* parameter is replaced by everything that follows the macro name on the command line. For example, given the definition

DOSKEY PR = PRINT $*

this command line will cause the files ONE, TWO, and THREE to be printed on the printer:

PR ONE TWO THREE

In this case, the $* is replaced by "ONE TWO THREE". This means that you can specify as many files as you want without knowing the exact number in advance. Although $* will seldom be used with DOS commands, you may have application programs for which the $* parameter is appropriate.

Since the $ is used to signal the beginning of a DOSKEY command, if you actually want a "$" use $$.

Some DOSKEY Options

To save your command history, DOSKEY allocates 512 bytes of memory. Because the lengths of commands differ, you cannot know precisely how many commands can be stored in that amount of memory, but a reasonable estimate is between 40 to 50, unless all of your commands are very long. Once the memory set aside for your command history is full, each new command eliminates one or more of the oldest commands. If you think you will want DOSKEY to remember more commands than will fit in 512 bytes, you can specify the amount of memory set aside for DOSKEY using this general form when you first install DOSKEY:

DOSKEY /BUFSIZE = *number-of-bytes*

For example, this sets aside 2000 bytes for DOSKEY to use:

DOSKEY /BUFSIZE = 2000

Remember that to specify the amount of memory used by DOSKEY, you must do so when you first install it. You cannot change the amount of memory set aside for DOSKEY once it is installed.

You can display your command history using this form of DOSKEY:

DOSKEY /HISTORY

The list produced by this form of DOSKEY differs from the one produced by pressing F7 in that it does not display any line numbers.

You can reinstall DOSKEY using this form:

DOSKEY /REINSTALL

You may need to reinstall DOSKEY when working with certain types of programs, but this will be rare.

As you know, by default the DOS command line uses overwrite input mode. You can change the default to insert mode using this form of DOSKEY:

DOSKEY /INSERT

To change back to overwrite mode, use this command:

DOSKEY /OVERSTRIKE

Summary

In this chapter, you learned to use DOSKEY to

- Reuse previous commands
- Expand your command line editing capabilities
- Create macros
- Switch between overwrite and insert mode

In the next chapter, you will learn how DOS 6 can help you recover from mistakes and accidents.

Key Terms

Command history   The list of previous commands that you have given DOS.

DOSKEY   The DOS command that expands the capabilities of the command line interface.

Macro   As it relates to DOS, a name that represents one or more commands.

Exercises

Short Answer

1. Briefly describe what DOSKEY does.

2. When using DOSKEY, how do you access previously entered commands?

3. How do you list your command history?

4. Describe how to issue more than one command at a time using DOSKEY.

5. What DOSKEY command makes LISTDIR another name for the DIR command?

6. Create a macro that executes the MEM command, then lists all files on the disk that have the extension .DOC, and finally sets the time and the date.

7. What DOSKEY command lists all currently defined macros?

8. What key combination erases your command history?

9. What key combination removes all macros?

10. What are the names of the replaceable parameters when creating a DOSKEY parameterized macro?

11. Show the DOSKEY command that sets the buffer size to 4000. Must this command be issued when you first install DOSKEY?

12. What is the difference between overwrite and insert mode when using DOSKEY?

Matching

Match the answers in the second column with the terms in the first.

_____ 1. $B	a. Nondestructively moves the cursor left one word
_____ 2. $G	
_____ 3. $L	b. Toggles between insert and overwrite modes
_____ 4. $$	c. Creates a pipe in a macro
_____ 5. (CTRL)-(T)	d. Creates a $ in a macro
_____ 6. (CTRL)-(←)	e. Nondestructively moves the cursor right one character
_____ 7. (→)	
_____ 8. (INS)	f. Separates multiple commands
	g. Redirects input in a macro
	h. Redirects output in a macro

Activity

Experiment with DOSKEY. Also, create macros that perform some common job-related tasks.

14

Recovering
From Mistakes

CHAPTER OBJECTIVES

After completing this chapter, you should be able to:

- Undelete a file.
- Use Deletion Tracking.
- Use a Deletion Sentry.
- Unformat a diskette.

Things in real life seldom proceed along the path of perfection. Being human means that we will make mistakes. Fortunately, relative to DOS, many mistakes can be remedied before any real harm has been done. In this chapter, you will learn some important DOS commands that will help you undo two common errors: accidentally erasing a file and accidentally reformatting a disk.

To follow along with the examples in this chapter, put a blank, formatted diskette into drive A. Also, remember that all the commands discussed here are external commands.

Undeleting a File

By far the most common error that occurs when using DOS is accidentally erasing an important file. For example, this can happen when you erase using wildcard characters, and a file that you didn't intend to erase matches the wildcard. Other times, a file is erased and you later realize that you need that file. Also, newcomers to DOS sometimes just do the wrong thing and accidentally erase one or more files. Whatever the reason, DOS will often let you recover a file using the *UNDELETE* command. The UNDELETE command has this general form:

UNDELETE *path*

> *UNDELETE   The DOS command that recovers a file that has previously been erased.*

where *path* specifies the drive and path name of the directory that contains the file or files that you want to unerase. If you do not specify a drive or path, then the current drive and directory are used.

Before trying UNDELETE, you should understand how and why a file can be undeleted. When you remove a file using ERASE (or DEL), the information in the file is not physically destroyed. Instead, the file is marked as deleted in the directory. When a file is marked as deleted, DOS is free to use that part of the disk for other purposes. However, as long as no other file has overwritten the erased file, it is possible to recover the file by simply restoring its directory entry.

Try the UNDELETE command now. First, create a small text file, called TEST.TXT, containing anything you like. Next, copy the file to the diskette in drive A. This should be the only file on the disk. Next, erase TEST.TXT on drive A. Now, enter this command:

UNDELETE A:

You will see something similar to the following:

```
Directory: A:\
File Specifications: *.*

    Delete Sentry control file not found.

    Deletion-tracking file not found.

    MS-DOS directory contains     1 deleted files.
    Of those,    1 files may be recovered.

Using the MS-DOS directory method.
    ?EST      TXT         15  7-16-93  4:09p  ...A Undelete (Y/N)?
```

Before continuing, note these two lines:

```
Delete Sentry control file not found.
Deletion-tracking file not found.
```

As you will learn in the next section, it is possible to help UNDELETE do a better job by using a *Delete Sentry* and a *tracking file*, but you don't need to worry about this now.

Notice also that the first letter of TEST now contains a question mark. When you erase a file, the first character of the file name is destroyed. (As you will soon see, UNDELETE will prompt for the correct first letter when you undelete the file.)

UNDELETE prompts you before undeleting each file because by default, UNDELETE restores all deleted files in the directory. However, it is likely that you want most of the files that you have deleted to remain deleted. By prompting you, UNDELETE allows you to decide on a file-by-file basis which files you want to undelete. Since you want to undelete the file, press Y (you don't need to press (ENTER) after pressing Y). Next, you will see this prompt.

```
Please type the first character for ?EST    .TXT:
```

Since the first character is T, press T once now. (Again, you won't need to press (ENTER) after pressing T.) Assuming that everything worked correctly, you will see this message:

```
File successfully undeleted.
```

If you list the directory of the disk in drive A, you will see that TEST.TXT has been restored.

IMPORTANT

As stated earlier, when a file is erased, DOS is free to reuse the portion of the disk that held the file. Therefore, if you erase a file and then create new files, copy additional files to the disk, or alter the contents of one or more files, the erased file may be physically overwritten. If this occurs, you will not be able to successfully restore the deleted file. For this reason, if you accidentally erase a file, use UNDELETE immediately. Do not perform any other operations on that disk until you have undeleted the file.

In some cases, you will be able to restore only part of a file. If the restored file is a text file, then you may be able to use the part that was restored. However, if the file is a program or data file, it is best to use a backup copy of the file instead of the partially undeleted file. (Trying to use a partially restored program will almost certainly crash your computer.)

Undeleting Specific Files

Instead of having UNDELETE attempt to restore all erased files on a disk, you can specify exactly which ones to undelete using this general form:

UNDELETE *filename*

The *filename* may include wildcard characters, a drive specifier, and/or a path name.

For example, this command undeletes only TEST.TXT.

UNDELETE A:TEST.TXT

On your own, try copying several files to the disk in drive A, delete a few, and try various forms of the UNDELETE command to learn their effects.

Using Deletion Tracking to Help UNDELETE

Tracking file   A file that keeps a record of deleted files.

You can greatly improve the operation of UNDELETE by maintaining a *tracking file*. A tracking file keeps track of which files are deleted. This information is used by UNDELETE to restore an erased file. To create a tracking file, you must execute the UNDELETE command using the /T option. This causes part of UNDELETE to remain resident in memory and to keep track of files that are erased. The general form of UNDELETE that is used to load the memory-resident part is shown here.

UNDELETE /Tx

Here, x is the letter of the drive that you want to track. After this command has executed, UNDELETE creates a hidden system file called PCTRACKR.DEL on the specified drive that stores recovery information about each file erased on that drive. For example, this command creates a tracking file for drive A:

UNDELETE /Ta

Deletion tracking A method of enhancing UNDELETE that uses a tracking file to keep a record of erased files.

To see how a *deletion-tracking* file can help UNDELETE, execute this command now. Next, erase TEST.TXT and then unerase it using UNDELETE. You will see the following output:

```
Directory: A:\
File Specifications: TEST.TXT

    Delete Sentry control file not found.

    Deletion-tracking file contains     1 deleted files.
    Of those,     1 files have all clusters available,
                  0 files have some clusters available,
                  0 files have no clusters available.

    MS-DOS directory contains     1 deleted files.
    Of those,     1 files may be recovered.

Using the Deletion-tracking method.

TEST     TXT       15  7-16-93  4:09p  ...A Deleted: 7-16-93  1:43p
All of the clusters for this file are available. Undelete? (Y/N)
```

Files that have all clusters available will be fully recovered. Those with some clusters missing will be only partially recovered. Files with no clusters cannot be recovered. Now, press Y to undelete the file. This time, UNDELETE is able to use the information in the tracking file to undelete TEST.TXT. Specifically, you do not need to specify the first letter of the file name. Notice that the date and time when the file was deleted are also displayed.

It is important to understand that each disk that you track must be specified individually. That is, all drives are not automatically tracked. You can specify as many drives as you like on the same command line. For example, this tracks drives A and C:

UNDELETE /Ta /Tc

Because the /T option causes part of UNDELETE to be installed in memory, you will need to specify all drives that you want to track the first time you execute this command. You cannot use the /T option a second time just to track another disk.

TIP

By default, the /T option automatically gives you room to store information for 25 to 303 deleted files. The actual number depends on the size of the disk that you are tracking. If the limit is reached and you erase another file, then UNDELETE removes the information about the oldest deletion and replaces it with the current deletion. You can specify the number of deletions that UNDELETE will store by including a number after the /T option using this general form:

UNDELETE /T*x-num*

where *num* is the number of deletions that will be held by the file. For example, this command specifies that 50 deletions will be stored for drive C.

UNDELETE /Tc-50

The number of files tracked must be in the range of 1 through 999.

It might seem like a good idea to always specify 999 files to track. However, the more deletions that you track, the larger the tracking file becomes. In general, room for 50 to 100 is generally sufficient.

Using a Delete Sentry to Help UNDELETE

Although using a tracking file enhances the performance of UNDELETE, there is an even better way to improve its reliability. This way is called a *Delete Sentry*, and it is the highest level of protection that you can obtain using the DOS error recovery system. The Delete Sentry maintains a special directory called SENTRY into which erased files are copied. That is, when a Delete Sentry is on duty, each time you delete a file, it is copied into the SENTRY directory. Using this method, if you need to undelete a file, the file is simply copied back into your working directory. Remember, when you use either a tracking file or UNDELETE unaided, it is still possible that your erased file will be overwritten by some other file in the time between when the file was erased and when you try to recover it. Using a Delete Sentry prevents this.

Delete Sentry
A method of enhancing UNDELETE that copies erased files into a special directory called SENTRY.

The SENTRY directory will use about 7 percent of each protected disk's space. If you delete more files than will fit, the oldest files are removed to make room for the new ones. This means that it is still possible to permanently erase a file if that file is removed to make room for newly erased files. However, the level of protection offered by the Delete Sentry is still very significant.

To use a Delete Sentry, use this general form of UNDELETE:

UNDELETE /S*drive*

Here, *drive* specifies the drive to be used. If *drive* is not specified, then the current drive is assumed. This form of UNDELETE installs part of itself in memory. The memory-resident portion provides the sentry. Because the Delete Sentry is memory-resident, you must specify all the drives you want to monitor when you first install the sentry.

The deletion sentry provides the highest level of file recovery protection. It is the best protection to use if you have the disk space available to support it. Remember, the deletion sentry trades away 7 percent of your disk space for the added protection. If you cannot spare the space, then you will need to use either deletion tracking or no UNDELETE enhancements at all.

Some UNDELETE Options

UNDELETE has several options that affect how it operates. The /LIST option lists all erased files that will be recovered. (However, the files are not actually recovered.) The /ALL option undeletes files automatically without prompting. (That is, you won't be asked if you want to undelete the file(s).) The /DT option causes UNDELETE to use only the tracking file when undeleting. The /DOS option tells UNDELETE to ignore the tracking file.

Users of DOS 6 or later versions will also have the following UNDELETE options available. The /DS option causes UNDELETE to recover only those files stored in the SENTRY directory. The /U option removes (unloads) the memory-resident portion of UNDELETE. This is useful when you need to reinstall it using a different set of options. The /PURGE option erases all files in the SENTRY directory. You may want to do this to free disk space. The /STATUS option shows the protection method in effect for each drive. The /LOAD option causes UNDELETE to load its memory-resident portion using the information in the UNDELETE.INI file. (This option is generally used only by system integrators and is not discussed in this book.)

Unformatting a Disk

Perhaps the most catastrophic error that you can make is to accidentally reformat a disk that contains important information. Accidentally reformatting a disk used to mean that all data on that disk was, for all practical purposes, irretrievably gone. However, DOS 6 contains the *UNFORMAT* command, which unformats the disk and returns it to its previous state.

UNFORMAT   The DOS command that undoes the effects of an accidental format.

A disk can be unformatted because reformatting does not necessarily destroy the preexisting information on the disk. Instead, it simply reconstructs the file allocation table. The old information is still physically present on the disk. (However, disks that have been reformatted using the /U option to the FORMAT command cannot be restored.) Keep in mind that you can only successfully unformat a disk that has just been accidentally reformatted. Once that disk has been used, any attempt to unformat it will be only partially successful because new information has replaced the old.

> **CAUTION**
> Unformatting a disk destroys its current state and returns the disk to its original condition. This implies that any information you currently have on the disk will be destroyed. Therefore, don't UNFORMAT disks that haven't been accidentally reformatted because you will lose data. Further, for safety *do not* try the example in this section. UNFORMAT is a valuable command, but it must be used only if you have accidentally reformatted a disk.

Using the UNFORMAT command is straightforward and takes this general form:

UNFORMAT *drive*:

where *drive* is the drive to unformat. For example, to unformat the diskette in drive A, use this command:

UNFORMAT A:

UNFORMAT uses the information still present in the root directory and the disk's file allocation table to unformat your disk. (Remember, the old information about your disk is not necessarily destroyed by reformatting.) If the disk has not been used since it was accidentally reformatted, then UNFORMAT can use this information to successfully restore your disk. If the disk has been used, only a partial restoration is possible.

UNFORMAT has three options. The first is /L, which causes all the files and subdirectories to be displayed as the disk is unformatted. The /TEST option causes UNFORMAT to display how the disk will be unformatted, but does not actually do it. You might want to use this option if you think that the result of an UNFORMAT will be less desirable than what you currently have. Finally, the /P option sends the output of the UNFORMAT command to the printer.

Summary

In this chapter, you have learned:

- How to undelete a file using UNDELETE
- How to use deletion tracking to improve UNDELETE
- How to use a deletion sentry to improve UNDELETE
- How to unformat a disk using UNFORMAT

In the next chapter, you will learn about DOS 6's anti-virus system.

Key Terms

Delete sentry A method of enhancing UNDELETE that copies erased files into a special directory called SENTRY. If the file is later undeleted, then it is simply copied from the SENTRY directory. This is the highest level of deletion protection.

Deletion tracking A method of enhancing UNDELETE that uses a tracking file to keep a record of erased files.

Tracking file   A file that keeps a record of deleted files.

UNDELETE   The DOS command that recovers a file that has been previously erased.

UNFORMAT   The DOS command that undoes the effects of an accidental format.

Exercises

Short Answer

1. Can an erased file always be recovered? If not, why?

2. What command unerases a file?

3. What command unformats a diskette?

4. What is a tracking file?

5. What command unerases all files on drive B?

6. When no tracking file is present, what character must be specified when unerasing a file?

7. In some cases, an unerased file can be only partially restored. If this happens to a program file, can the program still be used? If not, why? Further, what types of files might be of some value if only partially restored?

8. What command do you use to cause a tracking file to be maintained for drive D?

9. If you want to undelete a file called WORKRCD.DAT that is on drive E, what command would you use?

10. What does the UNDELETE /LIST option do? What does the /ALL option do?

11. What command unformats the diskette in drive B?

12. If you accidentally UNFORMAT a diskette, will its data be lost or can it be recovered?

13. How does the Delete Sentry protect erased files?

14. What is the one disadvantage to using a Delete Sentry?

True or False

1. The /TEST option is used with UNFORMAT. _____

2. You can have tracking files for more than one disk. _____

3. Using UNDELETE, files must have been erased one at a time. _____

4. A tracking file will save information about an unlimited number of erased files. _____

5. If a tracking file is not found, neither UNFORMAT nor UNDELETE will work. _____

6. Since DOS includes UNDELETE and UNFORMAT, there is no need to be careful when erasing files or formatting diskettes. _____

7. Using the Delete Sentry means that you can always restore an accidentally erased file. _____

8. The Delete Sentry encodes erased files into a special, compacted format so that they are very small and don't take up too much disk space. _____

Activities

For the following activities, put a *copy* of your Student Data Disk into drive A.

1. Erase YOURFILE and then use UNDELETE to recover it. Notice that you must specify the first letter of the file.

2. Excute the following command:

   UNDELETE /Ta

   This causes a tracking file to be maintained for the diskette in drive A. Now, erase YOURFILE and then restore it. This time, because the tracking file is in use, you do not need to specify the first letter of the file.

3. On your own, format a diskette, copy some files of your own choosing to it, and then reformat it. Next, confirm that the diskette is reformatted and that the files you copied there are gone. Finally, UNFORMAT the diskette and confirm that the files have been restored.

Business Case Study

You and your coworkers have been using your computer to perform various business tasks, including word processing, spreadsheet analysis, and generating graphics images. One day, while you are out at a sales conference, a coworker makes a serious mistake. Here is what happens. The fellow employee wants to reuse a diskette for a new purpose. He puts the diskette into drive A and issues the command "ERASE *.*". When prompted by DOS whether he wants to erase all files, he answers "Yes". However, to his horror, after pressing (ENTER), he notices that he has forgotten to log into drive A! Instead, he is still logged into the DOS directory on drive C and has just erased all of the DOS external commands! Unfortunately, instead of stopping immediately and awaiting your return to undo the damage, he continues to use the computer for the rest of the day. When you return the next day, he tells you of the incident and asks you to repair the damage. Since he continued to use the computer, it is unlikely that you can use UNDELETE to recover all the files. It is most likely that portions of them have been overwritten. However, you try it anyway. But, just as you suspected, most of the DOS commands cannot be fully recovered. Fortunately, you have at your disposal your master DOS disk that contains all of the external DOS commands. You know that you can restore your DOS directory using this disk, but to make sure that no further mistakes occur, you first map out the steps that you must follow.

1. To prevent additional troubles, you first prepare your computer.

    a. Write-protect your DOS master diskette. This will prevent it from being accidentally erased.
    b. Insert your DOS master diskette into drive A.
    c. Make sure that you are logged into drive C and that the DOS directory is current.

2. Now that everything is ready, you restore the external DOS commands to your DOS directory.

    a. To copy the DOS files from drive A to C, you issue this command: **A:COPY A:*.* /V.** Because your DOS files are very important, you specify the /V (Verify) option, to double-check that all files are copied without error.
    b. To make sure that you did everything correctly, you list the contents of the DOS directory and of the master DOS disk in drive A. Both directory listings should report the same number of user files.

PART 5

Managing Your System

CHAPTER 15

Defending Against Viruses

CHAPTER OBJECTIVES

After completing this chapter, you should be able to:

- Understand how a virus infection takes place.
- Use MSAV.
- Use VSAFE.
- Put VSAFE in your AUTOEXEC.BAT File.

In recent years, the computer virus has caused more fear and controversy than any other type of potential trouble that can befall a system. A *computer virus* is a malicious program that differs from other programs in two ways. First, it is harmful, or at least annoying, to your computer. Second, it is capable of reproducing itself and spreading from machine to machine. Viruses are created by deviant programmers for the sole purpose of inflicting suffering on others. However, DOS 6 includes a powerful tool to help you combat viruses. This tool is called MSAV (Microsoft Anti-Virus), and its diligent use can help prevent a disastrous viral attack.

> *Computer virus*
> *A program that causes harm to your system and can duplicate itself.*

257

How a Virus Infection Takes Place

Just like with human diseases, the first line of defense against a virus is avoiding infection. If your computer is currently free from all viruses, you NEVER put any foreign disk into your computer, your computer is not part of a network, and you never connect a modem to your computer, then your computer will never get a virus. However, meeting these restrictions is difficult. Short of complete isolation, a computer system is vulnurable to a virus infection in two ways: by coming into contact with an infected disk or by communicating with another infected computer either via a network or a modem. The most likely method of acquiring a virus is by inserting an infected diskette into your computer and then copying the file or files that contain the virus to your system. It is this route of infection that makes putting unknown diskettes into your computer so risky.

Once a virus has access to your computer, the infection will generally occur in one of three ways. First, some viruses attach themselves to one of DOS's system files that contains the initial part of DOS that is loaded when your computer is first turned on. This is called a *boot-sector virus*. (In the early days of computing, starting a computer was called "boot strapping" the system, and the term *boot-sector* is commonly used to refer to that part of a disk in which the initial part of DOS resides.) Once a boot-sector virus is loaded, it is free to perpetrate its harm. It is also free to copy itself to any other diskette that is inserted into the system.

Another type of virus attaches itself to a program. When the program is executed, the virus takes over and can then perform its malicious acts, as well as copy itself to other programs on your disk or other diskettes inserted into the computer. This type of virus is called a *file-infector virus*.

The third basic type of virus is called a *Trojan horse*. A Trojan horse looks like and, in some cases, will even act like a legitimate program. However, the program is really a virus that causes damage when it is executing in your system. Once the Trojan horse is executed, it is free to copy itself to other diskettes.

Once a virus has infected your system, it will act one of two ways. First, the virus may damage your system when it is first executed. For example, a virus may erase files or corrupt files each time it is run. A second type of virus will wait until some predetermined event occurs before it harms your system. For example, a virus may wait until a certain date or until you run a certain sequence of DOS commands. This type of virus is particularly infectious because it may go unnoticed for a long time.

Whatever the type of virus, with DOS 6 you can mount an effective defense if you follow the procedures described in this chapter.

Boot-sector virus
A virus that attaches itself to the boot sector.

Boot-sector *The part of a disk on which the initial part of DOS resides.*

File-infector virus
A virus that infects a program.

Trojan horse *A virus that masquerades as a normal program.*

Using MSAV

Your first line of defense against viruses is MSAV. This command searches for viral infections on your drives and reports any that it finds.

It can also remove a virus. MSAV uses two general methods to search for viruses. First, it has a list of known viruses that it seeks. Second, it watches for signs of a virus infection. Signs of infection include changes to the boot-sector, changes to your DOS files, and changes to other executable programs. To look for changes, MSAV maintains a *checksum* of each program (and program-related) file on your disk. Loosely, a checksum is a number that is derived from a file by adding together the values of each byte in the file. MSAV then records the checksum of each file. The next time you run MSAV, it again computes the checksum for each file. If the new checksum does not agree with the previous checksum, then the file has been changed. If you did not alter this file, then the file was altered by some outside entity (probably a virus) for potentially malicious purposes. MSAV also looks for other suspicious activity.

Checksum   A number derived from a file by adding together the values of each byte in the file.

NOTE

The MSAV command supports a large number of different options to handle a number of different unusual situations. However, you will generally want to use MSAV in its default mode of operation, and it is this operation that is discussed in detail here.

The simplest way to execute MSAV is to enter it without any options on the command line. For example, enter **MSAV** now. You will see the screen shown in Figure 15-1.

As you can see, MSAV is a window-based command that provides a menu of options. You select an option using either the keyboard or the mouse. To select an option using the keyboard, use the arrow keys to position the highlight on the desired option and press (ENTER). To select an option using the mouse, position the mouse pointer over the option you want and press the left mouse button. (That is, you "click" the mouse on the option you want.) You may also select an option by pressing its associated function key. The function keys are shown on the bottom of the screen. For example, to select Detect & Clean, press the (F5) key. The drive that will be checked for viruses is shown as the

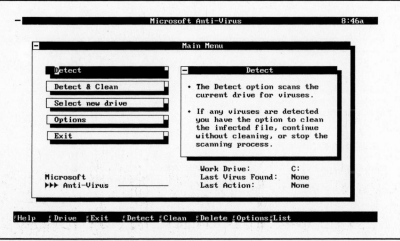

FIGURE 15-1   **The MSAV main screen**

Work Drive. By default, this will be the drive that was current when you executed MSAV.

If you want to scan your drive for viruses, but not necessarily remove any, select the Detect option. You might select this option for two reasons. First, you might simply want to know if the drive is infected with a virus, but leave any actual disinfection to a specialist. Second, when a virus is found, the Detect option asks you if you want it removed. However, you may not want to remove a virus until you have shown it to a system manager. Rarely, a file can be modified in a way that MSAV thinks is a viral infection when it isn't. In this unusual case, you can tell MSAV to skip a file that is not actually infected.

To automatically check and remove viruses from your disk, use the Detect & Clean option.

After either Detect or Detect & Clean has concluded, you will see a report similar to the one shown in Figure 15-2 regarding the status of your drive.

To select a different drive to scan for viral infection, use the Select new drive option. You will see a list of drives in your system, and you can select a new drive by using either the keyboard or the mouse. To use the keyboard, press the arrow keys to move the highlight to the desired drive and then press (ENTER). Alternatively, simply press the letter of the drive you want. To use the mouse, click on the new drive. (To leave the drive unchanged, press (ESC).)

MSAV allows you to set a number of options by selecting the Options option. For the majority of users, the default settings will be appropriate. (Also, some options are best used only by system managers.) However, feel free to explore these options on your own. You can obtain a description of each option by first highlighting it and then pressing the (F1) (Help) key. To change the state of an option, position the highlight over that option and press the space bar. (You can also change the state of an option by clicking on it using the mouse.)

To exit MSAV, either press the (ESC) key or position the mouse pointer on the small box in the upper-left corner of the MSAV screen and press the left mouse button. Then, select the Close option. Next, you will be

```
┌─────────────────────────────────────────────────────┐
│ ─        Viruses Detected and Cleaned                │
│                                                       │
│                   Checked      Infected     Cleaned  │
│                                                       │
│   Hard disks   :     1            0            0     │
│   Floppy disks :     0            0            0     │
│   Total disks  :     1            0            0     │
│                                                       │
│   COM Files    :    49            0            0     │
│   EXE Files    :   251            0            0     │
│   Other Files  :   920            0            0     │
│   Total Files  :  1220            0            0     │
│                                                       │
│   Scan Time    : 00:01:33                            │
│                                          ┌────────┐  │
│                                          │  O K   │  │
│                                          └────────┘  │
└─────────────────────────────────────────────────────┘
```

FIGURE 15-2   **A sample MSAV status report**

prompted by the double-check window shown in Figure 15-3. To terminate MSAV, press (ENTER) or select the OK box using the mouse. To cancel, press (ESC) or select the Cancel box. If you have changed an option, you can save this change by checking the Save Configuration checkbox. To do this, either click on it using the mouse or move the highlight to it (by pressing the (TAB) key) and then press the space bar. Saving the configuration causes your changes to become part of MSAV's default operation when you next execute it. (Save Configuration usually should not be checked.)

How to Use MSAV

For MSAV to be effective, it must be run whenever your computer is vulnurable to infection. This generally means on a daily basis if your computer is used in an office environment. You can either run MSAV manually or include it in your AUTOEXEC.BAT file. If you do the latter, you might want to use the /N option, which suppresses the graphical display. MSAV will then check your disk and report any problems, but does not require any user interaction. If you also specifiy the /R option, then any problems that are found are written in a file called MSAV.RPT, which you may examine using the TYPE command.

> **TIP**
> If your computer begins to act abnormally, try running MSAV. Your problems may be due to a virus.

If you want to check more than one drive when using the /N option, specify the drives on the command line. For example, this causes MSAV to check drives C and D:

MSAV C: D: /N

> **CAUTION**
> New viruses will always be invented. It is, of course, possible to create a virus that will circumvent MSAV's protection capabilities. Therefore, always be careful about what software enters your computer. If you don't know where a diskette or program came from, don't put it in your computer.

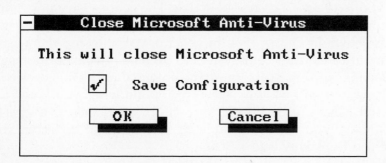

FIGURE 15-3   **The close confirmation box**

Listing Known Viruses

When running MSAV, you can obtain a list of viruses that MSAV knows about by pressing the (F9) key. To move through the list, use the (↑) and (↓) keys or use the mouse to operate the scroll bar. To receive information about a virus, first highlight it and then press (ENTER). You can also click on the desired virus using the mouse.

The virus window contains several command buttons that work like the ones you encountered when using EDIT. To select a button, first move the highlight to it by pressing (TAB) and then pressing (ENTER). Or, you can select a button by clicking on it using the mouse. (You can also select a button by holding down the (ALT) key and then pressing the highlighted letter.) The Find Next option highlights the next virus in the list; Info displays information about the highlighted virus. (This is the same information that is displayed if you select a virus from the list.) The Print option prints the list of viruses.

If you know the name of a virus and you want to see if MSAV has it listed, you can type it into the box below the list and, if it is found, it will be highlighted in the virus list window. To exit the Virus list window, press (ESC) or select the OK button.

Using VSAFE

While MSAV is effective at finding viral infections, it finds only those that are present when it is run. However, DOS also includes a program called VSAFE that monitors your system at all times, watching for any action that may indicate that a viral infection is taking place. VSAFE is an installed command. Once installed, it monitors the activity that takes place in your computer and reports any suspicious activity.

To install VSAFE, simply execute VSAFE from the command line. VSAFE supports several command line options, but most are used only by system integrators and require specialized technical knowledge beyond the scope of this book. However, a few will be examined later in this section.

When VSAFE detects an action that might indicate that a virus is attempting to infect your system, it will display a window that allows you to choose a course of action. The actions vary depending upon the type of potential trouble detected. A sample warning window is shown in Figure 15-4. In general, you can stop the activity that might be causing your system to become infected or damaged by selecting Stop. You can ignore the potential problem by selecting Continue. You will want to select this option when you know that the activity that caused VSAFE to react is normal and not a viral infection. Finally, if you are completely unsure about the error, your can reload DOS by selecting Boot.

Once you have installed VSAFE, you can alter its function by setting or clearing various options using the VSAFE control panel. To

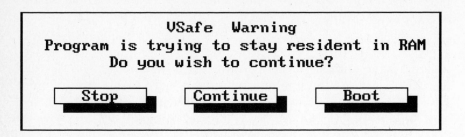

FIGURE 15-4   **A VSAFE warning window**

activate the control panel, press (ALT)-(V). You will see a window that contains eight options. These options are:

1. Warn if fixed disk is about to be formatted
2. Warn if a memory resident program is installing
3. Prevent a program from writing to the disk
4. Check program files before they are executed
5. Check all disks for boot-sector contamination
6. Warn if fixed-disk boot-sector is being altered
7. Warn if a floppy-disk boot-sector is being altered
8. Warn if a program file is being altered

By default, options 1,4, 5, and 6 are on. You can turn on or off an option when the control panel is displayed by pressing its corresponding key. For example, to turn on option 2, type 2. Each time you press the key, the option is turned on or off.

If you want to remove VSAFE from memory, press (ALT)-(U) while the control panel is displayed. You can also remove VSAFE from memory by executing it using the /U option. To close the control panel, press (ESC).

CAUTION

While it may seem wise to turn on all the VSAFE options, you may not be able to do this. For example, most application programs maintain data files that are frequently changed or updated. If this is the case with your computer, you will not be able to turn on option 3, which prevents the disk from being written to.

Putting VSAFE in Your AUTOEXEC.BAT File

Since VSAFE is an installed command, you will probably want to have it executed automatically from your AUTOEXEC.BAT file each time your computer is turned on. If you find its default settings acceptable (as most users will), then simply include VSAFE without any options.

However, if you want to turn on additional warnings or turn off any of those set by default, then you can use this form of VSAFE:

VSAFE /*n* /*n* /*n* ...

where *n* is the number of the warning (as shown previously). To turn the warning on, follow the number with a +. To turn it off, follow it with a -. For example, this executes VSAFE with warnings 3, 4, 5, and 6 on. (Remember, by default, VSAFE has warnings 1, 4, 5, and 6 on, so this command turns off number 1 and turns on number 3.)

VSAFE /1- /3+

Bear in mind that VSAFE's default warnings are adequate for most users.

Final Thoughts on Virus Protection

Protecting your computer from viral infection is an important but not cost-free endeavor. Using the highest level of virus protection provided by DOS makes your computer more cumbersome to use. For example, turning on all options to VSAFE makes your computer practically unusable for several normal, day-to-day tasks. Therefore, you must balance the level of virus protection you use against the threat level that you feel viruses pose to your system. If you work by yourself, install only name-brand software on your system, and don't put strange diskettes into your system, then your risk from a virus is quite low. However, if you work in a large office, often use strange diskettes, or if your computer is frequently used by others, then the chance of viral infection is greatly increased. The best protection against viral attacks is common sense combined with prudent use of MSAV and VSAFE.

Summary

In this chapter, you learned

- What a virus is and how one attacks your system
- How to check your system for viruses using MSAV
- How to monitor your system for possible virus attack using VSAFE

In the next chapter, you will learn how to configure your system.

Key Terms

Boot-sector   The part of a disk on which the initial part of DOS resides.

Boot-sector virus   A virus that attaches itself to the boot-sector.

Checksum   A number derived from a file by adding together the values of each byte in the file.

File-infector virus   A virus that infects a program.

Trojan Horse   A virus that masquerades as a normal program.

Computer virus   A program that causes harm to your system and can duplicate itself.

Exercises

Short Answer

1. In your own words, explain how a computer can become infected with a virus.

2. In general terms, what does MSAV do?

3. In general terms, what does VSAFE do?

4. Why is a combination of MSAV and VSAFE necessary to protect your system from harm?

5. If you want to scan your drive for viruses, but not necessarily remove any using MSAV, what option do you use?

6. What MSAV option automatically detects and removes viruses?

7. Why should you put MSAV into your AUTOEXEC.BAT file? What special command option should you use?

8. Why won't you normally want to turn on all of VSAFE's options?

9. Once installed, how do you activate VSAFE's control panel?

10. Since VSAFE is an installed command, how do you remove it from memory?

Activities

1. Check your Student Data Disk for viruses. (There shouldn't be any.) If you find a virus, report it to your instructor immediately.

16

Configuring DOS

CHAPTER OBJECTIVES

After completing this chapter, you should be able to:

- Use the MODE command.
- Change the DOS prompt.
- Create and modify your CONFIG.SYS file.
- Understand several configuration commands.
- Utilize extra memory in your system.
- Use the PATH command.
- Use the APPEND command.
- Use the ASSIGN, SUBST, and JOIN commands.
- Understand international configurations.
- Use SETVER.

You can change several things about DOS. Some affect the way DOS operates or appears, while others alter the way DOS accesses disk drives or defines devices. You can also configure DOS for use in a foreign country. In this chapter, you will learn the commands that let you configure DOS to best meet your needs.

Using the MODE Command

As you know, DOS controls the devices that constitute the computer. Some of these devices have various modes of operation. When DOS starts, these devices are set to operate in a way that applies to the widest range of situations. However, you can change the way some of the devices operate to take best advantage of how your system is configured. One of the most versatile configuration commands is MODE. You can use *MODE* to change the operation of the video adapter, the keyboard, the serial communication ports, and the printer. MODE is an external command.

> **MODE** *The DOS command that determines the operation of several devices attached to the computer.*

MODE has many forms, some of which apply only to very specialized situations. Here, we will look at the most commonly used ones.

Controlling the Video Adapter

The *video adapter* is a circuit card inside the computer that controls the monitor. Its purpose is to generate and maintain the text and graphics that you see on the screen. The two basic types of video adapters are the monochrome adapter, which can display text characters only in black and white, and the various color/graphics adapters, which can display text and graphics in color. Though uncommon, it is possible for both of these adapters to be in your computer. You can use MODE to select a video adapter or set the way that it displays information. The general form of MODE used to do this is

MODE *video-mode*

where *video mode* is one of the adapter codes shown in Table 16-1.

If you have a color/graphics adapter, you can set it to either 40- or 80-column mode and to display in either color or black and white. For example, if you have a color/graphics adapter, enter

MODE CO40

The screen will clear, and you will see the DOS prompt displayed at twice its usual size. In 40-column mode, the letters are twice as big, so only 40 can fit from side to side. For this reason, 40-column mode is almost never used. To reset the display to the normal 80-column mode, enter

MODE CO80

If you have a monochrome adapter, you cannot change its mode of operation. However, if you have two adapters in your system, you can enter

MODE MONO

to switch to the monochrome adapter.

Although fairly rare, there can sometimes be a mismatch between the color/graphics video adapter and the monitor, which causes the image to be off center (left and right) on the screen. You can shift the display left or right by using the following form of MODE:

MODE *video-adapter*, R/L, T

Video-mode	Effect
40	sets a color/graphics adapter display width to 40 columns
80	sets a color/graphics adapter display width to 80 columns
BW40	activates the color/graphics adapter and sets the width to 40 columns and the display mode to black and white
BW80	activates the color/graphics adapter and sets the width to 80 columns and the display mode to black and white
CO40	activates the color/graphics adapter and sets the width to 40 columns and the display mode to color
CO80	activates the color/graphics adapter and sets the width to 80 columns and the display mode to color
MONO	activates the monochrome adapter—the display width is always 80 columns

TABLE 16-1   **Video adapter codes**

Use R to shift the display to the right or L to shift it to the left. The display is shifted two spaces in 80-column mode and one space in 40-column mode. The T is optional; when present, it causes a test pattern to be displayed and asks you whether the screen is correct. For example, the following command

MODE CO80, L, T

produces this display:

```
01234567890123456789/.../01234567890123456789
```

```
Do you see the rightmost 9 (Y/N)?
```

If you press N, the display is shifted left and you are reprompted.

Setting the Autorepeat Rate and Delay

You can control the rate at which characters are automatically repeated when you hold a key down and set the delay before the autorepeat begins. (DOS refers to the autorepeat rate as the *typematic rate*.) To do these things, use this form of the MODE command

MODE CON RATE=*rate* DELAY=*delay*

Here, *rate* is the number of characters generated per second and *delay* is the number of quarter seconds before the autorepeat begins. The maximum value for *rate* is 32; the maximum value for *delay* is 4. You must always specify both the rate and the delay value; you cannot leave one off.

The following command sets the autorepeat feature to 25 repetitions per second with a delay of ¼ second.

MODE CON RATE=25 DELAY=1

The typematic rate will not be able to be changed on all computers.

Configuring the Printer

You can set the maximum number of characters per line and the number of lines per vertical inch that the printer will display with the following form of MODE:

MODE LPT# COLS=*length* LINES=*lines-per-inch*

where the # must be printer number 1, 2, or 3 (there can be up to three printers on the system). The *length* must be either 80 or 132, and *lines-per-inch* must be either 6 or 8. When DOS begins, the line length is 80 with 6 lines per inch. You should understand that when you select 132, the printer automatically makes each character smaller so that 132 characters can fit on one line. Selecting 8 lines per vertical inch simply puts the lines closer together.

For example, this configures the first printer for 132 columns, 8 lines per inch.

MODE LPT1 COLS=132 LINES=8

This form of mode can also accept an option called RETRY, which takes this form:

RETRY=*x*

where *x* is either E, B, P, R, or N. (The meaning of these options requires a technical knowledge beyond the scope of this course.) This option is generally used only by system integrators. However, if an application program tells you to use this option, simply append it to the end of the MODE LPT# command. Don't change this option without reason.

Configuring the Serial Port

To transfer data to external devices, a computer can use two types of ports: parallel and serial. The parallel ports are usually used for printers, and the serial ports are used for such things as modems, plotters, and other special devices. However, a printer can be connected to a serial port. The full name for the serial port—and the way it is referred to in the IBM user manuals—is the asynchronous serial communications adapter. However, *serial port* is much shorter and is the commonly used term.

The most important difference between the two is that a parallel port transmits eight bits of data (one byte) at a time, while the serial port transmits data one bit at a time (hence the name "serial"). The rate at which the bits are transmitted is measured in *bits per second* and is abbreviated as *baud*. In order for the serial port to communicate with an external device, the baud of the device must match the baud of the serial port. This is usually done automatically by the application pro-

Serial port *The type of port used for modems, plotters, and other special devices and that transmits data one bit at a time.*

Baud *The speed of transmission measured in bits per second.*

grams, but you may occasionally be told to manually set the baud. You can do this by using the MODE command with the general form

MODE COM# *baud*

where # is the adapter number 1 through 4, and *baud* is the baud setting, which must be one of the following numbers: 110, 150, 300, 600, 1200, 2400, 4800, 9600, 19200. The larger the number, the faster the transfer rate. Though only the first two digits are necessary, you can use the whole number. For example, to set COM1 to 9600 baud, enter

MODE COM1 9600

The default setting for the serial ports is 1200 baud.

The serial ports have several other attributes that may need to be set to something other than their default values. Occasionally, you may have to set these values. Though it is beyond the scope of this book to explain the technical details of these attributes, we will present a brief overview. A serial port uses one of the following: even, odd, or no parity. The *parity* setting determines if and how error checking will be performed. No parity means that no error checking occurs. The parity of the serial port and the external device communicated with must be the same. The default setting is even. The number of *data bits* determines how many bits are used to transfer information. This number can be between 5 through 8, with the default value being 7. The number of *stop bits* determines how many nondata bits occur between the data bits. This can be either 1 or 2; the default is 2 for 110 baud and 1 for the others. The general form of MODE used to set all the information for the port is

MODE COM# *baud*, *parity*, *data-bits*, *stop-bits*

where *parity* is "E" for even, "O" for odd, or "N" for none. The *data-bits* and *stop-bits* are numbers. For example, to set the COM1 to 300 baud, even parity, 8 data bits, and 2 stop bits, enter

MODE COM1 300, E, 8, 2

A final parameter that you can optionally specify when configuring the serial port follows the stop-bits. This value is called *retry*. It is similar to the retry option when configuring the printer and it may have these values: E, B, P, R or N. (An explanation of these parameters is beyond the scope of this course.) You should only specify the retry parameter if you are told to do so by your instructor or by the instructions that accompany an application program.

Redirecting Printer Output

If you have a serial printer, you can redirect all printer output to it by using this form of MODE:

MODE LPT#=COM#

where # is the number 1 through 3 for LPT or 1 through 4 for COM. For example, the following command switches the default printer to COM1:

MODE LPT1=COM1

> **NOTE**
> Some computers also allow the parity value to be specified as M (mark) or S (space), but this is quite rare.

Now all printer output, including that produced by the PRINT SCREEN command, will be directed to COM1.

To reset the printer to its default, use this form:

MODE LPT*n*

where *n* is a number between 1 and 3. For example, this resets LPT1.

MODE LPT1

Redirecting the printer is most useful when you have two or more printers attached to your computer.

Checking Status

You can see the status of each device controlled by MODE by entering MODE by itself. To see the status of a specific *device*, use this form.

MODE *device*

For example, to see the status of COM1, use this command:

MODE COM1

Changing the DOS Prompt

By default, the DOS system prompt displays the current drive followed by a > symbol. However, you can change the prompt to display practically anything you want by using the *PROMPT* command. The general form of the PROMPT command is

PROMPT *message*

> **PROMPT** *The DOS command that changes the form of the command line prompt.*

where *message* is a string that will become the new system prompt. For example, enter

PROMPT My Computer:

Now DOS displays the prompt as

`My Computer:`

To return the DOS prompt to its default message, enter PROMPT without a message.

Though short prompts are usually best, the prompting message can be up to 128 characters long. For example, you might use a prompt like the following to discourage unauthorized use:

`PROMPT Warning: authorized users only!`

You can include special characters and other information in the prompt by using one or more of the codes shown in Table 16-2. All PROMPT codes begin with a dollar sign. Because the characters >, <, | , and = have special meanings when they appear on a DOS command line, you must use the proper code if you want one of these characters to appear in the prompt.

One of the most popular prompts is created with the following command:

PROMPT PG

Code	Meaning
$$	dollar sign
$b	| character
$d	system date
$e	escape character
$g	> character
$h	a backspace
$l	< character
$n	current drive letter
$p	current directory path
$q	= character
$t	current time
$v	DOS version number
$_	carriage return-linefeed sequence

TABLE 16-2   **The PROMPT codes**

This causes the current directory path name to be displayed, followed by the > standard DOS prompt. For example, if the current path is C:\ACCOUNTS\AP, the DOS prompt will look like this:

```
C:\ACCOUNTS\AP>
```

This prompt is so popular because it makes it easy to tell what directory you are in. You might want to put this prompt command into the AUTOEXEC.BAT file so that it automatically executes upon startup.

Another popular prompt is formed with the following command:

PROMPT $D $T PG

This causes the current system date and time to be displayed along with the directory path. If the date were 12/2/94, the time 12 noon, and the root directory were current, the prompt would look like this:

```
Fri 12-02-94 12:00:00.00 C:\>
```

Experiment to see what sort of prompt you like best and then place that PROMPT command into the AUTOEXEC.BAT file. A custom prompt is a good way to personalize your system.

Using the CONFIG.SYS File

DOS has a number of features that can be set only when it begins execution. That is, some aspects of DOS may not be changed after the DOS prompt has been displayed because they affect the fundamental operation of the system. To alter these types of attributes, you must use a special configuration file called *CONFIG.SYS* and some special DOS configuration commands. When DOS begins execution, it looks in the root directory of the disk from which it was loaded for the file CONFIG.SYS. If it is present, DOS reads the given configuration commands and sets the specified parameters accordingly. If CONFIG.SYS is not found, DOS uses its default settings. When you create or alter

CONFIG.SYS A special file that contains configuration information used by DOS when it first starts executing. It must be in the root directory of the disk that loads DOS.

the CONFIG.SYS file, none of the changes will take effect until you restart DOS.

If DOS was installed on your computer in the normal way, then you will already have a CONFIG.SYS file. In general, you will not want to remove anything from the file. The instructions contained in the file are necessary to support the operation of DOS and other application programs you may have. However, you may want to change a few of the commands to work differently, as you will see in the next few sections. You may also want to add one or more commands to this file. The common configuration commands are discussed now.

CAUTION

Many configuration commands are intended only for programmers or people specifically in charge of configuring a system. For example, several configuration commands deal with networks, extended memory management, and work groups. All of these areas require specialized knowledge that is beyond what the average user has. Also, changing your CONFIG.SYS file in an incorrect manner can cause your system to function incorrectly. Therefore, if you have any reservations about using the commands discussed in this section, consult your instructor or computer laboratory monitor before proceeding. This book explains those configuration commands that you, personally, are likely to need.

BREAK

As you know, the (CTRL)-(BREAK) or (CTRL)-(C) key combinations are used to cancel a command or application program and return to DOS. However, DOS's default method of operation only checks for a (CTRL)-(BREAK) when I/O operations take place to the standard input, output, or printer devices, or to the serial port. Some programs may not perform any of these operations for quite some time and, therefore, may not respond quickly to a (CTRL)-(BREAK) command. For example, a database program that is doing a sort operation on a very large file may not perform any I/O operations for several minutes. You can instruct DOS to check for a (CTRL)-(BREAK) more frequently by placing the *BREAK* command in the CONFIG.SYS file, as shown here:

BREAK=ON

Keep in mind, however, that this will cause all commands and programs to run slower because DOS is spending more time checking to see if you have pressed (CTRL)-(BREAK).

BREAK   The configuration command that causes DOS to check more frequently for the (CTRL)-(BREAK) (or (CTRL)-(C)) keypress.

COUNTRY

Different countries and different languages may vary in how they display and define the time, date, and currency symbols. Also, collating sequence and certain capitalization conventions may differ. For example, in Europe the comma is used as a decimal separator instead of the period. Generally, if you live in a country other than the United States, your computer will, by default, be configured to that country's standards. However, should you need to change DOS to conform to the conventions of a different country, you can use the *COUNTRY* command to accomplish this. The COUNTRY command takes the general form

COUNTRY = *code*

where *code* must be one of the codes listed in Table 16-3.

For example, the following command configures DOS for Spain:

COUNTRY = 034

If the country you want is not listed, you must choose the one whose conventions are the closest to what you need.

DOS contains extended support for countries with special character requirements, and a character set definition can be specified with the COUNTRY command. This issue is covered at the end of this chapter when we discuss foreign language versions of DOS.

DEVICE

The parts of DOS that control the various devices of the computer are called *device drivers*. All the drivers necessary for the operation of a standard configuration of the computer are included in DOS when it begins execution. However, some special device drivers are optional, and you must tell DOS to load them if you want to use them.

Some device drivers are supplied by application programs and some are supplied with DOS. The ones supplied by DOS 6 are shown here.

COUNTRY   *The configuration command that determines a number of country-related items.*

Device driver   *A special program used by DOS to help control a device.*

ANSI.SYS	**EGA.SYS**	**RAMDRIVE.SYS**
CHKSTATE.SYS	**EMM386.EXE**	**SETVER.EXE**
DISPLAY.SYS	**HIMEM.SYS**	**SMARTDRV.EXE**
DRIVER.SYS	**INTERLINK.EXE**	
DBLSPACE.SYS	**POWER.EXE**	

Country	Code	Country	Code
Arabic	785	**Israel—Hebrew**	972
Australia	061	**Italy**	039
Belgium	032	**Japan**	081
Brazil	055	**Korea**	082
Canada—English	001	**Latin America**	003
Canada—French	002	**Netherlands**	031
Czechoslovakia	042	**Norway**	047
Chinese	086	**Poland**	048
Chinese (Taiwan)	088	**Portugal**	351
Chinese (mainland)	086	**Spain**	034
Denmark	045	**Sweden**	046
English (generic)	061	**Switzerland**	041
Finland	358	**United Kingdom**	044
France	033	**United States**	001
Germany	049	**Yugoslavia**	038
Hungary	036		

TABLE 16-3   **The DOS country codes**

Also, you may have other device drivers to handle special hardware. For example, a mouse typically requires a special device driver. An overview of the most commonly used of these device drivers is presented here.

To tell DOS to load a device driver, use the DEVICE command, which takes the general form

DEVICE = *device-driver*

We will examine the function and use of the DOS device drivers in turn.

ANSI.SYS

Occasionally, an application program will instruct you to load the ANSI.SYS device driver, which enables DOS to understand an additional method of controlling the cursor's position on the screen. ANSI.SYS can make it easier for some types of application programs to use the screen.

If you need to load this driver, use the following command in the CONFIG.SYS file:

DEVICE = ANSI.SYS

NOTE

If your device drivers are not in the root directory, then be sure to specify the correct path so that DOS can locate them. For example, if they are in the DOS directory on drive C, then use this line:

DEVICE = C:\DOS\ANSI.SYS

Since all modern versions of DOS store the DOS files in the DOS directory of drive C, the commands in this section will reflect this. However, if your computer is organized differently, be sure to make the appropriate corrections.

RAMDRIVE.SYS

The one device driver that you will probably want to use is RAMDRIVE.SYS, which is used to create a virtual disk drive in RAM (sometimes referred to as a *RAM-disk*). A virtual disk simulates the operation of a disk drive using RAM rather than the magnetic surface of the disk to hold the files. As far as your programs are concerned, a virtual disk looks and acts just like a regular disk drive. But, there is one big difference that you will see and appreciate: virtual disks are much faster than standard disk drives because they run at the speed of the computer's memory, which is always faster than the transfer rate of a disk drive. However, this speed has its price. The virtual disk effectively reduces the amount of available memory of the system. While this is often not a problem, some application programs may require so much memory that a virtual disk cannot be used. You should also be aware that when the power is turned off, or if the computer is restarted, the contents of what is stored in the virtual disk are lost. Therefore, be sure to copy files that you wish to save to an actual disk before concluding a session at the computer.

The basic form of the RAMDRIVE.SYS command is

DEVICE = RAMDRIVE.SYS *total-size sector-size entries*

where *total-size* is the size of the virtual disk in kilobytes, which must be in the range 4 through 32,767. The default value is 64K, but this is usually too small to be of any value. If you specify a value larger than can be allocated, RAMDRIVE adjusts it to the largest amount that will fit in memory. The *sector-size* specifies how large to make the sector size and must be 128, 256, or 512 bytes. The default value is 512, which is generally adequate. The *entries* argument specifies the number of directory entries to be allowed in the root by the virtual disk. This value is 64 by default and is usually a good choice, though you can specify any number between 2 and 1024.

The following command in CONFIG.SYS creates a virtual disk that is 384K bytes in size, uses 128-byte sectors, and has 64 root directory entries.

DEVICE = C:\DOS\RAMDRIVE.SYS 384 128 64

Several computers have what is called extended memory, which is memory that is not directly usable by DOS but may be used by programs running under DOS. (You will learn more about extended memory, and its close cousin expanded memory, later in the next section.) If you have extended memory, you can use it for the virtual disk by placing the /E option at the end of the RAMDRIVE command. For example, the following command tells RAMDRIVE to use the 512K bytes of extended memory of the computer.

DEVICE = C:\DOS\RAMDRIVE.SYS 512 /E

If your computer has expanded memory, which is another form of memory not normally usable by DOS but which RAMDRIVE can use, then you can tell RAMDRIVE to use it by specifying the /A option.

When RAMDRIVE.SYS is installed during startup, you will see a message similar to this:

```
Microsoft RAMDrive version 3.07 virtual disk X:
```

where *X* will be the letter of the virtual disk.

CAUTION

Use of a virtual disk is highly recommended because of the dramatic increase in speed. But, once you turn the computer off, or restart DOS, anything stored on a RAM disk is lost unless previously copied to a real disk.

SMARTDRV.EXE

Another device driver that you will probably want to add to your CONFIG.SYS file is called SMARTDRV.EXE. SMARTDRV.EXE speeds up disk operations. After it is installed, some of your application programs that make heavy use of the disk will run faster. This device driver requires either extended or expanded memory.

To speed up disk operations, put this line in your CONFIG.SYS file:

DEVICE = C:\DOS\SMARTDRV.EXE

SMARTDRV.EXE has several options that can affect its performance. However, the use of these options requires significant knowledge about how your computer and DOS function. As such, they are best left to specialists.

FILES and FCBS

File control block   A region of memory used by DOS to store information about an open file.

FILES   The configuration command that specifies the number of files that may be open at any one time.

FCBS   The configuration command that specifies the number of file control blocks that are available for use.

You can specify the number of files that may concurrently be open and the number of file control blocks (FCBS) that may concurrently be in use. (A *file control block* is a region of memory used by DOS to store information about an open file.) The default values given to these items are acceptable in most cases, but some application programs may require you to change them in order to run correctly.

The number of concurrently open files is 8 by default. If you need to change this, use the *FILES* command, which has the general form

FILES = *num*

where *num* is a number between 8 and 255. For example, the following command sets the number of files to 10:

FILES = 10

To change the number of file control blocks, use the *FCBS =* command, which has the general form

FCBS = *num*

where *num* is the total number of file control blocks. It must be between 1 and 255; the default is 4. For example, the following command tells DOS to allow 12 file control blocks.

FCBS =12

> **NOTE**
> **Many application programs require 20 or more files or FCBs, so don't be surprised if you need to change these values in your CONFIG.SYS file. (However, only do so if the instructions that accompany your application program tell you to do so.)**

INSTALL

INSTALL   The configuration command that is used to install one or more of DOS's installable commands.

The *INSTALL* command is used to install the following DOS commands from within your CONFIG.SYS file: FASTOPEN.EXE, KEYB.COM, NLSFUNC.EXE, and SHARE.EXE. SHARE is used in networking, and NLSFUNC is used to provide extended foreign language support. We will look at KEYB later in this chapter and FASTOPEN in another chapter. Depending upon how you use your computer, other commands may need to be installed using INSTALL.

The commands installed by INSTALL may also be executed at the DOS prompt. Thus, the use of INSTALL is largely a convenience.

The general form of the INSTALL command is

INSTALL *filename*

where *filename* is the name of the file to be installed.

LASTDRIVE

DOS automatically knows how many *physical* disk drives are on your system. However, because it is possible to have more *logical* drives—such as those created using RAMDRIVE—you can use the *LASTDRIVE* command to increase the number of drives allowed. The general form of LASTDRIVE is

LASTDRIVE = *letter*

where *letter* is the drive letter and must be between A and Z.

> *LASTDRIVE The configuration command that specifies the letter of the last disk drive in the system.*

REM

You can put a comment into your CONFIG.SYS file by preceding it with the REM command. Whatever follows REM on the same line is ignored when DOS processes the file.

Bypassing the CONFIG.SYS File

Beginning with DOS 6, you can cause DOS to ignore the configuration file when your computer starts. There is one good reason why you might want to do this: If you incorrectly change the CONFIG.SYS file, your computer may not work at all! Therefore, if you make a change to CONFIG.SYS and your computer will not work, press and hold the (F5) key after DOS prints the message "Starting MS-DOS". Hold the key until the command prompt is displayed. Once you see the command prompt, you can correct your CONFIG.SYS file and then restart your computer.

Pressing (F5) also causes the AUTOEXEC.BAT file to be skipped. Because both the CONFIG.SYS and AUTOEXEC.BAT have been by-passed, your computer will be configured in its default state. Therefore, some things will function or look different than normal.

If you know which configuration command is causing the trouble, you can still make DOS execute the rest of the CONFIG.SYS file by pressing and releasing the (F8) key when the "Starting MS-DOS" message is displayed. This causes DOS to ask you before executing each command, which allows you to manually bypass the incorrect command while leaving the rest of the configurations intact.

Using NUMLOCK

You can control whether Num Lock is on or off when DOS begins running. As you know, the numeric keypad generates either numbers or arrow keys, depending upon the state of the (NUM LOCK) key. Generally, Num Lock is on by default. However, to turn Num Lock off when DOS begins, include this line in your CONFIG.SYS file:

NUMLOCK = OFF

If Num Lock is off by default on your computer and you want it on, use this command to turn it on when DOS starts:

NUMLOCK = ON

Using Extra Memory

In its default mode of operation, DOS can utilize only 640,000 bytes of memory in your computer. However, it is possible for your computer to actually contain far more memory than this. In fact, many application programs routinely use this extra memory. The extra memory can take three forms: *extended*, *expanded*, and the *upper memory area*. *Extended memory* follows normal memory. Most computers today come with extended memory. *Expanded memory* is specialized memory that is accessed only as needed and requires special software drivers. (Only a few computers come with expanded memory.) The upper memory area is the 384K of memory that is left over in the first one megabyte of RAM in your system. Some of this memory is used by the computer to support the video adapters, but some is generally free for other uses. DOS 6 has some options that allow you to utilize more than just the first 640K of memory.

> **NOTE**
> The commands and device drivers discussed here are technical in nature. For this reason, they are presented with little discussion of the details to their operation. However, you should feel free to use them; they will increase the efficiency of your computer.

The device driver HIMEM.SYS aids in the management of your extended memory and is required by other memory management commands. To use HIMEM, put this line in your CONFIG.SYS file.

DEVICE=C:\DOS\HIMEM.SYS

> **NOTE**
> HIMEM can be used only if your computer has an 80286, 80386, or 80486 processor that has extended memory. Specifically, HIMEM will not work with an original IBM PC or XT.

You can have the resident portion of DOS loaded into extended memory by putting this command in your CONFIG.SYS file:

DOS=HIGH

This command must follow HIMEM.SYS. The advantage of loading DOS into extended memory is that it frees normal memory, allowing more memory for application programs.

The DOS configuration command has a second function, which has this form:

DOS=UMB

This command is used to help DOS manage extended memory and is required by some other DOS commands.

Extended memory
Memory in your computer that begins with the first 384K bytes above normal memory.

Expanded memory
Memory in your computer that is other than normal or extended.

> **NOTE**
> If you use the UMB option, then you will also need to use the EMM386 device driver, described shortly.

You can combine both HIGH and UMB by putting this command in your CONFIG.SYS:

DOS=HIGH,UMB

If your computer has an 80386 or an 80486 processor, then you can use the EMM386.EXE command to allow programs that use expanded memory to be run in extended memory by simulating expanded memory. This command also helps DOS further manage extended memory and the upper memory area. In addition, it is needed if you use the DOS=UMB command. To use expanded memory, put this line in your CONFIG.SYS file:

DEVICE=C:\DOS\EMM386.EXE

Once you install the DOS and EMM386 configuration commands, you can use the *LOADHIGH* (LH for short) command to run programs in your computer's upper memory area. It takes this general form:

LOADHIGH *filename*

where *filename* is the name of the program you want to run. (It can include a path and drive specifier, too.) For example, to run CHKDSK in the upper memory area, use this command:

LOADHIGH CHKDSK

Keep in mind that if, for any reason, LOADHIGH cannot load the specified program, then it is loaded into normal memory and executed.

> *LOADHIGH   The DOS command that runs a command in expanded memory.*

REMEMBER

LOADHIGH is used to execute a program in the upper memory area. However, from your point of view, the following two command lines will produce identical results:

C>CHKDSK
C>LOADHIGH CHKDSK

The only difference is where the programs reside while executing.

After you have installed EMM386, you can use the DEVICEHIGH configuration command to load device drivers into the upper memory area. Unlike LOADHIGH, DEVICEHIGH works only in your CONFIG.SYS file. DEVICEHIGH uses the same syntax as DEVICE. If it cannot load a device driver into extended memory, it will load it into normal memory.

Because memory management varies widely among computers, consult your owner's manual for further instructions about managing and maximizing memory of your own computer.

Using the PATH Command

Until now, whenever you needed to execute a command or program, the file had to be in the current working directory. However, if you are using the command prompt, you can tell DOS to look in other directories for external commands, programs, and batch files by using the *PATH* command. The general form of PATH is

PATH *path-list*

where *path-list* is a list of paths, separated by a semicolon, that will be searched. You cannot use spaces in the path list.

To understand how PATH works, assume that a disk has the directory structure shown here.

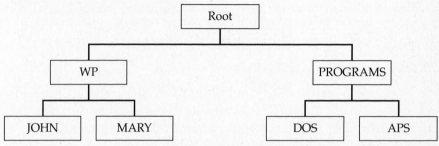

Further assume that all DOS external commands are in the DOS directory and all application programs are in the APS directory. To allow the access of any DOS external command or application program from any directory, enter

PATH \PROGRAMS\DOS;\PROGRAMS\APS

Now, whenever a command is given to DOS that is not internal, DOS will first check the current directory. If it is not found, DOS then begins checking, in order, those directories specified by the PATH command, beginning with the \PROGRAMS\DOS directory. If the command is not found there, DOS next searches the \PROGRAMS\APS directory.

To see what the current path is, simply enter PATH with no arguments. To reset the path to its default, enter

PATH ;

Remember, setting a search path with PATH causes DOS to search the specified directories for .EXE, .COM, and .BAT files. You cannot access data files with the PATH command.

The APPEND Command

The *APPEND* command gives you access to files in other directories and operates much like PATH except that it can work with any type of file. The general form of APPEND is

APPEND *path-list*

where *path-list* is a semicolon-separated list of paths. APPEND is both an internal and external command. The first time that APPEND is executed, it is loaded from disk. After the first time, however, it becomes part of DOS's internal commands. As with PATH, there can be no spaces in the path list.

Assume the same directory structure that we used with the PATH command. This APPEND command allows you to access data files in the JOHN and MARY directories:

APPEND \WP\JOHN;\WP\MARY

Now the data files in these directories can be accessed from any other directory. However, they will not show up in a directory listing of any other directory. Nor can you execute commands or programs in the appended directory.

To see which directories are currently appended to the current one, enter **APPEND** with no arguments. To cancel an APPEND, enter

APPEND ;

The APPEND command has several options. To allow application programs to be executed from appended directories, specify the /X:ON option. To prevent this, use /X:OFF. The default is off. This option must be specified the first time you execute APPEND.

The /PATH:ON option allows a program to search the appended directories even if a certain directory is specified. This option is on by default. /PATH:OFF suspends searching when a full path is specified.

Finally, the /E option gives DOS access to the appended directory list. The /E option may be used only the first time APPEND is executed. It is primarily of use to programmers, but you might have an application program that requires this option. If so, just follow the instructions that come with that program.

CAUTION

At this point you might be tempted to simply APPEND all directories together so that you can reach any file in any directory at any time. But this is a bad idea for two reasons. First, it negates the basic philosophy of tree-structured directories and can easily make it impossible for you to correctly manage your files. Second, although you can read a file from any directory, if an application program writes a file, it will be written in the current directory. This means that if you edit a file in the JOHN directory while the current directory is MARY, then saving that file writes it to MARY, leaving the original version in JOHN unchanged.

ASSIGN

You can cause DOS to reroute an I/O request for one drive to another by using the *ASSIGN* command. For example, you can make all disk I/O options that specify drive A actually go to drive B. The general form of ASSIGN is

ASSIGN *old-drive = new-drive*

ASSIGN is an external command.

If you have two floppy drives, try the following command:

ASSIGN A = B

Now put your DOS work disk in B and enter

DIR A:

ASSIGN   The DOS command that reroutes an I/O request for one drive to another.

NOTE

ASSIGN may not be included in your version of DOS 6. If it is not, skip this section.

As you can see, the B drive is activated.

If you have a fixed disk, put a DOS diskette in A and try this sequence of commands:

ASSIGN C = A
DIR C:

This activates the A drive.

You can specify more than one drive reassignment at a time. For example, the following command switches drives A and B:

ASSIGN A = B B = A

To reset the drive assignments to their original values, enter ASSIGN with no arguments. To see the current drive reassignments, use this form of ASSIGN:

ASSIGN /STATUS

The ASSIGN command's principal use is to allow application programs originally written under the assumption that the computer would have two floppy drives called A and B to take advantage of a fixed disk.

Using the SUBST Command

SUBST The DOS command that lets you specify a drive specifier that refers to either another drive or directory.

The external command *SUBST* lets you specify a drive specifier that may refer to either another drive or a directory. This drive specifier is conceptually similar to a nickname. SUBST has the general form

SUBST *nickname: drive-name:\path*

where *nickname* is the new drive letter that can be used to refer to *drive-name\path*. For example, the following command allows you to refer to the A drive as E (as well as A).

SUBST E: A:

You can also substitute a drive specifier for a subdirectory that is on the same disk. For example, assume the directory structure below on drive C:

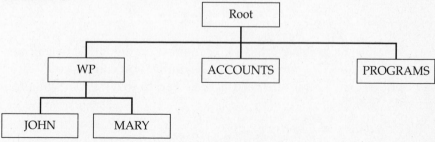

After executing the following command,

SUBST E: C:\WP\MARY

you may now refer to the \WP\MARY directory as if it were drive E.

The drive letter that you select as a nickname must be less than or equal to E unless you have used a LASTDRIVE command to the contrary in your CONFIG.SYS file.

You can display the current substitutions by entering SUBST with no arguments. If substitution of E for \WP\MARY has been made, for example, SUBST will display the following:

```
E: => C:\WP\MARY
```

To remove a substitution, use the general form

SUBST *nickname* /D

The SUBST command exists to allow application programs to be used that do not recognize path names. Although most programs available today recognize full DOS path names, very early programs did not. But these early programs do recognize drive specifiers, so you can use SUBST as a way of making a program work correctly with directories. However, the likelihood of your coming across a program that does not recognize path names is becoming increasingly small.

JOIN

The *JOIN* command allows the directory of one disk to be connected to a directory on a different disk so that the second directory can access the first disk's files. JOIN is an external command with the general form

JOIN *first-drive joined-drive:\directory*

where *first-drive* is the drive specifier of the drive that will be joined to *joined-drive* as directory *directory*.

For example, the following command joins the A drive to the B drive in the directory B:\ADRIVE.

JOIN A: B:\ADRIVE

If drive B is made current, a directory listing will show the directory ADRIVE. You can switch to this directory the way you switch to other directories by using the CD command. To put it differently, after the preceding JOIN command, all references to files on A will be made as if they are in the ADRIVE directory of B.

You can see what is joined to what by entering JOIN with no arguments. To cancel a joining, use the general form

JOIN *first-drive* /D

JOIN has a number of restrictions to its use. The directory name that you specify for access to the joined drive must be empty or nonexistent. You cannot join the currently selected drive because the drive name for the joining drive becomes invalid immediately following the JOIN command. Further, do not use JOIN if SUBST or ASSIGN has been used on either of the drives participating in the command. Finally, do not use the commands BACKUP, DISKCOPY, FORMAT, RESTORE, LABEL, RECOVER, CHKDSK, SYS, FDISK, or DISKCOMP when one drive has been joined to another.

> *JOIN*   The DOS command that joins one disk to another.

> **NOTE**
> **Your version of DOS 6 may not include the JOIN command. It it does not, skip this section.**

> **REMEMBER**
> **The commands ASSIGN and JOIN are largely obsolete. It is possible that your version of DOS no longer includes them. They are included in this book for completeness.**

International Configurations

As you learned when reading about the CONFIG.SYS file, several conventions differ among countries such as how the time, date, and currency symbols are defined. However, beyond that, several non-English languages require some additional characters, some accented characters, or both. Also, the exact layout of the keyboard will differ because of the inclusion of these different characters. (For the keyboard layouts for other countries and languages, refer to your DOS manual.) DOS allows you to change the configuration of the keyboard and which characters are actually displayed through the use of the KEYB command.

Keep in mind that configuring DOS for a language other than English does not cause DOS to translate any messages—all DOS prompts and commands remain in English.

The KEYB Command

KEYB   The DOS command that configures the keyboard for use with a language other than English or for use in another country.

Using the *KEYB* command, DOS allows you to change how it interprets the signals from the keyboard to accommodate the alternate layouts used by foreign countries. Fortunately, if you live in the country in which the computer was purchased, the proper keyboard layout has, most likely, been correctly configured by the dealer. This section presents a brief overview just so you know something about the KEYB command.

DOS supplies several files with the extension .CPI. These are *code page information* files, which hold the codes for the various keyboard and printer character sets. Table 16-4 shows the countries supported along with their keyboard and code page codes. (Because this list is frequently updated, your copy of DOS may be somewhat different from that shown in the table.)

If you live in a country that uses code page 437, you needn't worry about code page switching. If you do not, refer to your DOS user manual for explicit instructions on how to switch to the proper code page. (Generally, if you live in one of these countries, your computer will be preconfigured for you.)

The general form of the external KEYB command is

KEYB *keyboard, code-page, path*

where *keyboard* is a keyboard code for the country desired, *code-page* is the proper code page, and *path* is the path to the KEYBOARD.SYS file. You don't usually specify the last two arguments, allowing them to default to the current code page and the root directory. For example, to switch to a French-speaking Swiss keyboard, enter the following command:

KEYB SF

You should try this now. Notice that the positions of the Y and the Z are reversed on the French keyboard.

Country	Keyboard Code	Code Page Code
Australia	US	437
Belgium	BE	437
Brazil	BR	437
Canada—English	US	437
Canada—French	CF	863
Czechoslovakia	CZ	850
Denmark	DK	865
Finland	SU	437
France	FR	437
Germany	GR	437
Hungary	HU	850
Italy	IT	437
Latin America	LA	437
Netherlands	NL	437
Norway	NO	865
Poland	PL	850
Portugal	PO	860
Spain	SP	437
Sweden	SV	437
Switzerland—French	SF	437
Switzerland—German	SG	437
United Kingdom	UK	437
United States	US	437
Yugoslavia	YU	850

TABLE 16-4   **Code page and keyboard codes**

TIP

If you have used the KEYB command to switch the keyboard for use in another country, you can switch back to the U.S.-style keyboard at any time by pressing (CTRL)-(ALT) (F1). To return to the other language, press (CTRL)-(ALT) (F2).

If you want to put KEYB in your CONFIG.SYS file, use this form:

INSTALL=C:\DOS\KEYB.COM *keyboard, country-code, path*

If the KEYBOARD.SYS file is not in the root directory, then be sure to specify its location. For example, this KEYB configuration command sets DOS for French Canadian use. It assumes that KEYBOARD.SYS is in the C:\DOS directory.

INSTALL=C:\DOS\KEYB.COM CF, 863, C:\DOS\KEYBOARD.SYS

You can also specify a keyboard ID code using the KEYB command. The reason for this is that some foreign countries use more than one keyboard. These countries and codes are shown in Table 16-5. In most cases, you will never need to use them. To specify a code, use the /ID option, which takes this general form:

/ID:*nnn*

Country	Keyboard ID
France	120 and 189
Italy	141 and 142
United Kingdom	168 and 166

TABLE 16-5   **The KEYB keyboard ID codes**

where *nnn* is the keyboard ID. For example, this specifies the French keyboard using the ID 120.

KEYB FR /ID:120

Using SETVER

SETVER   The DOS command that tricks a program into thinking that it is using a different version of DOS.

For somewhat complex, technical reasons, some programs are very sensitive to the version of DOS being used to run them. In some cases, a program that is designed to run using DOS version 3.3, for example, will not work correctly with DOS 6. To circumvent this problem, DOS includes the *SETVER* command, which allows you to tell DOS what version it is supposed to act like when running a specific program. It takes this general form:

SETVER *filename version*

Here, *filename* is the name of the program, and *version* is the DOS version number that the specified program requires. For example, if your word processor is called WP.EXE and it requires DOS version 4 to run correctly, then specifying this command will allow you to use the word processor with DOS 6:

SETVER WP.EXE 4.00

When you use SETVER as shown here, you are changing the DOS *version table*. However, DOS reads this table only when it first begins execution, so you will need to restart your system in order for the command to be effective. You can add as many programs as you like to the version table.

You can view the version table by entering **SETVER** without any parameters. Most likely, you will see some predefined entries, which are provided by DOS.

You can remove a program from the version table using this general form:

SETVER *filename* /DELETE

If you want no output displayed when deleting a file from the version table, you can add the /QUIET option. (This may be useful in batch files.)

> **CAUTION**
>
> It is best not to "fool" your program into working correctly. Undesired or harmful side effects may occur. It is better to obtain a new version of a troublesome program that runs correctly with your version of DOS. In

general, avoid old versions of either DOS or your application programs. The best procedure to follow is to keep your computer's software current. The reason for this is simple, if aggravating: software vendors typically provide customer support for only their latest software versions. If you have an old version, you might be out of luck if you encounter trouble!

Summary

In this chapter, you learned a number of ways to configure your system, including

- Using the MODE command
- Changing the DOS prompt
- Creating a CONFIG.SYS file
- Setting up a virtual disk
- Using PATH and APPEND
- Changing the way that DOS accesses the disk drives
- Using extended and expanded memory
- Using the SETVER command

   In the next chapter, you will learn about managing your disks.

Key Terms

APPEND   The DOS command that tells DOS what directories to search to find any type of file.

ASSIGN   The DOS command that reroutes an I/O request for one drive to another.

Baud   The speed of transmission measured in bits per second.

BREAK   The configuration command that causes DOS to check more frequently for the (CTRL)-(BREAK) (or (CTRL)-(C)) keypress.

CONFIG.SYS   A special file that contains configuration information used by DOS when it first starts executing. It must be in the root directory of the disk that loads DOS.

COUNTRY   The configuration command that determines a number of country-related items.

DEVICE   The configuration command that is used to load a device driver.

Device driver   A special program used by DOS to help control a device.

Expanded memory   Memory in your computer that is other than normal or extended.

Extended memory   Memory in your computer that begins with the first 384K bytes above normal memory.

FCBS   The configuration command that specifies the number of file control blocks that are available for use.

File control block   A region of memory used by DOS to store information about an open file.

FILES   The configuration command that specifies the number of files that may be open at any one time.

INSTALL   The configuration command that is used to install one or more of DOS's installable commands.

JOIN   The DOS command that joins one disk to another.

KEYB   The DOS command that configures the keyboard for use with a language other than English or for use in another country.

LASTDRIVE   The configuration command that specifies the letter of the last disk drive in the system.

LOADHIGH   The DOS command that runs a command in expanded memory.

MODE   The DOS command that determines the operation of several devices attached to the computer.

PATH   The DOS command that tells DOS in what directories to search for executable files.

PROMPT   The DOS command that changes the form of the command line prompt.

Serial port   The type of port used for modems, plotters, and other special devices and that transmits data one bit at a time.

SETVER   The DOS command that "tricks" a program into thinking that it is using a different version of DOS.

SUBST   The DOS command that lets you specify a drive specifier that refers to either another drive or directory.

Exercises

Short Answer

1. What does the MODE command do?
2. What command puts the screen into 80-column color mode?
3. What command configures COM1 for 19200 baud, no parity, 8 data bits, and 1 stop bit?
4. What command causes the printer to print 132 characters per line and 6 lines per inch?
5. What command sets the autorepeat feature of the keyboard to repeat 12 times per second with an initial delay of ½ second?
6. What command redirects printer output to COM2?

7. What form of MODE reports the status of various devices?

8. What command creates a prompt that looks like this?

   `|<`

9. What command returns the prompt to its default?

10. What command creates a prompt that looks like this?

    `Drive A:`

11. What purpose does the CONFIG.SYS file serve?

12. What does BREAK ON do?

13. What configuration command loads the device driver ANSI.SYS?

14. What does RAMDRIVE do?

15. To execute a program in the high memory of your computer, what command do you use?

16. What PATH command allows DOS to look for executable files in the \SPSHT directory?

17. How can you display the current path?

18. Briefly, what do APPEND, ASSIGN, SUBST, and JOIN do?

19. What does SETVER do? Assume that a program called PROG.EXE requires version 3.3 of DOS. What SETVER command will you use to allow this program to run under DOS 6?

20. How do you make your computer ignore the contents of the CONFIG.SYS file?

21. What does NUMLOCK do?

Matching

Match the answers in the second column with the terms in the first.

_____ 1. $$	a.	The current drive
_____ 2. $b	b.	The dollar sign
_____ 3. $d	c.	The | character
_____ 4. $v	d.	The current date
_____ 5. $g	e.	The current time
_____ 6. $h	f.	The current directory path
_____ 7. $l	g.	The DOS version number
_____ 8. $n	h.	The > character
_____ 9. $p	i.	The < character
_____ 10. $t	j.	The (BACKSPACE) character

Activities

1. Create a batch file called PR.BAT that prints a file. This batch file should take two arguments. The first argument is the name of the file to be printed. If the second argument is NORM, then the file should print using 80 characters per line and 6 lines per inch. However, if the second argument is CONDENSED, the file should print using 132 characters per line and 8 lines per inch.

2. Experiment using PROMPT. Once you find a prompt that you like, add it to your AUTOEXEC.BAT file.

3. Extra Challenge: Add RAMDRIVE.SYS to your CONFIG.SYS file. (You may need to use LASTDRIVE, too.)

Floppy Disk Management

CHAPTER OBJECTIVES

After completing this chapter, you should be able to:

- Balance DOS and your applications on your work disk.
- Understand the trade-offs involved when using subdirectories on floppy disks.
- Back up your floppy disks.

Aside from the invention of the microprocessor that makes personal computers possible, no device has contributed as much to the development and success of the personal computer as the floppy disk drive. The reasons for this are threefold. First, floppy disk drives are inexpensive compared to fixed disks (though fixed disks are cheaper in terms of bytes of storage per dollar). In the early days of microcomputers, a fixed disk could easily cost several thousand dollars, while a floppy drive might sell for just a few hundred dollars. Second, compared to the only other cheap method of data storage—cassette tape—floppy disks are fast. Finally, the floppy disk gives users an easy and inexpensive way to share programs and transfer files. (Also, software developers found floppy diskettes the perfect medium on which to sell their programs.) For these reasons, the floppy disk has earned a lasting place in the world of computing.

How the floppy disk is used depends upon whether it is the main disk of the system or only a companion to a fixed disk. In most fixed-disk systems, the floppy disk is no longer the main disk drive. In fact, in most such systems the floppy is used for only two purposes: to back up information from the fixed disk for off-site storage, and as a transfer medium for data and programs. While most new computers today come with at least one fixed- and one floppy-disk drive, it is still possible to purchase floppy-only systems. Also, a great many older computers do not contain a fixed disk. In floppy-based systems, the floppy drive performs not only those functions that it performs in a fixed-disk system, but also provides the main storage device for the computer. In this chapter we will concentrate primarily on the floppy disk as it is used in floppy-only systems. Its use as a backup for the fixed disk is covered in Chapter 18.

Balancing DOS and Applications on Your Work Disk

It is difficult to balance DOS and your application programs when running DOS from a floppy-based system. As you know, DOS is a very large system. In fact, it is so large that you cannot even fit all of DOS on a single floppy disk. Thus, if you are running DOS using only floppy disks, DOS may be spread among two or more diskettes. The size problem is further compounded by your application programs because, typically, you will want at least part of DOS available on your application work diskettes. Fortunately, there is a solution to this problem. When running your applications, you generally need access to only a small part of DOS. Thus, when you create your work disks, you can carefully select only those parts of DOS that you will actually be needing. In this way, you can reduce the amount of disk space allocated to DOS.

In this section are some suggestions for files it makes sense to eliminate, and in which situations they can be eliminated from your DOS work disks. However, the following suggestions are not exhaustive, and you will want to experiment on your own. (Remember: Don't delete files on your master DOS diskettes or backups.) To begin, let's first see what files you cannot eliminate.

Which DOS Files Are Needed?

If a disk is not going to be used to load DOS, then no part of DOS is required on that disk. However, any disk capable of loading DOS must contain the DOS system. This includes the hidden files MSDOS.SYS and IO.SYS. The file COMMAND.COM must also be present. If you are using the Shell, then all files with the filename of DOSSHELL must also be present. What DOS files you include beyond these is determined by your needs and how you use your computer. For example, if you frequently sort a file using SORT, then SORT.EXE must be on your disk.

U.S. English-Language Usage

If you speak English and use your computer in the United States, you can eliminate the following files, which are used to support foreign languages and countries:

EGA.CPI
COUNTRY.SYS

DISPLAY.SYS
KEYBOARD.SYS
NLSFUNC.EXE

If you live in a country other than the United States, you might still be able to eliminate all but COUNTRY.SYS. (See the section in Chapter 16 on multinational versions of DOS.)

Removing Device Drivers

If you don't need or use them, you can remove one or more of the following device drivers:

ANSI.SYS
CHKSTATE.SYS
DBLSPACE.SYS
DRIVER.SYS
RAMDRIVE.SYS
SMARTDRV.EXE
HIMEM.SYS
EMM386.EXE

Removing Formatting and DOS Transfer Commands

On a work disk, you will probably not need any of the commands that are used to create new disks or install DOS. You will usually perform such tasks with your DOS disk rather than an application work disk. If this is the case, you can erase the following files:

FDISK.EXE
FORMAT.COM
SYS.COM

Programmer-Related Commands

Unless you are a programmer, you can remove the following files:

QBASIC.EXE
QBASIC.HLP
DEBUG.EXE

> **NOTE**
> If you intend to use DOS 6's editor EDIT, you will need to have QBASIC.EXE on your disk. (EDIT uses QBASIC's editor.)

Fixed-Disk Commands

If you don't have a fixed disk, you can erase the following commands:

BACKUP.EXE
FASTOPEN.EXE
MSBACKUP.EXE
MSBACKUP.OVL
MSBACKUP.HLP
RESTORE.EXE

Seldom-Used Commands

It is often useful to remove commands you seldom (or never) use. For example, you will probably never use the following commands:

APPEND.EXE
ASSIGN.COM
ATTRIB.EXE
GRAFTABL.COM
JOIN.EXE
SETVER.EXE
SUBST.EXE

If you have your own text editor, you can remove EDIT.COM and EDIT.HLP. If you do not use the Shell, you can remove DOSSHELL.*. You can also remove DOSSWAP.EXE, which is used by the Shell to support the Task Manager. In general, remove any command that you do not use on a daily basis.

> **NOTE**
>
> **If you have a dual-floppy system, then the best way to balance the needs of DOS and those of your application is to let the diskette in drive A hold DOS while you use the one in B to hold your application programs and files.**

Floppy Disks and Subdirectories

Because of the limited storage on a floppy diskette, extensive subdirectories are seldom used because it is easier (or necessary) to simply keep logically separate applications on separate diskettes. However, this is not meant to discourage you from creating and using subdirectories on your floppies. If you do use subdirectories on floppies, you should be aware of two performance issues.

First, each additional level of subdirectories increases the access time to the files in those subdirectories. On fixed disks this extra time is not much of an issue because they are so much faster than floppy drives. However, on floppies this additional access time can become annoying. You should use heavily nested subdirectories only when you can justify them.

The second performance issue is that each subdirectory uses disk space to hold its directory entries. Because space on a floppy is already limited, an unwarranted number of subdirectories could seriously decrease the amount of information that you could store on the disk.

Backing Up Floppy Disks

You must back up the floppy disks that contain your application programs and data on a regular basis. To put it bluntly, not making copies of important data is negligence of the highest order.

Sources of Data Loss

Before discussing the backup routine, let's look at the four ways that valuable data can be destroyed.

Computer Failure

The least common way that important information can be destroyed on a diskette is through computer failure. Few machine errors will destroy a file. But if the software that accesses the information is writing to the disk when a hardware failure occurs, the file could be damaged or destroyed. The most common causes of hardware failures are static electricity, overheating, line current transients, and physical abuse. Age is not as significant a factor in hardware failures as it once was because the integrated circuits now used to construct the computer have a very long mean time to failure.

It is difficult to guard against machine errors except by trying to maintain a clean environment and a steady source of power. If power transients are a problem in your area, you might want to invest in a surge protector.

Medium Failures

The next least-frequent source of data loss is physical destruction of the magnetic medium of the floppy disk. This can result from negligence on the part of the user or from a poorly manufactured diskette that simply disintegrates. Fortunately, with care, floppy diskettes tend to last a long time. However, any diskette that has been in heavy daily service for more than a year is a good candidate for replacement.

Software Errors

Programmers are not perfect. Hence, your application programs could contain one or more errors capable of destroying information. For the user who is not computer knowledgeable, it is sometimes difficult to distinguish between software and hardware errors. However, if data is consistently lost when you perform the same sequence of actions, software is likely the culprit.

Often you can work with the developers of your application software to get these errors fixed. If not, you must find different, more reliable programs to use.

Human Errors

Computers are one of the most reliable devices in use. People are not! The accidental erasure of important data is epidemic. So is accidentally reformatting a disk! Guarding against it is impossible—it is simply too easy to erase a file or reformat a diskette. As you know from reading Chapter 14, if you catch an accidental erasure immediately, you can often recover your file(s) by using the DOS error recovery command UNDELETE or UNFORMAT. However, human nature being what it is, it is not often that accidents are discovered in time.

The Backup Routine

Your only protection against having the data on a diskette destroyed is the backup routine. As you will come to understand, it is not enough just to make copies of important diskettes. *When* to make them, *how many* to maintain, and how to *recover* from a loss are also crucial.

Many data processing managers recommend the rotating triad method of backup. With this method, you have three backup diskettes for every work disk. The first, called the daily backup, is used to back up the work disk on a daily basis. Actually, you may find that it is better to back up after a shorter period, such as every two hours, if your data is volatile. The daily disk substitutes for the work disk should failure occur. (Actually, a copy of it should be used, as will be discussed shortly.)

The next disk in the triad is the weekly backup. Every Friday at 5 P.M., the contents of the daily disk are copied to the weekly disk. Thus, if both the master work disk and the daily disk are destroyed, the weekly disk can be used as a fairly close starting point.

At the end of each month, the weekly backup is retired and put in a safe place. A new copy of the daily disk is made and becomes the next month's weekly backup. The retired monthly backup completes the triad. In this way, if an error is not discovered for some time and has already corrupted the daily and weekly disks, the monthly backup can be used.

Because the nearest backup is potentially one month out of date, some managers employ the snapshot method in addition to the rotating triad. With this method, four diskettes are created for each work disk and are labeled One through Four. Every Wednesday, a copy of the daily disk is placed on one of the snapshot diskettes, beginning with One the first week, Two the second week, and so on. After Four has been used, the process cycles back to One. In this way, an error will not perpetuate itself through all the diskettes.

Backing Up a Disk

The best way to back up a diskette is by using DISKCOPY. Using COPY or even XCOPY is not as good because it permits human error—you could forget to copy a file or two.

Recovering Data

If you have to go to a backup diskette, use it only to make a copy; then use the copy. If a hardware or software problem has caused the loss of a file, it could happen again. You can never risk the destruction of a backup diskette. Be sure to write-protect the disk before putting it in the computer.

Remember also to restore all files, even if only one is lost, because many application programs use two or more files that work together. If these files are out of synchronization, you could be heading for even more trouble.

Mailing Diskettes

To close this chapter, a few words about how to mail or ship floppy disks are in order. The best way to mail a diskette is in a diskette mailer. If one is not available, place the diskette between two strong pieces of cardboard and put it in a large envelope. Be sure to write on the package, in large letters, that a floppy diskette is enclosed and should not be bent or exposed to magnetic fields.

Summary

In this chapter, you learned the following:

- How to free space on your DOS work diskette
- The effects of subdirectories on floppy disks
- How to maintain a backup routine
- How to mail a diskette

In the next chapter, you will learn to manage and back up your fixed disk.

Exercises

Short Answer

1. List three foreign language support files that you can remove from your work disk if you use your computer in the United States.

2. List three device drivers that can be removed from your work disk if they are not used.

3. List three seldom-used commands that probably don't need to be on your work disk.

4. What are the two reasons that you should use subdirectories sparingly on a floppy disk?

5. What are the four main causes of data loss?

6. Briefly describe how the rotating triad backup scheme works.

CHAPTER 18

Managing Your Fixed Disk

CHAPTER OBJECTIVES

After completing this chapter, you should be able to:

- Understand BACKUP.
- Restore files using RESTORE.
- Back up and restore your fixed disk using MSBACKUP.
- Use FASTOPEN.
- Defragment your disk using DEFRAG.
- Prepare the fixed disk for shipment.

With storage capabilities in excess of 300 megabytes, the fixed disk is a system resource that demands attention. In fact, most users will not consider buying a computer without a fixed disk because its extra storage and speed are generally judged to be worth the extra expense. In this chapter, you will learn some valuable techniques to help you manage this important device.

How Fixed and Floppy Disks Differ

The most fundamental difference between fixed and floppy disks is that the fixed disk, unlike the floppy, cannot be removed from the drive. It is not removable for two main reasons. First, the read/write head is mounted very close to the surface of the disk and is quite delicate. Second, even if the drive head were retracted to a safe position, the fixed disk is easily harmed by dust, so just opening its case is a bad idea.

From the aspect of performance, the fixed disk runs much faster than a floppy and stores from 10 to 200 times as much information. It is this increased storage that really distinguishes how fixed disks tend to be used. Unlike floppies, a fixed disk tends to have a complex directory structure that holds a wide range of information and application programs. In a way, a floppy disk is like a single-family dwelling, while a fixed disk is like a high-rise condominium.

Backing Up the Fixed Disk

The single most important fixed-disk management function is making a copy of its contents. Making and maintaining copies of the information on your fixed disk is seldom as easy as it is with floppy disks because of the amount of information usually found on the fixed disk. Unless you have some sort of tape backup system attached to your computer, you cannot copy an entire fixed disk in one smooth operation. Instead, you will need to copy the information on the fixed disk to several floppy diskettes. The trouble is that often just one directory on a fixed disk will contain more information than will fit on a single floppy. Using only the copying commands you have learned so far, there is no easy and trouble-free way to back up a hard disk. Instead, you must use a special fixed-disk backup command.

In this chapter, two different backup commands and related procedures are discussed. The first command is called BACKUP. BACKUP is *not* included in DOS 6. However, *BACKUP* was the backup command included in all versions of DOS prior to 6. You need to know about BACKUP even though you are studying DOS 6 because you are likely to encounter it frequently as you continue to work with computers. (As you may know, many computers will be using versions of DOS prior to 6.) Also, any backups made prior to DOS 6 will have been done using BACKUP. Further, some computer installation managers may elect to continue using BACKUP rather than the new DOS 6 backup command. For these reasons, BACKUP is covered in this chapter even though it is no longer included with DOS.

The second backup command—and the one provided with DOS 6— is called MSBACKUP, and it is much easier to use than BACKUP. In DOS 6, MSBACKUP replaces BACKUP.

We will begin our examination of backing up the fixed disk with BACKUP.

BACKUP   *The old DOS command that backs up the fixed disk to one or more floppy disks.*

Backing Up Your Fixed Disk Using BACKUP

The BACKUP command has several forms and numerous options. In this book, we will examine the most common forms. All the examples use drive A as the floppy drive receiving the information, though you may substitute drive B if you wish. Drive C is assumed to be the fixed disk. You should substitute a different drive letter if necessary. BACKUP has the general form

BACKUP *source target options*

where *source* specifies the drive, path, and file names to be copied to *target*.

The number of diskettes that you will need to back up the entire contents of your disk is directly related to the amount of information on your fixed disk. Sometimes this number can be quite large. To compute the number of diskettes that you will need, run CHKDSK to find the total storage size, in bytes, of the fixed disk and the amount of free storage. Subtract the amount of free storage from the total storage, and then divide this number by the storage size of the floppy drive that you will be using for backups. Rounding this number upward tells you the number of diskettes required. This formula in mathematical notation is

number of diskettes = (total–free)/size of floppy

You must number your backup diskettes because you will have to insert them in order. The exact order in which the diskettes are written is important because a large file may be spread across two or more diskettes.

If you are going to back up only part of the disk, you can roughly compute the number of diskettes needed by adding the amount of space taken up by the files you are going to copy and then dividing this number by the storage capacity of your floppy drive.

Backing Up an Entire Drive

The most important and by far most common backup scenario is backing up the entire contents of a fixed disk. This is the safest way to ensure that all the data on the disk is copied. To back up the entire contents of the fixed disk, use the following form of BACKUP.

BACKUP C:*.* A: /S

BACKUP will automatically format the diskettes for you, but you will save time if you use pre-formatted ones. (BACKUP uses FORMAT to format the diskettes, so this command must be available for BACKUP's use.)

The path C:\ ensures that the backup will begin with the root directory, and the /S option specifies that all subdirectories will be copied. As the backup procedure begins, you will see this message:

```
Insert backup diskette 01 in drive A:
```

```
Warning! Files in the target drive
A:\ root directory will be erased
Press any key to continue . . .
```

As BACKUP continues, you will be prompted to insert additional diskettes until all the information on C has been backed up. If your fixed disk is very full, the backup procedure will take a fairly long time—possibly an hour or more. Be prepared for this.

If you have more than one fixed-disk drive, then repeat the backup command using the next drive specifier.

Backing Up Portions of the Fixed Disk

In situations where several people use the same computer, it may make more sense for each user to back up his or her own directories rather than the entire disk. For example, assume that the directory structure shown below exists on a fixed disk.

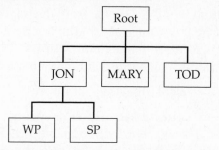

The command that Jon will use to back up his workspace, including the JON directory and its two subdirectories, is

BACKUP C:\JON*.* A: /S

In general, you specify a path to the directory where you wish to start the backup.

If you leave off the /S, then only the contents of the directories explicitly specified are copied. For example, the command

BACKUP C:\JON*.* A:

copies only the contents of the JON directory and not its subdirectories WP and SP.

Adding Files to Backup Diskettes

The forms of the BACKUP command shown so far erase any previously existing contents of the diskettes. However, suppose that you perform a complete fixed-disk backup only once a week, and you have simply added three files while leaving the others unchanged. How can you add these files to the backup diskettes without having to recopy the entire fixed disk? The answer is to use BACKUP's /A (add) option. When you specify this option, the target diskettes are not overwritten; rather, the specified files are added to them. For example, to add the file FORMLET.WP to backup diskettes for Jon, enter

BACKUP C:\JON\WP\FORMLET.WP A: /A

When this command begins execution, you will see the following:

```
Insert last backup diskette in drive A:
Press any key to continue . . .
```

As is implied by this message, new files are added to the last diskette used by the previous backup.

Adding new or modified files is a good way to keep your backups current without going through the time-consuming process of a full backup.

Backing Up Files Modified on or After a Specified Date

You can back up only those files that have been changed on or after a specified date by using the /D: option. For example, the following command copies those files that have been changed on or after 7-10-93.

BACKUP C:*.* A: /D:7-10-93

The format of the date is determined by the country specified with the COUNTRY command in the CONFIG.SYS file, or as mm-dd-yy (standard U.S. format) if no other country is specified.

Keep in mind that use of the /D: option does not prevent the target diskette(s) from being overwritten. To add new files with dates after a certain date, also add the /A option to the command line. For example, the following command will add any new files modified after 7-10-93 to the target diskette(s).

BACKUP C:*.* A: /D:7-10-93 /A

Backing Up Files Modified on or After a Specified Time

You can tell BACKUP to copy only those files with times equal to or later than a specified time on a specified date by using the /T: option along with the /D: option. For example, the following command only backs up those files created after 12 noon on 7-10-93.

BACKUP C:*.* A: /D:7-10-93 /T:12:00

Again, the format for the date and time will vary in countries other than the United States. Remember, the existing set of backup diskettes will be overwritten.

Backing Up Only Files That Have Changed

By using the /M option, you can tell BACKUP to copy only those files that have changed since the last backup. As you will recall from earlier in this book, all files have an associated archive attribute that can be either on or off. If the archive attribute is on, it indicates that the file has been modified. The BACKUP command automatically turns off the archive attribute. Therefore, only files that have been changed will actually be copied. For example, the following command backs up only the modified files of the fixed disk.

BACKUP C:*.* A: /M /S

Adding a Log File

With the /L: option, you can have a record of the time and date of the backup, the path and file name of each file backed up, and the number of the diskette that each file is on. You can specify a file name for the log file. If none is specified, BACKUP.LOG is used and is placed in the root directory of both the source and target. If the specified file exists, information is appended to the end. If it does not exist, then the file is created. For example, the following command writes to the file called MYLOG.

BACKUP C:*.* A: /S /L:MYLOG

This command uses the default BACKUP.LOG file:

BACKUP C:*.* A: /S /L

The first line of the log file will contain the date and time of the backup. Each subsequent line lists the disk number and file name. The first few lines will look something like this:

```
1-12-93 10:30:37
001   \AUTOEXEC.BAT
001   \ANSI.SYS
001   \ASSIGN.COM
```

The *log file* provides a record of which backup diskette any specific file is on. This can speed up the process of restoring a file, as you will shortly see.

If for some reason you want to have BACKUP automatically format the target diskettes to a size other than the capacity of the floppy drive being used for the backup, you can use the /F option. One reason you might want to do this is so that you can restore a fixed disk on a computer that uses different capacity diskettes. The /F option takes this form:

/F:size

where *size* must be one of these:

size	capacity	applicable diskette size
160	160K	5¼" single sided
180	180K	5¼" single sided
320	320K	5¼" double sided
360	360K	5¼" double sided
720	720K	3½" double sided
1200	1.20MB	5¼" double sided
1440	1.44MB	3½" double sided
2880	2.88MB	3½" double sided

Log file As it relates to BACKUP, a file that keeps a record of the files backed up.

If you are just backing up your fixed disk for your own use on your own computer, then you won't need to ever use the /F option.

The BACKUP options are shown in Table 18-1.

Backing Up Floppies With BACKUP

You can use BACKUP to back up the contents of a floppy disk, although this is rarely done because DISKCOPY is clearly superior. However, you can specify any target and any source drive that you desire (except that they cannot be the same drive) as arguments to BACKUP.

Restoring Files Using RESTORE

Backups that you made using BACKUP must be restored using the *RESTORE* command. That is, if a file is lost on your fixed disk and you used BACKUP to back up your fixed disk, then you will use RESTORE to recover that file. Assuming that you are restoring to a fixed disk, the general form of the RESTORE command is

RESTORE *bkdrive: target options*

where *bkdrive* is the drive that will hold the diskettes created by BACKUP and *target* denotes the drive, path, and file name specifiers that tell where information will be written to the fixed disk.

During the restoration process, you will be prompted to insert one or more of the backup diskettes beginning with diskette number 1. When you restore the entire fixed disk, all backup diskettes will be read in order. If only certain files are being restored, RESTORE will search through the backup diskettes until it finds them. The RESTORE prompt tells you which diskette to insert next and waits until you press a key. The first prompt will look like this:

```
Insert backup diskette 01 in drive A:
Press any key to continue . . .
```

Keep in mind that restoring a file means overwriting any existing file with the same name, so use the RESTORE command carefully.

> **RESTORE** *The DOS command that restores files previously backed up using BACKUP.*

> **REMEMBER**
> **RESTORE only restores files created by BACKUP.**

Option	Meaning
/A	add files instead of overwriting the backup diskettes
/D:	copy files with dates on or after the specified date
/F:	specify capacity of target diskettes
/L:	create a log file
/M	copy only those files that have been created or changed since the last backup
/S	back up all subdirectories starting with the specified path
/T:	copy files with times equal to or later than the one specified on the given date

TABLE 18-1   **The BACKUP options**

Restoring the Entire Fixed Disk

To restore all the files on the fixed disk, you must have backup diskettes containing all these files; that is, you must have recently used a BACKUP command similar to the following:

BACKUP C:*.* A: /S

With the diskettes that hold the backed up information, you should use the following form of the RESTORE command to restore all the files.

RESTORE A: C:*.* /S

The /S option tells RESTORE to restore all files and subdirectories. Notice that you specify the path name for where the files will be placed on the fixed disk, not from where they are stored on the backup diskettes.

In general, only two occasions will arise when you will completely restore a disk. The first, and most unfortunate, is when a hardware error destroys your fixed disk and a new one is put in the system. In this case, you must reload all your files. If you have been following a proper backup procedure (such as the one described later in this chapter), then the disruption should be minimal. However, if the fixed disk crashes and your backups are either out of date or nonexistent, you are in for a painful experience.

The other time that you will want to fully recover a fixed disk is when you are bringing up another system that is intended to have the same function as the first.

Restoring Individual Files

To restore individual files, you must specify the complete path and file names. RESTORE accepts wildcards, so it is possible to restore groups of files. For example, to restore the files LETTER.ONE, LETTER.TWO, and FORMLET.ONE found in the JON\WP directory, use the following commands:

RESTORE A: C:\JON\WP\LETTER.*
RESTORE A: C:\JON\WP\FORMLET.ONE

Restoring Files by Date and Time

RESTORE can restore files modified on (or before) a certain date when you add the /B: option. Alternately, the /A: option allows you to restore files that have been modified on or after the specified date. For example, the following commands restore all files changed before or on 3-3-92 and after 3-3-91—a period of one year.

RESTORE A: C:*.* /S /B:3-3-92 /A:3-3-91

In like fashion, you can use /L: to restore those files modified *at or later* than a certain time on a given date, and /E: to restore all files modified *at or prior to* the specified time on a given date. For example, the following commands restore all files modified on 2-28-91 after 12 noon but earlier than 5:01 that afternoon.

RESTORE A: C:*.* /S /D:2-28-91 /L:12:00 /E:17:00

Restoring Modified Files

The /M option lets you restore only those files that have been modified since the last backup was made. For example, the following command restores all files in the WP directory that have been changed.

RESTORE A: C:\JON\WP*.* /M

The RESTORE command simply checks the archive attribute of each file and restores those that have it turned on.

Similarly, you can use the /N option to restore only those files that have been deleted from the fixed disk.

Prompted Restoration

If you specify the /P option, RESTORE will prompt you whenever a file on the fixed disk has been changed since it was last backed up.

Special Considerations When Using RESTORE

- RESTORE cannot be used with backup files created using MSBACKUP. RESTORE is only for files created using BACKUP.
- RESTORE does not restore the files IO.SYS and MSDOS.SYS. You should use SYS restore for these system files.
- You must always start with diskette number 1 to recover a file unless you have created a log file during backup that will tell you the number of the diskette that the file is on.
- Files stored on backup diskettes are not the same as standard DOS files. Don't try to use the COPY command to restore files.
- You must always restore files into the same directory from which they came.
- If you want to restore only those files that do not exist on the target disk, use the /N option.
- To see the backup files that match the file specifier in the RESTORE command, use the /D option.

The RESTORE options are summarized in Table 18-2.

Backing Up Using MSBACKUP

As explained at the start of this chapter, DOS 6 does not include the BACKUP command. (RESTORE is included in DOS 6 so that backup files created using an earlier version of DOS can be recovered.) Instead, you will use *MSBACKUP* to back up your fixed disk and to restore files. Although MSBACKUP provides the same essential features as BACKUP and RESTORE, it operates in a much different manner and is

MSBACKUP   The DOS 6 command that backs up and restores your fixed disk. It replaces the older BACKUP and RESTORE commands.

Option	Meaning
/A	restore all files modified on or after the specified date
/B	restore all files modified on or before the specified date
/D	display backup files that match the file specifier
/E	restore all files modified at or earlier than the specified time on a given date
/L	restore all files modified at or later than the specified time on a given date
/M	restore all files that have been modified since the last backup
/N	restore only those files that do not exist on the fixed disk
/P	prompt before restoring a file
/S	restore all subdirectories

TABLE 18-2 **The RESTORE options**

a substantial improvement. Also, MSBACKUP is fundamentally easier to operate and provides visual feedback about what it is doing.

> **IMPORTANT**
>
> **If you need to recover files that were backed up using BACKUP, you *must* use RESTORE no matter what version of DOS you are currently using. However, new backups made with MSBACKUP must be restored using MSBACKUP.**

MSBACKUP is a window-based, menu-oriented program that fully manages the backup procedure. It performs the backup phase as well as the recovery phase. Unlike its predecessors (BACKUP and RESTORE), MSBACKUP combines the tasks of backup and recovery into one program. This makes it much easier to use.

MSBACKUP is a sophisticated program that allows substantial control over how your fixed disk is backed up. However, many of MSBACKUP's options and settings require knowledge about the operation of the computer beyond that which most users will have. Also, some options are highly specialized and apply only to unusual situations. Therefore, this book describes only its most common usage. However, this usage applies to most backup needs. (The advanced options are used mostly by system integrators and specialists and do not apply to the general user.)

Menu and Window Selection in MSBACKUP

MSBACKUP uses windows and menus in much the same way that the Shell does. If you can use the Shell, then you will have no trouble using MSBACKUP. However, since menu selection is fundamental to MSBACKUP's operation, it is reviewed here.

To select an option, first highlight it using an arrow key and then press (ENTER). To select an option using the mouse, position the mouse pointer over the option and then press the left mouse button. (As you should recall, this is referred to as "clicking on" an option.) You can also select an option by pressing the highlighted letter. For example, one of MSBACKUP's options is called Restore. To select it, you could simply type **R** when the menu containing it is displayed.

When MSBACKUP displays multiple windows, menus, or options on the screen, you can move between them by pressing the (TAB) key. Some MSBACKUP options are selected by using *check boxes*. If the box is checked, then the option is active; if it is not checked, then the option is not active. To change the state of a check box, first tab to it and then press the space bar. Each time you press the space bar, the state of the check box will change.

MSBACKUP is easy to navigate and you should have little trouble, but if you need help while running MSBACKUP, simply press the (F1) key. This causes context-sensitive information to be displayed that relates directly to what you are currently doing.

Executing MSBACKUP for the First Time

The first time that you execute MSBACKUP, you will need to run a compatibility test. This procedure helps MSBACKUP configure itself to best take advantage of the hardware in your computer, including its floppy-disk drives. It also confirms that reliable backups can be made. (MSBACKUP works with virtually all computers, including all major brands.)

MSBACKUP is an external command. To execute it, simply enter **MSBACKUP** at the prompt.

Once MSBACKUP begins executing, to run the compatibility test, simply follow the prompts that MSBACKUP displays on the screen. You will also need to have ready two blank floppy diskettes that are the right size for the drive that you will be using.

If you have two different types of diskette drives in your system, select the drive that has the greatest capacity for backing up your fixed disk.

If your computer system is never changed, then you will need to run the compatibility test only one time. However, if you enhance or alter your computer—by adding a new type of floppy drive, for example—then you should rerun the test. (To do this, select Configure from MSBACKUP's main menu and then select Compatibility Test.)

To terminate MSBACKUP, either select the Quit option or double-click on the box in the upper-left corner of the main window. (A double-click is two presses of the left mouse button in quick succession.)

Backing Up Your Entire Drive

The most important backup procedure is backing up all the files on a drive. Backing up all files ensures that all files are protected and can be recovered. To begin, execute MSBACKUP and then select the Backup option from the main menu. (This is the default selection, so you can just press (ENTER).)

After selecting Backup, you will see a screen similar to that shown in Figure 18-1.

Next, activate the Backup From window, move the highlight to the drive you want to back up (if it is not already on it), and then press the space bar. This will cause the message "All files" to be displayed. This means that the backup will copy all files.

If the method of backup displayed in Backup Type is not Full, then you must select that option and change it to Full. To change the backup type when the Backup Type window is displayed, press the space bar until Full is selected. (You can also click on Full using the mouse.) Finally, select OK to return to the main Backup window.

To back up all files on the specified drive, select Start Backup. This will copy all files on the Backup From drive to the drive specified in Backup To.

REMEMBER

You will need to have several blank floppy disks available to hold the files that are backed up. The exact number is displayed in the Backup window.

If you have more than one fixed drive, then continue to back up files by repeating the processes just described. Just change the drive selected in the Backup From window.

Methods of Backup

As the preceding discussion hinted, MSBACKUP allows you to back up your fixed disk in different ways. Specifically, it supports three methods of backup: Full (the default), incremental, and differential. Before proceeding, it is important that you learn what each backup type does. Here is a brief description of each.

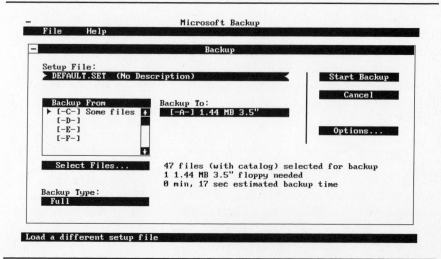

FIGURE 18-1   **The Backup screen**

Full Backup

A full backup copies all files on your disk. This type of backup ensures that all important files have been protected. This is also the type of backup that you must perform first. Both the incremental and the differential backups assume that you have performed a full backup. A full backup also turns off the archive attribute associated with each file.

REMEMBER

The archive attribute is turned on whenever a file is modified or when it is first created. Performing a backup turns off this attribute.

Incremental Backup

Once a full backup has been performed, you can use an incremental backup to have MSBACKUP copy only those files that have been added or that have changed. In the process, the archive attribute is turned off. Thus, each time you perform an incremental backup, only those files that are new or that have been modified since the last incremental backup will be copied. This means that in order to ensure that you have a current copy of every file, you will need to have your full backup disks and every incremental backup disk that you have created.

Differential Backup

A differential backup is similar to an incremental backup in that it copies only those files that have changed or been added. However, unlike the incremental backup, a differential backup copies all files that have been added or changed since the last *full backup*. This means that to have current versions of all files, you will need your last full backup disks and the latest differential backup. Performing a differential backup does not affect the setting of any file attributes. Specifically, it does not change the archive attribute of the files that it copies.

A Suggested Backup Strategy

Given the three different types of backups, you might wonder which you should use when. One effective and efficient method of backing up your disk is as follows. First, perform a full backup. Then, perform a differential backup periodically—every week, for example. Using the periodic differential backup takes only a little time, and it ensures that all new or changed files have been copied and are within easy reach. Occasionally, start over and perform a new, full backup. While other approaches are equally valid, this method requires the fewest diskettes and minimizes the possibility of a file becoming lost.

REMEMBER

Your backups are only as current as when they were made. Back up frequently to maintain accurate files.

Back Up Selected Files

By default, all files on a disk are copied when a full backup is performed. (Or, in the case of a differential or incremental backup, all files with their archive attribute on are copied.) However, you can select only specific directories and files to back up by using the Select Files option in the Backup window. When you do this, you can select the directories and files that you want to copy.

One time for backing up only selected directories or files is when the computer is used by several people and you want to back up only the portion of the disk that you used. Or, you might have loaded all new software into one directory and simply want to obtain a temporary backup of the programs before running your usual full backup.

> **NOTE**
>
> **Keep in mind that it is generally best to back up an entire disk rather than just selected files or directories. The ability to back up selected parts is intended to handle special situations.**

To begin the file selection process, first choose the Select Files option in the Backup window. This causes a window to be displayed that lists all directories on the disk and all files in the selected directory. This window is titled Select Backup Files.

Before you can select specific files, you must select the directory that contains them. To do this, highlight the directory (or directories) in the directory list and then press the space bar. Using the mouse, position the mouse pointer on the directory and press the right button (or double-click the left button). To select multiple directories, position the mouse pointer on the first directory, press and hold the right mouse button, and drag the mouse to the last directory. All directories in between will be selected.

To deselect a directory, follow the same procedure as described to select one. Any preselected directory will be deselected.

Once you have chosen the directory, you select files using the same basic approach as you did when selecting directories. First, move the highlight to the file list window by pressing (TAB) or by using the arrow keys, or by "clicking" on it using the mouse. Next, if using the keyboard, position the highlight over the file you want and then press the space bar. If using the mouse, press the right button while the pointer is on the file you want to select. Multiple files are selected in the same way that multiple directories are. To deselect a file, simply use the same process. Any preselected files will be deselected.

> **NOTE**
>
> **You can also select or deselect directories and files using the Include and Exclude buttons, respectively. To use these options, simply specify the path and the file names when prompted. (You can use wildcards in the file names.) The specified files will then be either selected or deselected.**

After you have selected the desired directories and files, select the OK button. Now, only the files you have selected will be copied by whatever type of backup you next perform. To confirm this, the message inside the Backup From window should be Some Files instead of All Files. (If it isn't, make sure that you have correctly selected only those files that you want to back up.) To actually back up the files, select Start Backup from the main Backup menu.

Some Options When Selecting Files

Several options are available when selecting files. To set these options, select the Special option in the Select Backup Files window. The first option allows you to back up only those files that have dates that lie within a certain range. To do this, first check the Apply Date Range box. (To do this, Tab to it and then press the space bar or click on it using the mouse.) Next, Tab to the From date and enter the starting date. Then, Tab to the To date and enter the ending date. After doing this, only files with dates between those two dates will be copied.

Other options allow you to exclude copy-protected files, read-only files, system files, and hidden files. While these options apply mostly to specialized situations, you may want to explore them on your own.

Catalogs

When MSBACKUP backs up your drive, it creates a special file called a *catalog* that contains a list of the files that have been backed up. Catalog files make restoring files faster and easier. In general, MSBACKUP will handle catalog files automatically. However, you should know that all catalog file names are eight characters long and are encoded like this (from left to right):

Catalog   As it relates to MSBACKUP, a catalog is a special file that contains a list of the files that you backed up.

Letter	Meaning
1	**first drive in catalog**
2	**last drive in catalog**
3	**last digit of year**
4, 5	**month**
6, 7	**day of month**
8	**letter of backup when more than one is made on a given day**

All catalog files will have one of these extensions, which indicate the type of backup performed.

FUL	**full**
INC	**incremental**
DIF	**differential**

For example, the following catalog file contains the file names for drives C, D, and E, was made in the year 1993 on the 28th of February, and was the second backup of that day. It was a full backup.

CE30228B.FUL

Restoring Files Using MSBACKUP

To restore files from backup disks, execute MSBACKUP and then select Restore from the main menu. It will look similar to Figure 18-2. By default, the most recent catalog file is used. If this is not the catalog

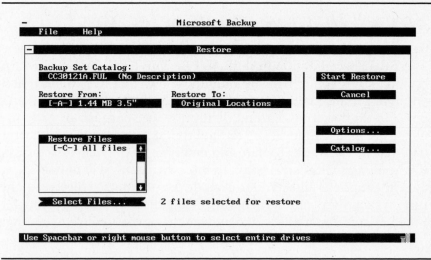

FIGURE 18-2   **The Restore window**

that you want, you can select one using the Catalog option. If either the Restore From drive or the Restore To drive is wrong, then change it by selecting the appropriate option. (Generally, you restore from the same diskette drive that you backed up to and restore to the same place that the files were originally from.) Next, you need to select the files to restore. To restore all files, first select the proper drive in the Restore Files window and then press the space bar. This causes the message "All files" to be displayed. However, if you want to restore only selected files, activate the Select Files options and select those files. (Files are selected using the same procedure described when backing up selected files.)

Once you have selected the proper drives and files, select Start Restore to begin restoring files.

Restore has several options that you might want to explore on your own. Generally, its default mode of operation is suitable to most file recovery situations.

Your backup diskettes are typically your only protection against data loss. If you lose or misplace these diskettes, you cannot recover your files. Be sure to keep backup disks in a safe place.

The Backup Routine for Fixed Disks

Whether you use BACKUP or MSBACKUP, the basic philosophy for backing up the fixed disk is the same. You should use the rotating triad method of backup; that is, you should maintain daily, weekly, and monthly backup diskettes. (The rotating triad backup method was discussed in Chapter 17 relative to floppy disks, and its method also applies to the fixed disk.)

Because backing up a fixed disk that contains a lot of information is a lengthy process, after an initial backup, you copy only those files that have changed to the daily backup disks, and then perform a full

> **REMEMBER**
> **When restoring files created using a version of DOS prior to 6, you must use RESTORE and not MSBACKUP.**

backup procedure at the end of the week. This will save you time and still ensure protection of your files.

Because the nearest backup is potentially one month out of date, you should use the snapshot method of backup (also described in Chapter 17) in addition to the rotating triad method. This way, an error will not perpetuate itself through all the diskettes.

Who Is Responsible?

Someone must be in charge of backing up a fixed disk if the system is used by many people. This may sound simple, but the failure to assign this task to a trusted individual is a major cause of backup diskettes being woefully out of date. When no single person is responsible, everyone assumes that someone else is doing the backups. If you are a manager, make sure that someone's job description includes backing up the fixed disk.

Using FASTOPEN

The external *FASTOPEN* command allows DOS to quickly access files that are several levels of subdirectories deep. For somewhat technical reasons, it normally takes DOS a lot longer to reach a file with a long path name than to reach one in the root. However, FASTOPEN allows DOS to remember the location of a file and, therefore, makes accessing that file much faster. The general form of FASTOPEN is

FASTOPEN *drive-specifier=num*

where *drive-specifier* is the name of the drive to which the FASTOPEN command applies. You can use FASTOPEN to provide fast access to the files on only one drive in the system. The optional *num* argument specifies the number of files and directories that FASTOPEN can remember and must be between 10 and 999. If *num* is not present, the default is 48. There can be no spaces between the drive specifer, the equal sign, and the number.

For example, the following command gives fast access to the files on drive C and allows 48 files and/or directories to have fast access.

FASTOPEN C:

FASTOPEN will display this message:

`FASTOPEN installed`

The following command allows the last 50 files and/or directories to be remembered.

FASTOPEN C:=50

You will usually want to use the default setting for the number of files or directories. For technical reasons, making it too large could actually increase rather than decrease access time. If you make it too small, you will not receive any benefit.

FASTOPEN   *The DOS command that helps DOS access files in deeply nested subdirectories more quickly.*

FASTOPEN installs itself the first time it is invoked, which means that you can execute it only once. For this reason, you should put it in an AUTOEXEC.BAT file.

If you have expanded memory, then you can have FASTOPEN use this memory by specifying the /X option. (This will leave more room for your application programs to run in normal memory.)

Defragmenting Your Disk

> **NOTE**
> **DEFRAG is a window- and menu-based command. You make selections the same way you do when using the Shell.**

> *DEFRAG   The DOS command that defragments your fixed disk.*

As you learned earlier in this book, DOS does not necessarily save a file in consecutive disk sectors. Instead, it uses the first available sectors. When the disk is newly formatted, the first available sectors are often also consecutive sectors. However, as the disk is used and old files are erased and new files are stored, gaps of available sectors develop between files. These gaps are then reused by DOS when a new file is stored. Thus, when DOS stores a file on a well-used disk, most likely that file is stored in non-consecutive sectors. Over time, this causes many files to be scattered throughout the disk. This is called *fragmentation*. When a disk is fragmented, it takes longer for the drive to read the file. This, in turn, slows down the performance of your computer. However, using DOS 6 you can defragment your disk using the DEFRAG command.

The *DEFRAG* command works by rearranging your disk so that files are stored in consecutive disk sectors. This improves the performance of your disk and generally speeds up all programs that access that disk. The DEFRAG command has this general form:

DEFRAG *drive*:

where *drive* is the drive to defragment. Thus, to defragment drive C, use this command:

DEFRAG C:

For example, enter this command now. You will see a screen similar to that shown in Figure 18-3.

The screen shows a map of the drive. The legend displayed on the screen explains the map. When DEFRAG is first executed, DEFRAG displays its opinion of what action to take in its Recommendation window. If you agree with DEFRAG's opinion, then you can begin the defragmentation process by choosing the Optimize option. If you want to perform a different action, choose Configure, which allows you to change various settings. (The DEFRAG options will be discussed shortly.) If DEFRAG detects that your disk does not require any optimization, then it will tell you this, as well. Most of the time, you will want to defragment the disk as suggested by DEFRAG.

To select an option inside the Recommendation window, first highlight the option using the left and right arrow keys and then press (ENTER). You can also select an option using the mouse by positioning the mouse cursor on the desired option and pressing the left mouse button.

FIGURE 18-3   **The DEFRAG screen**

The defragmenting process will take several minutes (perhaps as long as an hour). Therefore, only execute this command when you won't need your computer for a while. A good time to defragment a drive is over your lunch hour, for example.

If you do not want to use DEFRAG's recommendation, select Optimize inside DEFRAG's Recommendation window. This causes the Optimize menu shown in Figure 18-4 to be shown.

Using this menu, you can begin the optimization, select a different drive to optimize, select the optimization method, change the way the files are arranged on the disk, obtain an expanded legend of the disk map, display DEFRAG's copyright message, and terminate DEFRAG. Each of these options is described here.

To make a selection from the Optimize menu, position the highlight over the desired item using the ⊙ or ⊙ keys and then press (ENTER). Or, if you have a mouse, position the mouse pointer on the desired item and press the left mouse button.

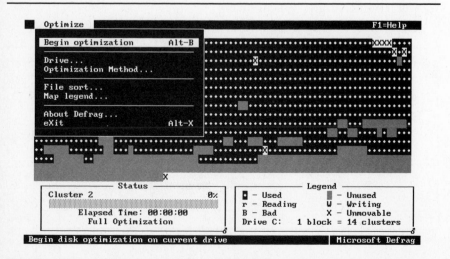

FIGURE 18-4   **DEFRAG's Optimize menu**

When the Optimize menu is displayed, you can also select an option by pressing the highlighted letter associated with each item. For example, to terminate DEFRAG, you can type X when the menu is shown.

To begin disk optimization, select Begin Optimization.

To change the drive being optimized, select Drive. You will see the drive selection menu. To switch drives, select the desired drive from this menu.

DEFRAG is optimized in two ways: full optimization and unfragment files only. To choose between them, select Optimization Method. You will see the window shown in Figure 18-5.

Using full optimization produces the best results and greatest increase in disk performance. It defragments all files, moves all subdirectories to the start of the disk (this makes access time faster), and moves all free space to the end of the disk. Use this optimization when your disk is highly fragmented.

Unfragmenting files only does precisely that; it defragments files but does not rearrange the disk in any other way. This takes much less time than full optimization, but does not increase the performance of your disk as much. However, in cases where your disk is only slightly fragmented, this is the best choice.

To switch between Full Optimization and Unfragment Files Only, press the space bar. Each time you press the space bar, the option selected will change. You can also use the mouse to select an optimization by "clicking" on the appropriate selection.

While DEFRAG optimizes your disk, it can sort the file list in each directory on the disk. By default, DEFRAG does not sort directories. However, you can change this by selecting File sort. You will see the window shown in Figure 18-6. This allows you to sort each directory by name, extension, time and date, and size. You can also sort the directory in ascending or descending order.

You can select a new sort criterion or sort order by pressing the space bar or using the mouse by clicking on the option. To move between the Sort Criterion and Sort Order, press the (TAB) key. When done, either press (ENTER) or click on the OK box using the mouse. You can also choose Cancel if you change your mind.

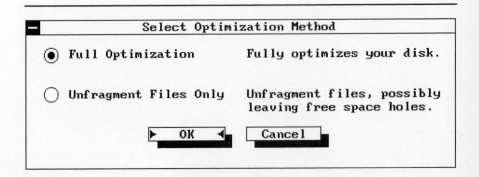

FIGURE 18-5   **The Optimization Method window**

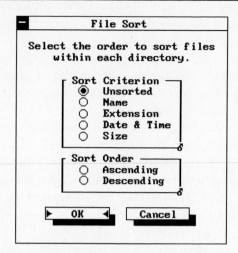

FIGURE 18-6 **The File Sort window**

To see an extended description of the symbols used by DEFRAG's disk map, choose Map Legend.

About Defrag displays copyright information about DEFRAG, and Exit terminates DEFRAG and returns to the DOS prompt.

You can obtain help information about DEFRAG at any time by pressing the (F1) function key.

In general, you will not want to use DEFRAG on a daily basis. Instead, use it every so often, as your computer usage dictates. For most users, once a month is sufficient. If you frequently create and erase files on your computer, use temporary files, or alter the purpose of your computer, then you will want to run DEFRAG more frequently. Also, if file accesses seem to be slowing down, try running DEFRAG.

Loading Applications to the Fixed Disk

No hard and fast rules apply to every situation involving loading applications to the fixed disk. However, some general guidelines will help you make the right decisions. We will examine these here.

Application Subdirectories

The first and most important rule is that each separate application should be loaded into its own directory. Do not put all applications into the root directory. If you do this, the root directory will become unmanageable and you will eventually run out of directory entries. It is also not wise to place all applications into one general-purpose applications directory because, again, that directory will become unmanageable.

For example, imagine that you have three applications: a spreadsheet, a word processor, and an inventory package. You should create three subdirectories, with descriptive names such as SPSHT, WP, and INVENT, and place the files associated with each application area into their respective directories.

Sometimes you will add an application that is really a subsystem of an already existing application. For example, if you add a spelling checker to the word processor, it does not make sense to create a new subdirectory off the root for it. Instead, you can simply add it to the WP directory because it is dependent upon the word processor. (In some special situations, it might be a good idea to place it in a subdirectory of WP, but this is not commonly the case.) In general, when one application depends on another, put the dependent one in the directory of the application on which it depends or in a subdirectory of that application.

User Subdirectories

If several different users will be using an application once it is loaded, it is best to create a subdirectory for each user off the application area so that each user's files will be separate. Further, because one user may use two or more applications, it is doubly important that individual subdirectories be created off the application directory and not the root. This way, each user can have a directory bearing his or her name in each application area. For example, if Jon does both word processing and spreadsheet analysis, then the proper directory structure will look like the one shown below:

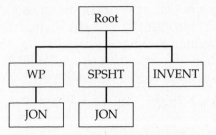

Preparing the Fixed Disk for Shipment

The fixed disk must be properly prepared for travel prior to moving it. This requires that the read/write head be retracted to a position that is not over the magnetic medium of the disk. Most modern fixed disks retract the head automatically, but some require that you give a command that retracts the head. Failure to retract the head could result in the read/write head contacting the disk, causing damage and loss of data. When the read/write head contacts the disk, it is called a *head crash*.

If you must manually retract the head (sometimes called *parking*), the exact method of doing so is determined by the type of computer that you have. Consult your owner's manual for details.

Head crash   *A situation in which the read/write head of the fixed disk comes in contact with the disk medium.*

Summary

In this chapter, you learned how to manage the fixed disk, including:

- How to back up the fixed disk using BACKUP
- How to restore data using RESTORE
- How to back up and restore data using MSBACKUP
- How to use the fixed-disk backup routine
- How to use FASTOPEN
- How to defragment your fixed disk to improve its operation
- How to load applications onto a fixed disk
- How to prepare your fixed disk for shipment

In the final chapter of this book, you will learn about some advanced commands that help you manage the entire computer system.

Key Terms

BACKUP   The old DOS command that backs up the fixed disk to one or more floppy disks.

Catalog   As it relates to MSBACKUP, a catalog is a special file that contains a list of the files that you backed up.

DEFRAG   The DOS command that defragments your fixed disk.

FASTOPEN   The DOS command that helps DOS access files in deeply nested subdirectories more quickly.

Head crash   A situation in which the read/write head of the fixed disk comes in contact with the disk medium. (This generally results in a catastrophic error.)

Log file   As it relates to BACKUP, a file that keeps a record of the files backed up.

MSBACKUP   The DOS 6 command that backs up and restores your fixed disk. It replaces the older BACKUP and RESTORE commands.

RESTORE   The DOS command that restores files previously backed up using BACKUP.

Exercises

Short Answer

1. What BACKUP command backs up the entire fixed disk in drive C to floppies in drive A?

2. What BACKUP command backs up all files on drive C that were created on or after Jan. 10, 1991?

3. What BACKUP option backs up only files that have their archive attribute set?

4. What BACKUP option creates a log file?

5. Should you label the diskettes used by BACKUP? If so, why?

6. Why can't you restore backed up files using COPY?

7. What RESTORE command restores a file that is called INFO.DAT to the \INVTRY\BACKORD directory?

8. What does the /M option to RESTORE do?

9. What RESTORE command restores all files created or last modified on or after 2:00 P.M. on 10-20-92?

10. What RESTORE command restores all files created or last modified on or before 2:00 P.M. on 10-20-92?

11. How do you back up your entire fixed disk when using MSBACKUP? What command restores files created using MSBACKUP?

12. Relative to MSBACKUP, explain what is meant by full backup, differential backup, and incremental backup.

13. What is a catalog?

14. Can MSBACKUP restore files created by BACKUP? Why or why not?

15. Since BACKUP has been replaced by MSBACKUP in DOS 6, why is the RESTORE command still included in DOS 6?

16. How do you back up selected files using MSBACKUP?

17. What does FASTOPEN do?

18. What command installs FASTOPEN for drive D and allows it to remember up to 45 files?

19. What command defragments your disk? Explain what fragmentation is.

20. When using DEFRAG, what is the difference between full optimization and Unfragment Files only?

21. What benefit is gained by defragmenting your disk?

22. Why should you prepare your fixed disk for shipment?

Activities

1. If your computer has a fixed disk, try backing it up. When you are finished, put the diskettes in a safe place.

2. Design a backup routine that meets the needs of your work environment.

CHAPTER 19

Miscellaneous Topics

CHAPTER OBJECTIVES

After completing this chapter, you should be able to:
- Use the FDISK command.
- Use the SET command.
- Recover damaged files using RECOVER.
- Increase disk space using DBLSPACE.
- Move files using MOVE.
- Delete directories using DELTREE.
- Use MEMMAKER.
- Understand POWER.

Congratulations! You have come a long way since Chapter 1. If you have read and worked through the examples in the preceding chapters, you will have no trouble using DOS. This final chapter will cover topics and commands that you will not need on a daily basis. However, you may find some of them useful in special situations. They are discussed briefly so that you know they exist. Also presented is a short guide to system maintenance.

FDISK

Before the fixed disk can be formatted, it must be partitioned. A partition is a portion of the fixed disk that can be either part or all of the disk. You can partition the fixed disk so that it can be used with two or more different operating systems, or so that it has multiple DOS partitions, which are given separate drive letters. If your system needs to support another operating system, such as UNIX, you must refer to the specific instructions in your DOS manual. To partition the fixed disk, use the *FDISK* external command.

> *FDISK   The DOS command that partitions your fixed disk.*

> **NOTE**
>
> **The FDISK command is used when a fixed disk is first brought into service or if you want to change the size of its partitions. Either way, whatever is on the disk is lost.**

The FDISK command lets you do these four things:

- Create a partition
- Set an active partition (from which DOS loads)
- Delete a partition
- Display disk information

In general, your fixed disk is partitioned and formatted by the supplier of your computer. If you need to use this command, refer to the documentation that came with your computer.

The SET Command

The *SET* command is used to create and give a value to a name that becomes part of DOS's environment. Although this name may not be of any direct value to you, it may be used by application programs. The general form of SET is

> *SET   The DOS command that sets an environmental value.*

SET *name=value*

where *name* is the string that is placed into DOS's environment with the value of *value*.

For example, the following command sets the name APPSDAT to the path \PROGRAM\APPS.

SET APPSDAT=\PROGRAM\APPS

Once this is done, an application program that wants to locate application program data files can check the value of APPSDAT in the DOS environment.

To remove a name from the environment, use the general form

SET *name=*

For example, the following command removes APPSDAT:

SET APPSDAT=

You can use the value of a name stored in the environment in a batch file by placing the name between percentage signs. For example, the following batch file uses the value of APPSDAT to copy data files from the path specified by the value of APPSDAT into the current working directory:

```
REM copy the data files into the working directory
COPY %APPSDAT%*.*
```

When this batch command runs, it will look like this:

```
COPY \PROGRAM\APPS\*.*
```

You can see the names and values active in your system by entering SET with no parameters.

Recovering Files From a Damaged Disk

In rare cases, a disk will become physically damaged in such a way that part of a file will still be readable. In such situations you can partially recover the file by using the *RECOVER* command.

The RECOVER command is only for use on physically damaged files. If you accidentally erase a file, use UNDELETE. If you accidentally format a disk, then use UNFORMAT.

Recovering data from physically damaged files will be useful only on text files where a small amount of text will have to be reentered. If part of a program file is lost, the program will simply not run. The general form of RECOVER is

RECOVER *file-name*

where *file-name* is the name of the file to recover, which may include a drive specifier and a path.

For example, to recover a file named FORMLET.WP, use the command

RECOVER FORMLET.WP

You can use RECOVER to recover an entire disk when it is the disk's directory that has become damaged. When a disk's directory is damaged, it is unreadable so DOS cannot know which files are on the disk. In this type of recovery operation, the program files may be recovered in a usable form, but it is best not to rely on this. To recover an entire disk, use this form of RECOVER:

RECOVER *drive-specifier*

As RECOVER recovers the files, it does not know their names (because the directory is unreadable), so it puts them in files using the form FILE*num*.REC, where *num* is a number between 0000 and 9999.

Never assume that you can successfully recover a damaged file; often there is no way to do so. It is usually better simply to go to a backup copy. But as a last resort, you can try RECOVER.

RECOVER   The DOS command that attempts to recover damaged files. (This command may not be included in your copy of DOS 6.)

Using MOVE

MOVE   *The DOS command that moves a file or renames a directory.*

Although versions of DOS prior to 6 included a command to *copy* files, they did not include a command to *move* files. However, DOS 6 has added the *MOVE* command, which allows you to move a file from one place to the other. Moving a file first copies the file to the new destination and then erases it from its original location. While you can move a file manually by first using COPY followed by ERASE, the MOVE command automates the process. Here is the general form of MOVE:

MOVE *source destination*

Here, *source* is the file or files that you want to move, which may include wildcard specifiers, and *destination* is a drive specifier and/or directory. You can also specify a new file name if you are moving only one file. For example, this moves the file TEMP from the C drive to the A drive:

MOVE C:TEMP A:

You can also use MOVE to change the name of a directory. To do this, use this general form:

MOVE *old-dir-name new-dir-name*

where *old-dir-name* is the full path name of the directory to be renamed and *new-dir-name* is its new name.

Removing an Entire Directory Tree Using DELTREE

As you learned earlier in this book, before you can remove a directory using RMDIR, it must be empty. This means that it cannot contain either files or subdirectories. Thus, if you want to remove an extensive subdirectory system, you must manually remove each subdirectory, starting from the top and moving down—erasing all files and removing directories as you go. In the case of complex directory trees, this process can be tedious and time-consuming. Prior to DOS 6, it was the only way that this process could be accomplished. To simplify this procedure, DOS 6 has added a new command that removes an entire directory system. The command that will remove an entire tree is called *DELTREE* and it has this general form:

DELTREE *directory*

DELTREE   *The DOS command that deletes a directory, including all of its files and subdirectories.*

Here, *directory* is the name of the top-level directory of the directory tree that you want to delete. (Remember, in the language of DOS, a directory system is referred to as a *tree*.)

The DELTREE command automatically erases all files in the entire directory tree and then deletes all of the directories.

For example, assuming the directory structure shown in Figure 6-1, which you created on your directories work disk, the following command removes all word processing files and directories:

DELTREE A:\WP

Before DELTREE actually removes the directory tree, you will be asked to confirm the deletion. If you don't want this confirmation, specify the /Y option. This option must go immediately after DELTREE, before the directory to be deleted. For example, this deletes the tree associated with /WP and does not ask before doing so.

DELTREE /Y A:\WP

> **CAUTION**
> **Use DELTREE with care. If you misunderstand what it is deleting, you might erase several files by accident.**

Using DBLSPACE to Increase Disk Space

Disk space is often at a premium. It seems that no matter how large your fixed disk, you can always use more. In the past, to increase your disk space, you had to either buy an additional fixed disk or replace your existing drive with one with larger capacity. However, if you are using DOS 6 or a later version, then you can increase the effective size of your hard disk using a special technique called *disk compression*.

Disk compression is the process by which information on your disk is encoded in a special way so that it takes up less disk space than it does in its non-encoded form. When disk compression is used, a special device driver automatically converts the data between its compressed form and its regular form so that as far as you (and your application programs) are concerned, the data will appear normal. Using disk compression, you can increase the storage capacity of your fixed disk by a factor of two or more.

Disk compression is not all gain without pain. When disk compression is used, the data on your disk is altered and may not be read without the special disk compression device driver. Therefore, if, for some reason, you need to access the information on the disk and you don't have access to the compression driver, you won't be able to read the files. Disk compression will also slow down your system slightly. In addition, some application programs may not be able to use compressed data if they bypass DOS and perform low-level disk accesses. Therefore, you may not want to use disk compression before you discuss the matter with a computer professional to see if it will be compatible with the way you use your system.

> **CAUTION**
> **Disk compression is an advanced operation. Once you compress a drive, you cannot decompress it! Therefore, do not use disk compression until you fully understand all its ramifications. It is best to discuss using disk compression with your instructor or another knowledgeable person first.**

The command that compresses your fixed drive is called *DBLSPACE*. To compress your fixed disk, simply run DBLSPACE. After passing through a series of safety checks, you begin disk compression by choosing either Express or Custom setup. Unless you are a very knowledgeable computer user, choose Express Setup. (Because it requires specialized knowledge, Custom Setup is not discussed here. Refer to your DOS manual for details.) The Express Setup causes DBLSPACE to compress your disk, install the necessary DEVICE

DBLSPACE   The DOS command that compresses your disk. Use this command with extreme care.

command in your CONFIG.SYS file to load the compression driver, and then restart your system. After the process is complete, your drive will have more room on it.

REMEMBER

Disk compression will create more disk space but may cause your disk to be incompatible with some software. Be sure to use DBLSPACE only after thoroughly considering the consequences. If you are new to DOS, do not use this command until you fully understand what you are doing.

Using MEMMAKER to Free Memory

MEMMAKER The DOS command that automatically optimizes the memory in your computer.

You can automatically optimize your system's use of memory by running the *MEMMAKER* command. This command automatically determines which device drivers and installed commands or programs can be run in the upper-memory area. In this way, it frees memory for your application programs. MEMMAKER only optimizes your memory if your computer uses an 80386 or an 80486 processor.

CAUTION

MEMMAKER may perform alterations to your system that are incompatible with your existing software. You may want to consult your instructor or other knowledgeable person before using this command.

To use MEMMAKER, simply execute it and then, when prompted, choose Express Setup. (If you are a very experienced user, you can choose Custom Setup. But, if you are knowledgeable enough to use Custom Setup, you probably don't need MEMMAKER to optimize your system!) MEMMAKER then optimizes your system and, in the process, may make changes to your CONFIG.SYS and AUTOEXEC.BAT files. Once the optimizations have been made, it then restarts your computer so that the changes can take effect. Next, you will be asked if everything seems OK. If it does, answer "Yes"; if not, answer "No." If you answer "No," MEMMAKER will attempt to fix the problem. (Generally, you won't have any trouble.)

NOTE

If your computer "locks up" when it attempts to restart after MEMMAKER has been used, just turn your system off and then on again. MEMMAKER will fix itself. Some of your programs may be incompatible with MEMMAKER's optimizations, so be patient if you encounter trouble.

If you cannot get MEMMAKER to work correctly or are unhappy with its optimizations, you can return your system to its original configuration by entering this command:

MEMMAKER /UNDO

Therefore, if you do encounter trouble and all else fails, simply return your system to its previous configuration.

If you are happy with the way your computer is working and have not run out of memory while using any of your application programs, then there is no reason to use MEMMAKER.

Using POWER to Conserve Battery Power

If you have a battery-powered computer, such as a laptop, then battery life is important to you. You can use the *POWER* command and device driver to help conserve battery power. The POWER device driver automatically manages your computer's devices so that minimum power is used. To use POWER, first put this line in your CONFIG.SYS file and then restart your computer.

DEVICE=C:\DOS\POWER.EXE

Once the POWER.EXE device has been installed, power conservation will be in effect. To see the status of power conservation, enter the command POWER at the prompt. You will see a display similar to this:

```
Power Management Status
-----------------------
Setting = ADV: REG
CPU: idle 71% of time.
```

Of course, the power setting and the CPU idle time may be different.

You can control the way power is conserved by using the ADV: option. This option has the following three forms: ADV:MAX, ADV:REG, and ADV:MIN. These correspond to maximum conservation, normal conservation (the default), and minimal conservation. For example, this POWER command sets power conservation to its maximum:

POWER ADV:MAX

While maximum power conservation may seem attractive, it may cause inconvenience or poor performance. (The exact effects will vary with your software and computer.) For the most part, the default conservation level provides the best power conservation. However, if you encounter problems, try the ADV:MIN setting.

To turn off power conservation, use this command:

POWER OFF

The POWER device driver is most effective when your computer conforms to the Advanced Power Management specification. (This is a hardware specification that you cannot change.) However, even if it doesn't, you will still get some savings in power by using the POWER device driver.

> *POWER   The DOS command that conserves battery power when using a laptop or portable computer.*

NOTE

The default settings of POWER are generally the best for normal use, but be sure to check the manuals that come with your computer. It is possible that a different setting will be advised.

Linking to a Network

Computer networks are becoming increasingly common. DOS 6 contains substantial network support that makes using a network easier. However, since each network has its own design and configuration and because networks are generally run by a network manager, this book will not discuss them or their related commands. If your computer is connected to a network, be sure to discuss its use with the person in charge.

Maintaining Your System

A computer is much like an automobile. With proper care and attention, it will run for several trouble-free years. But if you neglect the maintenance, it will be plagued with troubles. A computer system requires two types of care: physical maintenance of the computer and maintenance of the software.

Maintaining the Hardware

The golden rule of maintaining the computer's hardware is to keep it clean. Dust is the computer's worst enemy. It can build up on the circuits inside the computer, causing them to overheat by reducing their normal heat-dissipation capabilities. Furthermore, dust and dirt on diskettes reduces the life of both the diskettes and the disk drive read/write heads.

Though it may be hard to believe, static electricity is a major cause of computer failure. Walking across a carpet on a dry winter day can cause your body to develop a charge of several thousand volts. If you touch the wrong part of the computer, this voltage could flow into the circuits and literally blow their insides apart. If static electricity is a problem in your environment, you can either use antistatic sprays on the carpet or invest in a grounded metal strip that you always touch first before touching the computer.

Along the same lines as static electricity is lightning. If lightning strikes very near the computer, enough of the charge can be picked up by the circuits to destroy them. You cannot prevent lightning, but you can minimize the risk by unplugging the computer from the power. The wires that carry power act like a large antenna, which can pick up the lightning charge. If your computer is unplugged, there is much less chance of damage.

Finally, don't put liquids on top of the computer. Although this seems like a simple statement, users unfamiliar with computers will often put coffee cups or soft drink cans on top of the system. Obviously, a spill can cause significant damage.

Maintaining the Software

The most important thing that you can do to protect the software in the system is to maintain a rigid backup schedule. The average system usually has several years of information stored in it, and the dollar value of this information is often far greater than the cost of the computer. It is a resource to be protected.

In large (or even small) offices, it is important to restrict access to any computer that contains important information. Though deliberate destruction of information is rare, it can happen. Most of the time, however, the damage is done by someone who doesn't know what he or she is doing—the bull in a china shop syndrome. Every employee must have a clear understanding that the information in the computer is a valued asset. The fact that it is invisible does not reduce its importance.

Application programs are often improved by their developers, and you will want to take advantage of these new versions. To avoid trouble, you must switch to the new version correctly. Never destroy an old version of the program! Sometimes, though rarely, the new version will have an unknown problem that prevents it from being used. If you have destroyed the old version, you will have no way to run the application. Also, always follow the installation instructions that come with the new version. Unless specifically told otherwise, make sure that all the old programs are replaced by the new ones. Mixing different versions of the programs that make up an application can cause serious trouble.

The Shell Versus the Command Prompt

Now that you know how to run DOS using both the Shell graphical interface and the command prompt, you may think that you have to choose one of these two methods and use it exclusively. This is far from the truth. The best way to use DOS is, first and foremost, the way you feel the most comfortable. If you like the Shell, use it. If you like the command prompt interface, use it. But, don't be afraid to mix the two. For example, for simple file manipulations and running your application programs, the Shell is very convenient. The Shell also supports the Task Manager. However, for some repetitious operations, the command prompt interface is better. (Remember that DOSKEY makes reusing commands at the prompt very easy indeed.)

In the final analysis, how you use DOS will, in large part, be determined by how you use your computer. Feel free to experiment and use what works best for you.

Final Thoughts

DOS is somewhat like a living animal because it continues to evolve and change as the ways in which it is used evolve. The knowledge and understanding that you have gained about DOS will benefit you both now and in the future, because the same basic concepts can be applied to other environments. In fact, you will probably be using DOS on one computer and a different operating system on another in the not-too-distant future. You can easily generalize your understanding of DOS, and you will have no trouble using virtually any type of computer or operating system.

Key Terms

DBLSPACE The DOS command that compresses your disk. Use this command with extreme care.

DELTREE The DOS command that deletes a directory, including all of its files and subdirectories.

FDISK The DOS command that partitions your fixed disk.

MEMMAKER The DOS command that automatically optimizes the memory in your computer.

MOVE The DOS command that moves a file or renames a directory.

POWER The DOS command that conserves battery power when using a laptop or portable computer.

RECOVER The DOS command that attempts to recover damaged files. (This command may not be included in your copy of DOS 6.)

SET The DOS command that sets an environmental value.

Exercises

True or False

1. Before a fixed disk can be formatted, it must be partitioned. _____

2. Generally, you will not need to use the FDISK command. _____

3. SET is the command that is used to create and give a value to a name that becomes part of the DOS environment. _____

4. Damaged files can always be fully restored using RECOVER. _____

5. MOVE copies a file and erases it from its original location. _____

6. DELTREE erases the entire directory structure of the disk, starting from the root. _____

7. Before DELTREE can operate, you must write-protect your disk. _____

8. DBLSPACE doubles the length of each file on a disk. _____

9. Since DBLSPACE causes no permanent change to your disk, you don't have to worry about using it. _____

10. MEMMAKER applies only to portable computers. _____

11. When you need your computer to run really fast, use the POWER command. _____

Short Answer

1. What SET command gives the name WP the value WPDIR?

2. How can you use the value of a name stored in the environment in a batch file?

3. What command displays all environmental names and values?

4. What command attempts to restore a damaged file called TIRES.DAT?

5. How does MOVE differ from COPY?

6. What is the main advantage to using DELTREE over RMDIR?

7. Why must you be careful when using DELTREE?

8. What does the /UNDO option to MEMMAKER do?

9. To what type of computers does the POWER command apply?

10. What device driver must be installed before you can use the POWER command?

11. What command turns the POWER monitor off?

12. Name some causes of hardware failure.

Activity

On your own, continue to explore your computer and DOS. The more you know about both, the better you will be able to use them.

Business Case Study

A member of your company has decided to retire. At his retirement party, it is announced that you will be taking his place. As you are being shown around the department you are going to manage, the retiring employee explains that the department has recently acquired a few computers from another department. "Since I don't know much about these things," he admits, "you might like to make some changes." At your first opportunity, you start one of the systems and find things to be in good order. There are only a few minor changes you would like to make. Here are the steps you follow. (As a final activity, try to fill in the missing details on your own.)

1. Assume that your newly acquired systems are equipped with one hard drive and one 3½ inch floppy drive. The system is on and the prompt reads C:>.

   a. View the root directory.
   b. After you execute the directory command, you notice the following: a DOS directory, a WP directory, and a SPREADST directory.
   c. You need to know if this is the most current release of DOS. After you execute the proper DOS command, you realize that it is.
   d. You now want to know how much memory the system has and how many megabytes the hard disk system contains.
   e. You want to view the AUTOEXEC.BAT file to see if you need to make any changes. After you issue the appropriate command, you see the following:

   ```
   @ ECHO OFF
   DATE
   TIME
   CLS
   ```

   f. You make a few changes to the AUTOEXEC.BAT file by adding the following:

      • A prompt statement to display the > symbol and the current path.
      • A path statement to include the directories listed above.

2. You are notified that a delivery will soon be made to your department of five new printers. This changes a few things, and now you need to add another statement to the AUTOEXEC.BAT file.

   • Modify the AUTOEXEC.BAT file with a command that will cause the printer to print 132 characters per line and 6 lines per inch.

3. You have also been informed that you will be getting a new database program, which you assume will require an update of the CONFIG.SYS file. As you issue the DIR command again, you notice that you don't have a CONFIG.SYS file, so you will need to create one.

Create a CONFIG.SYS file to include the following:

a. Check for (CTRL)-(BREAK) more frequently.
b. Set 30 open files.
c. Create a virtual disk that allocates 256K of storage, has sectors 128 bytes long, and allows up to 64 directory entries.

PART 6

Appendices

APPENDIX *A*

EDLIN: The Original DOS Text Editor

E DLIN is the text editor provided by early versions of DOS. Although you will want to use the DOS screen editor EDIT described in Chapter 7 when working with DOS 6, this editor is not included in versions of DOS prior to DOS 5. However, it is possible that on occasion you will need to use a computer that is running an earlier version of DOS. In this case, you may need to use EDLIN to create or modify text files. For this reason, this appendix teaches you how to create, modify, and maintain text files using EDLIN.

You will need your DOS work diskette in drive A to follow along with the examples in this chapter unless you are a using a fixed disk.

NOTE

The only reason to learn to use EDLIN is if you might, in some situation, have to use a computer running a version of DOS that predates version 5. If this will never be the case, then there is no reason to learn EDLIN. It is better to use DOS 6's screen editor EDIT.

What EDLIN Is and Isn't

Formally, EDLIN is a line-oriented text editor. It is not a screen-based editor, nor is it, in the proper definition of the term, a word processor. Its sole function is to allow the creation and modification of text files on a line-by-line basis. As far as text editors go, EDLIN is of a rather old style. It contains no flashy features. But it is sufficient.

If you are new to microcomputers, keep in mind that EDLIN is not representative of the types of editors in general use. It is a simple editor supplied by all versions of DOS to allow you to create and modify short text files that will help you customize and tailor DOS to your needs. It is not intended to take the place of either a full-featured, screen-oriented text editor or a word processor.

Most editors today use the WYSIWYG (wiz-ee-wig) approach. That is, "What You See Is What You Get." This means that what appears on the screen is the way the file will look when printed. However, EDLIN does not follow this principle—the way the file looks in the editor will be somewhat different from the way it will look if printed.

Another difference between EDLIN and most modern-style editors is that EDLIN does not use the arrow keys to move around on the screen. This is because EDLIN is not screen-oriented. Instead, EDLIN is line-oriented, which means that it can only deal with a line of text at a time—not a screenful.

Executing EDLIN

EDLIN is an external command, so you will need a copy of EDLIN.COM on your work disk. To execute EDLIN, use the general form

EDLIN *file-name*

where *file-name* is the name of the text file you wish to edit. If *file-name* does not exist, EDLIN will create it. Remember that the *file-name* may include a drive specifier and a path name.

Some EDLIN Basics

In this section you will learn some of the essentials of EDLIN's operation, including entering text, listing the file, saving the file, and exiting EDLIN. Once you understand its basic operation, the later sections in this chapter will discuss EDLIN's commands in detail. Let's begin with some examples.

Creating a Text File

Execute EDLIN by entering

EDLIN EDTEST.TXT

When EDLIN begins executing, you will see the following:

```
New file
*_
```

As you expect, the message "New file" simply means that the specified file did not exist and EDLIN has created it. The asterisk (*) is EDLIN's prompt. Whenever you see it you know that EDLIN is ready to accept a command.

This is an important point: EDLIN operates a little like DOS by displaying a prompt and waiting for commands. Each time you give EDLIN a command, it does what it is told.

Entering Text

When EDLIN displays its prompt, it is in command mode and is *not* ready to accept text. To cause EDLIN to accept text you must give it the I (insert) command. (You may enter this and the other EDLIN commands in uppercase or lowercase, as you like.) For example, enter the **I** command and then enter these lines of text.

Now is the time
for all good men
to come to the aid of their party.

Your screen will look like this:

```
*I
        1:*Now is the time
        2:*for all good men
        3:*to come to the aid of their party.
        4:*_
```

In insert mode, EDLIN tabs in, displays the current line number and an asterisk—which in insert mode indicates the currently active line—and waits for input. Each time you press (ENTER) a new line number is displayed. Remember that when the asterisk follows the line number, it is not a command prompt but simply an indicator of the active line. (This is one of the most confusing aspects of EDLIN.)

The line numbers are not part of your file and will not be on the disk when the file is saved. Rather, they are supplied by EDLIN as both a convenience and a means of referring to a line.

If you make a mistake while typing you can use the same commands, function keys, and control keys that DOS accepts to correct your mistake. However, once you have pressed (ENTER), you must use special EDLIN commands to make corrections.

To stop entering text you must press (CTRL)-(BREAK). Try this now. As you can see, a "^C" is displayed and EDLIN's prompt returns once more.

Listing the File

To list the contents of the file currently being edited, you use the L (list lines) command. To execute its simplest form, simply type **L** and press (ENTER). Do so now. You will see the text you just entered displayed like this:

```
1: Now is the time
2: for all good men
3: to come to the aid of their party.
```

Terminating EDLIN

There are two ways to terminate EDLIN. The one you will use most often is the E (end edit) command, which causes EDLIN to save the contents of the file and then terminate. The other is the Q (quit edit) command, which causes EDLIN to abort without saving the file to disk.

Exit EDLIN using the **E** command at this time.

Re-editing a File

EDLIN behaves a little differently when you are editing a pre-existing file than when you are editing a new file. To begin, edit EDTEST.TXT again by entering

EDLIN EDTEST.TXT

When EDLIN begins execution, you will see this:

```
End of input file
*
```

The message "End of input file" is EDLIN's way to tell you that it has loaded the entire file into memory. The only time you will not see this message is when (and if) you edit a file large enough that it cannot all fit into memory. In this case, EDLIN reads the file until 75% of the memory is used. To edit the remainder of a large file you will need to use some special commands, discussed later, that write part of the file back to disk and read in some more of the file from disk. It is very likely that you will never have a file larger than will fit into memory.

List the file at this time using the **L** command. It will look like this:

```
1:*Now is the time
2: for all good men
3: to come to the aid of their party.
```

Notice that the asterisk is at the start of line 1. This is EDLIN's way of telling you which line is current. The current line determines where certain editor commands will take place. For example, if you enter the **I** command and begin inserting text, the text that you enter will be inserted *before* line 1. Try this now by entering this line: **This is before line one**. Press (ENTER) and then (CTRL)-(BREAK). List the file. Your screen will look like this:

```
1: This is before line one
2:*Now is the time
3: for all good men
4: to come to the aid of their party.
```

Notice that line 2 is now current. The next section will discuss more fully the meaning and manipulation of the current line.

At this point, enter the **E** command, which saves the file to disk and exits the editor. At the DOS prompt enter this command:

DIR EDTEST.*

Two files will be displayed. One is EDTEST.TXT, as you would expect because this is the name of the file that you are editing. The other is called EDTEST.BAK. This file contains the previous version of EDTEST.TXT. The ".BAK" extension stands for "backup." Each time EDLIN saves text to an already existing file, it first renames the extension of the existing file to ".BAK" and then writes the text to disk using the actual file name. In this way you always have the old version of your file to fall back on if you accidentally corrupt the current version. Periodically, you may want to erase backup files that you no longer need in order to free disk space.

The Current Line

Intrinsic to the operation of EDLIN is the concept of the *current line*. You can think of the current line as being the one you are "on" or "at." As stated earlier, EDLIN identifies the current line with the asterisk. When you first begin editing a file, line 1 is current. As you will shortly see, a number of EDLIN commands change the current line.

When you insert text, it is placed before the current line and the rest of the existing text is moved down.

EDLIN Commands

Now that you know the basics of EDLIN's operation, it is time to study its commands in greater detail. EDLIN has 14 commands. These commands are listed in Table A-1. Let's look at each of these commands in turn.

Command	Meaning
A	**Append lines (from disk file)**
C	**Copy lines**
D	**Delete lines**
E	**End edit and save file**
I	**Insert lines**
L	**List lines**
M	**Move lines**
P	**Display a page (23 lines)**
Q	**Quit (does not save file)**
R	**Replace text**
S	**Search text**
T	**Transfer lines (merges one file into another)**
W	**Write lines (to a file)**
line-num	**Intra-line edit *line-num* line**

TABLE A-1   **The EDLIN commands**

Inserting Text

At this point, edit EDTEST.TXT. (Use **EDLIN EDTEST.TXT**.) Enter **2I** and
this is new line two followed by pressing `ENTER`. Then press `CTRL`-`BREAK`.
Use the **L** command to list the file. It will look like this:

```
1: This is before line one
2: this is new line two
3:*Now is the time
4: for all good men
5: to come to the aid of their party.
```

By placing a line number in front of the I command, you told EDLIN
to begin inserting text immediately before that line. The general form
of the I command is

line-num I

where *line-num* is the number of the line in front of which you wish to
begin adding text. If you don't specify the line number, text is inserted
before the current line.

   To add text to the end of a file, simply specify a line number that is
greater than the last line number of the file. To add lines to the end of
the EDTEST.TXT file, for example, you can enter **6I**. Try this now. Add
the lines

Text editors
are fun to use
as long as you know the
right commands.

and then press `CTRL`-`BREAK`. If you list the file you will see that the lines
have, indeed, been added to the end.

Deleting Lines

To delete lines of text, use the D command. The delete command takes
this general form:

*start-line, end-line*D

where *start-line* and *end-line* are line numbers. The delete command
will delete all lines from *start-line* to *end-line*. For example, using the
EDTEST.TXT file, try the command

3,5D

and then list the file. Your screen will look like this:

```
1: This is before line one
2: this is new line two
3:*Text editors
4: are fun to use
5: as long as you know the
6: right commands.
```

If you do not specify the starting line number, then the delete command will delete all lines from the current line to the ending line. You must start this form of the command with the comma, however. For example, this deletes lines 3 and 4 in this example:

,4D

You can delete any one line simply by specifying its line number. For example, this deletes line 2.

2D

Notice that no comma precedes this form of the command.

Finally, if no line number is specified, the current line is deleted.

Listing the File

So far you have seen only the simplest form of the L command. Its general form is

*start-line, end-line*L

where *start-line* and *end-line* specify a range of lines to list on the screen. For example, to list lines 3 through 5, enter

3,5L

This will display

```
3:*Text editors
4: are fun to use
5: as long as you know the
```

If you omit the starting line number, then EDLIN will display 11 lines before the current line and stop at the specified ending line. You must start this form of the command with a comma.

Omitting the ending line causes EDLIN to display 23 lines beginning with the specified line. If fewer than 23 lines remain, then EDLIN will display lines until the end is reached. For example, still using EDTEST.TXT, the command

4L

causes this display:

```
4: are fun to use
5: as long as you know the
6: right commands.
```

If no line numbers are specified, then 11 lines before and after the current line are displayed. This makes a total of 23 lines (if the file has that many).

Editing Lines

You can edit (modify) an existing line in a file by entering its line number. The specified line will be displayed and the cursor positioned beneath the first character in the line. You can use any of the DOS command line editing keys to make changes to the line. The process of editing an existing line is called *intra-line editing*.

For example, enter **2** now. You will see this:

```
2:*this is new line two
2: _
```

You may now edit this line exactly as you would the DOS command line. For example, press (F1) until the cursor is positioned past the space following the word "is." Now press (INS) and enter **a new addition to**, then press (F3) followed by (ENTER). When you list the file, line 2 will look like this:

```
2:*this is a new addition to new line two
```

Once you press (ENTER), any changes you have made to the line will be part of the file. You can cancel the edit at any time by pressing either (ESC) or (CTRL)-(BREAK). Also, if you have not moved the cursor from the start of the line, then pressing (ENTER) will also cancel the intra-line editing process.

You may edit the current line by entering a period instead of its line number.

You should try some examples of intra-line editing now. Restore all lines, including line 2, to their original condition before moving on.

Copying Lines

The C (copy) command is used to copy a range of lines. It has the general form

*start-line, end-line, dest-line, count*C

The lines between *start-line* and *end-line*, inclusive, are copied before *dest-line, count* number of times. If *count* is not specified, the default is one.

For example, once again using the EDTEST.TXT file, enter this command:

1,3,6C

The file will now look like this:

```
1: This is before line one
2: this is new line two
3:*Text editors
4: are fun to use
5: as long as you know the
6: This is before line one
7: this is new line two
8: Text editors
9: right commands.
```

REMEMBER

A copy duplicates lines. This means that the lines copied are still in their original place as well as in the new location. The move command, discussed next, is used to move lines from one spot to another.

If you specify a count value, then the specified lines are duplicated that many times. For example, try this command:

1,1,4,3C

Your file will now look like this:

```
1: This is before line one
2: this is new line two
3: Text editors
4:*This is before line one
5: This is before line one
6: This is before line one
7: are fun to use
8: as long as you know the
9: This is before line one
10: this is new line two
11: Text editors
12: right commands.
```

You should keep in mind that the destination line must be outside the range of the lines to be moved.

Moving Lines

The M (move lines) command is similar in nature to the copy command except that it moves the specified range of lines from one spot in the file to another. Its general form is

start-line, *end-line*, *dest-line*M

Before proceeding, let's clean up the EDTEST.TXT file. First, delete all existing lines by entering **1,100D**. Now, insert the following lines.

one
two
three
four
five
six
seven
eight
nine
ten

Once this is done, try this command:

2,5,8M

List the file; it will look like this:

```
1: one
2: six
3: seven
4:*two
```

```
 5: three
 6: four
 7: five
 8: eight
 9: nine
10: ten
```

As you can see, the original lines 2 through 5 have been relocated to the position immediately before line 8.

If you leave off either the starting line or the ending line (or both) then the current line is used by default. For example, this moves line 4 to the top of the file:

,,1M

As with the copy command, the destination must not be within the range to be moved.

Searching

To find a specific string in the file, use the S (search) command. A *string* is simply a sequence of characters. The search command takes this general form:

start-line, end-line ? S*string*

The search command searches the file between *start-line* and *end-line* looking for an occurrence of *string*. The "?" is optional and is used to find multiple occurrences.

To begin, delete all the lines in the file and enter the following:

This is a test
of the search command.
From time to time,
you will find this command useful -
especially when the file is very large.

Once you have entered this, try this command:

1,5Stime

EDLIN will display

```
3: From time to time,
```

The line in which a match is found is also made current.

If you want to search for a specific occurrence of a string that appears more than once in the file, use the "?" option. For example, enter this command:

1,5?Sthe

You will first see

```
2: of the search command.
O.K.? _
```

As you can see, the "?" causes EDLIN to ask you whether the proper occurrence of the string has been found. If it has, press Y or (ENTER); otherwise, press any other key. Press **N** at this time. EDLIN will find the second "the" in line 5 and will once again prompt you. Press **N** again. Since "the" does not appear again in the file, EDLIN prints the message "Not found".

The search command is case sensitive. This means that uppercase and lowercase versions of the same character are considered to be different. For example, try

1,5?SThis

EDLIN finds the match with "This" in the first line, but does not report any other matches because the "this" in line 4 begins with a lowercase "t."

If you omit the first line number, the search command begins with the line immediately following the current line. Omitting the second line number causes the search to continue until the last line in the file. If you omit the search string, then the previous string is used.

You should try some examples of searching at this time.

Replacing Text

To replace one string with another, use the R (replace) command. The general form of the replace command is

start-line, end-line ?R*old-string*(F6)*new-string*

The first two line numbers define the range over which the replacement will take place. The "?" is optional. If you use it, you are prompted prior to each replacement. The old string is the one to be replaced by the new string. The old and new strings are separated by pressing the (F6) key.

Using the file developed in the section on searching, try the following command.

1,5Rtime(F6)day

Note that the (F6) key displays as "^Z". This command will change line 3 from

```
From time to time
```

to

```
From day to day
```

If you do not want to change all occurrences of a string, use the "?" option. You will be prompted at each occurrence as to whether you want to change it or not. For example, to change the sentences to past tense use this command:

1,5?Ris(F6)was

The first thing you see is

```
      1: Thwas is a test
O.K.? _
```

As you can see, EDLIN found the "is" in "This." Since you do not want to change this "is" to "was", answer **N**. EDLIN will then look for other occurrences. The next one is the one that you want to change. You will see

```
        1: This was a test
O.K.? _
```

Since you want to change this "is", answer **Y**. This process will continue until the full five lines have been searched.

You can use the replace command to remove unwanted text by leaving the new string blank. For example, try this:

1,5Ra⟨F6⟩

As you can see, all occurrences of the letter "a" have been removed from the file. The ⟨F6⟩ is technically unnecessary in this case.

Like the search command, omitting the first line number causes the replacements to begin with the line immediately following the current line. If the ending line number is not present, the replacement process ends with the last line in the file. If no strings are specified, then the strings from the previous R command are used.

Try some examples at this time.

The Page Command

The P (page) command is used to list a block of lines on the display. It differs from the list command in that it resets the current line to the last line displayed. In its simplest form, it pages through a file 23 lines at a time. This is done by simply entering P repeatedly. Its general form is

*start-line, end-line*P

If present, *start-line* and *end-line* specify a range of lines to display. If *start-line* is omitted, the line following the current line is used. If an *end-line* number is not specified, then 23 lines are listed.

End Edit and Quit

End edit, E, terminates the editing process and saves the file as described earlier. Quit, Q, terminates the editor but does not save what has been edited.

Transferring Text Between Files

EDLIN allows you to read the contents of a file on disk into the file you are currently editing by using the T (transfer) command. So that you can follow along, create two files called TEST1.TXT and TEST2.TXT using EDLIN. Into TEST1.TXT enter these lines:

one
two
three
four

Into TEST2.TXT, enter

This is a test

Now edit TEST1. Try this command:

3TTEST2.TXT

Now list the file. It will look like this:

```
one
two
This is a test
three
four
```

As you can see, the contents of TEST2 were read into the TEST1 file immediately before line 3.

The transfer command takes the general form:

*line-num*T*filename*

where *line-num* is the number of the line before which the text from the disk file will be placed. The *filename* is the name of the file to read in and may include a drive specifier and path name. If no line number is specified, the text is placed before the current line.

There are three things to remember about the transfer command. First, the text is read in immediately before the line specified. Second, if the file is not in the current directory, then you will receive the message "File not found." Finally, the entire contents of the disk file are read in—it is not possible to read in just part of a file.

Append and Write

When you are editing a file that is too large to fit in memory, EDLIN reads in the first part of the file until 75% of free memory is used. You can tell EDLIN to read in more lines using the A (append) command. The append command has the general form

*num-lines*A

where *num-lines* is the number of lines to read in. If no number is specified, then one line is read. For example, "45A" reads in 45 more lines.

In order to edit the end of a large file, you will need to write part of it out to disk to free memory before issuing the append command. To do this you use the W (write) command, which has this general form:

*num-lines*W

Here, *num-lines* refers to the number of lines to write to the disk. If a number is not specified, then text is written until 75% of memory is free. The write command writes lines from the top of the file starting with line 1.

B

Quick Command Reference

This appendix contains a short summary of all commonly used DOS commands presented in alphabetical order. (The few not covered here are used mostly by programmers and system integrators.) This appendix will help you quickly learn what a command does or find which command you should use for a certain operation. As such, only the most common forms and options of each command are shown. For a full discussion of each command, please refer to the chapters of the book.

The following notational conventions will be used. Items enclosed between square brackets ([]) are optional. Except where explicitly noted otherwise, the term *path* refers to the full path name, including an optional drive specifier. The term *file name* may include a drive specifier and/or a path name. Finally, three periods (...) indicate a variable-length list, and two periods (..) indicate a range, such as 1..10.

NOTE

Only those commands that can be executed from a command prompt or from a batch file are contained here. Shell commands, configuration commands, and device drivers are discussed in their appropriate sections inside the book.

APPEND

The external APPEND command is used to join one directory to another. If directory B is joined to A, it will appear to the user that directory A contains all of A's and B's files. APPEND is executed the first time using one of the following two forms:

APPEND *path1*[*;path2;...pathN*]

or

APPEND [/X] [/E]

The first form uses APPEND's default method of operation. APPEND only applies to data files. The second form only applies when APPEND is first installed. (APPEND is an installed command.) The /X option allows DOS to search appended directories when executing a program. (This option must be specified the first time you execute APPEND.) The /E option causes the appended paths to be held in the DOS environment area. APPEND is used to allow access to data files, much as PATH is used to allow access to program files.

You can see the currently appended directories by entering the APPEND command with no arguments. The following form disassociates any appended directories:

APPEND ;

For example, the following command appends the \WP directory.

APPEND \WP

ASSIGN

> **NOTE**
> **ASSIGN may not be included in your copy of DOS 6.**

The external ASSIGN command is used to redirect input/output (I/O) operations from one disk drive to another. It takes the general form

ASSIGN *drive1=drive2* [*drive3=drive4* ...]

For example, to reverse the assignments of drives A and B, you could use the following command.

ASSIGN A=B B=A

Now all I/O operations for A will go to B, and all I/O operations for B will be redirected to A.

You reset the drives to their original assignments by entering ASSIGN with no arguments. Remember, do not use ASSIGN with the BACKUP or PRINT commands.

ATTRIB

The external ATTRIB command is used to set or examine file attributes. It takes the general form

ATTRIB [+R] [-R] [+A] [-A] [+H] [-H] [+S][-S] [*file-name*] [/S]

where *file-name* is the name of the file(s) that will have its attributes set or examined. Wildcard characters are allowed. +R turns on the read-only attribute, while -R turns it off. +A turns on the archive attribute, while -A turns it off. +S turns on the system-file attribute; -S turns it off. +H turns on the hidden-file attribute; -H turns it off. If one of these is not present, the current state of the file attributes is displayed. The /S option tells ATTRIB to process files in the current directory and any subdirectories.

For example, the following command turns on the read-only attribute for all .EXE files in the current directory.

ATTRIB +R *.EXE

BACKUP

The external BACKUP command is used primarily to back up the contents of a fixed disk by copying it to several floppy diskettes. Used in this way, it takes the general form

BACKUP *source-drive[file-name] target-drive* [/A] [/D:*date*]
        [/F] [/L] [/M] [/S] [/T:*time*] [/F:*size*]

The *file-name* may include wildcard characters.
The meaning of each BACKUP option is shown below:

Option	Meaning
/A	Add files to existing target diskettes
/D:*date*	Copy only those files with dates the same as or later than *date*
/F:*size*	Specifies capacity of target disk
/L	Create and maintain a log file
/M	Copy only those files that have been modified since the last backup
/S	Process all subdirectories
/T:*time*	Copy only those files with times equal to or later than *time* on the specified date

> **NOTE**
> **BACKUP applies only to versions of DOS prior to 6. For backing up files using DOS 6, refer to the MSBACKUP command.**

The /F option is used to specify the capacity of the target disk when you want it to be something other than its normal capacity. See Chapter 18 for a full description.

For example, if executed from the root directory of drive C, the following command backs up the entire fixed disk.

BACKUP C:*.* A: /S

BREAK

The internal BREAK command tells DOS how to check for the (CTRL)-(BREAK) key combination, which is used to cancel commands. It takes the general form

BREAK [ON]

or

BREAK [OFF]

Setting BREAK ON causes DOS to check more frequently for
(CTRL)-(BREAK). BREAK is off by default.

Though setting BREAK to ON may seem tempting, it is usually
not a good idea because it slows down the execution of all commands
and programs.

The following command tells DOS to check more frequently for
the (CTRL)-(BREAK) key combination.

BREAK ON

CALL

The CALL batch command is used to execute another batch file command from within a batch file. The general form of CALL is

CALL *batch-file*

where *batch-file* is the name of the batch file command that you wish to
execute.

For example, the following command calls the batch file named
COPYALL.BAT.

CALL COPYALL

CHCP

The internal CHCP command is used with code page switching for
extended foreign language and country support. This little-used command is seldom required. Refer to your DOS manual.

CHDIR

The internal CHDIR command (CD) is used to change the current directory. The general form of the command is

CHDIR *path*

where *path* is the path name of the directory to which you are changing. For example, the following command makes the \WP directory
current.

CHDIR \WP

CHKDSK

The external CHKDSK command reports the status of the specified
drive and repairs certain types of disk errors. It takes the general form

CHKDSK [*drive-specifier*] [*file-name*] [/F] [/V]

If *drive-specifier* is absent, the current disk is checked. The /F option instructs CHKDSK to fix any errors that it can. The /V option displays all files and their paths. Specifying a *file-name*, which may include wildcard characters, causes CHKDSK to report the number of noncontiguous (nonadjacent) sectors used by the file(s).

For example, the following command reports the status of drive A and attempts to fix any errors.

CHKDSK A: /F

CHOICE

CHOICE is used to allow the user to select between two or more options. CHOICE is too complex to synopsize here. Refer to Chapter 11 for details.

CLS

The internal CLS command clears the screen of the computer's display monitor.

COMP

COMP is the file comparison command that was included with versions of DOS prior to 6. It is an external command that may not be included in your copy of DOS 6. (FC is the new file comparison command.) COMP has the general form

COMP *first-file second-file* [/D] [/A] [/L] [/C] [/N=*num*]

where *first-file* and *second-file* are file names that may contain wildcard characters.

For example, the following command compares the contents of the file ACCOUNTS.DAT on drive A to the file by the same name on drive B.

COMP A:ACCOUNTS.DAT B:ACCOUNTS.DAT

By default, the output of COMP is displayed in hexadecimal. To display in decimal, use the /D option. To display the results as characters, use the /A option. To display line numbers of mismatches, use /L. To have COMP ignore case differences, use /C. Using the /N=*num* option, you can have COMP compare only the first *num* lines in the file.

COPY

The internal COPY command is used to copy the contents of one file into another. It takes the general form

COPY *source destination* [/V]

where *source* is the name of the file to be copied into *destination*. Both file names may use wildcard characters. The /V option causes COPY to automatically verify that the information was copied correctly into the destination file. The /V option is not available in the Shell version of COPY.

For example, the following command copies all files that end with the extension EXE to the C drive.

COPY *.EXE C:

CTTY

The internal CTTY command is used to switch console control to a different device, such as a remote terminal. It takes the general form

CTTY *device-name*

where *device-name* must be one of DOS's standard device names. Do not try this command unless another device is attached to your computer that can control it.

DATE

The internal DATE command is used to set the date of the system. It takes the general form

DATE [*date*]

where *date* is the current date. You must use the proper date convention for the country you live in. For the United States, it is mm-dd-yy. If you do not specify date on the command line, DATE reports what it thinks is the current date and waits for you to either enter the correct date or press (ENTER), indicating that you accept the date reported.

For example, the following command sets the date to June 26, 1993.

DATE 6-26-93

DBLSPACE

> WARNING
> **Use DBLSPACE only after you are sure you understand its consequences. Once you have compressed your disk, it cannot be decompressed.**

The external DBLSPACE command increases the effective storage capacity of your fixed disk by using data compression. Refer to Chapter 19 for details.

DEBUG

The external DEBUG command is used by programmers to help find problems in programs.

DEFRAG

The external DEFRAG command rearranges the files on your disk to eliminate fragmentation. Removing fragmentation causes access to your files to be faster and, thus, increases the overall effective speed of your applications. Because DEFRAG is a window-based, menu-driven command, refer to Chapter 18 for details.

DEL

The internal DEL command erases files from a disk. It takes the general form

DEL *file-name* [/P]

where *file-name* is the name of the file to be erased. You can use wildcard characters in the file name to erase groups of files. ERASE is another name for DEL.

If you specify the /P option, DEL will ask for your OK before erasing a file.

For example, the following command erases all files that begin with INV from the disk in drive B.

DEL B:INV*.*

DELTREE

The external DELTREE command deletes the specified directory tree and any files in that directory tree. The specified directory and any of its subdirectories need not be empty. The general form of DELTREE is shown here.

DELTREE [/Y] *directory*

where directory is the top-level directory of the tree to be deleted.

By specifying the /Y option, you prevent DELTREE from prompting you before deleting the directory.

DIR

The internal DIR command is used to list a disk's directory. It has the general form

DIR [*file-name*] [/P] [/W] [/A:*attr*] [/O:*order*] [/S] [/B] [/L]

If a *file-name* is present, only those files that match will be displayed. Otherwise, the entire directory is listed. Wildcard characters are allowed in the file name. The /P option pauses the display every 23 lines, while the /W option causes the directory to be displayed in four columns across the screen. The /A option specifies what types of files are displayed.

The latter uses the same attribute codes as the ATTRIB command. They are shown here. (You may use any combination of these attributes.)

Attribute	Files Listed
a	**files with archive attribute on**
–a	**files with archive attribute off**
d	**directories only**
–d	**files only**
h	**hidden**
–h	**non-hidden**
r	**read-only files only**
–r	**nonread-only files**
s	**system**
–s	**nonsystem**

The value of *order* determines how the /O command sorts the directory. The values of *order* are shown here.

Order	Sort By
c	**compression ratio**
–c	**reverse order by compression ratio**
d	**date and time**
–d	**reverse order by date and time**
e	**extension**
–e	**reverse order by extension**
g	**directories before files**
–g	**directories after files**
n	**name**
–n	**reverse order by name**
s	**size**
–s	**reverse order by size**

To list all files that match *file-name* in all subdirectories, use the /S option. To list filenames only, specify /B. To display output in lowercase, use /L.

For example, the following command lists only those files with the extension BAT in lowercase.

DIR *.BAT /L

DISKCOMP

The external DISKCOMP command is used to compare two diskettes for equality. Its most common form is

DISKCOMP *first-drive second-drive*

where *first-drive* and *second-drive* are drive specifiers.

For example, the following command compares the diskette in drive A with the one in drive B.

DISKCOMP A: B:

DISKCOPY

The external DISKCOPY command is used to make a copy of a diskette. Its most common form is

DISKCOPY *source destination* [/V]

where *source* and *destination* are drive specifiers. DISKCOPY cannot be used to copy the fixed disk.

To have DISKCOPY verify that the copy was made correctly, use the /V option.

For example, the following command copies the diskette in drive A to the one in drive B.

DISKCOPY A: B:

DOSKEY

The external DOSKEY command gives you greater control over the way the command-line interface works. Refer to Chapter 13 for details.

DOSSHELL

The external DOSSHELL command restarts the Shell after leaving the Shell by pressing (ALT)-(F4). (If you leave the Shell by pressing (SHIFT)-(F9), use EXIT to reactivate the Shell.)

ECHO

The ECHO batch command is used to write messages to the screen and turn on or off the echoing of other batch commands. It takes this general form

ECHO [*on*] [*off*] [*message*]

For example, the following command prints the message "Backing up all files" to the screen.

ECHO Backing up all files

EDIT

The external EDIT command is the DOS screen editor. See Chapter 7 for details.

EDLIN

The external EDLIN command is the old, outmoded DOS line editor. See Appendix A for details.

ERASE

The internal ERASE command erases files from a disk. It takes the general form

ERASE *file-name* [/P]

where *file-name* is the name of the file to be erased. You can use wildcard characters in the file name to erase groups of files. DEL is another name for ERASE.

If you specify the /P option, ERASE will ask for your OK before erasing a file.

For example, the following command erases all files that have the extension DAT from the disk in drive B.

ERASE B:*.DAT

EXIT

This command reactivates the DOS Shell from the command prompt interface. Use it only if you activate the command prompt by pressing SHIFT-F9.

FASTOPEN

The external FASTOPEN command allows DOS to remember the location of files that are in deeply nested subdirectories, thus providing faster access to these files. Its general form is

FASTOPEN *drive-specifier*[=*num*]

where *num* determines the number of files that DOS will remember. This number can be in the range of 10 through 999; the default is 48. FASTOPEN is an installed command; that is, you can only execute it once each time the computer is turned on.

For example, the following command causes DOS to remember the location of 48 files on the fixed disk.

FASTOPEN C:

FC

FC compares two files. It replaces the older COMP command. Its simplest form is

FC *file1 file2*

Here, *file1* and *file2* are the files to be compared.

The two principle advantages to FC over the older COMP command are that it can compare files of differing sizes and it will resynchronize the files after a mismatch. Resynchronization enables FC to provide a more accurate picture of the differences between the files than COMP does.

This command is fairly complex. Refer to Chapter 10 for details of its operation.

FDISK

The external FDISK command is used to partition the fixed disk when it is first prepared for use. Refer to your DOS manual for information.

FIND

The external FIND command searches for occurrences of a string in a list of files. FIND is a filter that sends its output to the standard output device, which may be redirected. The general form of FIND is

FIND [/C] [/N] [/V] [/I] *"string"* *file-list*

where *string* is the string searched for, and *file-list* is the list of files to search. Notice that the options must precede the string.

The /C option causes FIND to display a count of the occurrences. The /N option causes the relative line number of each match to be displayed. The /V option causes FIND to display those lines that do not contain the string. The /I option causes FIND to ignore case differences.

For example, the following command searches the files REC1.DAT and REC2.DAT for the string "payroll."

FIND "payroll" REC1.DAT REC2.DAT

FOR

The FOR batch command is used to repeat a series of commands using different arguments. The FOR command takes the general form

FOR %%*var* IN (*argument list*) DO *command*

where *var* is a single-letter variable that will take on the values of the arguments. The arguments must be separated by spaces. The FOR will repeat *command* as many times as there are arguments. Each time the FOR repeats, *var* will be replaced by an argument moving from left to right.

For example, the following command prints the files TEXT1, TEXT2, and TEXT3.

FOR %%F IN (TEXT1 TEXT2 TEXT3) DO PRINT %%F

FORMAT

The external FORMAT command is used to prepare a diskette for use. Its most common form is

FORMAT *drive-specifier*

The diskette to be formatted must be in the specified drive. Remember that formatting a disk destroys any and all preexisting data, so use the FORMAT command with care.

For example, the following command formats the disk in drive A:

FORMAT A:

FORMAT takes several options. Refer to Chapter 10 for details.

GOTO

The GOTO batch command is used to direct DOS to execute the commands in a batch file in a non-sequential order. Its general form is

GOTO *label*

where *label* is a label that is defined elsewhere in the batch file. When the GOTO is executed, it causes DOS to go to the specified label and begin executing commands from that point. With GOTO, you can cause execution to jump forward or backward in the file.

For example, the following command causes execution to jump to the label DONE.

GOTO DONE

GRAFTABL

The external GRAFTABL command loads a character table that gives DOS extended foreign language support. It requires a color/graphics adapter. If you speak English, you will not need this command.

GRAPHICS

The external GRAPHICS command enables graphics images to be printed on the printer using the print screen function. Its general form is

GRAPHICS [*printer*] [/R] [/B/] [/LCD]

where the name of *printer* is determined according to the list below:

Printer Type	Name
IBM Personal Graphics Printer	GRAPHICS
Wide-carriage IBM Personal Graphics Printer	GRAPHICSWIDE
IBM Proprinter	GRAPHICS
IBM PC Convertible printer	THERMAL
IBM Color printer with black ribbon	COLOR1
IBM Color printer with red, green, blue, and black ribbon	COLOR4
IBM Color printer with black, cyan, magenta, and yellow ribbon	COLOR8
Any Hewlett-Packard DeskJet printer	DESKJET

Hewlett-Packard LaserJet	**LASERJET**
Hewlett-Packard LaserJet II	**LASERJETII**
Hewlett-Packard PaintJet	**PAINTJET**
Hewlett-Packard QuietJet	**QUIETJET**
Hewlett-Packard QuietJet Plus	**QUIETJETPLUS**
Hewlett-Packard PCL printer	**HPDEFAULT**
Hewlett-Packard Rugged Writer	**RUGGEDWRITER**
Hewlett-Packard Rugged Wide Writer	**RUGGEDWRITERWIDE**
Hewlett-Packard ThinkJet	**THINKJET**

If no printer name is specified, the IBM Personal Graphics Printer is assumed. The Epson series of printers is quite commonly used with microcomputers and is also specified with the GRAPHICS printer name.

By default, white on the screen is printed as black on the printer, and black on the screen is printed as white. The /R option causes black to print as black and white to print as white. The background color of the screen is usually not printed, but if you have a color printer, you can print the background by specifying the /B option. Finally, the /LCD option should be specified for computers using the IBM PC Convertible Liquid Crystal Display.

For example, the following command enables graphics images to be printed using the default GRAPHICS printer.

GRAPHICS

HELP

The HELP command gives you information about other DOS commands. It takes this general form

HELP [*command*]

where *command* is the command for which you want information. The information provided by HELP serves only as a reminder. It is not a substitute for a thorough understanding of DOS.

For example, this displays information about the COPY command.

HELP COPY

If *command* is not specified, then the menu-based help system is activated and you may select the command that you want help with from a list.

IF

The IF batch command takes the general form

IF *condition command*

If the *condition* evaluates to TRUE, the *command* that follows the condition is executed. Otherwise, DOS skips the rest of the line and moves on to the next line (if there is one) in the batch file. (See Chapter 11.)

JOIN

The external JOIN command joins one drive to the directory of another. Thus, files on the first drive may be accessed from the joined drive as if they were in a subdirectory. JOIN takes the general form

JOIN *joining-drive joined-drive\directory* [/D]

The *joining-drive* will appear to be in the specified directory of the *joined-drive*. The /D option is used to disconnect a join.

For example, this command joins the A drive to the C drive using the directory ADRIVE.

JOIN A: C:\ADRIVE

KEYB

The external KEYB command loads keyboard information for foreign language support. Its most common form is

KEYB *keyboard-code,code-page*

where *keyboard-code* and *code-page* define the keyboard code and code-page code. (See Chapter 16 for details.) If you speak English, you will not need this command.

For example, the following command configures the keyboard for use in Germany.

KEYB GR,437

LABEL

The external LABEL command is used to create or change a disk's volume label. It has the general form

LABEL [*drive-specifier*] [*name*]

If no *drive-specifier* is used, then the current disk is assumed. If you do not specify the volume *name* on the command line, you will be prompted for one. Disk volume labels may be up to 11 characters long. You cannot use the following characters in disk volume labels:

* ? / \ | . , ; : + = < > [ ] "

For example, the following command changes the volume label on the current disk to MYDISK.

LABEL MYDISK

LOADHIGH

The LOADHIGH (LH for short) command is used to load a program into extended memory. It has this general form

LOADHIGH *file-name*

where *file-name* is the name of the program that you want executed in extended memory.

Before you can use LOADHIGH, several conditions must be met. Refer to Chapter 16 for details.

MEM

The external MEM command displays information about the memory in your computer.

MEMMAKER

The external MEMMAKER command is a menu-based command that organizes and optimizes any extra memory in your system. Refer to Chapter 19 for details.

MKDIR

The internal MKDIR command (MD for short) is used to create a subdirectory. Its general form is

MKDIR *path*

where *path* specifies the complete path name to the directory. The path name may not exceed 63 characters in length.

For example, the following command creates the directory \WP\FORMS.

MD \WP\FORMS

MODE

The external MODE command is used to set the way various devices operate. MODE is a complex command with several different forms. (Refer to its description in Chapter 16.)

MORE

The external MORE command allows you to page through a text file 23 lines at a time. It is a filter that reads standard input and writes to standard output. Its most common form is

MORE < *file-name*

where *file-name* is the file to be viewed.

You can also use MORE in conjunction with other commands, such as DIR, to provide a convenient way to page through displays that are larger than one screen. For example, the following command displays the directory 23 lines at a time.

DIR | MORE

MOVE

The external MOVE command moves a file from one disk and/or directory to another. It has this general form

MOVE *source destination*

where *source* is the file (or files) to be moved, which may include a path specifier, and *destination* is the drive or directory that will receive the file(s). Wildcards are permitted. You can also specify a new file name if you are moving only one file.

In addition, you can use MOVE to change the name of a directory. To do this, use this general form

MOVE *old-dir-name new-dir-name*

where *old-dir-name* is the full path name of the directory to be renamed, and *new-dir-name* is its new name.

For example, this command moves the file MYFILE from the C drive to the A drive.

MOVE C:MYFILE A:

MSAV

The external MSAV command is a window-based, menu-driven command that provides protection against computer virus infection. Refer to Chapter 15 for details.

MSBACKUP

The external MSBACKUP command backs up the fixed disk. It is a window-based, menu-driven command and replaces the older BACKUP command. Refer to Chapter 18 for details.

NLSFUNC

The external NLSFUNC command is used by DOS to provide extended support for non-English users. You will probably never need to use it. For details, refer to your DOS user's manual.

PATH

The internal PATH command is used to define a search path that DOS uses to locate program files in directories other than the current one. It takes the general form

PATH *path*[;*path*...;*path*]

where *path* is the specified search path. You define multiple search paths by separating each path with a semicolon. There cannot be spaces in the path list.

For example, the following command defines a path to the \WP\FORMS directory.

PATH \WP\FORMS

PAUSE

The PAUSE batch command is used to temporarily stop a batch file's execution. It takes the general form

PAUSE [*message*]

If the *message* is present, it will be displayed. PAUSE waits until a key is pressed.

POWER

The external POWER command is used to conserve battery power when running a portable computer. Before you can use the POWER command, the POWER.EXE device driver must be installed. For the correct procedure and usage, refer to Chapter 19.

PRINT

The external PRINT command prints text files on the printer. Its most common form is

PRINT *file-name file-name* ... *file-name* [/T] [/C]

where *file-name* is the name of a file you want printed. The /T option cancels the PRINT command. The /C option cancels the printing of the file name that it follows.

For example, the following command prints the files LETTER1.WP and LETTER2.WP.

PRINT LETTER1.WP LETTER2.WP

PROMPT

The internal PROMPT command is used to change the DOS prompt. It takes the general form

PROMPT *prompt*

where *prompt* is the desired prompt. The prompt string can contain one or more special format commands that allow greater flexibility. The commands are shown below:

Code	Meaning
$$	dollar sign
$b	| character
$d	system date
$e	escape character
$g	> character
$h	a backspace
$l	< character
$n	current drive letter
$p	current directory path
$q	= character
$t	current time
$v	DOS version number
$_	carriage return-linefeed sequence

For example, one of the most popular prompts is created by the following command.

PROMPT PG

It displays the current directory path followed by the > symbol.

RECOVER

The external RECOVER command attempts to recover damaged files. It has the general form

RECOVER [*drive-specifier*] [*file-name*]

If only *drive-specifier* is present, RECOVER attempts to recover all files on a disk. Otherwise, only the specified *file-name* is recovered. When the entire disk is recovered, RECOVER creates file names following this convention: FILE*num*.REC, where *num* is a number between 0000 and 9999.

Remember, not all files can be recovered. Further, recovered program files are very likely unusable. It is best to use RECOVER only on text files—and then only as a last resort.

For example, the following command attempts to recover the file FORMLET.WP.

RECOVER FORMLET.WP

REM

The REM batch command has the general form

REM *remark*

The *remark* can be any string from 0 to 123 characters in length. No matter what the remark contains, it will be completely ignored by DOS.
    For example, the following remark is ignored.

REM this is a test

RENAME

The internal RENAME (REN for short) command is used to change the name of a specified file. It takes the general form

RENAME *old-name new-name*

where *old-name* and *new-name* are file names.
    For example, the following command changes the name of the file originally called INV.DAT to INV.OLD.

RENAME INV.DAT INV.OLD

REPLACE

The external REPLACE command replaces files on the destination disk with those by the same name on the source disk. It takes the general form

REPLACE *source destination* [/A] [/P] [/R] [/S] [/W] [/U]

If you specify the /S option, all files in all subdirectories will also be examined and replaced. You can use /A to add to a disk only those files that are not currently on the destination disk. This prevents existing files from being overwritten. If you need to insert a different diskette before REPLACE begins, use the /W option. This causes REPLACE to wait until you press a key before beginning. The /P option causes REPLACE to ask you before a file is replaced. The /U option only replaces files that are older than files that will replace them.
    For example, the following command replaces the files on drive A with those by the same name found on drive B, including all subdirectories.

REPLACE B: A: /S

RESTORE

The external RESTORE command is used to restore files to the fixed disk from diskettes created using BACKUP. It is not used to restore files created by MSBACKUP. BACKUP takes the general form

RESTORE *backup fixed* [/ A:*date*] [/B:*date*] [/E:*time*] [/L:*time*]
       [/P] [/S] [/M] [/N] [/D]

where *backup* is a drive specifier defining the drive that holds the backup diskette, and *fixed* is a drive and path specifier for the fixed disk. The options are summarized in table below:

<u>Option</u>	<u>Meaning</u>
A:*date*	Restore all files modified on or after the specified *date*
B:*date*	Restore all files modified on or before the specified *date*
D	Display names of files to be restored
E:*time*	Restore all files modified at or earlier than the specified *time* on a given date
L:*time*	Restore all files modified at or later than the specified *time* on a given date
M	Restore all files that have been modified or deleted since the last backup
N	Restore only those files that do not exist on the fixed disk
P	Prompt before restoring a file
S	Restore all subdirectories

For example, the following command restores all files having the DAT extension into the DATA directory, using drive A to read the backup diskettes.

RESTORE A: C:\DATA*.DAT

RMDIR

The internal RMDIR (RD for short) is used to remove a subdirectory. It has the general form

RMDIR *directory*

where *directory* is a complete path name to the desired directory. The specified directory must be empty. It is not possible to remove a directory that still has files in it.

For example, the following command removes the WP directory.

RMDIR \WP

SET

The internal SET command is used primarily by programmers and system integrators to put a name and its value into DOS's environment. (Refer to Chapter 19 for details.)

SETVER

Some application programs are particularly sensitive to the specific version of DOS that you are running on your computer. In fact, some programs will not run correctly unless a specific version of DOS is used. To solve this problem and to let you use any application program, DOS includes the SETVER command. It allows you to tell DOS what version it is supposed to act like when running a specific application program. It takes this general form

SETVER *file-name version*

Here, *file-name* is the name of the program, and *version* is the DOS version number that the specified program requires. For example, if your word processor is called WP.EXE and it requires DOS version 4 to run correctly, then specifying this command will allow you to use the word processor with later versions of DOS.

SETVER WP.EXE 4.00

This command will, however, only take effect after you have restarted DOS.

SHARE

The external SHARE command is used in networked systems to prepare for file sharing and file locking. Refer to your networking and DOS manuals for complete information.

SHIFT

The SHIFT batch command is used to shift the command line arguments left one position. This allows for more than ten arguments.

SORT

The external SORT command sorts text files on a line-by-line basis. It is a filter command that reads standard input and writes to standard output. It takes the general form

SORT [<*input*] [>*output*] [/R] [/+*num*]

where *input* and *output* are either file names, devices, or pipes. If not specified, standard input and output are used. The standard default is ascending order (A to Z). The /R option causes the file to be sorted in reverse or descending order. The /+*num* option causes the sorting to begin with the *num*th column.

For example, the following command produces a sorted directory listing.

DIR | SORT

SUBST

The external SUBST command allows you to use a different drive specifier to access a drive and directory. That is, you can use SUBST to assign a drive specifier to a drive and directory and refer to that drive and directory by using the drive specifier. In essence, the new drive specifier is like a nickname for the other drive. SUBST takes the general form

SUBST *nickname drive-specifier path*

where *nickname* is the new drive specifier for the indicated *drive specifier*. The *path* is the path to the desired directory.

To undo a substitution, use this form of the command:

SUBST *nickname* /D

For example, this causes drive A to respond to both A: and E:.

SUBST E: A:

SYS

The external SYS command is used to copy the DOS system files to a disk. It has the general form

SYS *drive-specifier*

where *drive-specifier* indicates the drive that will receive the system files. SYS must be able to read the system files off the current drive.

For example, the following command puts the system files on the disk in drive B.

SYS B:

TIME

The internal TIME command is used to set the system time. It takes the general form

TIME [*hh:mm:ss*]

If you do not enter the time on the command line, you will be prompted for it. TIME expects the numbers 0 through 23 for the hours; that is, it operates like a 24-hour military clock. You can also enter the time in 12-hour format, but you must specify "a" for A.M. or "p" for P.M. You need not specify the seconds.

For example, the following command sets the time to 12 noon.

TIME 12:00:00

TREE

The external TREE command prints a list of all directories on the specified disk. It has the general form

TREE *drive-specifier* [/F] [/A]

where *drive-specifier* is the letter of the drive that will be examined. If /F is used, the files in each directory are also displayed. By default, the directory tree is displayed in a graphical form. If your computer cannot display DOS's extended character set, then specify the /A option, which causes the output of TREE to be displayed using normal characters.

For example, the following command displays the directory structure for the disk in A.

TREE A:

TYPE

The internal TYPE command displays the contents of a file on the screen. It has the general form

TYPE *file-name*

where *file-name* is the file to be displayed.

For example, the following command displays a file called TEST.

TYPE TEST

UNDELETE

The UNDELETE command lets you unerase a file that you have just erased. For guaranteed results, you must use UNDELETE immediately after an ERASE. If an intervening disk operation has occurred, you might not be able to recover the file. UNDELETE takes this general form:

UNDELETE *file-name*

where *file-name* is the name of the file.

UNDELETE is part of DOS's error recovery system. Refer to Chapter 14 for complete details and options.

UNFORMAT

UNFORMAT is part of DOS's error recovery system. It unformats an accidentally re-formatted disk. Refer to Chapter 14 for details on correcting accidents.

VER

The internal VER command displays the DOS version number. It takes no arguments.

VERIFY

The internal VERIFY command turns on or off verification of disk write operations. That is, when turned on, it confirms that the data written to disk is exactly as it should be and that no errors have taken place. It takes the general form

VERIFY [ON]

or

VERIFY [OFF]

where you specify either *on* or *off*.

For example, the following command turns verification off.

VERIFY OFF

VOL

The internal VOL command displays the volume label of the specified disk. It has the general form

VOL [*drive-specifier*]

where *drive-specifier* is the name of the drive whose volume label will be displayed. If not specified, the volume label of the current drive is displayed.

For example, the following command displays the volume label of the current drive.

VOL

VSAFE

The external VSAFE command helps guard your system against a virus infection by monitoring ongoing system activity, looking for suspicious events that might indicate that an infection is in progress. This command became available with DOS version 6. It is an installed, window- and menu-based command. Refer to Chapter 15 for details.

XCOPY

The external XCOPY command is a more powerful and flexible version of the COPY command. It takes the general form

XCOPY *source target* [/A] [/D] [/E] [/M] [/P] [/S] [/V] [/W]

where *source* and *target* are file or path names. The operation of XCOPY is largely determined by the options applied to it. These options are summarized in the following table.

Option	Meaning
A	Copy only those files with the archive attribute turned on; the state of the archive bit is not changed
D:date	Copy only those files whose date is equal to or later than the one specified
E	Create all subdirectories, even if empty
M	Copy only those files with the archive attribute turned on; the state of the archive bit is turned off
P	Prompt before copying each file
S	Copy files in subdirectories
V	Verify each write operation
W	Wait until a disk is inserted

For example, the following command copies all files on a disk in drive A to one in drive B, including all subdirectories.

XCOPY A: B:\ /S

Index

Note: Boldface page numbers indicate an illustration